Beyond Mud and Vines

Dear Craig,
May my story
enrich you + your
family

Jacqueline Jorgensen

To order additional copies of this book, contact:
Xlibris Corporation
1-888-7-XLIBRIS
www.Xlibris.com
Orders@Xlibris.com

Contents

Prologue

Wounds that never heal hurt forever. As I looked around the classroom, I felt as if my breakfast of cereal and coffee had turned to screws and nails, and were shredding the lining of my stomach. At age thirty-eight, I was older than the other students, and the only one without a high school diploma. I had been turned away from several jobs, which I had urgently needed, just because I had not graduated from high school.

"Give me a chance," I had pleaded to the manager of a yardage store. "I worked in a sewing factory in Puerto Rico for four years, and I know mathematics. I might do the job better than someone with a high school diploma, but you'll never know unless you give an opportunity to prove it."

My plea with that manager was wasted. A high school graduate who didn't even know how to cut fabric got the job. I moved on, and was turned away and humiliated more times than I care to remember. Finally, I made my way to the nearest junior college, where a kind man, a counselor, took the time to help me. Somehow, I managed to do well in the test he gave me, and I started classes the following Monday. I felt awkward from the start, knowing that I was the oldest among all the students. They never asked me why I was attending school at my age, but I knew the reason, and I would keep it a secret for a long time. The fear of having to admit that I was just beginning to learn how to spell, even my own name, kept me trembling inside my skin.

"Girls don't need an education," my parents had said, "all

they will ever be are wives and mothers. No one needs education for that."

I struggled to learn in two years what I had not been allowed to learn during my childhood. I finally went to a psychologist, looking for ways to accept the agony of not knowing much of anything, which had haunted me since running away from my turbulent upbringing.

"Write about your life," she advised. "Put it all on paper. Get it off your chest. Share your story. It will help others. You have come a long way. You fought, and didn't use your upbringing as a handicap. Look where you are now, and you can still accomplish a lot more. Write your story!"

Chapter One

My Escape

When the first rooster crowed, I stepped out into the chill of dawn, opening the kitchen door slowly, so that the squeak of rusty hinges would not awaken my parents. The image of my father's red face and bloodshot eyes, as he held his sharp machete at my throat the previous night, was still painfully vivid in my mind. I went under the house, which was on stilts, as most houses in the hills of Puerto Rico were, and I waited. The thick forest surrounding the house was still as dark as the bottom of an iron pot, and would stay like that for at least another hour.

At daybreak, I would run to the river, and follow it to the big city on the west end of the island, where I would make a good life for myself. I had heard my parents talk about kids who had run away from home. One girl had survived and became a nun, but others had never been heard from again. I hung onto the hope that I would survive. I had to—and one day come back to help my little sister and brothers escape from our parents' drunkenness and brutality.

The madness in our family began when Papa met Mama in 1926. At that time, in our hills, most parents didn't believe in long courtships. So my parents, Salvador Montalvo and Carmela Santos, married nine days after they met. All Papa knew about Mama then was that she came from a good family and was a hard worker. And all Mama knew about him was that, according to her girlfriend, his sparkling brown eyes and brilliant smile made women feel weak in the knees and have erotic dreams.

According to Mama's stories, which she told only when she was mad at Papa, they spent the honeymoon building their home on the five acres of land Papa had inherited when his father died. They cut down many trees to make the clearing, and made their own boards and beams out of those trees.

Within weeks, they had a three-room house on stilts, on a hillside overlooking the river. Actually, the house was one big room with two short walls dividing it into three spaces: *la sala* (the living room), *el aposento* (the sleeping area), and *la cocina* (the kitchen). One had to walk through the sleeping area to get from the kitchen to the living room and back. There was a door between the living room and the sleeping area, and one between the sleeping area and the kitchen. Those doors were to be closed only when someone needed to change clothes. A burlap curtain hung around Mama's bed for privacy when Papa made her bed squeak and when a new baby arrived.

The lumber from the cut trees had not been given enough time to dry before nailing it in place. Consequently, when the wood finally dried, cracks opened between the boards in the walls and floor. The breeze blew in through the cracks, and on cold nights everyone had to pull their covers up to their chins to keep out the chill.

Papa made a table and two benches for the living room. Then he made *el fogón* (the stove), a thirty-inch-square wooden box four inches deep, with three medium-sized rocks in the center and four wooden posts. He filled the box with a mixture of earth, water, and ashes, which dried as hard as concrete. Before the mixture hardened, he placed the three medium-sized rocks in the center. Once the mixture dried, the three rocks were secured in place, and they would hold fast even under a huge pot of rice and beans or green bananas boiling vigorously.

But before cooking anything at all, Mama had to go into the

woods and gather dried tree branches into a bundle, carry it into the kitchen, arrange the kindling between the three rocks, strike a match to it, and blow until the wood ignited. Ashes from earlier fires often rose as she blew and whirled down over her black hair. She'd brush the ashes off with her hands and continue with the preparation of our meals.

Mama kept her few dishes hanging above the *fogón* on a round net she made from flexible branches and vines. The smoke from cooking kept the roaches and mice away from the dishes.

In the beginning of their marriage, Papa bought lard cans for hauling water from the springs up to the house. Made for transporting ten pounds of lard, the cans were flimsy and rusted quickly, so Mama had to make *calabazos* for hauling water. First, she drilled a round hole near the stem of a large gourd which grew on trees and resembled a huge watermelon. Using a long, wooden spoon, she carved out the spongy stuffing. Then she put a handful of small rocks with a little water into the empty gourd. Finally, covering the hole with her thumb, she placed her other hand under the *calabazo,* brought it to chest level, and shook it vigorously. The scouring action from the rocks and water left the inside of the hard shell smooth.

Having a round bottom, a *calabazo* could not be carried on one's head like the lard cans. It had to hang from a hand, with two fingers inside the hole and the thumb pressing the base of the stem to keep it from tearing off.

Unfortunately, the gourd shell would rot after months of daily use, and a slight tap against a rock would break it. Mama made many *calabazos* for years, until her daughters grew old enough to take over that job.

*   *   *

My mother had been taught that using certain words, including *sex*, *pregnancy*, and *childbirth*, was morally wrong for a lady.

So her babies were brought to her by angels, saints, and kind old ladies from across the river.

Without going into details, she often mentioned the first baby brought to her by an angel ten months after she and Papa had married. Papa invited his friends to help him celebrate the arrival of his first son. The six men drank moonshine, smoked cigars, laughed loudly, and stamped the floor. The little house vibrated on its stilts, and Mama trembled in the sleeping area, watching the baby twist and squirm with the noises. He was only eight days old, and the only thing between him and the drunks was a short, thin wall.

When the men were too drunk to stand up straight, they began a contest of throwing bottles out the window, up in the air, and shooting them down with their guns. One shot rang louder than the others, and Mama saw the baby's little body spring up and then go still.

At that point in Mama's sad story, her eyes always filled with tears, and her words got stuck in her throat. I never heard whether the baby was shot or startled to death, or what Papa said or did afterward.

Mama was later blessed with a baby girl, brought to her by the Virgin Mary. That baby was my oldest sister Emilia. She grew to look like Papa: stout with wavy black hair, brown eyes, and dark skin with a reddish glow. She also inherited his temper and cruelty.

When Emilia was two years old, an old lady from across the river brought Mama another baby girl. That baby was named Gloria, and she looked like Mama, with ivory skin, straight black hair, a fine nose, and sad brown eyes.

Gloria wasn't quite two when I made my appearance during a storm. I didn't resemble my parents or any of my siblings. The only details about my arrival were told to me by Emilia. But Emilia made up stories quicker than she could sneeze, so I never knew when she was telling the truth.

Chapter Two

Dropped Like a Rock

"You were dropped by a storm in Mama's bed," said Emilia when I was five or six years old. We were on our way to the springs, each dragging an empty *calabazo*.

"How do you know that a storm dropped me?" I asked. "Did you see it?"

"I know because I'm the oldest, and the oldest kid in the family knows everything."

"Well, I don't believe that I was ever dropped."

"Oh, yes you were, Sabina!" She pointed a boney finger at me. "You were dropped, and that's why you are the only one in the family with milky-white skin, yellow hair, and white eyes. That is why you are so weird and different!"

I bit my lip and stared at her squinted eyes and clenched teeth, my stomach twisting and tightening. She was bigger than I, and had often threatened to pull my hair out by the roots the next time I called her a liar.

"Before I tell you the story," she went on, "you must promise never to tell Mama that I told you. She hates talking about that night, and she'll be mad at me for telling you, and I'll never tell you anything else ever again. So promise me."

I promised that I would never repeat a word, but only because I had been wanting to know for a long time just how a storm could drop a baby in somebody's bed.

"Okay, then. I'll tell you when we reach the springs."

That was Emilia's style. She would get me interested in something, and then make me wait and wait.

I followed her down the slippery path, which was so scary it gave me bad dreams every night. It was narrow, dark with shadows, and downhill all the way. It twisted around thick trees tall enough to reach the sky with intertwined branches that blocked the sun.

Emilia always ran much faster than I, and she never tripped on the rocks and vines, and never landed face down in the mud like I did. Sometimes I'd cry and beg her to be nice. But on that day, I didn't want to say anything that might cause her to change her mind about telling me the story.

"I saw part of the roof come down on Mama that night," she said when I finally caught up with her. "Put the *calabazos* under the stream, then I'll tell you the whole story." Emilia turned from me and looked up toward the ceiling of branches. It was her way of torturing me, but I stayed calm, letting her think that hearing the story wasn't that important to me.

One good thing about that day was that it hadn't rained for a long time, and the water filtering through the rocks had become a slow trickle. It would take a long time for the *calabazos* to fill up, and that would be enough time for Emilia to finish the story— but only if she talked straight, without stopping to scratch her ear, or to look over her shoulder, or to fake a cough. Those were things she often did to aggravate me.

I placed each *calabazo* under a trickle, then stepped back to watch the green fern fronds dance and reach for the water we would haul away.

"You have to promise me again that you will never ask Mama any more questions about the storm that dropped you in her bed," Emilia insisted.

I turned from the ferns and said calmly, "I promise, Emilia, I promise." Moving away from the *calabazos*, I took a short stick and sat on a little slope to draw animals on the ground. "Did the storm drop me like a rock from a hand?"

"That's right! It dropped you just like one of those rocks down there." Emilia's chin aimed at the sky, but her long finger pointed to a huge pile of rocks between the springs and the creek.

"Did you see me land on Mama's bed?"

"No, but I saw you after you landed. Do you want to hear the story, or not?"

"Yes! Emilia, I want to hear it."

"Then keep your mouth shut and listen! It all started with a breeze that made the hair on Mama's arms stand straight up. 'Oh, that breeze is kind of cold for the month of August,' she said, rubbing her arms. She then closed the bedroom window and went to the kitchen to cook our supper. Then the breeze increased and soon became a strong wind. Dark clouds gathered in the sky until there was no more blue. And suddenly, a flock of black and brown bats swarmed out of the woods, screeching and stretching their wings like black and brown umbrellas against the dark clouds.

"The bullhorn blared from the top of the mountain, and a man yelled something about higher grounds and getting away from the river, but the wind took away every other word. Mama ran to the window and made out that a storm was coming.

"At about the same time, Papa came home, his eyes startled and his hair rearranged by the wind. 'Got to pound more nails on the tin sheets before the wind takes them away,' he said, reaching for his hammer and nails. Mama and I watched him climb up to the roof. Then she told me to stay in the house with Gloria while she went out to milk the cow. I watched her walk against the wind, her dress pressing against her belly and legs, her hair straight back like a black banner.

"I was afraid that Mama and Papa would be taken away by the wind and I'd have to raise Gloria by myself. She was such a bundle of trouble then, always getting into everything, and I always had to keep a watch on her.

"Finally Mama staggered into the house through the kitchen, and Papa through the living room. They both looked like they had been tossed around and they couldn't figure out what was happening.

"Mama rolled our clothes into a bundle and tied the bundle to a corner post so the wind wouldn't take it away. Then she went to the kitchen to cook our supper. While Mama did all that, Papa closed all the windows and doors, then took a gallon jug of rum and stretched out in his hammock.

"Lightning flashed through the wall cracks, making quick stripes of light on the dark floor, and thunder blasted in the sky and then roared away to make room for the next blast. The first drops of rain tapped across the roof, and then it seemed as if the sky split open and all its water came gushing down over our house."

"Was that when it dropped me?" I asked, eager to get on to the most interesting part of the story.

"No! And don't interrupt again if you want to hear the rest of the story."

"I won't . . . but why are you taking so long, Emilia?"

"Because it's a long story, stupid!"

I shut my mouth, but I felt a bigger storm growing inside my chest. Emilia should have been the one dropped on the pile of rocks for being so mean. But she'd probably be lucky enough to bounce right up without a bruise or a scratch.

"The house shook like someone stronger than Papa was under it trying to knock it off the stilts. The corners crackled and popped, and the tin sheets twisted and screeched. I pressed my face to a wall crack to look out and got dirt in my eyes, but not before seeing Papa's white horse running around the house with his tail and mane up in the air, neighing like it was in pain. Even our poor cow ran into the woods with her tail tucked between her legs.

"A blast of thunder sent Mama running out of the kitchen to the living room, but all she found there was Papa in his hammock taking one drink after another. 'I don't intend to be awake when the house goes down with a mud slide all the way to the river,' he told her with a silly little laugh. She gave him a mean look and stamped back to the kitchen."

"Please, get to the part where it dropped me!" I cried.

She glared at me. "You're interrupting again."

"I'll shut up."

"Good! The rain sounded on the roof like a dozen hammers pounding at the same time, and the wind came through the cracks and made the flames on the *fogón* grow high enough to reach the ceiling. Mama worked frantically to keep the walls from catching on fire. I wanted to go help her, but she told me to sit under the table with Gloria and keep her from stumbling around. Gloria was healthy then, but a lot of trouble, always causing me to miss out on everything.

"Mama managed to finish cooking the meal and brought a plate of rice and beans to Papa, and one for Gloria and me. She went back to the *fogón* and heaped ashes over the burning wood so the fire would keep for the next day. Then she came with a plate of food for herself and sat on the floor to eat next to Gloria and me, 'cause she knew I was scared." Emilia rolled her eyes and tapped her chest. "My heart was pounding as hard as the rain."

It seemed that she expected sympathy from me for the fear she had experienced, but I had been warned not to interrupt, so I stared and said nothing.

"Well, anyway," she went on. "Shortly after Mama sat down to eat, we saw shadows dancing on the wall. The wind coming through the cracks had blown away the heap of ashes. 'Fire!' Mama yelled. Then she ran to the water barrels and frantically splashed water on the flames. Meanwhile, Papa flew past Gloria and me, and with a gunnysack he helped Mama put out the fire. When they finished, Mama returned to us with red eyes and smelling of ashes and smoke. Papa walked past us, looking startled, back to his hammock and his jug.

"Mama didn't eat after that. Her face was twisted with fear, or anger, as she tucked us in our gunnysacks and warned that we should stay under the table. 'Are you scared, Mama?' I asked, but she patted my head and without a word walked to the rum room and brought out her own jug of rum.

"From then on, I watched her at the edge of her bed, taking one drink after another." Emilia looked at the *calabazos* and smiled maliciously. "But you'll have to wait for the rest of the story, 'cause the *calabazos* are full."

I stood there with my mouth open, while Emilia grabbed her *calabazo* and hurried up the hill.

Chapter Three

The Rest of the Story

I reached the kitchen door out of breath. Emilia had dumped her water into the barrel and explained to Mama that the springs were drying up.

Mama turned from the heap of green bananas she was peeling for our lunch. "Then you'd better hurry back down and catch the last drops." She didn't even look at me, who stood there gasping and with a head full of questions.

Emilia whined, "But, Mama, I'm so tired!"

"You can rest while the *calabazos* fill up," Mama said.

From Emilia's look of frustration, I guessed that she'd tell me the rest of her story, if only to get back at Mama for making her work so hard.

She started talking as soon as we reached the springs.

"You have to swear again that you'll never breathe a word to Mama of what I'm going to tell you."

"I swear," I said eagerly. "I'll never breathe a word to Mama, or anyone else. Just hurry up with it, please!"

"So put the *calabazos* in place," she said, and then climbed up a low tree where she sat on a branch, swinging her legs. I did as I was told, then climbed up to another branch and sat across from her.

"Now where did I leave off? Oh yeah, I remember. I woke up

to the pounding sound of the storm. The house was dark and damp. I called out to Mama, but she didn't answer. I stretched my arms in front of me and made my way to her bed. She was snoring, and I smelled rum. Feeling around in the dark, I reached the living room, where Papa snored in his hammock with rum on his breath, too.

"I started back to Mama's bed, but a flash of lightning stopped me at the doorway. I heard the pounding and scratching outside the walls, and I imagined arms of ghosts reaching for me in the dark. I tried to scream, but my voice got lost in all the sounds.

"A big gust of wind sent a floorboard by Mama's bed flying against the closed window. Now we had a long hole on the floor, and when the lightning flashed again, I saw the muddy water rushing down beneath the house. Our goat was still fastened to a stilt, but her babies were gone.

"Then a chicken shot up into the house through that hole. Squawking fearfully, it flapped its wings into the kitchen. I thought I was going to die from shaking with fear, and I hated that Mama and Papa could not wake up.

"I heard a loud screech and looked up as a sheet of tin lifted off the roof. Gushes of rainwater came down into the sleeping area. I turned away and staggered to a corner near Papa's hammock, where I sat on the floor with my knees to my chest. Covering my eyes with my hands, I heard another loud blast that seemed to have split the house in half, but I was too scared to open my eyes.

"I sat there for the longest time, probably hours and hours. Finally, when the roaring and pounding of the storm calmed down, I opened my eyes and saw daylight coming from the sleeping area. Then I saw Papa lifting his head out of the hammock. 'What the hell?' he yelled. 'Carmela!' He lowered his feet to the floor and leaped to the doorway. Then he froze, his mouth open and both hands grasping the doorjambs.

"I walked over and stood next to him. Then I saw the huge pile of tree limbs and tin where the table and Mama's bed had been. Thinking that Mama and Gloria had disappeared in the wind, I started to cry really hard. But Papa said that everything was going to be all right, and he started lifting away branches and tin. 'Carmela!' he kept calling. Finally he spotted the gallon jug, broken, next to the collapsed bed. 'Damn drunk!' he shouted. 'How much of that stuff did you drink?'

"He found Mama under a tin panel, her eyes closed, her hair wet and stringy, streaks of blood from her forehead running down her face and neck. Papa put his finger under Mama's nose, then grabbed her wet hair and shook her. 'Wake up, you damn drunk!' Mama didn't move. She looked like a wet rag. Papa kept shaking her, yelling, 'Damn pig. Drunk pig!'

"I felt sorry for Mama and cried louder, begging Papa to stop. He finally quit shaking her and, with an angry face, looked around until he saw Gloria pinned under the collapsed table. Letting go of Mama's hair, he hurried to lift the tabletop and scoop Gloria off the floor. Gloria whimpered, and I saw a big bloodstain on her shoulder. The blood came from a deep hole on her head. That's why she's so fragile, fainting all the time and breaking out with tumors."

Emilia glanced at me as if to make sure I was listening. I was, but something was blocking my throat. I felt sad and scared for Mama and little Gloria.

"Papa looked at Gloria, then at Mama, and finally laid Gloria next to the broken bed. Then he went back to shaking Mama. 'Wake up! This girl is hurt! Damn you.'

"Mama didn't even blink. Then, as he turned away, we heard a cry that sounded like a cat. Papa froze again, his eyes wide and startled. He grabbed a corner of the wet blanket and yanked it off. His mouth dropped open. 'What in hell is that?'

"A wiggly, red, wrinkled thing lay squirming at the foot of Mama's bed. That ugly thing was you, Sabina. Now we'd better hurry home before Mama comes looking for us with her belt." Emilia jumped off the branch, grabbed her *calabazo*, and hurried up the hill. She never bothered to look back.

I stayed on my branch for a while, crying for the poor baby who must have been so scared on that stormy night. Then I took my time getting home. If Mama came after me with her leather belt, I would break my promise to Emilia. Even if I had really been dropped by a storm, no one should have told me. It made me feel awful about myself, like I wanted to die, like I wasn't human, or something like that.

Chapter Four

The Albino

When relatives came to see what the storm had brought to my mother, someone remarked that this new baby was an *albina*, which means albino girl. Since the hill people always added extra letters to their words, and sometimes chopped off a letter or two from other words, they said *sabina* instead of *albina*. My name then became Sabina. But to tease and torture me, my siblings and other people called me *La sabina*, which made me want to grow up fast just to punch them on the nose.

Through the coming years, Mama would be blessed with one more girl and four boys, but all of them were dark, with black hair and brown eyes.

Many years after hearing Emilia's story, I learned that a storm had not dropped me in my mother's bed, but that she had given birth while unconscious under the tin panel and branches. I also learned that Mama's grandfather, who had died when she was eight, had been blonde with green eyes, and I looked like him. My mother never told me that, but I heard her tell those who asked how she had come up with a blond baby while the rest of her children were dark.

Knowing that I looked like my mother's grandfather didn't make me feel any better about myself. First, Mama always seemed embarrassed when she answered questions about me. And secondly, a little girl who might look like a grandfather couldn't possibly be very pretty.

*　　*　　*

All the babies were brought to Mama, but Papa, being a man and the owner of the house and everything in it, ruled over all of us. Papa would decide what we would eat, what we would wear, and what kind of work we would do. He had his children do most of the work around the farm so he didn't have to hire anyone to help him. He would save all the profits from the harvests and from the animals he raised.

Since our island had become a territory of the United States, it was mandatory that parents register the birth of their children at the nearest city hall. However, Papa had made his own rules. He waited until there were two or three children, then made a trip to one town where he registered the newborn. From there, he went to another town and registered another child as a newborn.

One day he registered three children, all in different towns. Ultimately, all the registrations ended in one district, so we children appeared in the books as twins and triplets. The dates of our births got all mixed up, and we never knew our correct ages, which helped our parents to have better control over us. All we were told about our ages was that we were old enough to work hard without complaining, too old to play, and too young for things that the grownups enjoyed, like smoking, drinking rum, and dancing.

We couldn't ask how things were done or said, yet we got slapped across the face for being dumb enough to do and say the wrong things.

Our parents had a long list of rules for us to follow.

"Don't talk back."

"Do as you are told and don't ask questions."

"Don't repeat anything you hear."

"Don't ever lie, not even to save yourself from a beating."

"If you run from a whipping, you'll get double the punishment."

And the most important of all rules: "Honor your father and mother, no matter what." I honored my parents until I grew old enough to understand the meaning of that word.

We were baptized within weeks of our arrival, and were given a set of godparents who became our parents' *compadres* (parents in common). With the christening came more rules:

Girls belonged to the Virgin Mary, and weren't supposed to do anything that would disappoint the Virgin.

We must not be disloyal, dishonest, cruel, or lazy. We must pray a lot, honor our parents, and never, never lie.

During Holy Week, we had to walk as though our feet were feathers, for Jesus died for us. If we stamped, He would feel the blows, and that would make the Virgin cry. We'd better not cheat, either. If we did, a hummingbird would tell on us. For many years, I hated those poor little birds.

I was the only one of us children whose godparents lived only a few hills away. Emilia's godparents were Mama's parents, and they died before I came along. Gloria's godparents were one of Papa's cousins and his wife, who lived across the river. José's were one of Mama's brothers and his wife, who lived in a city called San Juan. Lorenzo's were Papa's brother Adolfo and his wife, who never came around. They owned the grocery store on top of the mountain, and Mama said that they thought of themselves as better than us.

My godparents were also Papa's cousins, Gregorio and his twin sister Maria. Godparents were usually older and married, but Gregorio and Maria were young and unmarried, so they came to see me often. They said they felt honored to be my godparents.

I knew that my godparents loved me. Godfather would read to me stories and poems he had written about the stars in the sky, the flowers in the fields, and a little girl with soft blonde hair like the silky wings of yellow butterflies. I would put my hands over my face and smile, hoping that Emilia and the other kids weren't watching. If they saw me smiling, they would make me regret the love I felt.

"I want to write like you," I said, watching my godfather write my name, *Sabina*, with a piece of charcoal on a board.

"I'll teach you," he said with a smile that made me feel loved and beautiful. Then, with his hand over mine, he helped me write my name for the first time. "You'll be a fine writer," he said, bringing his face close to mine.

I saw a girl's face in the center of his sparkling brown eyes, and told him so.

"Look again," he said. "It's you, the apple of my eye!"

Sitting on my godfather's lap always made me feel loved and protected by his big, warm arms.

Those moments of affection often turned to misery once my godparents left. Emilia would make fun of the way my godfather talked, laughed, and the way he read. Then she'd say that my godmother was ugly because she looked like her twin brother, and that she was stupid for saying that my hair was soft and curly like that of an angel. "As if she had seen angels!"

Being a girl, my godmother Maria had not attended school, but she knew how to embroider beautiful flowers on blouses and handkerchiefs. So while her brother taught me reading and writing, my godmother taught me fine needle work. This made Emilia even more cruel toward me. She couldn't stand seeing me learn things she hadn't been taught. Yet she refused to pay attention the one time my godmother tried to teach her, too.

Then my godparents suddenly stopped coming around. For a long time, I wondered if I had done something wrong and they didn't love me anymore.

Finally one day, Emilia told me that Mama had yelled at them for making me feel special, and for saying that someday I would make something of myself because I was smart and beautiful.

Chapter Five

Riverbed Babies

I have no recollection of the arrival of my brother José, who joined our family after I did. But I would never forget Lorenzo's arrival. I woke up one night to the sound of what I thought was a cat. I noticed light behind the burlap curtain that hung around my mother's bed. Hurrying out of my gunnysack, I ran under the curtain and found Papa talking with a toothless old woman dressed in black. And to my amazement, I saw Mama in her bed with a tiny baby to her breast.

"Where did you find that baby?" My voice echoed in the room, and the old lady and my father burst out laughing.

"Doña Ana found him by the river, cold and hungry, and brought him to me," my mother said. I saw her tiny smile and read it as joy. "His name is Lorenzo—your new brother. Now go back to bed."

I ran back under the curtain and into my gunnysack, picturing tiny babies with wet black hair, cold and hungry, clinging to the bushes on the riverbed.

At daybreak, I tiptoed out of the house and headed for the river, dragging my gunnysack, which I meant to bring back filled with little babies. I was sure that this would make Mama so happy she would start loving me more than she did the other kids.

I tripped over every rock in my path and got tangled in every vine, but the little babies had to be rescued. Suddenly, my father popped out from behind a bush and blocked my way.

"Where do you think you're going?"

His eyes told me that no answer would be good enough, so I responded with a question. "To find hungry babies for Mama?"

He grabbed my shoulder with one hard hand, turned me to face the hill, and swatted my behind. "Don't ever think of doing that again, do you hear me?" He gave me another swat and ordered me to hurry home.

"If those babies starve to death, it'll be your fault!" I yelled and started up the hill.

Papa took one giant step, grabbed the back of my skimpy dress, and pulled me back. "What makes you think you're big enough to talk back to me, eh?" His big hand pounded my behind all the way home.

*   *   *

There was a side of my father that surfaced a few times when I was very young, and for a long time I wished to see it again. Working near the house, he'd sing us a song in which he used our names and any word that rhymed: *Pan y café* (bread and coffee) for José, *una china* (an orange) for Sabina, and *una pana* (a breadfruit) for Gloria.

We would giggle and say, "Goody, goody! Thank you, Papa!" Then he added other words: a rotten egg, a dead frog, a fart, and other things that made us cry out, "Oh, no! You spoiled it." He'd laugh, and I felt happy. Those were joyful moments, but they were few and far between.

The tenderest memories I have of my mother are of the few times she sat on the front steps with a lap of oranges and a sharp knife. Squinting and pressing her lips tightly together, she peeled and sliced the juicy oranges, and handed each of us kids a portion.

"Ooh, sour!" she always said, watching us take our first bite. We kids laughed at the faces she made, and she looked at us with twinkling eyes and smiles.

*　　*　　*

I don't know at what age Emilia and I were assigned to a daily working routine, but I knew it wasn't fair. At daybreak, we'd head down to the springs and haul heavy containers of water up the hill to fill our barrels. Then, except for one day a week that we spent at the creek slumped over rocks and squeezing the dirt out of a huge pile of laundry, Emilia stayed in the house helping Mama, and I followed Papa everywhere as his helper. Emilia's work was in the shade, where she could nibble on whatever was cooking and never be hungry.

My work was out in the hot sun, which Papa claimed would make my skin dark so that I would eventually look like my sisters and brothers. I pulled weeds in the cornfield and planted beans, sweet potato vines, and coffee plants. I got stung by wasps and bees so often that I became immune to their poisons.

When I wasn't out in the fields, I had to go up on the roof and help Papa fix the rusted spots on the tin sheets. I handed him the nails, the hammer, the saw, and the little cans of tar he used to plug the nail holes. I handed to him whatever he asked for. When I couldn't quickly find what he wanted, he threatened to widen my "beady eyes" with his pocketknife. I lived in fear, and often dreamed that one day he would do just that.

From the hot roof, I could see Gloria and José playing and running around the house. I'd get a bitter taste in my mouth, for I wanted so badly to jump down and join them in the fun. I could hear Emilia in the living room, swinging Lorenzo in the hammock and singing. Why wasn't she up on the roof and I swinging Lorenzo?

The worst feeling came when the smell of fried onions and codfish drifting from the kitchen reached my nose. My mouth watered, and my stomach growled and twisted until it hurt. But Papa was the one who decided when I would eat. I had to bite my lip and swallow the pain, for I was the little girl, and my father was "the king."

I began to wonder if my mother made up the stories she told us. If little girls did belong to the Virgin Mary, why weren't my silent prayers answered? All I wanted was that Papa would get tired, or get hungry, or get a headache—anything so he would quit working, and I could get out of the sun. Couldn't the Virgin see that the hot tin roof was burning my bare feet? Papa protected his feet by wearing shoes. Did he think that my feet were tougher than his? And there were sun blisters forming on my shoulders, my nose, and the top of my head. Didn't anyone care that I was burning? Papa wore long sleeves and a hat.

The sun did not make me dark. Instead, it blistered my skin and covered it with freckles. I became "the dotted girl with yellow hair."

My mother was the first to call me that. I grew to hate her for coming up with the name, and for not stopping my brothers and sisters from repeating it. When I begged them to stop torturing me, they teased me more. I'd get a knot in my stomach that made me wish I could disappear.

One day I couldn't hold back my anger and threw a piece of wood at Emilia. She grabbed her head and screamed, "Mama, Sabina split my head!"

Mama came out with a flat board that was made to stir the roasting coffee beans. She took me by the hair and pounded my backside for a long time. When she stopped, I fell to the ground and couldn't get up. Through my tears, I saw Emilia grinning. I begged God to strike her and Mama dead, or to make me strong so I could run away from home, and one day come back to make them regret the things they did to me.

One time, while trying to figure out why Emilia was so mean to me, I watched her at the *fogón* blowing on the embers to ignite the wood. Clouds of ashes whirled over her, then settled on her hair and face. I decided that some of the ashes had crawled into her ears and that's what made her so mean. Momentarily, I felt sorry for her.

Although I hated working with my father, I had an advantage over Emilia. For one thing, my ears stayed clear of ashes, and I learned things Emilia would never learn from Mama. I learned to climb tall trees. Emilia would climb only the small trees at the springs, to jump off at the sound of our parents' steps. I wanted to tell her that I had climbed way up high just to watch men bathing in the river, but she would tell Mama and I would never be able to climb anything else for the rest of my life.

Another thing I learned was rope looping, and I kept that to myself, too. I learned it by watching from behind a bush or tree when Papa and his brother Luís looped the horses and cows just to see who could do it better. I didn't understand why that was a thing that only men were allowed to do. It was a lot of fun, and I didn't think that it would make the Virgin Mary cry. I practiced every chance I had, and on anything that stood erect. I looped the pigs, the goats, the cows, and even the chickens. I became very good at it, and felt proud that I could do something forbidden, and my parents and Emilia didn't know it.

Even though I was younger than Gloria, I had a great advantage over her, too. The poor girl could be making mud balls outside the kitchen, or chasing the chickens around the house, and suddenly her eyes would roll up toward the sky until all we could see was the white. She would let out a soft moan, her legs would become as limp as rags, and down to the ground she'd go. Several times, she rolled down the hillside behind the house, and was lucky that a tree trunk stopped her from landing in the creek or the rocks.

Whenever Gloria fainted, Mama carried her into the house and splashed water on her face, or slightly slapped her face to awaken her. After such an episode, Gloria broke out with boils all over her body, and she cried even in her sleep. Gradually, the boils turned bright red, and did not go away until Mama poked holes in them with a long thorn from an orange tree and squeezed out the infection.

This was all a matter of routine. I never saw much concern on my parents' faces about the sick little girl.

Chapter Six

Making Rum

Papa added another room to the house, *el almasen* (a storage room). There he kept his rum, tobacco, eggs, corn, beans, and the money he received from selling all those products. The room remained locked at all times, and no one, including Mama, could enter without Papa's permission. He carried one key, and a second one hung from a nail inside the storage room, far from Mama's reach.

Papa made his rum in a tin shelter he'd built against a bank of earth near the creek. He took pride in building that structure, and no storm ever knocked it down. The trees around it were so tall that by the time blue smoke from the still filtered through the thick branches, no one could pinpoint exactly where it came from. Making rum was illegal since Puerto Rico had become a possession of the United States.

A week or ten days before lighting the fire under the still, which Papa called *el aparato*, he filled two or three barrels with water, crushed oranges or sugarcane, and a lot of molasses. He covered the mixture and let it set until it fermented. One could tell when fermentation was complete by the heavy, sweet-sour smell that lingered around the barrels.

We children detested the days when Papa made rum. He would be up at the crack of dawn, demanding that everyone get out of their beds and start on their chores. There were cows, horses, goats, pigs, and chickens to tend to before we headed for the bean or cornfields to pull weeds. Our fear mounted as the day progressed. Maybe we would get supper and sleep in our corners that night, or maybe we would end up under the house, hungry and without our gunnysacks.

Brewing the rum was tedious. First, Papa lit a fire between three large rocks. He placed the metal drum on those rocks and filled it with the smelly mixture. It would take a long time for the mixture to boil, and someone had to stay there to keep the fire from going out.

As the drum heated, it crackled and popped, which spooked me when Papa left me in charge. Even on a sunny day, this place was scary with the shade from so many trees. On a gloomy, stormy day, it became dark and horrifying. It made me think that monsters and ghosts were watching me through the branches, ready to snatch me away. I always felt as if I were at the edge of a bottomless pit, and any sudden move might push me over.

When the mixture boiled inside the sealed drum, the hot vapor traveled up through a pipe twelve inches long, called the neck, sticking out from the upper part of the *aparato*. From there, the vapor pushed itself into a longer pipe, then dumped into *la serpentina* (a coiled tube) which sat inside a large barrel of water.

The water cooled the vapor and reduced it to liquid, which trickled into a gallon jug through a smaller tube at the bottom of the barrel. This rum, called *cañita*, was about eighty proof. By the time the first few drops hit the jug, my father's throat must have been dry. He drank the fresh-from-the-pipe stuff, which worked on his blood immediately and turned him into a vicious monster.

He walked into the house with bloodshot eyes, grinding his teeth and snorting. The first kid who looked at him got pushed out of the way. Whether Mama said anything or not, he started on her, saying she was nothing but a pig, a cow, a stupid woman not good for anything. After a while, she and some of us kids were thrown out, without supper or our gunnysacks, to spend the night under the house with the pigs and goats. The next day, everyone had to put on happy faces and do the chores as if nothing had happened.

The only thing that kept us from having a miserable night when Papa made rum was a visit from his cousins or *compadres*. They helped Papa sample the freshly brewed rum, and kept him too busy to pick on us.

Sometimes Mama made goat cheese in the kitchen while the men drank. Then she'd bring them some cheese, and Papa gave her some rum. Usually Mama couldn't walk a straight line after a couple of shots, but it didn't bother Papa while his guests were still there. The longer the visitors stayed, the better for all of us, for Papa would fall asleep as soon as they left instead of fighting.

One time, shortly after Papa brought all the gallons of freshly brewed rum into the house, his cousin Bartolo showed up with his wife and a guitar he had just purchased. That was the first time we children heard the sound of a guitar.

Things got even better after a while, as two *compadres* also dropped by with their wives, and before long our house was filled with music, laughter, and clapping. Papa kept passing a jug of rum around, and everyone, including Mama, took one drink after another.

We children weren't allowed in the living room, but we listened from the sleeping area and looked through the cracks in the wall. I felt like I was floating on air that night, and the sound of that happy time stayed in my mind forever.

Another night, two cousins came with their wives and stayed drinking and talking until the rooster crowed. Papa sat in his hammock, Mama and the wives on one bench, and the two cousins on the other. They talked about spirits that came in the dark to get even with those who had done them wrong in their lifetime. Then they talked about faraway places, where young men went to become soldiers and ended up getting shot and dying.

Finally one of the cousins mentioned a man named Manuel

Castillo, and Papa almost flew through the roof. Castillo lived on the other side of the river, but he had just purchased the farm adjoining ours. He intended to build a *cantina* (a small store) and a house for his family.

"When the hell did he do that?" My father's voice rang high. "He knew I wanted that farm! Build a *cantina*? Now I've heard everything. He's going to have people walking across my farm to get to his damn place. How in God's name am I going to put a stop to that?"

While Papa fumed on the other side of the wall, we girls made eyes at each other. We heard Mateo say that Castillo had ten children. This was great! We would get to see some of them from a distance, as their home would be only two hills away. We would hear their voices, which always traveled from mountain to mountain with the wind. Besides that, we'd get to see people walking past our house.

Up to that point in our lives, the only girl who came to our house some mornings was Pedra, Mateo's daughter. She lived beyond the creek, and came to buy milk for the baby in her family. She seemed close to my age, so even though we weren't allowed to play, we'd smile at each other and wave when no one was watching.

Chapter Seven

The Letter

My parents were still carrying on about how Castillo would change their lives when Uncle Adolfo's son Lumen showed up at our front door with a white envelope in his hand.

Papa didn't invite his nephew in. Instead, he stepped outside and, sitting on the step, asked the boy what had brought him here. Without a word, Lumen handed him the envelope.

Emilia and I had arrived from the creek and were in the kitchen finishing our lunch when we heard Papa's voice. We immediately rushed into the sleeping area and pressed our faces to a wall crack. There stood Lumen, whom I had seen only twice before, waiting for Papa's reaction.

Papa stood up, switched the envelope from hand to hand, then handed it back to Lumen. "Read it!"

Lumen's hands shook as he read:

> Señor Salvador Montalvo,
> I understand that you have children of school age, yet you have not come by the school to register them. It's the middle of August already and classes began two weeks ago. Please come by the school at once. Your children are already way behind the other students.
>
> Sincerely,
> *Rosa Blanca Traverso*

Papa's eyebrows went up and down. "Give me that!" He snatched the paper from Lumen's hands. "Who the hell told that damn teacher that I had children of school age?"

Lumen kept silent. Standing almost as tall as Papa but skinnier, he rolled his brown eyes, then turned and ran.

"You little blabbermouth!" Papa yelled, his cheeks quivering. "You told her! *Hijo e perra!* (Son-of-a-bitch!) Come around here again and I'll break your brown nose and kick your ass all the way up that hill!"

Lumen's black hair flapped up and down as he ran, and his tucked-in shirt became a huge blue bubble of air on his back.

Mama had gone out to stand quietly against the wall, her skinny arms crossed over her bulging belly, her face blank.

Papa walked in circles, yelling and cursing, the veins on his neck like ropes under the skin. He shook a big fist and shouted, "That's right! Keep running, you little bastard!" When Lumen disappeared into the woods, Papa exhaled like a raging bull, staring down at the ground. After a few minutes, he rubbed his chin and said to Mama, "Maybe there's no harm in sending that girl to school for a few months."

Mama's mouth popped open. "Send Emilia to school? That's too far for her to go alone."

Papa, still red-faced, slapped the wall above Mama's shoulder and said, "She'll have to go. I don't want anyone from that damn school coming around here asking questions."

"It's too far for Emilia to go alone," Mama said in a firm tone. "Besides that, the oldest daughter is always the mother's helper. No one can make you send her to school."

"Whether they can make me or not is beside the point. If anyone from the school comes around, they sure as hell will find my rum and the still. I'd end up paying a fine and going to jail. I'll take Emilia in on Monday." Papa pulled a roll of tobacco from his pocket, bit off a chunk, chewed rapidly, then spat so the wind would blow the saliva toward Mama. "Sabina can go with

Emilia, for a while anyway. See that they're ready." He took his machete and walked toward the cornfield.

Mama stretched her arms to the sky, mumbled some words we couldn't hear, then dropped her arms and wiped the brown spittle off her legs and arms.

I felt bad for Mama. She had to wipe off the spit drops with her hands. At the same time, it dawned on me that I would be going to school. Even though it might be for only a little while, the thrill made me smile and clasp my hands together. At last, I would get to see the school my godfather had described as a white building with a red roof far away from our house.

I had to wait for Emilia's reaction before expressing mine. If she didn't like what she heard and I appeared pleased, she'd make me regret it.

Emilia squinted as we turned from the wall. "Shit! I don't want to go to a stupid school!"

I kept quiet to avoid getting hit, but I thought she was definitely an idiot.

The next day, Mama stood at the rickety table, cutting a piece of yellow fabric to make our school dresses. "Who has ever heard of girls going to school? All they'll ever do is get married and raise babies. Nobody needs an education for that!" She complained while cutting the fabric, and while hunched over the table, turning the little wheel of the sewing machine by hand.

Meanwhile, Emilia cursed Lumen for bringing the letter, and the teacher who wrote it. Then she wished that someone would burn down the school before Monday morning.

Each night thereafter, I went to bed with a bubble of excitement in my chest, and two questions in my mind. *What if Papa decides to listen to Mama? And what if God answers Emilia's prayers?*

On Sunday night, Mama called us into the kitchen and squatted down next to the *fogón* with one hand on Emilia's wrist and the other on mine. "I want you girls to come straight home after school. Don't play with other children inside the school or out.

Don't eat anything somebody might give you, even if you're starving. Don't talk with anyone on your way to school or back. Stay together all the time. You don't need anyone but each other. Even to *la letrina*, you must go together."

"What's a *letrina*?" I asked, feeling spooked, as if hands were reaching from the darkness.

"*La letrina* is a shack with a round hole on the floor where you squat down to pee and do whatever. It's dangerous, too. You might fall in and drown."

"Oh, no! Will it stink?" Emilia wrinkled her nose.

"Not much, especially after you drown," Mama said with a grin that confused me. I knew that drowning wouldn't be good, so why the grin?

"Don't they have bushes around the school?" I asked.

"No, you can't go behind the bushes like we do here." Mama let go of our wrists and stood up. "There will be boys running around the school, and they spy on girls."

"I hate having to go to that stupid school," Emilia whined. "And I hate Lumen for bringing Papa that letter!"

"Well, your father said you have to go. Just make sure you watch out for each other, like I told you."

I went to bed trying to picture the shack with a hole in the floor. Then I thought about boys spying on the girls who'd go behind the bushes. I'd throw a rock at them if they did that to me. The fear of a few nasty boys would never take away my desire to attend school. As for *la letrina*, I made up my mind not to use it, no matter how badly I needed to go.

* * *

I woke up early the next morning thinking about school, and I smiled at the ceiling. I wanted to get up, put on my new dress, and leave. I had no room in my stomach for that morning's coffee; I was too full already with floating bubbles. Someone else would have to do my chores. I felt like singing, but I didn't because Papa might hear me and decide that Emilia didn't need anyone to accompany her to school. I'd be pulling weeds forever.

Pretending that going to school wasn't a big deal was not easy, so I forced down my coffee, ran to the bushes, and ran back into the house to put on my new dress. I felt the wide smile across my face, and feared that Mama might slap it off—but I couldn't stop it even when I tried.

"Get over here and I'll comb your hair," Mama said.

She started with Emilia, scraping her scalp and pulling at the tangled hair. Emilia's tears spilled to the floor. Emilia rubbed her eyes with her knuckles until the whites turned pink.

Mama tapped her on the shoulder. "Stop wiggling and whining, or I'll give you a good reason to cry!"

Emilia shoved her whole fist into her mouth and rolled her eyes toward me. I saw that look as a warning: She would take the anger she felt for Mama out on me, just as she had done other times when we had our hair combed. My hair was fine and thin, easy to comb without pulling and scraping. It bothered Emilia that I didn't suffer, so she would pull my hair and throw mud balls and do other things to pass her pain onto me.

What happened next nearly shocked me to death. Papa walked into the room clean-shaven and dressed in his black trousers and white shirt.

"I'll comb Sabina's hair," he said, and everybody froze where they stood. Mama held the comb inches above Emilia's head, and Emilia's eyes stared without blinking. Gloria couldn't close her mouth, and José backed against a wall. Lorenzo was the only one who didn't appear surprised, but he was too young to do anything but suck two of his fingers.

Papa ignored the questioning eyes and sat on a bench, motioning with a bent finger for me to stand between his knees. Expecting something awful, I walked over to him. The only times he had ever called any of us to his side had been for a hard whack on the head.

But he put his hands on my shoulders and turned me to face

away from him. Now I couldn't see his face, but I saw everyone else staring. I braced myself for the first blow, but instead I felt his little comb moving gently up the strands to the top of my head.

"What a white scalp she has," he said, and I felt his breath of stale coffee and tobacco on the back of my neck. The smell didn't bother me then, for he spoke in such a soft voice that it gave me tiny bumps on my skin. "Such soft hair," he said, trailing his hand behind the comb.

If combing my hair and saying nice things about it was a loving gesture from Papa, I had to keep it wrapped around my heart and never let on that it made me feel pretty. Mama and Emilia had often told me that I was nothing special, "just a white-eyed girl with yellow hair and freckles."

Papa stood up and reached for his machete. "It's time to leave," he said to Emilia and me. "Tell your mother goodbye."

Mama's eyes turned teary. "Don't forget what I told you girls last night." She reached out her arms, pulled us close to her rounded belly, and spread some loud kisses over our faces. "Now go. Your father's waiting."

Emilia headed up the hill behind Papa, and I followed, watching her yellow dress sway back and forth over the green grass. I turned once to look back and saw Mama at the kitchen door, dabbing her eyes with the hem of her dress. I didn't know if she was crying because she'd miss us, or because she would have to do all the work by herself. Either way, I felt bad for her, even though it made no sense that I cared at all.

We entered a part of the forest I'd never seen before, where the air felt cold and smelled of rotting leaves. Chills traveled up my legs all the way to my spine as I placed my bare feet on the wet, dark mush of rotted leaves. Dark, thick water shot between Emilia's and my toes, but I realized that it showed more on my white feet than it did on Emilia's.

Papa always wore shoes, so he didn't know how bad we felt. But he also didn't know I would go through anything to get to school and learn to read and write like my godfather.

"Make sure you look for these marks," Papa said, carving chunks of bark off the trees with his machete so we could find our way back home. "You don't want to go the wrong way and get lost in the woods." He stopped and looked at Emilia. "Are you going to remember that?"

Emilia nodded.

"I'll remember," I blurted out.

"Good!" he said. Then he looked at my muddy feet. "White skin shows everything." He grinned, and then turned away.

We went up one slope and down another. Emilia was only a short distance behind Papa, but I was way back, slipping, sliding, and scared. It would be scary to get lost in the woods. The trees were tall, with big trunks and thick branches that blocked the sun. The sound of water rushing down at the bottom of the hill echoed through the woods, and I shivered at the thought of being there in the dark of night.

After what seemed like hours of walking under the trees, we finally emerged onto a flat strip of land with green grass, yellow butterflies, and ferns wrapped in vines that had blue flowers shaped like dangling bells. The sky extended like a huge blue dome from the top of the mountain to the river and beyond. I thought my heart would soon fly out of my chest. I wanted to clap my hands, whirl around and yell, "Wow! What a big world!" But if I did that, Papa would make me turn around and go back home.

This stretch of flat land was divided by a narrow path of reddish earth that smelled sweet, like something one could eat. A narrower path branched off to the left, and another to the right. In the distance were little houses with blue smoke rising from their roofs, children's voices, roosters crowing, and dogs barking.

Our path continued straight until we reached a dark old house under a patch of trees.

Papa stopped suddenly and said, "Listen carefully, you two. The people who live here are very old, and a little crazy, especially the old man. Sometimes he disappears into the woods for days. I want you girls to always run past here and don't stop, even if you hear somebody calling you."

Papa's voice was little more than a whisper, which added to my chills, and the look in his eyes made me think this place was evil. Looking at Emilia didn't reassure me. She stood stiffly, rolling her eyes left and right, as if dark arms were reaching out to drag her away. I wondered then if the monsters in Mama's Bible stories came from around here.

Emilia finally whined, "Papa, why? Why do we have to go to school? What does a crazy old man look like, anyway? And what if he chases us? What shall we do?"

"Run as fast as you can. That's what you do."

I wished Papa hadn't said that. Knowing Emilia, she would run away and leave me behind for the crazy old man.

Maybe going to school isn't such a good idea, after all. But maybe if the old man grabs hold of me, I can bite his arm really hard and he'll have to let me go.

Chapter Eight

A Blanket on a Pole

Our path divided shortly beyond the old house. Papa took the one angling to the left, which led to a metal gate. A tall, thick hedge of red bougainvillea dotted with dewdrops stretched out for quite a distance on each side of that gate. Papa said it was a fence to keep *bandidos* out of the schoolyard.

I had my first impression of what magic would be like when Papa pulled out an iron bar and the gate swung open. Way out there against a line of trees, surrounded by a large expanse of green grass, stood the white school building with a red roof and two little houses (the latrines) behind it.

As I quietly cheered at the beauty of such a striking building, I noticed a brilliant piece of fabric or blanket hanging from a high pole above the red roof. Pretending that this wasn't the happiest day of my life hadn't been easy, but I couldn't hide my curiosity about the fabric on the pole.

"Is that a blanket up there, Papa?"

"That's more than just a blanket," he said. "It's the American flag."

"The American flag, Papa? What's American?"

Papa stopped, took off his hat, looked up at the flag, and said, "The American flag represents the United States."

"What's the United States?"

"A big country on the other side of the ocean."

"What's an ocean?"

"A lot of water all around this island, and don't ask any more questions."

I had asked too many questions, and I still needed to know what the United States, an ocean, and an island were.

Papa decided to hide his machete before reaching the school building. "I don't want to scare the teacher away," he said with a grin. He pushed the machete into a bougainvillea bush, smoothed the leaves over the hole he'd made, then wiped his hands on his trousers. "Now let's go meet the teacher."

Reaching a flight of steps, Papa stopped to give us yet another warning. "Now listen, you two," he said, a serious look in his eyes. "These steps are very slippery when it rains. They are made of something called concrete, which is much different than wood. You can easily slip and break your neck, if you aren't careful."

Emilia made a face and cried, "Oh, God! I wish we weren't coming to this stupid school! Everything's so scary."

Papa creased his forehead. "Well, you're here now, so stop your complaining. All you need to do is be careful."

Emilia cast her eyes to the ground and said nothing more.

As we reached the top step, a woman in a pink dress came to the door. "I am Miss Rosa Traverso." She extended a white hand with red fingernails that matched her lips.

Papa's eyes sparkled as he took her dainty little hand between his and held it for a long time. "It's a pleasure to meet you. I'm Salvador Montalvo, at your service." He finally released her hand and added, "These are my daughters, Emilia and Sabina. Only Emilia is of school age. This other one has come to keep her company because we live too far for one girl to walk alone."

I couldn't help staring at the teacher. She was the prettiest lady I had ever seen. Her shoulder-length hair shone like golden brown silk thread in the sun. And her eyes were as green as the grass outside, but with eyelashes quivering like the brown wings of a butterfly.

"Are they sisters?" she asked. "This one's so light. Beautiful hair. She's a doll."

Papa's smile disappeared. "Yes, they are sisters. And no, she's not a doll. Her name is Sabina, because she's so light, like her great-grandfather, but she is not a doll."

A flush spread quickly across the teacher's face. "My apology, Don Montalvo. I meant no disrespect. Both girls are beautiful. May I see your teeth, Sabina?" She placed a soft finger under my chin. I took my eyes off her and looked at my father for permission. When he nodded, I opened my mouth wide. She turned her head to the side. "I see that she still has her baby teeth. Not six yet, is that right?"

Papa stood firmly. "It's like I told you. Only Emilia is of school age. This one comes just to keep her company."

The teacher stood as firm as Papa. "I understand. Let's go inside. You need to sign some papers."

A hint of a smile on Emilia's face told me that she thought Papa didn't like the teacher, and he would soon change his mind about us attending school. But Papa motioned us to follow him as he walked behind the teacher.

The classroom looked bigger than our whole house. It had white walls and a smooth ceiling without rough beams or posts. The floor shone as if it had never been walked on before. Its boards were narrow and fitted closely together. No roaches or other bugs could crawl in between these boards, as they did in our house. Better yet, the chickens, if there were any under the floor, would not be able to push their beaks through and nip at a kid's bare bottom.

An aisle ran the length of this huge room to the teacher's desk. On each side of the aisle were desks that, except for three, were occupied by boys and girls, big and small, all staring at us.

We walked single file, the teacher leading the way, the hem of her pink dress swaying and her slender heels tapping across the shiny floor. Papa's steps were heavier and louder, although he'd been trying to walk softly.

Emilia followed Papa, her eyes on the floor, shoulders hunched, her feet shuffling across the smooth floor as if she hoped no one would notice the dried mud and scratches.

I stayed far behind, looking everywhere, trying to capture all these new things. I checked out all the strange faces, hoping to see a girl or boy with hair and eyes the color of mine. There were none. Some had brown hair, similar to the teacher's, but without the shine. And all the eyes staring at us were dark.

I had never seen so many boys and girls before, none of them milky-white. And I could tell that they saw me as weird. I smiled at them, but some stuck out their tongues at me. Only one girl, whom the teacher called Manuela, smiled back.

Still, I quickly turned my head toward the pictures of black horses, brown cows, and yellow baby chicks around two blackboards up on the walls. White letters and numbers were written on those boards, and I thought of my godfather writing with charcoal. I felt like crying. I wanted to see him again, to tell him that I had been to the school and had seen the blackboards he had described to me.

The teacher sat at a desk the color of Mama's cinnamon sticks, but as shiny as the floor. She asked Papa some questions, which he answered softly, as if to keep us from hearing. The teacher wrote the answers on a stiff yellow card that already had some black writing on it. When she finished writing, she pushed the card toward Papa and asked him to sign it. Papa wrapped his big fingers around her black pen, and slowly scribbled his name on the line. Then he shook her hand again, and with his hat over his chest, motioned for us to follow him.

"This is your seat," he said to Emilia, "close to the teacher so you can learn fast." Then he led me to a back corner of the huge room and said, "This is a good place for you to wait for your sister. It's out of everyone's way, but you can still see the teacher and all her students. Make sure you stay right here. Don't go outside by yourself." He patted my head and walked away.

I caught my tears on my skirt as I watched my father disappear beyond the door. If only he could stay as nice as he had been all morning. I would never forget the way he had combed my hair at home, or the gentle pat on my head before he left.

Chapter Nine

Three Bullies

The things I could see from the corner of the class-room were better than what we had at home—like the four windows that were so big that they had to be held open with iron rods. Through one window I could see a tree that didn't look anything like the trees on our farm. This one had long, green needles instead of leaves, and it whistled when the breeze blew hard. One of its branches kept reaching for the window ledge, sweeping it as it moved back and forth.

I kept myself entertained by looking from that branch to a hibiscus branch with red flowers peeking in and out the next window. I imagined the pine branch as an old woman sweeping the cobwebs from a window ledge, and the hibiscus as a girl dressed in red, calling me out to play.

Sitting there was much better than having to work in the heat of the sun with my father. But I wanted more. I wanted to be up on one of those wooden chairs with attached desks, swinging my legs like the other girls. They didn't seem embarrassed about the dry mud and scratches on their legs, so I wouldn't worry about mine, either. I would just listen to the teacher and learn faster than Emilia, and faster than anyone else in the whole school. I'd make Papa so proud that he would sign me up in first grade in spite of my age. I'd be the best student Miss Traverso ever had.

And one day my godfather would find out that I had learned how to read and write just like him, and he'd be happy for me.

The teacher walked to the blackboard and wrote numbers and words with a white stick. She took a flat, narrow board and pointed to her writing, asking the students on Emilia's side of the room to repeat after her. The room filled with several voices responding. I listened for Emilia's voice, but did not hear it. She was probably too shy to say anything.

Pointing to other words and numbers on the board, the teacher asked the other group of students to read. A few hands went up, and the high voices of boys and girls called out the answers. The two groups of students, I later found out, were first graders on one side and second graders on the other. Classes would end at 11:30 for the two grades, and the third and fourth grades would come in at 12:00. All grades were taught by Miss Traverso.

The time seemed to drag on forever while I sat there waiting for my sister. I leaned on one elbow, then on the other, took deep breaths and exhaled loudly. I turned over on my stomach, elbows on the floor, chin in my hands, and stared toward the teacher and the blackboard. I promised myself that one day I would be a teacher, but I would not have a little girl sitting in a corner all by herself. I would have her come up and sit with the other students.

After a long time, the teacher announced that it was time for recess. The students bolted from their seats and ran out, clapping their hands and shouting.

Emilia and I stayed in our places until the teacher said that we could go, too. I wanted to say thank you, but I couldn't, so I quietly stood up and followed my sister out of the classroom.

As our mother had suggested, we sat together near the door. Within seconds, we had a swarm of girls around us.

"Aren't you girls going to play?"

"Are you just going to sit there?"

"Hey, can't you hear?"

"Can't you talk?"

I waited for Emilia to speak up, but she stared at the girls and said nothing. The mean girls would not be ignored.

One of them, with kinky black hair and red sores on her feet, scooped some dried leaves from the ground and threw them on us. "Come on, you two! Don't sit there like dummies."

I saw Emilia cover her face with her hands, so I did the same. Then I felt more dirt coming at us, and heard different voices calling out.

"Are you girls stupid idiots?"

"Are you real sisters?"

"They don't look like sisters."

"Hey, why is she so white and you so dark?"

"They can't talk?"

"They are ugly! Ugly! Ugly!"

Emilia wiggled herself so close to me that I felt pinned against the wall. Then I felt something poking my ribs, so I opened my eyes and saw brown feet with red sores jabbing at me. I let out a shrill cry, and at about the same time I heard another girl calling the teacher.

"What's going on?" the teacher yelled out the door, and the girls ran in different directions. "Everyone return to the classroom! Right now!" The teacher seemed angry. Then she came over to us and asked, "What did you two do to provoke such behavior?"

My big sister finally spoke up. "We did nothing, teacher. We just sat here by ourselves like Mama told us to do."

"Well, next time don't sit there. I'm not coming to your rescue if it happens again."

That was the end of our first recess. We followed the teacher inside, and Emilia went to her seat while I went to my cold corner. I felt confused. Miss Traverso had said earlier that I was a doll, yet she had not even looked at me before recess, and then didn't show any concern about what those mean girls did to us. Worse yet, she went on teaching without yelling at the bullies.

And what about my big and tough sister Emilia? Why didn't

she try to beat up one of those mean girls like she had beaten me for years? So much for being the oldest.

I spent the rest of that morning wondering where all those kids lived, and how many of them had to work on farms and be afraid of their parents. I looked for scratches and cuts on their dangling legs, and for patches and banana stains on their clothes. I noticed two girls in each grade whose dresses were new. But unlike the new dresses that Emilia and I wore, theirs had lace and buttons. Most of the boys had mud and scratches on their bony legs, and many patches and stains on their trousers and shirts.

There was one boy, however, who was not like any of the others. The teacher called him Noel, and she talked to him softly and with a smile. His desk looked newer and shinier than all the others, and had been pulled closer to the teacher, away from the other students. He was the only student wearing shoes and nice clean clothes. His black hair had been nicely cut and combed; his light skin looked smooth, and his hands looked clean and soft.

We learned later that he was the son of the *haciendero* (owner of a big farm) who had provided hospitality to the teacher. Teachers couldn't come that far from the cities if they had to return to their homes each day.

Noel didn't go out during recess. He stayed in with Miss Traverso. Then, at 11:30, the *haciendero's* servant arrived with Miss Traverso's lunch and took Noel home on horseback. On rainy days, the servant wrapped him in a raincoat and carried him to the waiting horse.

I concluded—and was sure that all the other kids had come to the same conclusion—that the son of a rich man was better than the rest of us, and for sure the bullies would never push him around like they did Emilia and me.

When class ended, the students ran out and scattered in different directions through the tall grass and bushes, their black heads bobbing, long hair flipping, and their voices echoing as they yelled goodbye to each other. We watched them from the top step, and when they disappeared, Emilia jumped down to the ground and ran like a wild horse.

"Run!" she yelled to me, but by the time I reached the gate, she was beyond the dark house of the old couple.

Running really fast, I saw my feet like white flashes on the dark soil. Looking way ahead, I saw Emilia's hair swinging left and right like the black tail of a horse.

She finally stopped when she reached the forest, but only to have me help her find the marks Papa had made on the trees. As soon as I located a few, she took off. She didn't stop again until she reached our yard, so our parents would see us arriving together. She was well rested by the time I caught up with her. But I was gasping, and my throat felt so dry I couldn't utter a word.

"Mama's making lunch!" Emilia exclaimed as we neared the house, and the smell of fried codfish reached us. She leaped across the yard, grabbed the doorjambs, raised one foot to the floor, and pulled herself up into the kitchen.

My legs were too short to reach the kitchen floor, so I went in through the living room and followed the aroma into the kitchen. I found Mama hunched over with one arm around Emilia, her other arm stretched out waiting for me. Although she didn't say it, her hug told me that she had missed us. It was the warmest hug I had ever received from my mother.

"You two must be hungry," she finally said, pulling away from us. She reached above the stove and brought down two gourd-shells. "Now tell me all about the school." Mama handed each of us a shell filled with cooked bananas and tiny pieces of fried codfish. "I also want to know about the teacher, and about what you girls learned."

We sat on the floor with our food, each of us stuffing a chunk of hot banana in our mouths, and trying to blow out the heat as we chewed. Since the half-cup of black coffee that morning, we'd had nothing to eat or drink.

Emilia swallowed hard. "The school is bigger than this house, and I hate it because it's filled with mean girls."

Mama leaned against the *fogón*, looking down at us. "One day in school, and you already hate the other students? Why?"

Emilia swallowed again, lifting her chin. "They kicked us, threw dirt at us, and called us hideous and stupid."

With a chunk of hot banana burning down my throat, I cut in. "That's because we sat together on the top step and didn't play like everyone else."

Mama gave me a cross look. "Well, that's what happens in schools. That's one of the reasons my parents kept me home. You keep doing what I told you until those girls learn that not everyone has to jump around and play."

She reached up to a beam and brought down her little black pouch of tobacco, and proceeded to make a cigarette. She carefully unrolled the soft dry leaf and held it over a burning piece of wood from the *fogón*. When the leaf became brittle, she crushed it on a piece of brown paper, which she held between her thumbs and middle fingers. With her index fingers, she arranged the tobacco crumbs and slowly rolled the cigarette. Then she ran the tip of her tongue along the edge of the paper and quickly folded it over, sealing in the tobacco. She pinched the ends of the short roll, brought one end to her lips, and with the burning piece of wood lit the other end. She took a long drag and blew the smoke through her nose. It rose lazily to the ceiling.

"Now tell me about the teacher. What does she look like?" Another puff of smoke floated over us.

Emilia smirked. "She looks like your rose bush. Red lips, red nails, and pink dress with little green leaves and flowers all over. And shoes with heels as long as your middle finger."

"So," Mama said, "is she pretty?"

I quickly jumped in. "She's beautiful! You should see her! She has white, soft hands, and brown hair that shines in the sun. And she wears see-through stockings, Mama . . . silky ones."

Emilia looked at me with mean eyes. "You only like her because her eyes are white and ugly like yours."

I nearly choked on my last piece of banana. The teacher's eyes were white like mine? I knew the difference between green and white, and Miss Traverso's eyes were positively green and gorgeous.

I didn't hear the rest of Mama's questions or Emilia's answers. And I didn't want Emilia to see that what she'd said made me smile. I stood up and took my gourd-shell to the *fogón*, washed it, and put it up on the hanging net. Mama and Emilia were still talking, but I didn't hear them. The words *Her eyes are white like yours* occupied my mind. I would be just fine if my eyes looked anything like Miss Traverso's.

When Emilia finished eating, Mama told us to change our school dresses and to go fetch the water. The water barrels were empty.

Emilia complained all the way down the hill. "If it weren't for that stupid school, we would have filled the damn barrels this morning, not in the middle of the day. I hate that stupid teacher for sending Papa the stupid letter."

"No, Emilia, she's not stupid. She's very, very smart!"

Emilia looked me up and down. "Oh, yes she is! Red lips and nails. Stupid! If God wanted women to have red lips and red nails, we would have come to the world that way." Emilia spoke with fiercely burning eyes. "And the way she walked back and forth, tapping the blackboard with her piece of flat wood! I bet she felt big and mighty in her fancy dress and silly shoes."

I backed away slowly. "You wouldn't like to look like her someday?"

"Of course not!" Her eyes narrowed. "But I bet *you* would. Oh, I bet you wish you were her right now." She stopped right at the edge of the hill, aimed a bony finger at my forehead, and turned it like a screwdriver. "You wish you were like her, don't you?"

"No, I don't. And you're right . . . she is ugly and stupid." I felt the twist in my stomach, but I would say anything to keep from being pushed down the cliff.

After a half dozen trips up and down the hill, we went out to collect the eggs that the hens had laid under bushes around the house. We carried the eggs in our skirts without talking or arguing. It took complete concentration. If we tripped and broke the eggs that Papa would sell in town on Saturday . . . well, only God could save us from a whipping. And He seldom did.

By the time we finished our work, the sun had fallen behind the mountain, Mama was cooking supper, and Papa had returned from wherever he'd been. Now Emilia went to help Mama in the kitchen, and I had to scrub Papa's feet. He sat on the front steps, as he did every other day. I brought him a pan of water. He stuck his feet in, wiggled his toes, and the water turned brown.

"Scrub my feet," he said. "And tell me everything you saw from the corner of the classroom."

I told him about the branches peeking into the window, but I knew he wasn't listening. All I heard from him was, "Aha, aha, aha . . ."

Chapter Ten

Flapping in the Breeze

The school bell rang as we walked through the gate the next day, and all the boys and girls raced each other to the door. Up on the high pole, the flag flapped in the breeze, making a sound like that of a horsewhip. A whipping sound had usually scared me, as Papa always kept the horses moving by cracking a whip on the ground, and I had often worried that one day he would use the whip on me.

But the snapping and whipping of the flag filled my chest with a huge bubble that took my breath away. It was a feeling I would never try to explain to anyone, for I didn't know if other kids, including my sister, got any pleasure from hearing a flag flapping and whipping. I didn't even know if they found the flag as pretty as I did. Well, *pretty* doesn't describe it. To me, the flag was beautiful, gorgeous, brilliant, exhilarating. The look and sounds of it made me feel like climbing the pole and hugging the flag.

Burning heat spread over my face and ears as we walked into the classroom. All the students had taken their seats, and all those heads turned and thirty pairs of brown eyes beamed at us. The good feeling about the flag quickly vanished and, for that moment, I didn't know where to aim my own gaze. I felt as though Emilia and I looked like two shaggy dogs smeared with mud.

I made it to my corner with shaky knees in time to watch Emilia reach her seat. She did look like a shaggy dog—a scared little dog who knew that everyone else in the classroom was better and nicer-looking than she.

I felt her pain as I sat on the cool floor. She was bigger than most girls in both grades, and at home, especially with me, she was tough and mean. But on that day, Emilia appeared humble and distracted. I felt sorry for her.

Then I worried that I might end up being like her. I could not let myself look like Emilia, and I would not let myself appear scared and defeated in front of other kids, no matter how much nicer than us they looked. No. From that moment on, my ears and eyes would be directed to whatever Miss Traverso was teaching. I would learn fast, even from my lonely corner.

"Attention, class!" Miss Traverso's voice seemed to hit the walls and bounce back into the classroom. All the heads quickly turned toward her. "I'm going to read this little book to you, so pay close attention because I'll be asking some questions about the story." She walked back and forth in front of the class, holding a small red book open, the hem of her blue dress swaying back and forth, her black high-heeled shoes barely tapping the floor. She looked even more beautiful that day. I would be really happy to look like her.

I sat up so straight that I could feel the stretch on my spine, and tuned my ears to hear every word the teacher read. I had missed hearing my godfather read to me, so this was my chance to pretend that he was the one reading up there.

The story was about a girl who insisted on buying a bottle after her mother had advised her to save her pennies for something else. But the girl explained that she had never seen a blue bottle before, and she loved the color blue. When the mother and daughter returned home, the girl discovered that the little bottle was full of water. She dumped out the water, which she realized was blue, and the bottle was only clear glass.

The moral of the story was that children paid the

consequences when they did not listen to their parents. But by the time the teacher finished explaining the moral of her story, I had also realized that it was by following Mama's orders that we had been victimized the day before. I would still listen to my mother, but I would not follow all of her advice. I would play with the other girls during the next recess, and that way the bullies would not be mean to us. Of course, I forgot momentarily that I had been taught to follow my big sister's example.

For the next lesson, the teacher wrote numbers and letters on the blackboard. I had all I could do to keep from jumping up and yelling that I could read what she had written because my godfather had taught all that to me. I could easily copy her numbers and letters, if only I had some paper and a pencil, or one of those white sticks. Would she give me one if I walked up and asked her? What would I do if she ordered me back to the corner and all the students laughed?

I tried to look away and forget about whatever Miss Traverso was teaching her class, but it wasn't easy, especially when she called out the letters, a, e, i, o, u, just like my godfather had done.

I watched her gather a handful of papers and pass them to the first graders. *I must let her know that I can copy all of that if she would give me some paper and pencil.*

While building up my nerve to go ask her, I practiced writing the numbers and letters on the floor with my index finger. Then I got to my feet and marched up to the teacher's desk. It seemed to take me forever to get there. Everyone's eyes, including the teacher's, were on me now, but I wasn't going back to the corner without a piece of paper and pencil. I saw Emilia motioning me to go back, but I ignored her, too.

"Can I have some paper and a pencil, too?" My voice squeaked. My ears felt hot, and I knew everyone could hear my knees knocking.

Miss Traverso smiled. "Why? Do you want to draw pictures?"

"No, I want to copy that." I pointed to the blackboard.

The teacher's smile vanished. "I can't waste paper."

I looked into her beautiful eyes. "I won't waste it."

Her smile came back as she handed me a half sheet of paper and a short stub of a pencil. "Use both sides of the paper. I don't have any more."

"Thank you, Miss Traverso," I said and trotted back to my corner. I could feel the wide smile on my face as I sat on my legs to copy the numbers from the chalkboard. I did as my godfather had taught me. I made the zero like a ring for my little finger. The number one was a short line up and down with a tiny hook at the top. The number two was a little girl on her knees with her head so low that her chin poked into her chest. The number three, my godfather had said, was a crown with a dent in the middle. The number four was a straight line with another at its left which turned sharply to the right and over the first. The number five, my godfather had said, was the hardest to describe, but eventually everyone got it right. I started with a short straight line, then curved to the right, and quickly to the left. At the top of the short line, I drew a shorter line aiming right . . . and there I had a number five.

I finished the numbers and moved on to the five letters, remembering what my godfather had taught me. I practiced on the floor with my finger, then wrote on the paper, slowly, looking at the blackboard before and after writing each letter. I checked again when I finished, then leaned against the wall and waited.

The teacher stood up from her desk and went around the first grade section to collect the papers. I couldn't believe that she returned to her desk without even looking at me! I marched back up there again.

"You forgot mine," I said, putting the paper on her desk.

As she glanced at me, I hurried back to my corner, my ears burning and my legs shaking. Some of the kids giggled as I walked past, but I didn't look at them. I sat in my corner staring at the floor, waiting to hear what the teacher had to say about my work.

At the tapping of her shoes, I looked up and saw her coming

toward me with my piece of paper in her hand. My heart stopped. *She likes my work!*

"Have your parents been teaching you at home?" She smiled and crouched down next to me, smelling like a rose. "Have they?"

"No. My godfather taught me a long time ago."

"A long time ago?" The teacher's eyes sparkled. "You're pretty smart. Most of the first graders didn't even get the numbers right. Yet you did everything correctly."

I wanted to tell her that she was the most wonderful person in the whole world. But all I could do was stare at her beautiful face, her green eyes, and her shiny hair. I felt the corners of my mouth tighten, and my face froze.

"I think you're ready for first grade," she said, touching my shoulder. "I'll write a note to your parents. They'll be pleased to know they have a smart daughter."

No, they won't be pleased at all, I thought as the teacher walked away. My stomach rolled toward my throat as I pictured myself pulling weeds and planting beans for the rest of my life.

Such thoughts were painful, so I fantasized about being a first grader, sitting up there with the other students, learning everything the teacher taught. I would be the smartest girl in the school, and everyone in the class would want to be like me. I would make my father so proud that he'd want to keep me in school for years and years.

I was still dreaming about being a first grader, reading books and writing on paper with real pencils, when the teacher announced recess.

As my sister and I walked out behind the noisy students, we came face to face with the three bullies. Sand and crumbled dried leaves came at us like rain, catching us by surprise. We covered our faces with our hands and backed up against the wall. I peeked through my fingers and saw the sneering smiles across the girls' faces.

Then a dead lizard came flying toward us with a stiff tail and crooked legs. The girl who threw it waited wide-eyed for it to hit us, but it missed and hit the wall with a thud. She found this even funnier and laughed loudly, clapping her hands and jumping up and down. The two friends joined her. As they carried on, I looked behind me and saw the dead lizard still where it had landed.

I felt rage rushing through me. Without thinking of the consequences, I sprang to my feet and ran back inside, screaming all the way to the teacher's desk: "Some big girls are beating us! They're throwing dirt and dead lizards at us!" I turned and ran back outside, and saw even the bullies staring open-mouthed toward the school door.

"All right! Everyone back inside," the teacher yelled out the door. "I will not tolerate that kind of behavior!"

A big boy from second grade went up to her. "No, Miss Traverso, please let me explain. It's those three girls who are being mean to the new students." He picked up the dead lizard by the tail and held it up to show the teacher. She squirmed and told him to get rid of the poor thing. The boy threw it over the hibiscus bush, and it spun through the air as stiff as a stick, but with bent legs and crooked fingers.

Miss Traverso changed her mind and ordered only the bullies to go inside and wait to be punished. The rest of us were to stay out until she rang the bell.

"We need to find another place to sit," I told my sister. "The teacher told us yesterday not to sit where those girls would pick on us."

"No," said Emilia, "we're not going to sit anyplace. We can jump around and play like everyone else."

I stared at her in surprise. "What about Mama? Remember what she told us?"

"We won't tell her," Emilia said, and burst out laughing. "You should have seen those mean girls' faces when you screamed and ran. They looked shocked, as if they had expected us to sit here and let them kick us around."

"Yeah, no thanks to you," I said. "You should have made

them stop, since you're the oldest and the biggest." I leaned back on the wall, crossed my arms, and looked over my shoulder. "So much for being the oldest."

Luckily, Emilia didn't have time to clobber me. Manuela, the girl who had smiled at me the day before, came up the steps and asked, "Your mama doesn't want you girls to play, right?"

"How do you know that?" I jumped in while Emilia, looking surprised, studied the girl's face.

"That's what my mother tells me every morning," Manuela replied. "She says I might break a leg or an arm, and we live too far away from hospitals and doctors. But I don't pay much attention to my mother's rules. I can't sit here like you two did yesterday while the other girls play. Their mothers probably warned them not to play, either, but look at them having fun."

Emilia's eyebrows went up. "What will your mother do if she finds out that you disobeyed her?"

"Who's going to tell her? God?" Manuela hid her face in her hands and laughed. Her laugh was contagious. It made Emilia laugh, too. That laughter brought two other girls, Margarita and Mercedes, over to ask what was so funny. The question made all of us burst out laughing, and we all ran down the steps and chased each other around the flagpole.

Chapter Eleven

A Desk for Me

When the bell rang, Emilia and I walked with our new friends into the classroom. Even though I had to go to my corner, I felt that I was part of the class. From then on, whenever I looked up, I spotted three friendly faces. I didn't feel so alone anymore. And the best thing yet was knowing that Emilia felt better, too. She had a spark in her eyes, and she didn't stare at the floor anymore.

So we had made a few friends, and my sister didn't appear so mean anymore. But I still needed to be up there with the rest of the students. *If the teacher writes to Papa, will he sign me up for first grade?*

When class finally ended for the day, the teacher called me to her desk. "Take this letter to your parents. If they agree, you can start first grade tomorrow." Her smile made me feel that she really wanted me in her class. But while staring at her, speechless, I realized an even more important detail. She handed *me* the letter to my parents, ignoring my oldest sister who had always been trusted with important things. I suddenly felt a wide smile burning the corners of my mouth. At that moment, I could have sprung up off the floor and flown all the way home.

That day, Emilia didn't start running right away. She walked quietly ahead of me until we passed the old couple's house. Then she stopped and asked, "What's the teacher sending to Papa?" Her eyes narrowed. "Give it to me. I'll take it to him."

My stomach took a dive. "It's for Papa, not for you." Knowing that she couldn't be trusted, I felt suddenly sick. "The teacher sent it with me."

She clenched her teeth. "Let me see it!"

"No!" I stepped back and held the envelope high over my head. "The teacher sent it with me, because I'm going to be a first grader."

"Give it to me!"

"I can carry it myself."

Emilia reached up and snatched the envelope from my hand. "I'm going to tear it up and throw away the pieces."

Feeling desperate to save the letter, I yelled, "You do, and I'll tell Mama that we played, and that it was your idea!"

"Go ahead. I'm going to tell her anyway." She flipped the envelope, and the wind picked it up. With hate building up inside me, I watched it go up, down, and around until it came to rest on a bush. By the time I retrieved it, Emilia had run off.

I had felt good about her after we had made new friends, but now she'd turned mean again. Knowing how tricky she was, I expected her to be hiding behind a tree, ready to jump in front of me. I could not understand how she could turn mean so quickly. If she tore up the letter, Papa would never find out that I was ready for first grade. I felt nauseous, but there wasn't anything in my stomach to throw up.

Hoping that she wasn't watching, I lifted my skirt and stuck the envelope inside my underpants, then tightened the string we used in place of elastic. I felt the sharp corners over my navel, but knew that Emilia would not look there to find the letter.

It wasn't easy to run downhill through the forest, around so many trees, while still looking around for my mean sister. I didn't catch up to her until I reached our yard.

"Don't tell me you lost the envelope," she said with a smirk. "You're in trouble if you did."

My mouth felt so dry it made me cough, but I gave her a look of pure hate and dashed past her toward the front door. I found Papa in his hammock finishing his lunch. Turning away from him, I lifted my skirt, pulled out the envelope, and gave it to him.

"What's this?" he asked.

"A letter from the teacher," I gasped. "She wants me in first grade." I stood there, clearing my throat, pushing my hair from my face, exhaling hard, waiting for Papa's reaction.

He looked at the envelope, flipped it to the other side and back, then without a word put it in his shirt pocket. He took it with him when he left the house after lunch.

I went to the kitchen, hungry and disappointed. Papa could at least have looked at me, maybe raised his eyebrows and acted surprised. He didn't even tell Mama. I wanted to tell her what the teacher had said, and about Emilia threatening to tear up the envelope, then running and leaving me behind. But Mama seemed tired and uninterested.

"Hurry up and eat," she said, handing us each a gourd shell of cooked *panas* (breadfruit). "Here, feed this to Alejandro," she said to Emilia, giving her a small shell of *panas* mashed in goat milk. She then walked out of the kitchen and into the sleeping area, rubbing her lower back.

Sitting against the wall to eat my lunch, I wondered what had happened after we left for school that morning. Mama didn't look right, and Papa wasn't talking. It seemed as though something was about to happen, and Emilia had guessed it the minute she entered the kitchen. The look on her face told me she knew, but she wouldn't tell me even if I asked.

Mama didn't come out from behind the burlap curtain, and Papa, before he left, ordered Emilia to watch the little boys and make supper. He assigned me to carry water from the springs, bring the goats from the pasture and milk them, then gather dry wood for the stove.

"Gloria can help you gather the wood," he said, "but don't

take her to the springs. She might faint and roll down to the bottom of the hill."

Going down to the springs alone was good. I could dream about being a first grader, learning to read and write like Miss Traverso. Even the weight of the can of water on my head didn't bother me as I climbed the hill, picturing myself in school. It was thrilling to drift into my dream, imagining the cool breeze coming through the school windows, the smell of the chalk powder that fell to the floor when the teacher erased her writing. The best dream of all was that of me being a teacher, in beautiful dresses and high-heeled shoes.

By the third trip down and up, I had exhausted my fantasies about school, and I started thinking about Mama. *Is she really sick? Maybe dying?* Suddenly, I felt scared. *What would life be like without Mama? Who'd make our school dresses? Would Emilia become meaner and more controlling?*

The thoughts were devastating, and I could hardly breathe. Mama didn't look well. Her belly was huge. I wondered if maybe she had the kind of worms that grew in children's bellies.

Desperate to help her, I hurried home. I would remind her that a laxative, like the ones she gave us sometimes, would make her well again.

I found Emilia at the *fogón*, stirring the boiling beans.

"I know what's wrong with Mama," I blurted, gasping, lowering the can to the floor. "She might be full of worms, and she's forgotten to drink a laxative. You have to remind her! Hurry, before she dies."

Emilia turned from the *fogón* with a burst of laughter. "You're crazy. Better go get some wood before Mama comes out and whips some sense into you."

"It makes sense to me!" I shouted, running back to the woods. "If Mama dies, it'll be your fault!"

*   *   *

That night, after we children went to bed, I heard our parents whispering behind the curtain. Since Papa had taken the teacher's letter with him, I assumed that he had one of his cousins read it, and that he was now telling Mama about it. I turned my head, trying to hear, but couldn't make out their words.

The next day, Mama didn't get out of bed. Papa said that she had a bellyache but would be fine by the time we came home from school.

"I bet she has worms," I blurted out, and got a cross look from Emilia.

But Papa chuckled. "You could be right about that. Now you two get going."

On the way to school, it dawned on me that I should have asked Papa about the letter. With my concern about Mama, I had forgotten. Suddenly I felt as though I had lost the most important thing in my life. Every step from then on was a struggle. *What if Papa lost the letter? What if he chose to ignore it? What if the teacher thinks I lost it? What if she thinks I'm too dumb to deliver a letter?*

I walked into the classroom dragging my feet, keeping my eyes to the floor to avoid looking at the teacher, hoping she'd forgotten about the letter. I didn't know what I would say if she asked for a reply from my father.

From my corner, I chose to face the door rather than the blackboard. Hopefully, the teacher would wait until recess or noon to ask me for Papa's reply.

I shifted my weight from right to left and back, then turned on my stomach and began tracing letters and numbers on the smooth floor.

I traced the same numbers and letters over and over, covering a large area of the floor. Creeping backwards, I gave myself more writing space, pretending that I was at my own desk, writing with a pencil on paper.

The thumping of hooves interrupted my dream. I looked toward the door and was surprised to see Papa fastening his horse to a fence pole. Papa rubbed his hands together and walked up the steps. He was wearing his light-blue shirt, brown trousers, and a bright smile across his clean-shaven face.

He waited inside the door while the teacher finished writing on the blackboard. By the smile on Papa's face, I guessed that he was there to sign the necessary papers for me to begin first grade. I could hardly contain myself. I became two persons in one, arguing. One wanted to jump up and down and hug my father; the other me knew that Papa would not like to be hugged by his daughter. He would change his mind and refuse to sign the registration. I would simply die if that happened.

The teacher announced early recess, then invited Papa to come to her desk. He went forward gracefully, holding his hat over his buckle, still smiling.

Emilia and I stayed in our places until Papa reached the desk. Then we quietly walked out.

While Papa and the teacher talked inside, my sister and I waited in our old spot on the top step. We dared not let Papa find us jumping from the steps or running around the flagpole, as we had done the day before.

Manuela came up and sat between us. "Did you tell your father about the bullies? They think that's why he's here. Did you?" She motioned to the three mean girls, whose names we had learned were Joséfa, Carlota, and Concha. They were playing around the flagpole, but often looked toward the school door.

Emilia answered softly. "No, I only told my mother."

Manuela shrugged. "Parents tell each other everything."

Emilia winced, but didn't say anything.

Manuela wasn't shy. She cupped her hands around her mouth and said, "You don't want your father to see you talking with other kids, right?"

Once again, Emilia did not answer. She'd been staring toward the door, which paid off because Papa soon walked out. The teacher followed him out, and we all watched them shake hands again. Then the teacher went inside and Papa headed down the steps. But he stopped, looked down at us, and said, "You girls go straight home after school."

We nodded and watched as he mounted his horse and rode across the school yard and out the gate.

"He's like my father," Manuela whispered when he was out of sight. "Don't you hate being told again and again to hurry home? I'm so sick of hearing that from my parents that sometimes I want to run away. How about you? Do you ever feel like running away?"

Emilia looked startled. "Where would you go?"

"I don't know . . . someplace far away. But I might never be brave enough to do it."

Running away sounded exciting to me, but before I could say that I had thought about running away myself, the teacher rang her school bell, and the three of us followed the stream of students into the classroom.

Emilia and Manuela went to their seats, and I sat in my corner, wondering if Papa had signed the registration form. If the teacher didn't call me up there soon, I would have to walk up to her and ask.

She handed a sheet of paper to each kid in second grade, then said, "You can come up here now, Sabina. Your father moved a desk there for you." She pointed to one next to Emilia that hadn't been there before.

Even though I had been praying for this, I felt shocked when she called my name. I stumbled as I tried to stand up on rubbery legs. "Am I a first grader now?"

The teacher chuckled. "Yes, you are now a first grader."

I felt my chin quivering as I walked up, unable to tell the teacher that I was thrilled and liked her very much.

I ran my hand over the smooth desktop and climbed up on the seat, only to find out that I couldn't touch the floor even with the tip of my toes.

The teacher nodded. "Don't worry. Your legs will grow, and your feet will soon be flat on that floor."

I nodded back, still speechless. Then, as I watched her walk away, I saw four holes on the floor, left by the screws that had held my chair there. I pictured papa carrying the chair and desk to its new place, and I felt a sudden, warm rush of love for him.

Chapter Twelve

Alicia

A strong wind had begun to blow shortly after Papa left, and by the time the class ended, dark clouds covered the sky. The teacher told everyone to hurry home before the rain came, but Emilia and I barely made it beyond the old couple's home when the sky seemed to split open.

The downpour came so loud that, even screaming, we couldn't hear each other. It was terrifying. The raindrops blinded us, and the half sheet of paper with our first school work dissolved in our hands. The wind whipped us, pushed us back, spun us around, then threw us against each other. Muddy water splashed under our dresses, and thunder roared in the sky, trailing off just before the next blast. As we struggled through the fern field, keeping our eyes to the ground, lightning flashed on and off. We pushed forward against the wind, hoping to reach the forest, where the trees would shelter us.

The trees didn't help. Rainwater gathered in their branches, then spilled out in gushes on the back of our heads and necks as we bent to protect our eyes. Leaves and twigs also came down on us, stinging our skin. The wind whirled up from the bottom of the hill, forcing itself toward the sky and throwing us off balance. Staggering and falling, we rolled against a tree trunk, glanced at each other, then struggled to our feet, only to fall again.

Like two drunks, we finally emerged from the trees into the clearing of our house, the wind still pushing us back. Shielding my eyes with my hands, I saw the house standing inside the thick cloud of rain.

Fighting the wind, we pressed forward and at last reached the kitchen door. It was locked. We went around to the front door, hanging onto the wet walls. That was locked, too. We pounded on it until Papa finally opened it, but only a crack.

"Go around to the kitchen," he said, and quickly shut the door. Back around we went again, and finally the kitchen door opened and Papa stuck out a hand to pull us up into the house.

The kitchen seemed strange to me, with Papa there instead of Mama. There was no fire in the *fogón*, no sign of food. We were hungry and soaked to the bone, with water dripping from our hair, dresses, and underpants. The water hit the floor, then disappeared through the cracks.

The door to the sleeping area swung open, and Doña Ana, the old lady who had brought Lorenzo to Mama, came through with two rags and our old dresses and underpants draped over her arm. She closed the door quickly, put the dresses and pants in a corner, handed one rag to Emilia, and dried my hair with the other.

Papa, who had been leaning on the *fogón*, shaking his head as if he couldn't believe how wet we were, finally said, "Dry your hair and change your clothes. When you're dry, come and see your mother. She has a new sister for you." He pulled open the door and walked into the sleeping area.

My brain took off from there. *Papa said that Mama had a new sister for us. We just had a storm. Emilia didn't lie about a storm dropping me. At last, I'm not the only one dropped by a storm!*

I began to shake, not from being cold and hungry, but because it dawned on me that the storms dropped off girls, and for sure they all would be blonde. I would be happy if my new sister had green eyes and light hair.

I had never been more disappointed. Our new baby sister Alicia had thick black hair and dark red skin. As the days passed, the red faded, but her skin turned darker than Emilia's. Alicia's face was round, like Lorenzo's, but her eyes were large and far apart. Her hair was curly, and her nose short and wide. She could have passed for another race. But Alicia was blessed with an irresistible personality, and I grew to love her dearly.

The day she arrived had been surprisingly pleasant in the morning, terrifying in the afternoon, and very pleasant at the end. Mama stayed in bed. Doña Ana couldn't go home, for the river had swelled, and she lived on the other side. She cooked our supper early, since no one had eaten lunch, then helped Emilia feed our little brothers and get them settled in their hammocks for the night.

We had not been sent to the springs for water, and I got to stay in the kitchen and watch Doña Ana make some special tea for Mama and fry ripe bananas for us.

When the dark of night came, Papa hung a hammock for our guest in the sleeping area, between Mama's curtain and us girls. Doña Ana sat straight on the hammock, her eyes glistening with the lantern's light, and told us stories about horses galloping in the night to escape the witches chasing them to braid their manes.

I wished for that night to last forever—with Doña Ana telling stories, Papa chuckling in the living room, and Mama behind the curtain—no drunks, no fights.

I woke up to the sound of pots and pans, the smell of coffee brewing, and bright sunlight shining through the wall cracks. The first thing I did was run under the curtain, hoping that Alicia's hair had turned blonde. Mama was still in bed, and the baby's hair was still black.

"Mama, did the storm drop her in your bed?" I whispered. "No. Go get ready for school."

Feeling terribly disappointed in the curt answer from my mother—and in the color of my new sister—I ran to the kitchen. There, to my pleasant surprise, I found Doña Ana adding sugar to the steaming pot of coffee. She had milked the goat and taken it to the pasture. This was all too good to be true: a new family routine?

I still needed to know how the new baby had arrived. It was time for me to ask her some questions.

"Doña Ana, where are my father and Emilia?"

"Down at the springs."

This was great! Now I could ask Doña Ana a whole bunch of questions. "Did you bring Mama that baby?"

Doña Ana looked surprised. "Not exactly, but don't ask me who did. Your mother will tell you eventually."

I wondered why adults never gave a kid straight answers. They all acted mysterious and unfriendly.

I saw Papa coming from under the trees with two cans of water hanging from a long pole on his shoulder, one can at each end of the pole. That was the first and last time I saw Papa carrying water. Emilia was behind him with the usual can and a look of disgust. I felt sorry for her, but glad that this time Papa hadn't sent me.

Emilia complained all the way to school about another baby to take care of, about the muddy path, and about Papa making her go down for water and letting me sleep just because two days earlier I had brought up all the water by myself.

"I always end up doing the worst jobs," she said, punching a branch, which sent a spray of raindrops to the ground.

"What about me?" I demanded. "I always have to help Papa. That's worse than cooking and washing dishes."

Emilia stopped, pointed a finger at me, and through her teeth said, "Don't tell me which job is worse, Miss Brains."

"Why are you mad at me? I didn't do anything to you." I couldn't believe that we were back to the old routine after we had struggled through the storm together.

"Shut up and walk," she said, sliding in the mud.

I didn't want her to push me down the hill, so I walked way behind and thought about being a first grader. Those thoughts had been pushed to the back of my mind with all the excitement of the day before.

*   *   *

The first thing I told Manuela at recess was the news about our new sister.

"Oh, God!" she exclaimed. "I'll die if my mother comes up with another baby."

"Who brings her the babies?" I asked.

"Who brings them?" Her brow furrowed. "Nobody brings them to her. She *has* them. Don't you know?"

This was puzzling. I looked at Emilia, and she barked, "You're not supposed to be talking about that!"

"I'm not! *She* is."

"Yes, you are, and I'm telling Mama."

"Oh, my God!" Manuela cut in. "The same thing happened to me. For years, I believed Mama's stories about how different saints had brought seven babies to her. Then I felt stupid when my brother got married and his wife had my little nephew. She told me how babies were made and how they are born. Of course, I had to promise never to tell Mama that she told me, but I was sure glad to know the truth."

I was still confused, so I asked the ultimate questions. "Well, then, how are babies made? And who makes them? And how are they born?"

In spite of Emilia's look, Manuela explained the mysteries of our births. As she explained the large bellies mothers grew, I remembered that Mama's belly did not look as big this morning as it had been. Then Manuela said that men and women did the same nasty things pigs and dogs did to make babies, and that human babies came out the same way as piglets and pups.

It was the most incredible thing I'd ever heard, but I knew it was true. I remembered our dogs hooking up to each other, and felt totally disgusted with my parents. If they did such filthy things, I would rather go on believing that a storm was responsible for my arrival into the world. Since I didn't look like anyone in my family anyway, being dropped by a storm in Mama's bed finally sounded good to me.

Chapter Thirteen

An American Christmas

I lost my first tooth during the first months of school. Mama said it was no big deal. "It happens to everyone." Her answer didn't bother me, because Manuela and Miss Traverso had said that losing my first tooth meant I was six years old. Well, I knew that my birthday was in August, so I had just turned six, and knowing I was six made me feel really good.

This new discovery made Emilia stop to think about her own age. "If you're six, I must be ten," she said bitterly. "And if I'm ten, I shouldn't be in the same grade as you."

"You have to be in first grade before moving up," I reminded her. "First grade comes before second and third."

"I know that!" she yelled. "I'm not stupid, you idiot."

Emilia would win the argument one way or the other, so I kept my mouth shut. Still, as the days passed, she seemed to dislike me more. Learning was easy for me and difficult for her. She wrote the numbers three, seven, and nine backwards. Then she hated me for writing the numbers correctly, and cursed the teacher for telling her that she should take lessons from me.

"You're not so smart!" she would yell on our way home. "That stupid teacher just likes you best, that's all."

"No, Emilia, it's not the teacher. Don't you remember? My godfather taught me. And I can help you."

"I'm the oldest, and you're going to help me?" She would give me a push, and down I would go, swearing never to try to help her again.

One morning Papa woke up singing, "It's the first day of December, blessed be God forever." Emilia picked up the tune and sang the same words on the way to school. This made me think that her feelings about school had changed and she would be a happy sister from now on. But she soon revealed her reason for being so joyful.

"This is a great day!" she said as we reached the field of ferns and yellow butterflies. She stretched her arms straight over her head and clapped. "A new year is coming, and we won't have to go back to school!"

Emilia's words were like a sudden punch to my stomach. If she didn't go to school, I would not be allowed to go either. I stayed way behind her, wondering how I could change her attitude about school.

But later, in the classroom, I realized that Emilia was as serious about disliking school as I was about liking it. While I looked for the good things about school, she looked for reasons to dislike it, or to cause the teacher to throw her out.

The teacher began the class with a story about an American family at Christmas time. She handed a little book to a girl in second grade and told her to pass it around so we could all see the pictures.

"Christmas is not celebrated the same way everywhere," she said. "For example, here in Puerto Rico, we celebrate from December twenty-fourth to January sixth. But Americans celebrate only one day, which is December twenty-fifth. A fat man dressed in red and white crawls down people's chimneys to bring gifts to their children. Here in Puerto Rico, the Three Kings bring gifts to the children on the night of January fifth."

Emilia bolted out of her seat with rage in her eyes. "You're making that up! In our family, we don't celebrate. Our Three Kings on their wooden horses are up in a niche with the crucifix and the Virgin Mary, and they never bring us any gifts. All they do is stare and wait for the times when Papa makes us kneel and pray to them." She slammed herself down into her seat, crossed her arms over her chest, and fixed her eyes on the floor.

The teacher had stopped talking and stood very still. "You'll stay in the classroom during recess," she finally said, her voice loud and shaky. "I will not tolerate that kind of behavior in my classroom. Do you understand?"

Emilia didn't even blink. I trembled for both of us. I had seen her mad before, but I had never thought she would talk that way to an adult, especially to our teacher.

Miss Traverso paced back and forth in front of the class, then calmly said, "Those of you who have received gifts at Christmas, raise your hands."

Six hands went up, all girls. One had received barrettes for her hair, and another said she had received ribbons. One girl said she had received a new dress, and three had gotten dolls.

The teacher asked the ones with the dolls if they could bring them to school to show the class. Only one girl, Julia, said she would bring her doll; the other two said they weren't allowed to take theirs out of the house.

I could hardly wait for the next day to see the doll, but Emilia showed no interest. When the little book that the teacher passed around reached Emilia, she gave a sweeping motion with one hand, refusing to look at it.

I had been waiting anxiously for the book, so I took it with delight. It had a picture of a young mother and father with a boy and a girl. They were sitting on the floor, around a little tree decorated with red, blue, and silver shiny balls. Under the tree were packages wrapped in red paper with prints of yellow and pink flowers, tied with purple and red ribbons. Each person held a wrapped package, and they were all smiling.

But what I liked most was that they all had white skin, blue eyes, and yellow hair. I was not weird, after all. I looked like an American!

Emilia stayed in the classroom during recess, looking as though it made no difference to her. But on our way home, I thought she would set the forest on fire with her cursing. She wished the teacher would die, and that termites would eat our wooden saints. Then she cursed the tall, leafy trees for keeping the sun out and the ground wet.

I finally was able to cut in with one question. "Aren't you afraid the teacher might write to Papa and tell him what you said in school?"

"I hope she does!" Emilia's voice echoed in the woods. "I hope she tells him not to send me back to that stupid school."

I didn't say anything else, and she calmed down before we reached our house. To my vast relief, the teacher didn't send a letter to Papa, and he never heard about Emilia's rage.

*   *   *

On the night of January 5th, I tried my luck with the Three Kings. I put a handful of new grass and a gourd shell of sweet water in the corner by my gunnysack and prayed for a pink doll dressed in purple and red feathers, like the one Julia had brought to school. I went to sleep dreaming about the beautiful doll, red ribbons, and barrettes.

The next morning, I awoke to find that my grass and water were still there. Emilia laughed hysterically.

"That ought to teach you," she blurted, "not to believe everything the teacher says."

Even though the Three Kings didn't come around with my doll, I still loved my teacher. She was my idol and my inspiration. I wanted more than anything to return to school after Christmas vacation. For this, I prayed that God would not hear Emilia's prayers. I knew she prayed that Papa would not send us back to school.

My prayers worked, but my teacher disappointed me four months later. She told us about Mother's Day—a day in May for children to honor their mothers. Then she asked that we each bring ten cents to school, which she would use to buy little baskets, cookies, and candy. She would help us adorn the baskets and fill them with the sweet goodies. On the Friday before Mother's Day, we would take the delightful surprises to our mothers.

While Miss Traverso described the baskets, I imagined Mama smiling and hugging me for the beautiful surprise. Mine would be the prettiest basket, for on the way home I would add some ferns and a few bell-like blue flowers. Mama would eat some of the candy and cookies and give each of us kids a piece. Even Papa would join in the feast of sweets, and everyone in the family would feel happy.

"The teacher told us to bring ten cents each on Monday," I told Papa as we walked through the door. Emilia had said she wouldn't even mention the ten cents to him. She felt sure that he would say no. But I had never been afraid to be denied.

"What for?" Papa didn't look up from his hammock. "What does she want ten cents for?"

"So we can honor Mama with candy and cookies on Mother's Day." I stood by the hammock with damp palms, shifting my weight from one foot to the other.

"Ten cents each?" Papa finally looked up. "A total of twenty cents? Do you have any idea how much money that is?"

"This much?" I held my hands open twice. Papa closed one eye tightly, and stared at me with the other. "That much exactly. But those are fingers. Your teacher is asking for money, not fingers."

"Miss Traverso said to bring a penny a day if you don't have a lot of money. That makes it easier, right?"

"Wrong. Even a penny a day will soon equal twenty. I didn't send you girls to school to spend money like it grows on trees!"

I frowned. "So we don't get to honor Mama?"

"Oh, you can still honor your mother. Get down on your knees and kiss her feet. That's how I honored mine."

Everyone else brought the ten cents, some all at once and

others a penny or two at a time. The teacher kept announcing how many days were left until Mother's Day. It became painful having to show up at school day after day without the money, explaining that Papa had refused to give even one cent a day. Worse yet was knowing that Papa had a lot of money in his tin can, while most of the students' fathers were only farm workers who didn't even own the shack in which they lived.

Our situation grew more painful when the teacher insisted that Emilia and I weren't trying hard enough to get the money from Papa. "You need to keep asking and begging. Hang from his belt and follow him everywhere until he breaks down. That's what I did every time I wanted something that my father didn't think I needed. It worked for me, and it will work for you, too."

The teacher didn't know Papa. If we pulled a trick like that, he would blister our skin with a wet rope.

On the Friday before Mother's Day, Emilia and I had to stay in our seats, wiping away our tears while the teacher and the other students prepared the baskets. Murmuring and giggling, some of our classmates made faces at us, saying that we didn't love our mother enough to honor her. The other students looked as though they felt bad for us but were afraid to take sides.

"Since you didn't bring the money, you're not entitled to participate," Miss Traverso had said. A whipping would have hurt less than that statement. I couldn't believe how she could turn that mean after I had admired her so much. Not only was she punishing us for something that was beyond our control, but she permitted the students to make us feel worthless.

When they finished decorating the baskets, some of the students held theirs up.

"See how beautiful they are?" they said. "Don't you wish you had brought in the money?"

A multitude of voices echoed in the room. Emilia and I cast our eyes to the floor, pretending that we didn't care, but our hearts were broken.

When class ended, the students walked out with their

baskets. Then Miss Traverso came to us with two branches of red bougainvilleas. "Take these to your mother. It's better than going home empty-handed."

We each took a branch, and I thanked her, but Emilia didn't say a word. She looked straight ahead, her lips pressed together. As we walked out the door, she began cursing. "Damn the school and the teacher, too!" She beat the gate with her branch until all the leaves and flowers fell off. Then she snapped the limb into tiny pieces, slammed the pieces to the ground, and ran.

I agreed that a branch of flowers was better than nothing, so I carried mine, holding it above my head to keep it from hooking onto the fern bushes. But the sun wilted it, and by the time I reached the forest, its flowers were falling off. I hooked the bare branch to a tree and left it there.

Papa went somewhere with one of his cousins that afternoon, and since Mama was in a good mood, we told her about the humiliation we had been through in school.

"First of all," she said, "your teacher is from the city. Most city people are rich. They don't think like hill people. Secondly, your father refuses to buy dishes, beds, or blankets. What made you think he would spend money on things like baskets, candy, or cookies, especially for me?"

I saw sadness in Mama's face as she talked, stirring the rice without looking into our eyes.

"When I grow up, I'm going to buy you candy, blankets, and a whole lot of other things, Mama," I said, feeling terribly sorry for her.

"Don't let your father hear you say that," she said, and ordered us to get started on our chores.

That night I lay in my gunnysack, staring at the ceiling and wondering why Papa was so stingy. Didn't he realize that he had made us look bad in front of the whole class and the teacher? I needed to find a way to explain to the teacher that it wasn't our fault, that we really wanted to honor our mother with flowers and candy, but Papa had refused to give us the money.

*   *   *

Before I could find the right time and the right words to explain our problem to the teacher, she started on a new subject: toothbrushes and dental hygiene. Now we were instructed to tell our parents that we needed toothbrushes, and that if we didn't keep our teeth clean, we would end up with rotted teeth and bleeding gums.

I delivered that message to Papa. Emilia had sworn never to ask him for another thing as long as she lived.

Papa peered into my eyes. "Did you say toothbrushes?"

"Yes," I said softly, afraid that he would rap my head with his knuckles. "The teacher said that brushing will keep our teeth healthy."

My father reached into his pocket and pulled out his tobacco, which looked like a piece of black rope. Keeping his eyes on me, he brought the tobacco to his mouth and bit off a piece. Then he squinted one eye and said, "I'm not spending money on brushes. Not even if your teeth rot away."

"But the teacher said that a toothbrush only costs ten cents." I backed away from him, in case he swung at me.

"I am not spending twenty cents on brushes. That's final." The look in his eyes warned me to drop the subject.

A few days later, he called Emilia and me to the sitting area. "You girls can tell your teacher that I'll buy one toothbrush for the two of you to share."

Since neither of us wanted to use a toothbrush that had been in the other's mouth, we did not deliver the message, and he never bought a toothbrush.

Luckily, we weren't the only ones without a toothbrush, so the teacher scolded most of the class. "You didn't try hard enough. It'll serve you right if your teeth rot."

She didn't mention the toothbrushes again. I kept wanting to tell her that Papa had refused to give us the money, but somehow the right time never came, and she never found out that Papa was stingy and mean.

I went to bed every night worrying about losing my teeth. I dreamt again and again about the toothbrush the teacher had shown to the class. In my dreams, I held it in my hands for a long time, running my fingers up and down the red handle, and feeling each of the white bristles. Finally, in one of my dreams, I made my own toothbrush.

The very next day, I started working toward making that dream come true. I chewed sugarcane, swallowed the syrup, and saved the fibers. After rinsing the fibers well, I dried them in the sun. Then I tied the fibers into little bundles and trimmed them with Mama's scissors when she wasn't looking.

I had to make several brushes before I came out with a perfect one, but when I did, Emilia stopped laughing and asked me to make one for her. Using the fibers she'd chewed, I made her one.

To my great surprise, my toothbrush business began to grow. Before long, all of the kids were brushing their teeth with sugarcane brushes. That became my most impressive invention.

Even Papa, who caught us cleaning our teeth, admitted that I had created something important and requested a brush for himself. That made me feel very smart. Making a toothbrush for my father meant that I knew how to do something he had not learned to do. Of course, I never let him or anyone see how proud of myself I felt. The sad part about this was that when I offered to make one for Mama, she said that my invention had come too late for her. The teeth she had left weren't worth saving.

I didn't quit inventing after the toothbrushes. We still needed toothpaste. I chewed charcoal and swished it in my mouth with a little water before brushing. Soon everyone noticed that I had the whitest teeth. This time Papa said that my latest invention was even more clever than my first. From then on, we collected the burning wood from the *fogón*, stuck it in water, and we had charcoal to clean our teeth.

Chapter Fourteen

A Flying Rosary

Emilia and I attended school for three years. Miss Traverso was our teacher for two years, and when she didn't return for third grade, I cried, feeling devastated. Even though she had often been unfair, I liked her because she was beautiful and dressed nicely. Watching her walk back and forth in front of the class always made me feel good, and I dreamed of someday looking and dressing just like her.

The new teacher was Carmen Mendoza, another young woman, but with kinky brown hair, a stubby nose, and beady black eyes. She had hands of iron and was heartless. She would ask how much was three plus two, and if the student didn't know the answer, she whacked him or her with the ruler. She usually aimed for the back of the knee, where you'd get red marks that lasted a long time.

One would think that the other students would be sympathetic, but that wasn't the case. When one kid was whacked, the others teased him or her mercilessly for days, until the next student became the target. So we learned that being spanked and teased was part of our education.

During those years of school, Emilia and I suffered again and again from the same kind of humiliation. The teachers would ask for things Papa refused to provide; we'd be afraid to ask him and embarrassed to explain his stinginess to the teacher and nosy classmates.

On top of that, Mama made us miss a lot of school. She would say that someone told her the teacher was sick and the school would be closed. We'd spend those days working around the house, no questions asked. When she had another baby, Alejandro, we missed nine days. Every night, I went to sleep hoping she would let us go to school the next day.

"It's not fair!" I cried one day. "We'll never make up the classes we're missing. The other students will be ahead of us, and the teacher will whack us with her ruler."

"Never mind the other students," Mama said, giving me a hateful look. "You're not in school to compete with them! As for the teacher, tell her I'm your mother and I can keep you home from school as long as I please!"

Knowing how quick Mama was with her hand, I had no choice but to shut up. Then, when we finally returned to school, the teacher put us through more pain.

"I don't want to hear excuses," she said. "Bring me a written statement, signed by your parents, telling me the true reason why you missed nine days of class!" Her voice went higher and higher, while we shrank in our seats. Every wide-eyed student watched, waiting to see the teacher whack us with her ruler.

As if that wasn't bad enough, we came down with colds, the flu, mumps, chicken pox, the measles, and pinkeye. Each year, we barely passed to the next grade.

When we finished third grade, the school closed for summer vacation, with the possibility that it might remain closed for years. Some people said that it was because of the war. Others guessed that city teachers refused to come this far into the country, even on horseback.

With school out of the way, we became full-time farm workers. We started the summer with the bean harvest, then followed with the corn a few weeks later.

First, we had to make the *tordas* (burlap sheets). We took

apart four gunnysacks, carefully so as not to tangle the fine string which had held the sack together. The sack became a piece of burlap thirty-six inches square. With the old string and a big needle with a large eye, we stitched the four squares together, and there we had a *torda*.

Before heading for the bean field, Emilia and I filled the water barrels, then had our morning coffee. We spread out the *torda* and began pulling out bean plants by their roots. The plants were dried, which was normal at this time of year, and the only time to pull them. We pulled with both hands, alternating right, left, right, until the bunches were too thick for our grip. Then we carried them to the *torda*. If we threw the dried plants, the pods would pop open and the beans would bounce right out. Heaven help us if Papa found a few beans scattered around.

When the heap of bean plants reached my chest or Emilia's waist, Papa came with another *torda* and took home the full one. He picked up one corner of the burlap sheet, and one of us handed the opposite corner to him, which he tied together. After the remaining corners were tied, we helped him lift the heavy bundle to his shoulders, and he carried it up one hill and down another, all the way to the house. There he untied the four corners and dumped the dried plants on a few other *tordas* which had been spread out on the clearing in front of the house.

Sometimes Papa came back right away, so we had to work fast to have another heap ready for him. Other times, he took a nap, showing up an hour or two later. Meanwhile, we had been afraid to run under the shade for a few minutes, or to look down toward the river, hoping to spot someone fishing or bathing. One thing was as bad as the other. If we stopped momentarily, we'd get caught. If we didn't stop, time passed, and we realized we could have rested but hadn't.

Usually we pulled the whole field of beans in one day, finishing about 2:00 or 3:00 in the afternoon. The sun was constantly on us all day. Our only break came when Mama sent us our lunch of cooked bananas, *panas*, sweet potatoes, or plantains, whatever was available for that season. Maybe there was a pinch of codfish to go with the vegetables, but more likely, some of the goat cheese Mama had made.

José would bring the lunch, but was in no hurry to reach us since his belly was already full. He would put the gourd shells down and leave before we could ask for water, which we'd finally get when Papa returned.

A worse job awaited me when we finally went home. The pile of dried bean plants had been in the sun all day to make the next process easier. Easier for a man, but not for a little girl with skinny arms, the sun burning the top of my head, arms, shoulders, nose, forehead, and behind my knees.

With both hands wrapped around the end of a long wooden pole, I had to pound on the heap of dried plants until the branches and leaves turned to powder. Every now and then, Papa came and pounded the heap about a dozen times, then left again. Each time he walked away, I wished one of us would drop dead. If he died, I would be free to quit. If I died, he would be sorry for losing his best helper.

Once the leaves and pods were pulverized with all that pounding, the beans had to be separated from the debris. That was when Mama came out to do her part, because she was taller than I. She would lift a large gourd shell of beans and crushed leaves above her head and let the mixture come down slowly. The breeze blew the pulverized leaves away, and the beans came down onto a clean *torda*. We still had to pick out the heavier pieces of stems that came down with the beans.

Finally, we filled up the sacks, a hundred pounds each, and sealed them. By then, I would be sunburned and aching in every joint and muscle. I also felt hurt and jealous, for Emilia had been in the house, in the shade, supposedly helping Mama, but probably nibbling on leftover food while I burned in the sun and starved.

*   *   *

With all the work we had to do, we should have been allowed to sleep in peace after a long day's work in the sun. But in our family, fairness and consideration did not exist.

I woke up one night from a deep sleep and saw Emilia on the floor, on her hands and knees, peeking out through a wall crack. My other brothers and sisters, whimpering and trembling, were grouped in a corner near Mama's bed. The streaks of light from the living room lantern meant that our parents weren't asleep.

"It's about time you woke up," Emilia whispered. "Come see."

I thought my heart would leap out of my chest when I joined Emilia at the wall crack and saw our parents going round and round in the patch of light outside the front door. Papa had Mama's hair wrapped around his left wrist and his right hand around his machete's handle. The sharp blade glistened as it went up, and came down flat on Mama's back.

Mama looked horrified as she reached desperately for Papa's legs, probably trying to throw him off balance. He was much too strong and continued swinging, flattening Mama to the ground.

Each time the machete came down, I felt an excruciating pain in my racing heart. I knew how good Papa was with his machete. He could bring down a tree with a couple of strokes, and a banana plant with one. If he turned the machete the right way, my mother would become two halves. I shivered at that thought and moved back away from the wall. Emilia backed away, too.

"He's going to kill her!" she cried as we stared at each other. Then she covered her face with her hands and uttered words I couldn't understand. One thing became clear to me then: tough and controlling Emilia was a coward at heart.

The thought of all of us ganging up on Papa entered my mind, but there was no time to gather everyone and make a plan. Yet I knew someone had to do something fast. *Oh God!* The sound of the machete and Mama's moans chilled me. I looked around for something to throw at Papa—something that might make him stop without seeing who had thrown it.

With that thought, I leaped from the sleeping area into the front room, my feet hardly touching the floor. I saw Papa's rosary, a large circle of wooden beads, heavy enough to bruise us when he used it as a whip. I grabbed it by the cross, snatched it off its nail on the wall, and whirled it like a rope, making the circle spin faster and faster.

Then I let it fly out the door. It whirled and looped around the upraised machete, passed over Papa's wrist, and rested on his bent elbow. He froze with the machete up in the air, his left hand still wrapped around Mama's hair, and his eyes on the rosary. By the time he looked around and up toward the front door, I had flown back to the sleeping area and stood watching through the crack.

"Oh no," Emilia whispered. "He knows one of us did it, and I am not going to take the blame."

I kept silent. This was a miracle, too good to be true. My trick had worked. Papa had stopped hitting Mama. He stood motionless, looking around, his eyes confused and startled. Something bigger than himself had stopped his rage.

He looked at the machete and released Mama. I took a deep breath when I saw her run toward the dark woods. Finally, Papa switched the machete to his left hand, gathered the rosary into his right hand and kissed it, then made the sign of the cross.

"Let's pretend we're asleep," I said, and dove into my gunnysack.

"He's coming in!" Emilia said, going into her sack.

My heart was still pounding so hard that I feared Papa would hear it if he came looking for us.

I heard the stamping of his boots across the floor, coming toward the sleeping area. I stopped breathing. He stopped at the doorway, took a deep breath and exhaled loudly, then backed away.

At last, I could breathe. I quietly pulled myself up and peeked into the sitting area. I saw the look of fear on my father's face, as if he believed that something mysterious had sent his own rosary to stop him.

I felt great about myself. The practice of looping a goat or a pig by whirling a rope had paid off. Roping had been one of the biggest secrets I had kept. It was something I wasn't supposed to learn, and no one knew I had.

Papa hung his rosary on its nail, then went outside. Seconds later, he came back, leading Mama by the arm into the house. She mumbled, trying to yank herself from his grip. Papa held onto her, a mystified look still on his face. He led her toward the sleeping area. I crawled into my sack and heard Papa's steps backing away. Then I heard the squeaking of his hammock's ropes, and I knew he would soon be asleep.

Mama walked past us and into the kitchen, where she murmured to herself and rattled the pots and pans.

I pulled my gunnysack over my face and smiled into the darkness. All was well, if only for the moment.

Chapter Fifteen

Free to Laugh

Papa took everything we harvested and sold it in Lares or San Sebastian, two small towns many miles from our hills. He would wake up at daybreak and fit two horses with *aparejos* (cushions he'd made from banana or palm leaves). Then he loaded each animal with 300 to 400 pounds of beans, vegetables, and oranges.

Finally, he and his weighted-down horses headed up the hill, reaching the paved road by mid-morning. There he transferred his goods into the back of a public station wagon and paid a nickel to a boy from a nearby family to tend his horses. When he arrived in town, he displayed and sold his goods in the designated *mercado* (marketplace).

On the days he went to town, Emilia and I harvested the corn by ourselves. Although this work was just as hard as pulling the bean plants, we felt a sense of freedom and had fun doing it. Knowing that Papa wasn't hiding behind a bush to catch us wasting time, we ripped the ears of corn off the stalks and carried them home by the sackful.

The entire time, while the summer sun baked our skin, we talked and joked about whatever came to our minds. We recalled our school days, imitating the teacher, the bullies, and the other girls and boys. We laughed aloud, quieting down when we approached the house where Mama might hear us, then giggling louder as we ran back to the field.

For this harvest, we didn't have to bend over, but the dried corn stalks were as sharp as knife blades. We would have hundreds of cuts and scratches by the time we finished. Still, we talked and laughed. Those short times of freedom eased the pain of our cuts and scratches. Also, during those times I felt equal to my big sister and wished she would stay this friendly forever.

During the short moments when Emilia paused from talking, I fantasized that Manuela, Margarita, and Julia lived nearby and would soon appear to visit us. The thoughts took my mind off the corn picking. I pictured myself in the cool classroom, looking like Miss Traverso in soft dresses of different colors, walking back and forth in front of the class, teaching the students how to read and write. They would love me because I would never be mean to them. When I'd come home at the end of the day, everyone in the family, even Emilia, would treat me as they would an important visitor.

Emilia's voice always brought me back to the heat of the day and the job, but I never told her that my mind had wandered off to the place I'd rather be.

The process of this harvest didn't end with the picking. We still had to remove the first layer of husks, tie two ears together, and hang them from the rafters to dry more. This we did at night or during another rain. We'd sit on the floor, one cob in one hand, and knock off the kernels with our other thumb. By the time we finished the job, our thumbs were raw and bleeding.

*   *   *

One day we returned from the fields with our last sackful of corn just as Papa arrived from town. This time his face wasn't red, and he even brought home two long loaves of hard-crust bread.

Mama grabbed a big knife and cut the loaves into pieces,

giving the first piece to Lorenzo, then José, Gloria, and so on. We all sat here and there on the floor to enjoy the special reward for a hard day's work.

Emilia and I were sweaty, our hair tangled and stringy, our legs covered with cuts and scratches, our feet painfully dried and cracked around the heels and under the toes. Still, the bread soothed our misery. Before biting into it, we would bring it to our noses and inhale slowly. The aroma was great!

Papa reached into a gunnysack and pulled out a huge piece of plain blue fabric, folded many times over. He gave it to Mama. "There's enough material for two shirts for me, one for each of the boys, one dress for you and one for Gloria."

Mama nodded, running her hands over the fabric. "All of us dressed in blue?"

"That's right. There's less waste if you cut from the same piece. I paid twelve cents a yard for that fabric."

Mama nodded, but with a look of disgust. I knew she was afraid to say that she would have bought fabric in different colors to separate the boys from the girls.

Emilia and I looked at each other. She moved her lips without sound: "None for us?"

Then I saw a tiny smile on Papa's face as he reached into the sack again and pulled out a smaller package.

"For dresses for Emilia and Sabina," he said, handing Mama the package.

When she unwrapped the little bundle and pulled out a pink fabric with a small print, my heart leaped. My chest filled with a thrill that took away my hunger even for the bread. To me, the new dresses meant that the school had opened and we would soon return to class. I didn't say anything to Emilia, hoping she would stay friendly, but deep in my heart, I believed that the new fabric meant going back to school. Soon Papa would tell Mama that the school had reopened and we would be going back for fourth grade.

The very next morning, he awakened us at the crack of dawn.

I immediately thought it was to tell us that we had to go to school. Instead, he had the most disgusting job lined up for us.

"I need you girls to get up and hold the piglets," he said, walking out of the sleeping area before we were fully awake.

"What's he talking about?" Emilia finally asked Mama.

"Your uncle is coming to castrate the piglets. Your father can't hold them alone. Hurry up, he's waiting."

"Come on, you two, speed it up." Papa's voice came from behind the pigpen, as we shivered in the early morning air. Then we saw him dragging a shrieking piglet. "This is what I want you to do. Emilia, you hold this leg with both hands. Sabina, hold this one. Don't let go, no matter how hard the pig kicks. I'll hold these two." Papa wrapped one of his huge hands around each of the last two legs.

Uncle Luís came from behind the house with a sickening grin, clearly thrilled at the chance to torture the struggling little animal. He put a chunk of tobacco in his mouth, pulled a razor from his pocket, wiped it on his sleeve, and squatted at the pig's tail. Reaching for the piglet's testicles, he cut into the skin. The little pig jerked and wiggled desperately, piercing our ears with its shrieks.

Uncle Luís shaved down some of the tissue, made a cut, and with a flip of his wrist, the testicles flew over his shoulder. He laughed when the dogs ran after the flying meat, smeared his chewed tobacco on the cut, then sent the pig off to scratch his tail in the dirt.

They castrated three piglets that morning, one after the other. After the first one, Emilia and I turned our heads one way then another to avoid looking at our father and uncle and the gruesome thing they were doing.

"That's it, girls. Now go do your chores," my father said, showing no interest in our feelings.

We ran to the house, too sick to drink our morning coffee. Without a word, we grabbed the water cans and headed for the springs.

"I'd rather die than watch such a filthy thing again," Emilia complained. "I hope the pigs get an infection and die. Uncle Luís should die, too. Even Papa should die."

When we reached the springs, she stripped off her clothing and stood under the stream, scrubbing herself so hard I thought her skin would rub off.

"Wash that damn feeling out of my skin." She repeated the words again and again, then blew hard through her closed lips like a horse. Her arms reached to wash every inch of her. I knew that Emilia wouldn't care if one of our parents came along and caught her naked under the stream. They would whip her for bathing out in the open where anyone could come by and see her. I'd get whipped, too, for standing there watching, astounded, and afraid of what my sister would do to me if I said anything.

Chapter Sixteen

The Forbidden

Even though I feared Emilia, and she enjoyed bossing me around, we shared certain secrets. These were things we did together, and she couldn't tell on me without revealing herself.

Whenever our parents were out of our sight, we'd run up a hill just to look toward the river, hoping to see someone naked in the water, or someone fishing or washing clothes.

We also enjoyed a good lizard fight, which was considered evil by our mother. She insisted that if we didn't watch, the lizards would stop trying to tear each other apart. We didn't understand Mama's logic, for the lizards we watched never lost more than the tips of their tails.

In spite of Mama, we kept an eye out for lizards. We enjoyed watching the green ones more, for they were bigger than the brown or the gray, and they fought more vigorously. Sometimes we'd spot two on a rock, staring at each other and flicking their black or pink tongues. We'd get down on our bellies and creep up close for a better look.

The lizards stared and blinked, slapping the rock with their tails. One of them would make a quick move to warn the other. They would take a few steps forward, then back away, only to come forward again, ready to strike. They lashed at each other, locked their jaws together, and twisted their heads back and forth, creasing the skin of their necks. By then, their tails were swinging rapidly, raising dust and dried leaves off the rock.

The lizards' back legs, short and stocky, pressed firmly on the rock to push each other off. With jaws still locked, they turned and twisted to the point of exhaustion, then stopped suddenly. The skin on each side of their throats would balloon out, retract, and puff out again. Sometimes a streak of sunlight shone through their ballooned skin, and we could see the tiny branches of veins inside.

The lizards' bellies would rise and fall. Then they'd swing their tails and continue fighting, twisting and pushing each other until one would send the other rolling to the ground. The winner, seemingly proud of its strength, would remain in place, flicking its tongue. At that point, we'd look around for Mama, brush the dry dirt off our dresses, and go on with our work.

To watch the roosters mate with the hens, Emilia and I took more precautions. This would make the Virgin Mary cry for sure, and if the younger kids saw us, they would tell Mama. So we would hide behind a bush. The rooster, in his silky suit of burnt-orange, black, and yellow feathers, would dance on one leg around his lady-hen. He'd gurgle and slap his wings so hard, one could hear him from afar. He'd change legs, and circle the hen again and again.

Sometimes the hen teased the rooster. She would scratch the ground for seeds and worms, clucking as though uninterested, and then walk away. But the rooster persisted, and sooner or later he hopped on the hen, pinned her down, trembled, then was off. He would swagger away like a man who thought of himself as powerful and dominating. The hen would shake her feathers and go back to searching for whatever lived in the dirt.

One day we got really lucky and saw the biggest and most exciting show. On our way to the creek, each with a huge bundle of dirty clothes, we heard one of our mares neighing and kicking the corral.

"Let's go see what's happening," Emilia said, and started on a detour toward the corral. There, we found Uncle Luís's stallion snorting and trotting around the rails.

"Oh good! Let's climb a tree and watch," Emilia said. "They're going to make a baby."

"Climb a tree?" I asked. "We aren't supposed to climb trees! Mama will whip us if we do."

"She'll have to climb the tree to do it."

I wasn't about to argue with my big sister. I put my bundle next to hers, followed her up the tree, and sat next to her on a branch.

"Don't forget to keep an eye out for Mama," she said, her own eyes on the horses below.

The stallion seemed frantic as he trotted around the corral, kicking the rails and stretching his neck to reach the mare. She appeared restless, going around with her tail up, coming close to the stallion and then trotting away.

"She's teasing him," Emilia said with an unusual glow, and the brightest smile I'd ever seen. "This is why Mama talked Papa into getting rid of his male horses a long time ago. She didn't want us to see nasty things like this." Emilia briefly took her eyes off the horses to look around, then went back to watching the two animals.

"I think we should get down from here," I said, looking worriedly toward the house. I imagined Mama swinging her belt at both of us. "I don't want to get a whipping, Emilia."

"Shut up and watch. Mama has to climb up here to get us. Even if we get whipped, this is fun. Just watch."

I nodded and looked at the horses. They were both trotting now and kicking the rails. Suddenly, the mare reached over the rails and nipped the stallion on the neck. Next, they brought their fat lips together.

"Ah, they're kissing," Emilia said. She didn't even blink, afraid she would miss something.

I looked toward the house one more time, afraid that Mama would hear the horses and come running with her belt.

"Look!" Emilia said.

I turned just in time to see the stallion stretch his neck after the kiss and peel back his upper lip with a loud snort. We cracked up laughing, but quickly covered our mouths so Mama wouldn't hear us. She'd strip the skin off our backs with her belt if she caught us.

The stallion trotted around once more, then galloped, snorting, his hooves pounding the ground so hard it thundered. He ran faster and faster, and finally flew over the rails like a huge golden-brown bundle with a fluffy yellow tail and mane. He landed on his hind legs, with a huge sausage sticking out from under his belly. His front legs came over the mare, she stopped trotting, and he shoved the huge thing into her. Emilia and I looked at each other, open-mouthed.

"My body's tingling!" she said softly, her eyes still wide open.

I didn't know what I felt, but the fear of Mama had disappeared, if only for that moment.

The stallion pressed against the mare several times, and then got off. Emilia blinked and, without a word, looked toward the house, then climbed down from the tree. I followed her, and we quietly grabbed our bundles and hurried down to the creek.

Our first concern now was to submerge the clothes, and we began rubbing and squeezing the dirt off. This would make it look like we had been hard at work if one of our parents suddenly appeared.

When no one showed up, Emilia asked, "Did you see the hard salami?" She burst out laughing.

"Yeah, like a brown, scabby sausage," I said, joining her laughter.

That was one special experience my sister and I shared—our secret. We had watched the forbidden and hadn't gotten caught. The usual gloom that often hung over us on wash day had lifted away, if only for one day. But we rubbed and squeezed the dirt out of the rags with energy and hope for better times. We glanced at each other often, only to crack up laughing again.

Just as we were beginning to calm down, I looked up and saw a lizard that was bigger than the others we often saw. We knew of this type of lizard, which only lived near the water, but we had never seen one. Mama had told us that if we ever saw this type of lizard, we should walk away from it and never, never stare at it. If we did, the lizard would jump and hang from our earlobe, and stay there until thunder roared in the sky.

"What if it doesn't thunder for months?" I had asked.

"Then you'll have a lizard on your earlobe for months."

After that answer from my mother, I had been afraid of coming across that type of lizard. But since we were in a brave mood today, I told Emilia about the lizard, and we both went up and stared at it. The creature was big, and probably weighed more than a pound. It had rough bumps on its head and upper body. Its tail was thicker than that of regular lizards, and its color was a bluish green. It clung to a tree limb, sticking out its black tongue to snatch flies.

"Think he'll jump at us?" I asked.

"No, he won't. Those are stories Mama made up." Emilia grabbed her earlobes and called out, "Here, ugly lizard, jump!" The lizard didn't move.

I continued staring at it, and even stuck out my tongue and blinked. The lizard didn't bother to look my way. I clapped my hands, and it turned its head, then crept away. So much for Mama's stories.

Chapter Seventeen

A Raging Storm

With the month of August came the news that the school would remain closed until further notice.

This was devastating to me. I had prayed for at least another year of school. The words "until further notice" meant that there was still hope of finding a teacher willing to teach the hill children. Naturally, I clung to that hope. In the meantime, I practiced my math and writing on every board, rock, and hard patch of ground I could find, and I read every printed word on the pieces of newspaper and magazine pages that came wrapped around the codfish and salt from the store.

One day during the last week of that terrible August, my father exposed me to an experience so horrifying that it erased the school issue from my mind for a long time. It was one of those mornings when the sun could not make its way through the clouds, but Papa insisted that rain wasn't in the air, and headed toward the rum shack. Before leaving, he ordered all of us children to get an early start on our chores, then spend the rest of the day pulling weeds from around the new patch of coffee trees.

Knowing what to expect on a rum-making day, we hurried to get everything done as fast as possible, hoping to minimize whatever he would find wrong that night. I milked the goats and took them to pasture. Emilia rolled the hammocks, folded the younger children's gunnysacks, and swept the floor. Then we hurried down to the springs.

José and Lorenzo, then around seven and six years old, had the horses to brush and lead out to another patch of grass for the day. Once that work was done, we all headed to the waiting weeds. To get to the coffee tree field, we walked through a dense wooded area, then across a hillside of nothing but tall grass, which we would often cut to feed the horses and cows. We all liked this clearing because it had a clear view of the river, and we could see men bathing or fishing, or women washing clothes.

Today we couldn't spot anyone. The river looked like a reddish brown ribbon twisting through the greenery, widening over the valley. This meant, as we had learned through the years, that rain had saturated the hills at the head of the river. Since Papa had announced that rain wasn't in the air, none of us felt brave enough to run back and tell him that the river was muddy and swelling.

The air around the coffee trees felt thick and moist, and the branches were dead still. Flies and mosquitos swarmed around our sweaty bodies, buzzing in our ears and pricking our skin. We slapped the nagging insects, reached for the weeds, and pulled. We were there to work, not to talk or fool around. Papa had left for the rum shack, but we knew he could be hiding behind a bush, hoping to catch us wasting time.

Only by the growling in our stomachs were we able to guess that the noon hour was upon us. The sky had become darker since we arrived there, and we couldn't spot the position of the sun. As usual, Mama would figure out the time of day, and she or Gloria would show up soon with our lunch.

A mild breeze moved the branches so suddenly we stopped and looked around for some supernatural source.

"Ah . . ." Emilia sighed. "A breeze. Finally."

"That means it's going to rain," I said.

"Good," said bright-eyed Lorenzo. "Now we can go home. I'm starving." He always welcomed any reason to stop working.

Usually José would join him, but this time he suggested we wait for the rain. "It'll cool us down," he said.

The breeze grew stronger. Then the first streak of lightning danced through the trees, and thunder roared. A gust of wind swept past us, and thunder again followed the lightning. It was time to run home.

The wind whirled around us as we ran, and the rain began as we reached the grassy hillside. The tall grass swayed and twisted in the wind, and raindrops hit us sideways. We ran with our heads turned against the wind to protect our eyes from flying debris. Still, I managed to glance down at the river. It had widened, and its water looked darker than it had earlier.

"Look at the river!" I yelled. But I got no answer. Emilia and the boys were too busy running for safety. Or perhaps the wind swept away my words, and they didn't hear.

We were soaked by the time we reached our house. But when we entered the kitchen, the aroma of fried codfish met our noses, and I felt glad about the rain.

As I sat down in a corner of the kitchen to eat my lunch, I saw Papa walking from the woods with a huge banana leaf over his head. His face was red, and the vein on his brow bulged like a piece of rope under the skin. I looked at Mama and saw her face go pale. I turned to Emilia and saw her eyes roll toward the ceiling. Trouble had arrived, but I found out that it was only for me.

"Sabina!" Papa yelled.

Having been taught to jump to attention when my parents called, I put down my lunch and went to the door. "Yes, sir?"

"Take this leaf and go watch the still."

My heart sank. "What about my lunch?"

"Eat it later."

"Can Emilia go with me?"

"No. One of you getting wet is enough."

"But, Papa, please!"

"No buts! Take the leaf!" He arranged my hands around the

thick stem of the banana leaf and gave me a push. "Get going! The jug was half full when I left. Don't let the fire go out!"

I knew no one could reason with Papa, especially when he'd been drinking, so off I went into the blinding rain, down one treacherous hill and across another.

The banana leaf twisted and flipped over my head. The coffee trees leaned low with the weight from the water in their clusters of berries. Lightning flashed on and off like blinking lights, and thunder blasted above the ceiling of tree branches. Water rushed down the hills, filling the gullies.

I tightened my grip on the stem and prayed that my next step would not send me sliding down to the roaring creek on the other side of the trees. The steps Papa had carved on the sloping earth some time ago had washed away. I knew that one false step would send me sliding down to the huge rocks below.

I decided then that Papa hated me and wanted me dead. Otherwise, he surely would not have sent me out in the middle of a storm. The thought made me mad, and I made up my mind that I would not get killed. I would be careful, and live, if only to make him regret his cruelty. I didn't know when or how, but one day I would get even.

The rain pounded on the leaf as I stepped over the deep puddles, muddy water splashing up under the clean dress I had put on. The wind whirled and snatched away the banana leaf. Now the raindrops rapped on my head like hard knuckles.

I didn't expect to find the metal drum still on the three rocks, but there it stood like a black, evil monster from Mama's spooky stories. The rainwater rushing down the hill fell onto the trench Papa had made around the shack to protect his precious still, and then moved on forcefully toward the creek.

The flames, like brilliant red silk, danced freely under the drum, untouched by the rain. Papa had made this lean-to strong enough to withstand the worst of storms. He had built a platform of packed earth on the lower hillside, but away from the creek, which collected the rainwater from both hills and carried it to the river.

Even Papa found this place scary during a storm. That was why he had gone home to sleep and left me in charge, knowing I would be too afraid of him to ignore his orders and run to safety.

The rum shelter lay parallel to the creek, but with its entrance facing up the hillside. Its walls were only three feet high, which kept the wind from blowing out the fire but still let it flow freely through the openings without lifting the tin roof.

I stood in the rain, trembling and staring at the tin structure, afraid to go near the fire and the monster drum.

The thundering creek grew wider, its brown water rushing down, carrying away branches and soil. The light of day had been replaced by a dark gloom that made me shiver. From high overhead, the gray sky dumped water onto the ceiling of branches, and the branches spilled the water in gushes.

I could see that the jug had overflowed, yet I could not walk inside the shack to change it. I watched the crystal clear liquid run down the dry soil, then disappear into the muddy water. It gave me pleasure to see Papa's precious rum wasted. He shouldn't expect me to feel good about being sucked into the foot of two hillsides in the midst of a storm.

Chapter Eighteen

Tumbling Bodies

Through the roaring sound of thunder, wind, and rushing water, I thought I heard the faint voice of a man yelling. Thinking it might be Papa, I hurried in, pulled out the full jug of rum, and placed an empty one under the trickle. I put the full gallon in the corner of the shack where two other full jugs rested, added wood to the fire, and went back out.

There was no sign of Papa, and I was convinced now that the voice I had heard wasn't his. I had probably just imagined it. Who would be out in this storm?

I sat on a log near the shack entrance and stared at the fire, wanting to pray but unable to, wanting to run but too afraid of my father to do so.

Lightning flashed and thunder blasted. I screamed with all my strength, then realized that even God couldn't hear me through the raging wind and rain.

A gush of rainwater hit the tin roof, splattered on the fire, and sizzled. I knew the storm would soon take me away, and the world would end. I covered my face with my wet hands and sobbed.

After a while, I heard a man's voice again. This time I felt sure it was real. I looked around and saw only rain. Then I heard the call again, clearly now. "*Primo* (Cousin)!"

I thought of Mateo, who always called Papa *Primo*. My heart thumped, and I didn't feel so alone anymore. Still, I couldn't see anyone.

I stood on the log and cupped my hands over my eyes, desperately trying to see through the rain.

"*Primo!*" The chilling call came again through the uproar. I craned my neck to look across the creek, and saw something moving, waving like arms. It appeared that at least two people were at the edge of the creek, waving and shouting toward the rum shack.

I thought of running home to tell Papa, but he would be angry if I left the still unattended. So I cupped my hands around my mouth and shouted, "Papa is not here!"

I could see the moving figures, but the only word I could make out was "*Primo.*" I kept shouting, hoping they would come across. I yelled even louder, but felt sure they weren't seeing or hearing me.

Stepping away from the shack so they would see me, I slipped in the mud and went down on my backside, sliding toward the raging creek. I screamed as my body turned one way and then another, passing coffee trees so fast I couldn't grab one. This would be the end of me. The creek was waiting. Papa had gotten his wish.

The trunk of a cocoa tree at the ridge of the bank broke my descent. I wrapped my legs and arms around it and looked down at the creek. The brown water thundered over the rocks to the pool only a few feet away from me. The earth shook as water crashed in, and the heaps of foam on the outer edges were swept away as soon as they were formed.

With my heart pounding, I thanked God for the tree that saved me. Then, hanging onto the tree with one hand, I shielded my eyes with the other and looked up the creek. Through the rain, I saw a tall figure walk into the muddy water with something on each shoulder. Behind that figure were two others, and behind those, another seemed to be grasping a bundle, perhaps a child. I couldn't tell.

The figures bunched together quickly, struggling, the muddy water rushing around them, pulling them down the creek. I could see better now. The figures were people with arms reaching frantically. They went under and vanished. Then they came out again, bobbing in and out, with quick flashes of different colors: a red dress, a blue torso, a yellow shirt, black heads, and white feet.

A taller person, shouting, waving arms, jumped in behind the others, and soon they all spilled into the pool like seeds from a melon. They hit the pool one after the other, whirled around, and were washed down the river.

Just as the last body disappeared, a long hush temporarily broke the thundering roar. I knew I had been screaming, because my mouth was open and my throat felt as if something sharp had stripped out my tonsils.

I could not move from the spot, even though my fingers were cramped from squeezing the tree trunk. Some of my father's cousins had been washed down the creek. I would have been ahead of them if I hadn't grabbed the tree.

They would be coming back up the hill any minute. At least, I hoped they would.

I waited a long time. When no one showed up, I started back to the rum shack, sliding again as I reached for one tree, then another. It wasn't easy, the soil sliding from under my feet, and gravity pulling me down. I couldn't look up or around me, but I could hear the cascade only a short distance away.

It took forever to crawl up the bank, a distance I had covered in seconds. Reaching the platform, I thought of Papa and felt hatred for him, and for Mama, who didn't even try to stop him from sending me here.

I sat on the wet log, brought my knees to my chest, wrapped my arms around them, and trembled. The creek roared, and the raindrops became a little smaller, as if the storm was finally running out of energy. I knew the jug would soon be filled, but I had yet to decide whether to change it or let it spill over. So what if

Papa found his rum running and me sitting here? Nothing could be as bad as what I had already been through.

"*Primo! Primo!*" I heard the voice again and rejoiced.

They're alive! I thought. I looked around, straining to spot someone. Through the downpour, I finally saw a stumbling figure pushing the coffee tree branches to the side. At last, Mateo came through, his wife Angela staggering behind him. Their faces were yellow and twisted with pain. Blood trickled down Mateo's cheek. Half of his left eyebrow was gone, exposing red flesh around the bone. His dark trousers were ripped into strips that dangled from his waist. He looked at me with surprise, as though wondering why Papa wasn't there but couldn't find the words to ask.

"Papa isn't here," I said, surprised to hear a hoarse voice which didn't sound like mine.

Mateo didn't answer. He walked in a circle, making a ring of footprints in the mud. His bony knees shook inside the strips of fabric, and a streak of blood ran down through the black hair on his legs. His chest swelled up and down with his heavy breathing, enlarging and shrinking the twisted line of black hair from his breast to his navel.

Angela could hardly stand. She wavered on her feet, moaning, "Gone! All of 'em gone! The baby . . . I let him go to save myself." Her eyes were fixed wide open. Bloody cuts and scratches covered her face and arms. "All of them gone! All of them!" she cried.

"We'll find 'em." Mateo pulled twigs and leaves from her mud-covered black hair. Her dress was shredded. A wrinkled nipple, dark as a prune, showed through a tear in the bodice.

"Where's *el Primo*?" Mateo finally asked me.

"Home," I answered.

Mateo looked at the gallon jug, shook his head, and staggered toward it. He grabbed it with both hands, brought it to his lips, and gulped down some of the rum. Then he handed the jug to Angela. "Drink!" he ordered.

But she couldn't take her eyes off the rushing creek. "All of them gone! All of them!"

"Take a drink!" he shouted, and at last she blinked and drank. Mateo took another mouthful and returned the jug to the trickle. "Let's go get *el Primo*," he said.

The two went back under the trees toward my house.

Sitting on the log again, I stared at the rushing water. I didn't remove the jug, didn't add wood to the fire, didn't even care if Papa showed up and whipped me. If he did, I would not feel a thing. My fear had left me. It had gone down with the muddy water, and nothing would ever bring it back. I felt glad that the tree had saved me, but I wanted Papa to find me dead. It would be right to make him feel guilty for causing my death, but what good would that do if I couldn't witness his misery?

When I finally heard the splashing of steps in the mud, I did not turn to look.

"Sabina, go home and get dry." My father's voice sounded strange. I still didn't look up. "Careful of the gullies. They've turned into little lakes."

This made me turn. *Did he say to be careful?* He seemed shaky and confused. He dragged his machete across the mud, not looking at the still or the overflowing jug.

"Leave everything and go home. I'm going to help Mateo find his missing children."

It seemed right to look into my father's startled eyes and say absolutely nothing. For once, he didn't yell, "What are you looking at?" Peering into our parents' eyes was another thing we weren't supposed to do.

Turning to walk away from my father, I saw Mateo stumbling through the mud. Papa walked toward him, and I watched the two head down the slippery hill toward the creek.

Splashing through and jumping over puddles, I wondered how it would feel to drown in such muddy water, with twigs, leaves, and dead toads going down my throat. I shivered at the thought of how close I had come to falling into the raging creek myself. Then I thought about Papa. *He showed no concern over his precious rum. Was he that much moved by whatever Mateo told him?*

I thought of Mama, and believed that she would be looking out the kitchen door, anxious to see that I was okay. A long hug from her would make me feel much better. She hadn't hugged me since my first day of school.

The only one who met me at the kitchen door was Emilia, sucking on a chicken bone. "Did you see them jump into the creek? Did you see the water take them away?"

Without answering, I walked past her, and past the other kids who were sitting on the kitchen floor slurping chicken soup. I found my mother in the front room urging Angela to eat some soup.

"Eat a little more. It'll give you strength."

When she finally looked up and saw me, I turned and walked into the sleeping area. I couldn't help wondering why my mother was concerned about a grown woman when I had been out there all by myself.

"Wait a minute," she called after me. "You need to change your clothes and dry your hair. I'll get you something to eat."

"All I want to do is sleep!" I cried, still hoping that she would hold me and say she was glad I hadn't drowned.

"You'll get sick if you don't eat something warm."

"I'm already sick. I just want to sleep."

"Sleep after you eat," she insisted. "It's a miracle you didn't drown."

"I almost did. A tree saved me at the last minute."

"I'm glad you didn't," she said on her way to the kitchen. "I cooked something special for you. Fried plantains the way you like them." Cooking something special for me meant that she had been worried. Other times when she made chicken soup, I had to go hungry. I had to learn to like chicken soup, she would say.

"Are you really glad I didn't drown?" I asked when she returned.

"Sure I am. Eat this while it's warm, and don't ask silly questions."

"I'm cold, and I want to sleep," I said, getting into my gunnysack. "I'll eat later."

"At least drink the coffee. It'll warm you up." She handed me the steaming coffee, and placed the shell of fried plantains next to me in case I changed my mind.

I think she told the other kids to leave me alone, because none of them came to bother me until I finished eating.

"Are you going to tell me how it happened?" Emilia planted herself next to me. One by one, the other kids joined her. They looked like lumps and bundles sitting in the dark, damp, and gloomy sleeping area. The sky was still gray, and there was only one window in this part of the house.

"Why do you think I saw them jump, Emilia?" I asked.

"You were there. Angela said you watched the whole thing. She said it's a miracle the creek didn't take you away, too. Weren't you afraid?"

"No, I wasn't. I saw some people bobbing in and out of the water, but I didn't know who they were."

"Imagine that!" Emilia whispered. "Those dumb people jumped into the water with their kids, and lost them all. Can you believe such stupidity? Then they showed up here, banging on our door, screaming for help. You should have seen Papa jump out of his hammock from a deep, deep sleep."

"He'd been sleeping all that time? Through the noisy storm?" I pulled the gunnysack over my head, rolled up like a snail, and cried loud and hard. *I could have fallen into the rushing creek while my father slept through the storm. My mother didn't give me a hug, and my sister only wants me to entertain her with details about how the people died in the muddy water.*

I didn't hear when my mother came and chased the kids away, but there she finally sat, patting my back and assuring me that everything was okay. What would have comforted me then was my mother saying that she loved me. She didn't say it, but I felt that she did in a weird way. I held back my thought of saying that I loved her, that I needed her hug, that it would mean more to me if she made the first move.

At the sound of our dogs barking and running from under

the house, the kids stamped to the door, and Mama took back her hand. "You sleep," she said to me. "I'll see who it is."

I pulled myself out of the sack and followed her to the front door. There stood Mateo with his two older kids—a girl named Adela with a pudgy nose, maybe nine years old, and Tito, a boy who was seven. All three were cut and scratched, covered in mud, their clothing shredded and bloody.

"Please, Carmelita," Mateo said, "see what you can do for them. I've got to go find the others before dark. These two were clinging to a bush a half mile down the creek." He turned and hurried away. Mama stood watching, her eyebrows pushing up her forehead.

The two muddy and blood-covered kids stared into space as if they were paralyzed, their eyes unable to blink.

Angela became aware that the two kids were hers and ran out to sob over them. The kids stood traumatized, and Mama did all she could to pull the three apart and take the bloody kids inside, where she cleaned their scratches with her homemade ointments.

I went back to my sack, feeling disappointed that I had not even one cut for my mother to fuss over. I pulled my gunnysack closer to the window so I could listen to the *coquí* (a tiny frog) bring in the night with his usual sound: *"Ko kee, ko kee, ko kee."*

Chapter Nineteen

The Wake

The air seemed unusually still this morning. I stayed in my gunnysack, curled up like a snail, afraid to open my eyes. I couldn't hear the regular sounds of pots and pans and kids whimpering. Even the pigs and dogs outdoors were quiet.

"Where is everyone?" I called, pulling out of my sack.

"Oh, are you awake?" Mama walked into the sleeping area. Her voice didn't have its usual sharp, peevish tone.

"Where is everyone?" I asked again.

She didn't answer, but looked at me and walked away.

"Mama!"

Seconds later, she returned with a gourd-shell of steaming coffee, and the strangest look I had ever seen on her face. "Emilia's out with the little ones feeding the horses. You need to get up and go with me."

"Where's Papa?" I took a sip of coffee. "And why is Emilia feeding the horses?" She had never done that before.

Mama looked out the window. "We must go to your godfather's house."

Something was really strange. I had never been to my godfather's house. "Why?"

"Last night," she said, bringing her hands together. She looked everywhere except at me. I held the cup and waited.

"Well . . . a terrible thing happened last night." Her voice turned into a sob. I thought she was going to say that Papa had fallen into the creek while looking for Mateo's kids.

"Did Papa drown?"

"No. Not your father. But he and Mateo found your godfather dead on a bed of rocks near the river." Mama covered her face with her hands and wept.

I felt as if a huge hand had wrapped around my heart. I remembered seeing the tall figure jump into the creek. "My god-father?" I threw the shell to the floor, ran from the sleeping area through the kitchen and out the door into the woods, where my shriek startled the birds out of their nests.

The blurry image of the tall figure falling into the raging creek kept flashing through my mind. I wrapped my arms around a tree and screamed. When I finally turned, I saw my mother huddled on the ground with her face on her knees.

I couldn't hold back my anger. "Why are you crying?" I yelled. "You should be glad that he's dead! Now you don't have to worry about him making me feel special." I saw the surprised look on her face. Her eyes were wide and red. A daughter didn't speak to her mother in that tone. I turned my back to her, and then ran toward the springs to be by myself.

When I returned to the house, my mother said sternly, "You still have to go to your godfather's house. They need you to complete the crown of nine virgins for the wake."

She had often told us during her spooky stories that a soul couldn't reach heaven until a lot of rosaries were recited in front of a circle of nine virgin girls. There was something spiritual about the number nine, but I had no idea what qualified me as a virgin. So far, whatever holiness a virgin possessed had not given me any power. Years later, I learned that a virgin was a girl who had not been touched by a man; it had nothing to do with the Virgin Mary. Nine rosaries made a novena. Nine virgin girls pleased the Virgin Mary.

I didn't want to believe that my godfather had died. He was

too nice to die, and I hadn't seen him for a long time. I hadn't told him that I could read and write.

"Somebody made a mistake," I said, and then stamped into the sleeping area. Putting on my good dress, I yelled, "My godfather isn't dead! My godfather isn't dead! Someone's playing a joke!" I listened for an answer, but I heard none. Then I realized that something terrible had indeed happened. Otherwise, Mama would have slapped me silly for yelling at her so loudly.

We started silently up the slippery hill. She seemed sad and sorry, but I didn't care. I still felt angry with her for keeping my godfather away from me. If he in fact had died without knowing that I could read and write, I would never forgive her, or Papa for letting her get away with that.

"He jumped into the creek to help his brother," Mama mumbled, her eyes on the muddy path. "That's how he drowned. Mateo's three younger children also drowned."

"Pedra, too?"

"I guess so. Poor little thing." Mama's words softened me a little. *She really feels sad*, I told myself. Still, I kept quiet. After all, this was a special occasion. I didn't think she would slap me for not answering at a time like this.

"That's your godfather's house," she said as we walked from under the trees into a clearing.

Suddenly, I couldn't take another step. The house was huge, but it appeared cold and gray with two windows and a door as symmetrical as the nose and eyes of a face.

"They are waiting for us, Sabina," Mama said softly.

"That's an empty house. Nobody's there!"

"They probably got tired of waiting for you and started the rosary," she said.

"Why can't people live after they die, like the vine *morivivi*?" I wanted to change the subject. Maybe the nightmare would go away. "Why can't they, Mama?" I tapped the leafy vines with my foot, and the little leaves closed tightly.

"*Morivivi* doesn't die," my mother said. "The leaves go to sleep when we touch them, but they wake up again."

"Well then, why don't we call it *dormivivi*?"

"I don't know, Sabina. I didn't make the rules."

"Who makes the rules, Mama?"

"I don't know. God, I guess."

"God makes bad rules, then?"

She shook her head. "No, God doesn't make anything bad."

"He makes storms, doesn't he?"

"Yes, but we can't question God's ways."

"Why not?"

"Because we aren't smart enough."

I didn't get to say what I thought about that. My godmother came out of the house and ran to greet us.

"*Comadre!*" she cried, wrapping her arms around Mama. "My poor brother, my poor, poor sweet brother."

The two women held each other and sobbed. I wondered why my godmother would want to hug Mama, after she had kept her and my godfather from coming around to see me. I wanted her to at least yell at Mama as I had earlier. I guessed that grownups were weird. They stopped being mad at each other just because some people died.

Finally my godmother pulled herself from Mama's embrace and turned to me. "And look at you, my beautiful godchild. How you have grown!" She kissed one side of my face, then the other. "Your poor godfather loved you so. He has missed you. My poor, poor brother."

"I know how to read and write," I blurted. "I learned in school. I can write my name, and yours, too."

"I'm glad to hear that, but we have to hurry. They are waiting for you." She took my hand, and I could hardly keep up with her. Her bare feet, tough as leather, trampled over the *morivivi* as if the vines had no thorns. "It's getting late," she said as we entered the house through the kitchen door. "Your poor godfather can't reach heaven until we start the novenas. We couldn't complete the crown of nine virgins without you, his precious godchild."

An old woman whom I had never seen before stood in the next room giving instructions to eight girls, each holding a candle. She saw me and sighed with a smile. "Now the crown is complete, thanks be to God." She handed me a candle. "Come! Hurry."

The girls and I followed her into the front room, where a lot of people—Papa's cousins and their wives, and others I didn't know—sat on chairs, benches, and lard cans, staring at a stiff body in the middle of the floor. A candle flickered at his feet and another at his head, and bunches of flowers were placed around the body. I had never seen a dead person before, so naturally, I was shocked. But I refused to believe that the dead person was my godfather.

"You kneel here," the woman said to me. Then she ordered the other eight girls to kneel so that we would form a circle around the corpse. The old woman lit my candle, instructing me to light the one next to me, and that girl would pass the light on until all nine candles were lit. We had to remain on our knees through the rosary, which lasted about forty minutes. After a long break, we would kneel again for the next one. A total of five rosaries would be recited during the wake, the last one ending at dawn.

The woman, whose name I later learned was Doña Olga, stood at the foot of the dead man and made the sign of the cross. Her round, black eyes were fixed on the crucifix straight ahead. Now the other people crossed themselves, and the praying began.

I didn't want to look at the dead man. Instead, I let my gaze wander. This home had several bedrooms. I could see beds through the open doors. Later, Mama told me that the house didn't belong to my godfather, but to his mother. He and my godmother, neither of whom had married, lived there to care for their widowed mother.

Next, I looked from one grief-stricken face to another as the mourners repeated the blessed words of the rosary. Their red eyelids were heavy with sadness, but their lips moved steadily, their eyes traveling from the corpse to the crucifix, and the black rosaries dangling from their trembling hands. Papa wasn't there, and neither were Mateo, Angela, nor their son and daughter.

My eyes searched for the best dressed, the most ragged, for those who wore shoes, and for mud trapped between bare toes. Then I glanced from one girl to the other, and saw that their eyes were wandering, too. They smiled, and I smiled back. All these girls were related to me—first and second cousins, I guessed.

Yet the only ones I had ever met were Pola and Maria Elena, the daughters of Papa's cousin Bartolo. The two were as big as women, with breasts the size of oranges and hair on their legs. They were the best dressed, one in a blue print and the other in purple with cream-colored lace. They were the only ones wearing shoes—black, shiny ones with buckles. I decided that Bartolo must be rich, and his lucky daughters surely never had to work in the fields.

I kept telling myself that the dead man wasn't my godfather. This man's face looked purple, his eyes sealed shut with only the tips of black lashes sticking out between two blood-filled bubbles. Bruises, scratches, and open cuts were all over his swollen face and neck. Part of one ear was missing, a lump in its place. Dried blood had plastered this man's black hair. His fingers were reddish purple and as puffed as sausages. His wrists were so swollen that the cuffs of his white shirt could not be buttoned.

I heard the prayers being recited turn to deep hums. Then I saw orange circles grow around the flickering lights, and a blur covering the somber faces. The candle slipped from my hand, and I floated away in a dark, cool cloud.

Chapter Twenty

A Voice in the Dark

Someone called my name, and I ran toward my godfather, who sat on a log, waiting for me with open arms. My legs felt heavy as I ran. Mama was chasing me.

"Wake up, Sabina! Wake up!"

I felt the hard floor under my ribs, and warm air blowing from someplace. Opening my eyes, I saw the statue of the Virgin Mary up on a shelf. She was staring down at me with sad eyes. She wore light blue and white, and a black rosary dangled from her hands.

"Where am I?"

"In your godfather's room," my mother said. "You fainted, and I carried you in here. Are you sick?"

"No. Are they still praying?"

"They are, and you must go back to the circle."

I shook my head. "I can't. The smell makes me sick." I saw a narrow bed against the wall. "Is that my godfather's bed?"

Mama shrugged. "Maybe, but I don't know."

"It sags in the middle. The legs are pulling inward."

"They are, but the people are waiting. Let's go."

"Mama, is my godfather really dead?"

"Yes. He's really dead. He's in heaven now."

"Then who's the dead man out there?"

"The dead man is your godfather."

"But you said he's in heaven."

"His *soul* is in heaven; his body will be buried. Now stop the questions. I have to get back to your brothers and sisters. You can wait here for your father."

"Where is he?"

"He's with his brothers and cousins, searching for Mateo's children. They still hope to find them alive."

"But, Mama, the dead man doesn't look like Godfather."

"Sabina, the current in the creek was very strong. It picked him up and slammed him again and again against the rocks and crushed the life out of him."

"Is that what happened to Pedra?"

"Maybe. We'll know for sure when the men come back. Now I'm going back to finish the rosary. When it's over, I'll go home. Go back to the circle. They are expecting you."

I moved over to the doorway and watched, ignoring everyone's curious looks, until the last part of this first rosary was finished. When the mourners left their seats, stretching their arms and sighing, Mama left. Then I slipped outside and caught up with the other girls.

For a while, I felt as though we were having a party—all of us girls running around and giggling—no big sister or parents for me to fear.

But good times don't last long. Just as the sun shone directly over our heads, Papa showed up with the other men. They walked across the yard with torn, muddy clothing, dragging their feet and their machetes. Their eyes were bloodshot, their faces sweaty and yellowish with whiskers that appeared darker than black.

After one look at the men, the women knew that the rest of Mateo's children had not been found. Some of them threw themselves on the ground, and their shrieks made the pigs and dogs come out trembling from under the house.

I couldn't keep from weeping along with everyone else, but

deep inside, I still hoped that my godfather would come walking from under the trees with his brilliant smile and sparkling eyes.

When the screaming stopped, Papa and the other men went behind the house to wash off the mud. The women headed for the kitchen. Moments later, the aroma of onions, cilantro, and garlic filled the air. One woman peeled vegetables, while another washed dishes in the wood box hanging outside the window. Doña Olga sat down to mend some of my godfather's trousers for the muddied men to wear. Aunt Margarita ironed the shirts with two small irons that she heated against the fire on the *fogón*. She used one iron while the other heated up. Her tears fell on the shirts and sizzled under the iron.

When the women finished cooking the food, they served it on plates, gourds, leaves, and anything else that would hold it. People ate sitting, standing, and squatting, inside and outside, in the kitchen, in the bedrooms, and even near the corpse. After the food came hot black coffee with sugar.

Then Papa and Uncle Luís went behind the house to build the casket. Everyone else gathered around for the next rosary, and we nine girls returned to the floor on our already painful knees.

The afternoon dragged on, and everyone looked tired. Still, after the second rosary, the women cooked rice and beans to feed everyone again later. Some of the men went to haul water from the springs near the house, and others fell asleep in the corners, mouths open and snoring.

Papa went home to change his clothes, saying he would be back shortly. He had asked if I wanted to go with him or stay there. I had said I'd like to stay, and he didn't seem to mind. I had never been among so many people before, and had never been without Emilia, so even though this was a sad situation, I felt excited. I could talk and giggle like the other girls, and not be criticized by my sister or hit on the head by my parents for being friendly.

"You girls should get some sleep," my godmother said

lovingly. "It's going to be a long night, and you'll be on your knees for most of it."

She suggested that four of us lie across her bed, and the other five girls could sleep in gunnysacks on the floor. It was the most fun I'd ever had. All those girls and me in one room, no parents and no sister. But after a lot of giggles and whispers, the girls fell asleep one after the other.

Then I felt guilty for having fun. I realized that if it hadn't been for all those people dying, I wouldn't have been here. The thought made me sad. I turned on my stomach and cried.

I was the last one to come out of the room. By then, everyone had eaten and had gone behind the bushes for their habits. Papa had returned, and people who hadn't been there earlier had arrived. The house was packed. It trembled, and the sound of voices roared through its rooms.

I decided then that death must be a good thing if it brought this many people together, acting friendly toward each other. But I hated that my godfather had to die and miss out on the excitement.

The next three rosaries were spread out through the night, and coffee and soda crackers were served in between. We girls knelt down for each rosary, and when we finished, our knees were raw. During the rosaries, I often felt sick to my stomach and dizzy. The multitude of voices hummed deeply, as if the sound came from long tunnels, and people's faces appeared distorted, like wilted plants. The light in the kerosene lamp and candles flickered slowly, as if lacking sleep.

At times, I could not feel the floor under my knees, and my body seemed to float and come down again. It was a scary feeling, yet it would do no good to tell anyone. It wouldn't excuse me from being in the crown. *After all, I am the godchild, the most important virgin in the circle.* That's what I told myself to keep from falling facedown on the body.

At last, the first rooster crowed, and then another. The pigs squealed and the dogs barked. A new day was coming to erase the nightmare. Soon the shadows on the walls faded away and the candles became heaps of wax in the saucers we held.

Aunt Gala could hardly keep her eyes open, but she stood in front of the crowd and recited the closing prayer. When she finished, everyone stirred, stretched, and for a short time dispersed like small fish in shallow water.

Finally, Papa and two of my godfather's brothers picked up the stiff body and carefully laid it inside the casket. The heels of their shoes clicked on the wooden floor as they stood back for one more look before nailing the coffin shut.

They strapped a long wooden pole lengthwise over the casket, and two of my godfather's brothers, one at each end of the pole, lifted it to their shoulders and walked out the door. Two more brothers and four cousins followed them up the hill, all walking slowly, with their heads hanging low.

At that moment, the women stirred up. One let out a piercing shriek, and the rest of them joined in, one after the other. They all scattered around the yard like a flock of chickens trying to escape a hungry wolf.

Standing outside the front door under gray skies with no sign of the sun, the moist coolness of the morning creeping up my legs and making me shiver, I wondered if I was supposed to scream like the grown women, or barely whimper like some of the girls. My eyes gazed from the girls to the screaming women, then to my father, who sat on a rock carving the ground near his feet with the blade-tip of his machete, and then on to Aunt Gala, who stood straight as an arrow shouting, "Goodbye, my son! Goodbye!"

The men with the casket shrank as they moved farther up the mountain ridge. Gradually, the screams subsided into short sobs, and the sobs into sniffs. Bloodshot eyes wandered from face to face, and then came the time for everyone to say their goodbyes and head home.

I followed my father through the *morivivi* patch and into the woods, which seemed darker and colder than ever before, as if they were closing in on us and there was no way out. This cold and fearful feeling hung over me like a deep black basket. If its rims touched the ground, I would suffocate.

I had thought that once we were alone, Papa would ask me questions about what I had seen at the creek the day of the storm—a day which by now seemed so long ago. My father walked quietly, with his eyes on the ground and his machete under his arm.

Suddenly I remembered the still and the jugs of rum I had walked away from. *Who finished the brewing, cleaned the drum, and carried the jugs home?* If I asked, he would remember that I had let his jug overflow and the fire go out.

The rest of the way home, I worried that Papa would sooner or later punish me for neglecting the still.

He never spoke—around me, anyway—about the storm or the rum he lost. Even as an adult, I never asked who collected the jugs and cleaned the still the day of the storm. But for years after that event, I trembled every time he made rum and it rained. He never told me that I had nothing to worry about, yet he never again left me or any of the other kids minding his still while he slept through a storm.

*　　*　　*

A few weeks after that storm, an epidemic of influenza swept through our hills. I was the first in our family to get it. Within days, everyone else, except Papa, hit their gunnysacks. Some of us were sicker than others lying in the same corner, delirious with burning fever for days.

A whole month went by before we could resume our daily chores, which we started as if we hadn't been sick at all. We began early each morning and worked steadily through the day.

As if working a full day after being so sick wasn't enough torture, one afternoon Papa called me to the sitting area. I was scared, because being called to the sitting area usually meant we'd get a whipping or at least get hit on the head for whatever reason. This time Papa had stretched himself in his hammock, and what he told me turned out to be worse than getting hit by his hard knuckles.

"It's about your godmother," he started, looking toward the door instead of looking at me. "She couldn't cope with her brother's death." Papa pushed on the floor with two fingers, and the hammock swung back and forth, the ropes screeching on the round poles.

I waited, wanting to demand that he speak up and be done with whatever news he had.

"Right after her brother's funeral, your godmother isolated herself from friends and relatives and stopped eating. Pretty soon, she looked like a skeleton. Then she caught the flu, which quickly turned into pneumonia, and now she's dead and buried."

There was calmness in my father's voice that didn't seem right to me. He didn't appear sorry that I had lost my godmother so soon after losing my godfather.

A suffocating pressure grew in my chest, so I jumped out the front door and ran fast, screaming at the top of my lungs. I didn't even think about what my parents would do to me for acting like that. I ran until I got tired, and screamed until my throat felt raw.

When I finally returned, Papa pointed a finger at me and said, "If I hadn't been feeling so bad myself about your godmother's death, I would have gone after you and given you a good whipping for running off like that."

I lowered my head, but I did not apologize.

My parents did not drink that night. After supper, they called us into the front room to recite the rosary for my godmother. This time we did not have to pray on our knees, and we were free to sit with our legs stretched out on the floor. When the younger children fell asleep, Papa did not whack them with his belt or with his rosary.

Chapter Twenty-One

Mama Begs God

For the next few months, our family lived in near harmony. We children still had to work all day and follow the rules, but Mama and Papa, although they drank, did not get terribly drunk. Papa didn't make any more rum until after Christmas. Sometimes after supper, we were allowed to sit in the corners of the sitting area while our parents talked about how many new chicks had hatched and how many eggs had gone bad. Although those were good moments, we older girls knew that they could end any time for any little reason.

And sure enough, they did.

Emilia and I returned from the springs one afternoon and found Mama under the mango tree outside the kitchen door. She stood with feet apart and arms straight up toward the high branches, her long hair hanging like a black cape down her back.

She had put on her brown dress, which stopped two inches above her ankles. We had left her wearing a pale blue dress with a little print. In our family, we never changed our clothes at the end of the day. Now this brown and black figure under a dark shade had made us come to a sudden halt, almost causing us to drop our *calabazos*. Then our mother's cry terrified us.

"God, why have you punished me with so many children? What have I done to deserve all this misery?"

She didn't even know that we were watching her from behind.

"I can't bear to give birth one more time!" she cried. "Please, God, send me a deadly illness and take me out of this miserable world!"

Her cry made my legs feel weak. When I staggered, she turned quickly. She had a blank look and red eyes.

"I'm nothing but a damn slave around here!" she cried, and walked past us as if we weren't there. Emilia followed her in a daze, shoulders rounded, jaw hanging open and eyes glued to Mama.

I trotted behind them, wondering where this was leading. Something had happened while we were at the springs, but what? Everything had seemed peaceful before we left.

"All my life, I've been nothing but a damn slave!" Mama reached for the doorjambs and pulled herself up to the kitchen, the two of us behind her. "My old man split my head with a can because I couldn't keep my baby brother from crying. Another time my old lady hung me by my arms from the ceiling and set fire to my legs. I wasn't supposed to run from a beating, but I hadn't burned the rice on purpose. I learned to cook without burning the food after that, and I never ran from another beating, either." Mama reached above the *fogón*, brought down her tobacco, and rolled a cigarette. "They married me to a madman, a slave driver. Now I'm tired, with too many children, and I'm still being beaten."

I felt a rush of anger surge through me. "That doesn't make sense, Mama!" I blurted. "If you learned to cook without burning the food, then you shouldn't have been beaten. And if someone still wants to beat you, you should run fast." I expected her hand to come across my face, but she only stared at the floor and blew out cigarette smoke.

"That's right, Mama." Emilia frowned. "Is that why you don't run from Papa's beatings? Is that why, Mama?" Emilia spoke harshly, her eyes wide open.

"Where do you think I could run to?" Mama's words were

squeezed through her broken teeth. "If I had a place to run to, do you think I'd be here today?" She took another drag.

"She can't run. She's a lady!" Emilia lifted her arms and brought them down powerfully against her thighs. "I can't listen to any more of this! Let's go and get more water."

Emilia dragged the *calabazo* and snapped more branches. "He must have already beaten her today. I wonder what they fought about this time. Things couldn't stay quiet for much longer, anyway. Damn, she's going to have another *mocoso* (a snotty brat), and I'm sick of washing shit-covered rags. I'm sick of mothering a bunch of brothers and sisters. I'll never get married if it means filling a house with a dozen *mocosos*."

I didn't dare open my mouth. But I kept thinking about what Mama had said about her parents. I understood why she felt bad enough to want to die. But I couldn't see why she would be as mean to us as her parents were to her.

All of it was too confusing for me. Still, I promised myself that if I became a mother someday, I would show my babies love instead of anger. In the meantime, I'd pray for ways to help my mother so she wouldn't want to die.

Later that evening, Gloria told us about the fight.

"As soon as you girls left for the springs, and the boys went to tend the horses, Papa sent Alicia and me outside with Alejandro. Then he closed the door, and I heard him and Mama murmuring in the sleeping area. After a while, Mama cried, saying that she didn't have the strength to have another baby. I heard one loud slap after another. Finally, Papa flew out the door and disappeared into the woods."

I felt sick listening to Gloria and remembering my mother under the mango tree, asking God to let her die. There had to be something I could do to make her want to live. If God wanted to listen to either Mama or me, I hoped He'd listen to me, and forgive her for wanting to die.

The next day, I had to fill the barrels by myself because Emilia claimed she felt sick. I had hidden some old newspaper pages in a gourd shell under a bush, and being alone gave me the opportunity to read them while the *calabazo* filled up.

Like an answer to my prayers, I came across a good solution to my mother's problem. *God has answered my prayers*, I thought as I read. A woman and her three children in a town called Arecibo had tortured her abusive husband for two days. They tied him to a chair and pulled out his hair, one hair at a time, pulled back his fingernails, spread apart his fingers and toes, bent back his wrist, and tickled his ears with chicken feathers. They cooked good-smelling food and ate it in front of the starving, bound man.

According to the article, the woman mailed a letter to the police department, telling them where her husband could be found. Then she left for New York with her children.

My palms perspired and my heart pounded as I read. I imagined all of us doing the same thing to Papa. We would use more rope, and tie him to a beam, for he could break apart the chairs he had built. Fear came over me as I imagined him untying himself. We would never find a place to hide.

Still, I had to convince Mama that it was time for us to straighten out Papa. As soon as I got inside the house, I read the article to her.

"What's so good about that?" she asked. By the look on her face, I knew she wasn't going to like my answer.

"Well, Mama, if a woman with three children did that to her mean husband, imagine what you could do to Papa with the *six* of us. Can't you see? We can teach him a big lesson."

I got a long, hard stare from my mother's large, brown eyes, while Emilia and Gloria watched. Then Mama's hard hand swung across my face, and I flew against the wall with bloody lips.

"That will teach you to honor your father and mother, no matter what!"

Now I felt more confused than ever. First, she didn't run when Papa slapped her. Secondly, she begged God to take her because she felt too tired to be a mother. Thirdly, she broke my lips for trying to help her, and she still insisted that I honor my parents, no matter what.

Life was too complicated. I licked the blood off my lips and slowly rose to my feet. Without looking at my mother, I crumpled the old newspaper page and walked out.

I went under the house to find comfort with the goats. As I crawled in, Cielo Azul, who was the size of a small cat, unfolded his little legs and came running to meet me. I wrapped my arms around his fluffy white body and sat leaning against one of the stilts. As he sniffed at me, I whispered into his ear.

"Let's run away from home. These people are too mean to me, and I know that one day Papa will take you away from me. He'll take you to the market and sell you. I'll die when that happens. I've loved you since the first time I held you to Canela. You took to her tiny nipples so eagerly. Your mother had rejected you. She'd given birth to three babies and could feed only two."

Canela had given birth to six puppies, and all but one had died. She had been walking around with her full teats almost touching the ground.

"When Mama said you would starve to death, I called Canela and held you to her milk. At first, she tried to resist, but then realized that you were taking out some of her pressure. I could see your little belly rising. After a few feedings like that, you knew where to go for your next meals, and Canela stayed still while you and her pup suckled away.

"You grew some and put on weight. Soon you were a warm and fluffy white bundle. I named you Cielo Azul for your lovely blue eyes. By then, Papa had caught us and instead of clobbering me, he said, 'You should consider yourself lucky that dog didn't bite you.' Shortly after that, everyone referred to you as 'Sabina's goat.' 'Come get your goat out of my way,' they'd say. You became my sweet pet, and I love you very much."

Whispering to Cielo Azul while he sniffed my neck and hair and tried anxiously to grab my earlobes, I felt his warm breath, and the softness of his cotton-white fur always eased away my anger and misery.

Chapter Twenty-Two

Plucking Chickens

Against the odds, I still clung to the hope that one day the school would reopen and my parents would let me go back for fourth grade. But would my father be willing to lose his best helper? That question nagged at me day and night, and the thought of working at his side for the rest of my life terrified me.

Finally one day, one of Castillo's sons yelled the good news from the top of the mountain. "The war is over! The United States bombed Japan and put an end to the war! *Viva America!* Now the school will reopen and we can go back to class. *Viva la education!*"

I was walking up the hill with a can of water on my head when those words reached my ears, and I had all I could do to keep from throwing the can and running home to make sure that my mother heard the news. Surely she'd be really happy that the war ended, and would not protest the possibility of my going back to school.

"Mama!" I called as I reached the kitchen door, gasping for breath. "Did you hear the news?"

"I heard it. What about it?" She was at the *fogón*, lighting the wood.

"Did you hear what he said?"

"I did. He said the war's over. Thank God!"

"About the school, Mama, did you hear about the school?" I lowered the can to the floor and waited.

Mama blew on the little flame, then said, "Don't believe everything you hear. That's probably one of Castillo's boys having fun. Even if what he said is true, who cares whether the school reopens?"

"*I* care if the school reopens. It means we'll be going back to school for fourth grade."

My mother turned to me and placed her hands on her hips, elbows pointing out. "Never mind the school. Get back to the springs and bring more water."

I emptied the water into the barrel and looked for Emilia, hoping to see her react happily to the good news. She was still curled up in her gunnysack bed with stomach cramps, so I headed back to the springs, still too excited to suspect that I might not be allowed to return to school.

I made six trips. Each time I returned with another can of water, I said something to Mama about the reopening of the school.

"I bet the place is swarming with bees and roaches, after being locked up for two years."

"I had almost given up hope, after waiting for so long."

"Sure glad I didn't forget how to read and write."

Mama always gave me a sidelong look. On my last trip, she said, "Never mind the school. You aren't going back."

Shocked by her simple statement, I turned to stare at her. "I'm not? Why, Mama?"

"You're too old to be going to school, that's why."

"Too old? How old am I, Mama? Am I nine? Or am I ten?"

"Never mind, but you're too old. Now stop the questions and get over there. It's time you learned how to pluck a chicken."

I cringed in revulsion. "Mama, please! Don't make me watch that."

"Sit down and stop whining." Mama grabbed the sleeve of my dress and pulled me to the floor. "Just sit there and watch." She walked away, then returned with a black chicken in her hands. She tied the chicken's legs together and hung it from a nail on the wall. The chicken flapped its wings desperately, but Mama showed no mercy.

"It's important that you learn how to do this." She dug her thumb into the bird's neck and spun it fast.

I covered my eyes, but I heard the flip-flap of the wings. "Mama, please!" I looked between my fingers, and saw the flapping and small feathers flying. My stomach rolled.

"Stop being silly." Mama gave my hair a tug.

"It's not silly to feel sorry for a helpless chicken."

"It *is* silly," she said. "God made animals and birds for men to eat."

"But we are not men."

"God said *men*, meaning every human being. Now be quiet. I don't want to hear another word." She submerged the chicken in a pot of boiling water. The smell of wet feathers rose from the pot, and I had to cover my nose with my skirt.

"I don't want to learn how to kill chickens, or to make stinky soup! All I want is to go to school and become a teacher."

"Shut up! You need to learn how to do this. Besides, teachers eat chicken, too." Mama waved her feather-covered hand at my face.

The stench grew stronger, my stomach kept turning, and Mama kept plucking. When all the feathers were gone, she chopped off the chicken's head and cut open the body. The smell became unbearable when she pulled out a handful of blue and pinkish tubing. My mouth filled with warm water, and vomit shot out over the pile of feathers.

"Go!" Mama screamed. "Get out of here! Go pull weeds with your father. Go!"

I went under the house, grabbed my hoe, and ran to the pigeon-pea field, shaking off the smell of chicken blood, anxious to find Papa. He would decide which of us kids would go to school and which would stay working on the farm. If he decided to send me, Mama would not be able to change his mind.

He wasn't at the field, so I started pulling weeds where we had stopped the day before. I pulled crabgrass and thorny vines faster than ever before, thinking about my favorite classmates: Manuela, Julia, and Margarita. I could hardly wait to see them again. I wondered how much they had grown in two years. I hoped they had missed me as much as I had missed them.

I kept pulling weeds, waiting for Papa, but he never showed up. Finally, when I realized he wasn't coming, I walked home. Before reaching the yard, I heard his voice and stopped, with fear churning in my stomach.

"I am the king of this castle! What I say goes. I rule over everyone in this house. I decide everyone's destiny. Don't you forget it!"

At first I thought it was just another of our regular fights: Papa with a red face would stand unsteadily in the middle of the room telling Mama and us children that we had no rights to anything, that the sooner we faced that fact, the better things would be for all of us.

I hurried across the yard and peeked through the cracks in the wall. Papa's face wasn't so red this time. His eyes were large and soft brown, not the piercing black we had seen whenever he had a lot to drink. He was walking circles around the *fogón*, where Mama stood, stirring the chicken soup in the steaming iron pot.

"Just get those three ready. José, Lorenzo, and Alicia. School begins in two weeks."

My heart stopped. What about me? Was he going to send them to school without me?

I made my way inside without Papa seeing me, and asked Emilia what was going on.

"Same old story," she said. "Mama doesn't want Alicia to go to school because she's a girl, but Papa says she's going."

"What about you and me?"

"We're not going," she said, "because we're too old."

"*I'm* not too old."

"Mama said you are."

Feeling sick enough to die, I went behind the house to wash the dirt off my arms and legs. I cursed inside my head the whole time, wishing that something really bad would happen—something that would change the way my parents thought.

I was glad, however, that Alicia would be going to school. She was a bright girl with a warm smile. At age six, she was small and skinny, but healthy and eager to learn.

As for José and Lorenzo, who didn't seem very bright, all I could hope for was that the school would teach them to be nicer. They were already monsters at ages seven and eight. Emilia had said that if we weren't careful, our brothers would grow up thinking they could control us just because they were boys.

Somehow, I had to convince Papa that keeping me out of school would be a bad idea. I had been a good student for three years, always got my homework done, and had received better grades than Emilia.

Tomorrow, I told myself, *when we're working in the fields, I'll convince him that I'll be much more helpful to him with a few more years of school. That way, I'll be able to read his correspondence to him and write his business letters. I'll even promise to work twice as hard if he'll let me go back to school.*

Later, after supper, when we children settled down in our sacks, I heard my parents murmuring in the living room. I listened, tilting my head toward the wall, hoping to hear Papa say he would be sending me back to school . . .

The next thing I knew was Papa twisting my toes. "Time to get up, time to get up. We need to start work early. Might rain this afternoon." It was still dark when I opened my eyes, but he said, "Have your coffee and meet me at the oak patch. I'll be cutting trees for the new corral."

I usually dreaded the days when Papa cut trees to build something. It meant long days of working with him, holding the rails for him to nail them, handing him the saw, the hammer, the nails, then some water, and anything else he needed.

But this morning I didn't mind working with him. I had to

take the opportunity to convince him that sending me back to school would be the right thing to do.

I drank my coffee slowly, rehearsing in my mind what I would say. I would start gradually and politely, suggesting rather than asking directly, so he wouldn't suspect that I was anxious about it. If he stopped me at the beginning of my talk, I would apologize and drop the subject to keep from making him mad—then I'd bring it up later.

When I had it all together in my mind, I grabbed the hem of my burlap dress so I could pull it above my knees and run. This dress, made especially for working in the fields, was actually a straight sack, inches below the knee and narrow so the wind would not lift it and expose my underpants. I could not run without raising it above my knees.

Papa had already cut down one tree and was chopping off the branches, which I would pull out of his way.

"Stack them up over there." He pointed with his chin, then began to whistle. Papa whistled only when he was in a good mood, so this seemed encouraging. Still, I got busy pulling the branches without saying anything.

When the time seemed right, I said softly, "Papa, are you going to send Emilia and me back to school?"

His machete stopped in mid air. "No." The machete came down, striking hard into the tree limb. He wiggled it to pull it out. "You girls have work to do at home." He continued whacking the tree, and began humming.

My heart sank. "But, Papa—"

"No buts," he said, and stopped humming. "There's work to be done. Don't waste time talking."

Something happened to my rehearsed words. I suddenly felt choked up. I blurted, "I'll die if I can't go back to school! But dying is better than having to work like a man in the hot sun and mud!" I was bent over, reaching for a branch, and I looked over my shoulder and saw the machete freeze once more in the air. Immediately, I cried out, "I'm so sorry, Papa, really sorry!"

He finished the swing, striking the tree so hard I jumped. Squinting, he leaped toward me and grabbed my earlobe. "Don't you ever talk to me like that again!" He pulled me close, the cut branches scratching my feet, and twisted my earlobe as if it were an orange he was trying to snap off a tree. "Not another word out of you! Do you understand?" He pulled and twisted the earlobe again. "Now get to work." He gave me one hard push, and I landed on my back on the pile of cut branches. I wanted to die so he would feel guilty for being so cruel.

Papa went back to work, but he didn't hum or whistle any more. I got up and started pulling the branches, and I didn't say anything more.

I started thinking about running away from home. Maybe I could go to Arecibo, where the woman and her kids tortured her husband. That was the same town Miss Traverso had moved to when she stopped coming to my school.

She would probably be glad to see me. I imagined her smiling and asking me to enter her gorgeous home. A teacher as beautiful as she would not live in a wooden shack. She would live in a house as big as the school, with a shiny floor and big windows.

I needed to find out where Arecibo was. Once I got there, I'd find Miss Traverso's home. I'd even take my little goat with me so Papa would not sell him for meat. I could not let that happen to my Cielo Azul.

I suddenly realized that Papa was still watching me, and I felt hollow inside. I had to leave my dreams for later. He would beat the life out of me if he knew what I had in mind!

I worked, trying not to look at him, yet now and then our eyes met. I wished to be far from him, but he was so close I could smell his sweat. I hated to ask him where he wanted me to put one branch and where he wanted the others. I always got a mad look as he snapped, "Over there!"

That night, I prayed silently that Papa would disappear, or that an angel would take me far away from him.

Chapter Twenty-Three

Sweaty Money

It devastated me to watch the boys and Alicia leave for school every morning, while I worked with my father in the fields. The emptiness I felt tore me inside. The feeling was as bad as what I had felt when my godparents died. This time, something scraped out my insides and replaced them with rage.

Yet I had to follow my father around, doing whatever he ordered me to do without a whimper. Each time I looked at him or heard his voice, rage whirled inside me and I wondered how life would be without him.

As usual, Papa came up with something nice after being rotten for days. At times like that, I wondered if maybe one day he would turn nice and stay that way, even though I knew that behind his pleasant moments, there was always something to benefit Papa. He would never take a step for the sake of others. Every move he made was motivated by his own wants.

Well, this time he finally came up with an idea that would eventually ease my pain about not going to school, although his intentions weren't to make me feel better. He had money in mind.

"You two," he said to Emilia and me one afternoon, "out here." He motioned us to follow him into the sitting area.

"What did we do now?" I whispered to Emilia.

"It can't be too bad," she said. "His eyes are twinkling."

Still, Emilia and I made sure we stayed between him and the front door. If he made a sudden move, we'd jump out and run.

He shook the dust off his hammock and, stretching himself in it, said, "Now listen carefully. I've made arrangements for you girls to learn how to sew gloves."

We stared at him in surprise.

"Gloves?" Emilia said at last.

"Gloves are covers for the hands of people who live in cold countries," Papa continued. "Doña Isabel, the lady who will teach you, said that each of you can earn twenty dollars or more per month without leaving this house." He paused and brought the tips of his fingers together. "The sewing factory is in Mayaguez, a big city on the west side of the island. It's far from here, but a distributor lives only a short distance beyond the school. You can go there and bring the sewing home. If you learn the craft, that is."

Emilia and I glanced at each other. My heart began to dance, and it was all I could do to keep Papa from seeing that I had just heard the most beautiful words he had ever spoken. I remembered reading in the old newspapers about Mayaguez, a big city on an ocean with a port where big ships unloaded cargo.

Then I thought about the school. We would walk past it. Even though I would not be attending classes, I'd get to see it, and maybe even stop in for a visit sometimes. I felt like jumping around, clapping my hands and singing.

"The boys will do most of your chores so you two can sew gloves all day," Papa went on. "If you don't want to sew gloves, you can plan to work in the fields all your lives."

Papa wasn't trying to spare us from the hard work in the fields. He was interested only in the money we'd earn for him. Little did he know that I would do anything to stay out of the hot sun and the muddy fields. As for Emilia, I felt sure that Papa's new idea pleased her very much. But she did a great job acting as if one thing was as good as another.

"Whatever you say, Papa," she said.

Papa looked at me. "And you?"

"Oh, me too, Papa, I'll do whatever you say."

"Very well, then. Doña Isabel is expecting you tomorrow. Be sure to pay attention and learn fast, or else she might get tired and decide not to waste her time on you. Now go do your chores."

We bowed our heads, took our *calabazos*, and headed down to the springs. As soon as we entered the woods, Emilia whirled around with a wide grin and sparkling eyes. "God is finally on our side! Think of all the people we'll get to see!"

I had been waiting to see her reaction before expressing my own, so I jumped and skipped around her. "We'll get to see the school, too! Maybe even stop for a visit sometimes."

"Yeah, but we won't have to listen to a dumb teacher."

"That's right. We won't have to learn anything." I said that to keep her happy, but my brain was speeding faster than Papa's white horse.

The ripples in my stomach kept me from eating supper that night. Then I lay awake for a long time, praying for the night to pass. Isabel lived in a new housing development about a mile from our property line. We had looked over from our hills when the homes were being built, but only with the hope that someday we might get to see them. According to those who had stopped by our house for a few shots of Papa's rum, the homes were made of concrete. This was something new in the hills, and some people couldn't understand how concrete would make a sturdy building.

In the morning, Emilia and I hurried to fill the water barrels before leaving for our first sewing lesson. As we entered the woods, Emilia stretched out her arms and said, "Oh, give me wings so I can fly!"

"Would you fly far away if you had wings?"

"No. I'd just fly to the springs and back. The sooner we can fill up the barrels, the sooner we'll go to Isabel's."

It was better for me to see her happy about something, so I didn't tell her that if I had wings, I would skip Isabel and the distributor and fly directly to that city in the west.

On our third trip to the springs, we bathed in the pool of water a short way down from the *calabazos*. The whole time, Emilia raved about going to Isabel's. This was good, because when she seemed happy, I could be myself and she wouldn't hit or tease me.

At home, we changed into clean dresses and combed our hair while listening to Mama's complaints.

"Nothing good will come out of you two learning how to sew gloves. No one asked my opinion, but I would never have someone who had lived in a city teach my daughters anything."

We kept quiet until we walked out of the house.

"Mama's so jealous," Emilia said. "She doesn't want to lose her best helper. And she thinks we'll learn more than sewing gloves from Isabel."

"She didn't want us to go to school, either," I said.

"Yeah, but that was okay because I didn't want to go to school. But this is different."

I didn't want Emilia to get mad at me this morning, so I said, "Yeah, going to Isabel's is different. We can ask her what a city looks like and if it is fun to live in one."

"That's right! So let's run. The sooner we get there, the longer we'll have with Isabel."

We ran through the woods for a while, than emerged onto a path of sweet-smelling red earth that reminded me of walking to school. *When we learn to sew gloves, we'll walk past the school. That's better than not ever seeing the school at all.*

At last we reached Isabel's house. She had seen us coming and had stepped out to greet us.

"Ah, you girls have grown so much since the last time I saw you."

She didn't look familiar to me, so I had no idea when or where she'd seen us. But what mattered to me then was that she'd spoken as if we were more than just two ragged girls from the other side of the hills.

"I promised your father to teach you how to sew gloves in a week's time, so let's go in and get started."

We followed the vibrant lady inside. I guessed that she was probably Mama's age, but she looked and dressed much younger. She wore a black and white polka-dotted dress an inch above her knee, with a low neckline that Mama would call indecent. She wore lipstick, and her hair was cut short.

Truly, this wasn't a lady Mama would choose to teach us anything. I remembered how Mama looked minutes before we left. She seemed as angry as she did the day Papa decided to send us to school.

The house was huge. It had a real living room with four windows, two smooth benches made of dark wood, and a shiny black table with four chairs to match. It had two bedrooms with two windows each, and beds instead of hammocks. It also had a real kitchen made apart from the house. The walls and floor were smooth, with no cracks anywhere.

I couldn't help wondering why Papa couldn't build a house like that. Later, I learned that these homes—all nine of them, each on two acres of flat land—were projects initiated by the American Red Cross, offered only to people who did not already own property.

"You need to pay close attention if you are going to learn in a week." Isabel spoke softly, with a broad smile that almost closed her glittering brown eyes. She reached into a small basket and pulled out a piece of white cloth that looked like a flat hand with four fingers. She opened it up and spread it on her lap, and the piece became two flat hands side by side. Now she reached into the basket for the glove's thumb, which she told us had to be sewn before closing the fingers.

"One important thing to remember, girls, is that all the stitches must be made the same size. If they are not the same, the inspector will return the work, and you'll have to take the gloves apart and then sew them again before you're paid."

She finished the thumb and started on the rest of the glove, sewing a strip of the same fabric up one side of a finger then down another until all four fingers were closed. Now she put the glove on her hand to check her work.

"If the stitches are too tight, the glove fingers will crease," she said. "If they are too loose, my skin will show between the stitches."

Isabel did not let us touch the gloves. We would have to learn only by watching and listening. But I had learned regular sewing by watching Mama, so I felt sure that I would learn to make gloves.

We went to Isabel's house for eight days. Then, on Saturday morning, Papa took us to the home of Don Estrada, the distributor. This was the first time we'd been near the school since it closed. I saw it from a distance and felt like crying because that was where I wanted to go.

The road became wider beyond the school, and it had a lot of shoe prints and hoof marks. Narrower paths branched off to the left and to the right, and we could see people from the hills trailing down toward us. Two girls about Emilia's age merged into the wide road, and Papa removed his hat.

"Good morning, young ladies," he said, with the brilliant smile he reserved for people other than his family. "On your way to the city?"

"No," one of them said. "We're going to Don Estrada's."

"Ah, glove makers? So are my daughters, Emilia and Sabina." Papa swung a hand gracefully, so the girls would see to whom the names belonged. "How long have you been making gloves?"

"We have just learned, so the gloves we hope to get today will be our first." The two girls spoke at the same time, then giggled.

"Ah, it's my daughters' first time, too," Papa said.

We walked behind him, listening to his soft, friendly voice, and I wondered if he saw what was so clear to me. The girls were wearing shoes and socks to match their dresses. One girl had a lilac dress with white lace, buttons down the back, and a white belt around her waistline. The other had a royal blue dress trimmed with red. They both had barrettes in their hair, and they seemed happy and confident.

Emilia looked embarrassed, walking far behind the two girls, her eyes on the ground.

When other people joined us, Papa started talking with an older man, and the girls went ahead, never looking back at us. *We aren't good enough for them*, I thought. I hoped to see at least one ragged girl, so we would feel better.

Don Estrada's home was enormous. It was made of smooth wood, and it had a balcony all around the *sala*, where the gloves were distributed. There were no benches in this huge room, but chairs made of dark, shiny wood. I saw several closed doors, which I guessed led to bedrooms. Up on a shelf in the salon, I saw a black box with a little window and two buttons. Soft music came from it, and Papa told us later that it was a radio, operated by something called a battery.

There were a few women and young girls already there, and Don Estrada, a tall, skinny man with gray hair and a beard, sat at a table inspecting gloves. He used a long wooden tool that was shaped like a finger but opened like scissors. He inserted it into the glove's fingers and squeezed it. The tool opened inside, stretching the fabric to reveal any spaces between the stitches. He checked every finger in every glove while the woman who had sewed them waited, perspiring in fear that he would find flaws in her work.

Papa had a constant smile as he stood so straight with his arms crossed over his barrel-like chest, watching the inspection. His eyes twinkled when he looked at us and nodded, but I knew he was only thinking of the money we'd be bringing home.

When Don Estrada finished inspecting the gloves, he turned to my father, who seemed proud and thrilled to introduce his daughters, the future money-makers. After their handshake, Don Estrada had us girls look at a finished glove, then he gave us one glove each to sew on the spot. If we did them right, he said he would let us take two dozen each to sew at home.

We had practiced on pieces of rags at home, but I felt shaky when my fingers touched the real glove fabric. It was a soft, light pink, which could easily turn the color of mud if we weren't careful. I saw beads of sweat on Emilia's forehead and knew she was nervous, too. We would be back in the fields if Don Estrada found our samples wrong and dirty.

"You might not get them right the first time," Papa said, probably guessing that we were worried. "Maybe you'll be better off working outside in the shade," he added with a friendly smile, and led us to a bench under a large tree. "Oh, look at that." He pointed to a long metal pipe that had some kind of hook at the end. "You can wash your hands here." He turned the hook, and water gushed out immediately.

"Water from a pipe?" Emilia asked, scrubbing her hands.

"Yeah, people in these parts aren't lucky enough to own land out in the country," answered Papa, seeming proud for being a farmer.

"But water from a pipe means that people who live around here are rich, right?" I asked.

"No, that's not what it means. You girls get busy. I'll leave you alone so you don't get nervous. It's important that you do the test right."

We dried our hands on our skirts and started with the glove's thumb, carefully pushing the needle in and out of the thick fabric. We were slow at first, and even had to take out some stitches, but we soon got the hang of the craft. We finished the thumb and started sewing the strips of fabric to the fingers. Once again, we had to take apart some stitches, which made us more nervous.

"Oh, shit!" Emilia whispered. "If Papa comes back and sees us taking this apart, he'll decide that we're wasting too much time. We'll be back in the fields in no time."

I felt more concerned about being embarrassed if some of the women came to wash their hands and saw us struggling.

"Don't worry," I whispered back. "Papa will not give up that easily. He's thinking money, not time."

Emilia cracked a little smile, and I knew she agreed.

Sewing the strips of fabric on the glove fingers was a slow

process, and we were nervous. But Papa stayed away for a long time, so we slowly sewed up one side of the glove finger and down another. I finished before my sister, but I didn't let her know it. When she tied her last stitch, I tied mine, and at last we tried on our first gloves.

My heart was really racing now, and I could see Emilia's eyes gleaming. We both smiled and sighed with joy, for neither of our gloves had spaces or creases between the stitches.

Papa's eyes lit up, and he smiled at us when Don Estrada checked the samples and handed each of us two dozen pairs of red gloves. We would be paid three dollars for every dozen, a total of twelve dollars for ninety-six gloves.

I must have had a thousand bubbles floating through my chest and stomach as we walked home. For the first time in our lives, we would be paid for working. I knew that Papa would take most of the money, but surely he would let us keep some. I'd save my share to buy a real toothbrush. Then I'd buy a pair of shoes, some ribbons for my hair, and a doll.

Yes, sewing gloves would mean a better life all around. We would see a lot more people than we did at home. We would travel past the school, and maybe even stop in sometimes.

These thoughts were like breathing fresh air. Perhaps our lives would be different from then on. If earning a lot of money for Papa would make him be nicer to all of us, I'd sew like crazy. I felt sure that Emilia was having the same thoughts. She had a trace of a smile as she followed Papa down the path to our home. I knew Papa was adding up the dollars in his mind, for he had not just a smile, but a wide grin across his face.

*   *   *

We could finish only three gloves a day in the beginning, but gradually we picked up speed and completed the four dozen in fifteen days. Papa went with us again to return the finished work and bring home more.

We stood side-by-side, watching Don Estrada as he shoved the wooden tool inside each finger of Emilia's gloves. If he squinted or creased his brow, I would know he had found hers wrong, and I would faint. If he found hers wrong and mine correct, she would torture me. If he found hers and mine wrong, Papa would torture both of us. So it was crucial that he would find both of our work done well.

Emilia had been shifting her weight from one foot to the other, sweat beads shining on her forehead, her eyes on Don Estrada's hands and the wooden tool.

Then she gasped and smiled as he said, "You did good work, young lady."

Well, I knew I was smarter than Emilia. So if her work was good, mine would be even better. He started on my gloves right away, and I waited, anxious but confident.

"Your stitches are perfect," Don Estrada said as he finished inspecting my gloves. "It's the work of a perfectionist."

I felt my smile and saw the one on papa's and Emilia's faces. Life was delicious for that particular moment. There stood the three of us, thrilled beyond belief, waiting for the fortune of precious money.

I felt a tingling sensation in my stomach. I'd soon be holding six dollars in my hands—six whole dollars! Papa might take three dollars and let me have the other three. I could buy a lot of toothbrushes, ribbons, and dolls with three whole dollars! I wiped my palms on my skirt often so the perspiration would not moisten the bills.

Don Estrada gave us girls each three dozen pairs of white, ready-to-sew gloves to do at home. Then he unlocked a wooden box and pulled out two five-dollar bills and two ones. Moisture accumulated in my hands, and I wiped them on my skirt, not wanting to damage the bills. Now I thought Papa would probably keep the fives and let us have a dollar each. But that was okay. Even a single dollar would be a fortune to Emilia and me.

Don Estrada held a five and a one in each hand and gave it

to us. I wiped my hands again, and then held out one to receive my pay.

Papa's huge paw dropped between Emilia and me, and we watched with opened mouths as our hard-earned money was lifted over our heads.

"It'll be safer in my pocket," he said, and I saw the look of anger in Emilia's face as she rolled her eyes at him.

"I think you should let us keep the ones," I said, not worried that he might hit me in front of Don Estrada. A hit on the head wouldn't have been as painful as seeing our hard-earned money disappear before we even had a chance to feel it in our hands.

"The money is safer with me," he said, shoving the folded bills into his deep pocket.

I felt a squeeze in my throat. "Aren't you going to let us keep even one dollar?"

"I'll be in charge of the household money," he said, and motioned for us to follow him. We did, but we stayed far behind, murmuring about how fast his tin can would fill up with our hard-earned money. I felt pain deep inside, but I couldn't tell if what Emilia felt was pain, or hatred.

Chapter Twenty-Four

Cielo Azul

One afternoon, Papa announced another brilliant idea: Emilia and I would make more money if we had more time to sew gloves.

"I'll sell some of the goats, and Alicia can take charge of the ones I'll keep for milk."

My heart skipped a beat. *He'd better not be thinking of selling Cielo Azul.* But I didn't say anything. If he hadn't thought about the little goat, I didn't want to remind him.

"Gloria can help your mother with the chores Emilia has been doing, and the boys can do most of Sabina's chores after school." Papa seemed to enjoy laying out his new plans for our future. "You two can still fill up the water barrels before sitting down to sew. In the evenings, Emilia can roast the coffee beans, and Sabina can milk the goats. Alicia's hands are still too small. One day a month should be enough time for you two to get the wash done. The rest of each day, you'll sew. Until a crop comes due for harvest, that is. Breaking away from the sewing will give your eyes a rest, anyway."

We kept pushing needles as Papa talked. Neither of us would say what was going through our minds. If we made him mad, he might decide to return the finished gloves to Don Estrada's himself, and we would no longer have that little trip to look forward to.

"I'm taking the goats to the market tomorrow," he went on, talking to me now. "You'd better leave the sewing for a while and take them all to the pasture. Let them eat all the grass they want so they'll weigh more."

"*All* the goats?" I blurted, unable to stop myself. "You're not going to sell Cielo Azul, are you?" I hated to sound alarmed, but I needed to know, even though there wasn't anything I could do if he said yes.

"No. Not that one." Papa took off his hat, scratched his head, and repeated, "No, I'm not selling that one."

Papa sounded sincere, so I left the gloves and went out to gather the goats, all nine of them, including Cielo Azul.

When I reached the pasture with the goats, I groomed Cielo Azul under a tree while the bigger goats feasted on the green grass. He sniffed and licked my hands, and I felt around the two little wattles dangling from his neck. Cielo Azul seemed content to be touched and groomed by me. I could rub and hug him for a long time, and he would not walk away—not even to follow his mother and his two siblings. Every now and then, he stretched out his neck to reach for a blade of grass. He chewed it slowly for a long time, and I would finally feel the tiny lump of chewed grass sliding down his throat.

This little animal was the first thing I had ever loved. I wanted him to grow up with me, and to stay under my care forever.

I felt so good that afternoon, down at the gorge with my goats where no one would bother me. The sky was blue, dotted with cotton-ball clouds. The breeze swayed the tall grass gracefully, and black birds screeched as they cruised overhead. And best of all, I had my Cielo Azul at my side, the first thing I had ever loved.

Suddenly I heard a man's voice calling me. Looking up toward the top of the gorge, I saw Uncle Luís sliding down on his seat toward me. I could not imagine what could have happened that would cause my parents to send him for me.

When my uncle came closer, I saw the vicious grin across his disgusting face, and my heart sank. I couldn't utter a word, but I wrapped my arms around Cielo Azul. That made my uncle's grin stretch wider, displaying a line of brown, crooked teeth. He reached out and grabbed my little goat's hind legs.

"What are you doing?" I shrieked, hoping that my parents would hear me and come running. "Let go of him!"

"You'll get him back later," he mumbled through his sickening laughter. "In little pieces, you'll get him back."

He tugged so hard on Cielo Azul's legs that if I had not let go, the little legs would have ripped right off. The poor little goat let out a loud bleat that was probably heard miles away. Still, no one came to my rescue. I stood yelling as my horrible uncle headed up the hill with Cielo Azul under his arm, his huge hand tight around the little goat's hind legs.

I'll never forget how Cielo Azul bellowed as he tried to get loose, his blue eyes staring back at me. He expected me to save him, but my mean uncle ran fast up the hill, ignoring my pleas.

"Why are you doing this? Put him down! He's my pet! Please!" I ran after him, yelling, my heart pounding so hard it seemed to be moving up to my throat. I knew that my uncle was evil. He did cruel things to old people and children, and laughed at their distress. He would tell a lie to watch a child get a spanking. Once he cut the rope of an old hammock in which I lay sick with chicken pox. I hit the floor hard, disoriented and with stars floating in front of my eyes. He had stood over me laughing.

I reached the top of the hill and ran toward the house, hoping to find Papa. Up to that moment, it had not occurred to me that my horrible uncle was following Papa's instructions.

As I reached the yard, Emilia came out of the house and pointed to the woods. "He's taking it to the creek."

I still didn't think that Papa was behind this, but while running across the yard, I heard the piercing cry from the bottom of the hill, and knew it was too late.

"Oh God!" I shouted.

Mama came out of the house, barking, "Quit yelling! Lucky your father didn't hear you!"

"What do you mean *lucky*?" I shouted back at my mother. "Didn't you hear my Cielo Azul? Did Papa send his nasty brother to butcher my little goat? Only minutes ago, he said he would not sell it."

Then I realized what Papa had meant when he said that he would not sell my little goat. I hadn't thought that he had other plans for the sweet little animal I loved.

Mama's face turned white as cotton as she stood still while I yelled at her. Finally she said with her nasal voice, "It's only a goat." Her words cut through my heart like a sharp blade.

"No! It's not just a goat, Mama! It's my Cielo Azul!"

"Nothing here is yours, so stop yelling before your father hears you."

I shut up suddenly, gave her a long, hard look, then ran back toward the remaining goats. A vine caught my foot, and I tumbled down the hillside, hitting every rock and hole in my path, finally landing face down on the grass. My head was throbbing and spinning, and it didn't matter if I died there.

Soon, I felt a moist warmth on the back of my neck. It was Cielo Azul's mother sniffing me. I wrapped my arms around her neck and sobbed. Another mama goat licked my tears. The rest of the herd gathered around, rubbing their soft coats against me as though they knew something bad had happened. I ran my hand over the soft, furry backs of the shiny black, gray, and white goats, wondering how anyone could butcher such beautiful animals.

I stayed with my goats for a long time, wishing that I never had to go home. If only I knew a place where I could go and take the goats with me. My gaze followed the ridge of the mountain to the horizon, then down to the valley. *If only I knew where to go.*

The thought of going home paralyzed me. I didn't want to find out what had happened to Cielo Azul, so I watched the goats flipping their tails and snapping blades of grass. None of them went too far from me as they filled their bellies.

Finally the pregnant goat, Cuca, plopped herself down next to me. She sniffed my foot, my leg, and my dress all the way up to the side of my neck. Her breath, smelling sweetly like chewed-up grass, spread down my shoulder and made little bumps on my skin. I ran my hand over her coat, tracing her backbone, then down the side and over the bulging belly where her unborn kids rolled like ripples on a pool. Visions of Cielo Azul flashed through my mind, and my tears spilled to the grass like raindrops.

The other goats looked at Cuca and, one by one, folded their long, skinny legs under them and settled down. I marveled at their rounded bellies, their shiny black, white, brown, and beige coats. I looked at their long necks, pointy ears, innocent eyes, and rapidly moving jaws. One fluffy white kid was missing. In my mind, I could still hear the agonizing cry. I wished never to see my mean uncle again.

A long time passed, and no one came looking for me. I decided to get even by stealing some of the goat milk. This was forbidden, as most of our milk was sold, and the rest used to make cheese. I pulled down a large leaf from a malanga plant and made it into a cup by making pleats around the edge. Holding the pleated leaf with one hand, I milked one of the goats, then leaned against a low tree to drink the warm milk. I didn't lick the white foam moustache under my nose. I wanted everyone to see that I would not obey every rule.

Later, I gathered my goats and headed up the hill, reluctantly, slowly. I reached the top of the gorge much too soon, and saw smoke rising above the roof of the house. The smell of spices hit my nose, and I recognized the other smell mixed in with that of onion, garlic, and cilantro.

Suffocating anger wrapped around my throat. I imagined myself as a gigantic woman with powerful arms, grabbing the house, squeezing it and turning it into dust with my parents and my mean uncle inside.

After a while, I took a deep breath and walked the goats across the yard, hiding my face so no one would see how miserable I felt. I would not give them the satisfaction of seeing me cry over something precious they had taken away.

After securing the goats under the house, I went inside through the kitchen door, past the iron pot that sat over the three rocks. I saw the stew boiling vigorously, with drops splattering and sizzling on the burning wood. The chunks of meat with white bones swam among the vegetables, and the steamy smell filled the kitchen and spread through the whole house.

My mother had been standing near the *fogón*, watching me. She gave me one of those looks that always made me wonder if she felt bad for me or disappointed in me.

She reached for my arm as I walked past her. "Don't let your father see you with a long face. You know that everything in this house is his. You were stupid to think that goat was your pet."

I looked her in the eye and pulled my arm free. Then I went to the water barrels and washed my face, arms, and legs before crawling into my gunnysack. On the way, I saw Emilia and some of the other kids, but I didn't speak to them.

From my sack, I heard my father and his brother arrive from wherever they had been. They went into the rum room, and then came back to the sitting area. I listened to the squeaking of the hammock and the clicking of the glasses against the gallon jug. Soon afterward, I heard the sound of dishes and slurping and the smacking of lips.

"You'd better get up and eat some stew," my mother said, standing over me.

"I'm not hungry . . ."

"Well, you won't find any food later."

"I feel sick, not hungry."

When Mama walked away, I cried, hearing Cielo Azul's loud shriek over and over again, and seeing his blue eyes as my mean uncle carried him up the hill. I prayed that the stew would make everyone sick, especially my father and his brother. By ordering his evil brother to butcher my little goat, my father proved what he'd always said: "I am the king. What I say goes. No one else has any rights."

Chapter Twenty-Five

The Sewing Hut

The first thing on my mind when I awakened the next morning was the cruelty against my little goat. Still, going around with a long face could only bring more pain, as my mother had said. I would get teased for loving a goat, and hit for staying mad. It was a losing battle for me.

I would be better off pretending that my lovely goat hadn't meant that much to me. I'd keep the hurt to myself for self-defense, but inside my head I would concentrate on running away from this bunch of mean people.

"You really didn't think you owned that little goat, did you?" Emilia asked on our next trip to the springs. "Didn't you feel like killing that mean uncle of ours?"

"No, I never feel like killing anyone," I lied.

"I would have thrown a big rock at him and knocked him flat to the ground if he did anything like that to me," she said. Emilia was always bold when it came to talking about what she would do.

"Yeah. But I really didn't own the goat, remember?"

Emilia walked ahead without another word, for which I was glad. Anger was building up quickly inside me, and soon I might forget how big and mean she was.

By the time we returned home, Papa had left for town with

most of the goats. He left only two: the pregnant one and Cielo Azul's mother.

Maybe it was my imagination, but I sensed that Mama felt bad for me. She didn't talk about the goats Papa had taken away, and she did the noontime milking herself. I figured that she did it to spare me, but it was too late. Her way of kindness would not make up for the loss of my little goat.

That afternoon, Papa came home with still another idea. He would build a sewing hut so Emilia and I could sew gloves out in the fresh air and no one would bother us. I figured he'd been thinking about what had happened and was feeling a little guilty.

Well, he could build ten huts, but I would never forgive him for being so cruel.

Later, Emilia pointed out that sewing away from the rest of our family would be good for us. "We can talk and joke while we sew, and no one will hear us. It'll be like we live someplace else. The sooner he builds it, the better for us."

I agreed with her only so she would stay friendly.

Papa wasted no time. He started on the hut the next day, and had it all finished two days later. He built it on stilts so we could sew even when it rained. The floor was made out of boards from a palm tree. He made the roof out of the tree fronds, for that would be cooler than tin. He made the walls short so that we could feel the breeze on our shoulders. Attached to those walls were two benches, one across from the other. Now Emilia and I could sit facing each other instead of side by side.

Sewing in the hut, with a little sense of freedom to talk and laugh, brought Emilia and me a bit closer. Sometimes it made me think we were becoming friends, although it was only as long as I agreed with everything Emilia did and said.

We had been sewing in the hut for over three weeks when Papa came to us with another idea—a huge surprise.

"Since you girls are bringing in money, I'm going to buy you some shoes." He stood at the entrance of the hut with a hint of a smile, waiting for our reaction.

Too shocked to speak, we glanced at him from under our brows and quickly returned our eyes to the sewing.

"Of course, that means a trip to town so you can try on the shoes. Sew like crazy, and we'll go Saturday." He lifted his hat, ran his hand over his thinning hair, and waited like a little boy who didn't know what else to say.

"We'll do whatever you say, Papa," Emilia said.

I kept pushing my needle in and out of the glove fabric. *Even a pair of shoes is not going to erase my little goat from my mind.*

"We'll go Saturday, then," he said, and walked away.

"Shoes and a trip to town?" I whispered to Emilia.

"I'll wait until Saturday to get excited," she said. "He hasn't started drinking yet, and this is only Thursday."

*   *   *

Papa followed through with this one. He rose early Saturday morning and told us to hurry and get ready to go.

I felt better this morning, as if my brain had decided to put aside the bad memories and get some thrills out of the upcoming event. I imagined a wall of sadness in one corner of my brain, which would remain there until the next act of cruelty took place in our family.

A trip to the city had been one of my biggest dreams, and a pair of shoes had been another. Even though I had to hide my feelings and not let anyone see that my chest was about to burst, I was determined to get all the joy I could out of this unusual day.

Emilia and I ran to the bushes, then splashed water on our faces, legs, and arms, put on our pink dresses, and combed our hair with an almost toothless comb. Throughout the whole time, we hardly spoke. Saying too much or the wrong thing could jeopardize the event.

Mama had not said a word about our first trip to town, or about our first pair of shoes, until now. Making the morning coffee, she muttered, "I'm nothing but a slave around here—not important to anyone. I'm sick of working so hard for people who don't give a shit about me." She poured the steaming coffee into cups and gourds, then went out to milk the cows without saying goodbye. She didn't even remind us to be little ladies.

Following Papa and Emilia up the hill, I felt guilty, as if I was taking something away from Mama. But why should I care about my mother's feelings when she'd never shown me any compassion?

I wondered then if I would ever be free to say what was on my mind, and not be afraid of my parents or my sister.

Papa stopped suddenly and said, "We'll stop at the fabric store, too, and get you some material for new dresses."

Things were getting more complicated by the minute. Papa kept coming up with more surprises. If the trip to town and new shoes made Mama feel bad, what would she think upon seeing fabric for new dresses?

As we got farther from the house, I thought of something that gave me a little hope. Papa had gone to Don Estrada's with us twice, but on the third time he had sent us alone. Now we were on the way to town. Perhaps later on, he would let us go alone. That would be a good opportunity for me to run away. I would start out with Emilia, and disappear in the crowd. She would have to go home alone to face Papa. Whatever he did to her would be payback time for all the cruel things she'd done to me.

All I knew about a city was what Isabel had told us. She'd said that the streets were made of *brea* (tar), and the sidewalks were made of concrete. The houses were painted in different colors and had curtains over the windows and doors. The stores and doctors' offices were so close to each other that nobody could walk between them. She had said that trees were rare in the city, and that people had to pay for everything, including water. The light at night didn't come from kerosene or candles, but from something called electricity, which reached stores and homes through wires, and people had to pay to use it. But the best thing about living in the city was that people didn't have to walk in the mud.

"People are going to think we're rats from the jungle," Emilia said suddenly.

Papa stopped abruptly. "What makes you say that?"

"Look at our muddy feet, and our dresses—they don't even fit." She gave her skirt a few tugs.

Papa gazed at her. "They have water at the shoe store so you can wash your feet before trying on the shoes. And I already told you that we'd buy material for new dresses."

Emilia didn't say anything else, and I was glad. If she made another complaint, Papa might change his mind and I would never get to see the town or the shoes.

"I was twenty years old the first time I came to town to buy my first shoes, and no one laughed at me," Papa said.

"Yeah, but you weren't a girl,' Emilia said softly.

"Well, no one's going to laugh at you, not as long as I'm with you. Stay close to me so we won't lose each other. And you must look both ways before crossing the streets. A car can come around the corner and hit you before you hear it." Papa bent down to look at his shoes. "Don't step in the mud. Watch where you place your feet. There are a lot of dry spots. See how clean my shoes are? That's because I don't step in the mud."

Emilia turned her head and didn't say anything else. We passed Don Estrada's place, and from there on, everything was new to Emilia and me. The road widened even more, and the houses on both sides were closer together. In the distance to our right, we saw a stream of people coming down a path toward the main road. The colors they were wearing looked like a line of blue, pink, yellow, and red moving through the tall, green grass. All those moving colors gave me a jolt of joy.

Soon the stream of people merged in with us, smiling and saying "Good morning." More appeared from another path, also dressed in pretty colors, smiling and greeting. I wondered if those people were always friendly, or if they were like my father, who saved his smiles and kind words for others.

Emilia and I were the only ones quiet, serious, and shy.

Everyone else talked and laughed. The smell of face powder and perfume lingering behind the women made me wish I was the daughter of one of them. I couldn't remember Mama smelling like anything other than tobacco smoke, onions, garlic, and other spices.

I looked to see how the women were dressed, if they had pretty buttons and lace, and what kind and color of shoes they wore. This was important to me, for I would want to buy the right things for myself when I grew up.

I had pictured in my mind what a paved road would look like, but I couldn't believe my eyes when I actually saw it, incredibly smooth and shiny. The morning sun heated the surface, and a vapor smelling of tar rose into the air.

"We'll wait here for *el publico*," Papa said. That was the public car, a station wagon. It was the only form of public transportation available on the island at that time.

A stout man cut through the group of people, smiling and calling, "*Tocayo* (Namesake)! How nice to see you!"

Papa put out his hand, also smiling, seeming glad to have met an old friend.

Then the man said something he shouldn't have. "Well, *tocayo*, anyone can see that this young lady is your daughter, but the little blonde doesn't look anything like you. What happened?"

I saw Papa's face change to a bright pink, and my heart sunk. *That's the end of the shoes and fabrics.* I was sure Papa would have us turn around and go back home.

"Don't insult me, *tocayo*. Both girls are my daughters. The little one here takes after her great-grandfather. But I don't owe you an explanation. Do you understand?"

The glow on the man's face disappeared. "Please forgive me for being stupid. I was only joking in friendship. God knows I've known you and Carmelita for a long time, and I can't think of a finer and more respectable couple."

"I accept your apology," my father said stiffly. "But I advise you not to stick both feet in your mouth the next time you feel like joking." Without another word, Papa put one hand on Emilia's shoulder and the other on mine. "Come, we'll wait over there."

The look on Papa's face gave me a twisting feeling in my stomach. I knew he would hate me even more after the stupid man's remark.

Luckily, a horn sounded from behind a line of trees, and Papa said, "*El publico* is coming."

It was the most exciting thing I had ever seen. The black station wagon came bearing down on us with three little red and white flags dancing on its hood. It turned around at the end of the pavement, and the sun reflected on its glossy roof, sending a flash of bright light into our eyes.

Now everyone rushed to be the first into the station wagon, which could hold nine passengers and the driver. Papa motioned us to follow him, and the three of us sat in the middle seat. Three men and a woman squeezed into the back seat, and two other men sat up front with the driver.

The *tocayo* stayed behind with a dozen other people waiting for the next station wagon. I was glad that he didn't try to ride with us. Only God knew what Papa would have done if he caught his *tocayo* looking at us.

As soon as everyone was seated, the driver turned a key, and the station wagon rolled forward, leaving a puff of blue smoke behind. Trees and houses zoomed by quickly, and the breeze blew through the windows and flushed away the fragrance of perfume and face powder. I hated having to hold back my feelings. I wanted to clap and shout that roaring down a road in a car packed with strangers was my most thrilling experience ever.

As my eyes darted everywhere to take in as much of the scenery as possible, I noticed the sad look on Emilia's face. She was trying to hide her feet under the seat. The ill feeling came back into my stomach as I looked down at my own feet. I eagerly rubbed one foot with the other to knock off the dried mud between my toes. But I wasn't going to dwell on that problem when there was so much to see.

I elbowed Emilia and pointed with my chin at all the things flying past us: trees, houses, high poles alongside the street with black wires from one to the other. Soon she was pointing things out to me, too. So we continued our dialog with our eyes and chins all the way into town, raising our eyebrows at big homes with balconies so close to the road, and at young couples walking and holding hands.

Chapter Twenty-Six

The Green Shoes

The town was more beautiful and more exciting than I had imagined. It had a space in the center with concrete benches and huge pots with blooming geraniums and bougainvilleas. Papa said it was *la plaza*. It appeared to me as a good place to sit around and watch the people move about. A young couple sat on one of those benches, holding hands and staring into each other's eyes as though they were the only people in the world.

Papa caught me staring. "Those are people who have nothing better to do," he said.

I quickly took my eyes off the couple. Appearing disinterested in what I saw and heard wasn't easy. The whole city seemed festive with all those people, and music blaring from cars and buildings.

We walked down a sidewalk, and through a wide door we saw a tall, glossy box with quivering lights.

"That's where the music comes from," Papa informed us knowledgeably. "It's called a jukebox."

Two doors down, we saw men playing a game with long sticks and hard balls on a green table, their cigarette smoke rising and drifting out onto the street.

Papa said, "Let's walk across the plaza. Those are lazy men who spend their lives playing games. Don't even look at people like that."

The tapping of his shoes on that warm concrete made me look down at my feet, and then I noticed that the scowling expression had returned to Emilia's face, and with good reason. We would stand out in any crowd: a clean-shaven man in dark trousers, white shirt and hat, and black shoes, walking across the plaza with two ragged girls.

Passing by a large store, Emilia and I caught our images in a long looking glass inside its window. "Oh, God," Emilia whispered. "Look at our tangled hair, the scratches on our legs, and dried mud between our toes. We are a disgrace."

Before I could say what I thought, we were startled by Papa who stood behind us, one huge hand on Emilia's shoulder and the other on mine. "This is not what I brought you girls to town for. Do one more stupid thing like this, and I'll take you back home without the shoes or the fabrics."

"Maybe you should take us back, Papa," Emilia said. "It's embarrassing to walk through a town filled with people, looking like we do."

I felt the blood drain from my face. *There go the shoes.*

"Hey, that is why we are here," he said, "to make changes. Now keep your heads high—no need to show everyone that you're bothered, and don't talk to me like that again." The look on Papa's face was enough to scare the whole town, so Emilia said nothing else. I was just glad that no one saw us being scolded.

From then on, Papa had us walk ahead of him. He told us when to turn right, when to turn left, and when to stop so he could tell us what was here and what was there.

"That's a pharmacy," he said as we came up to a wide door where we were met by a strong smell of rubbing alcohol. The spacious floor was made of black and white squares, and it shone like porcelain. Behind a large glass counter stood a clean-shaven man wearing a long white coat. "That man is the pharmacist."

He pointed out a lawyer's office and a hardware store, which looked ugly to me, with rough shelves, hammers, saws, and wooden tubs filled with screws and nails.

"What's a lawyer?" I asked.

"A lawyer is someone who defends people who get in trouble with the law—and they live in town because this is where most law-breakers live."

"What kind of people break the laws?"

"Crooks and criminals. Turn left here. I'm going to show you girls the marketplace." That meant no more questions.

As we walked on, I looked at the men and women, young and old, who rushed up one sidewalk and down another. I wanted to see someone, girl or boy, woman or man, with green eyes and blonde hair like mine. Just one blonde person—that was all I needed to feel that I wasn't odd.

There were some children and grownups with light skin and light brown hair, but I saw no one as white as I was.

Next to the sidewalks were homes with balconies, where little girls in pretty dresses played with dolls, and their mothers rocked babies in wooden chairs nearby. They smiled at passersby.

"See that?" Papa asked. "Those ladies have nothing better to do because they aren't lucky enough to own a farm, like we do."

"Yeah, too bad they aren't as lucky as we are," said Emilia, and by the expression on her face, I knew that we would be laughing about Papa's statement for a long time.

We came to a place that smelled of coffee, bread, and fried onions. This, Papa said, was a cafeteria, where people had to pay five cents for a cup of coffee and a piece of bread smeared with butter. "Maybe we'll stop in after the shoe store," he said.

"To look, or to eat something?" Emilia asked boldly.

"Oh, we'll have coffee and a piece of bread." Papa's first soft and friendly words practically knocked me over. I had been starving ever since we had left home with only a shell of black coffee in our stomachs.

We walked past stores that had rainbows of colors in clothing and material hanging from racks and swinging in the breeze. I saw dolls and other toys in glass cases, and watches, gold chains, face powders, and perfumes. I gasped at the abundance of things a person could buy.

Then I wondered why life was so unfair. Why did we have to live in a wet jungle instead of a place like this, with all the things I liked?

We reached the open market, where Papa came once a month to sell his beans, fruit, vegetables, and animals to the city people. I felt a stab in my heart when we came to the part of the market where the animals were sold. Immediately, I thought of our goats. Fortunately, I didn't see one as white as my Cielo Azul. That would have made me start crying, and I knew I would not have been able to stop.

The next stop was a shoe store, where a tall man in a dark blue suit with a red tie greeted us.

"Welcome! How may I help you?"

"My daughters need to try on some shoes." Papa stood tall and businesslike.

"No problem," the shoe man said, glancing at us. "But first I must ask the lovely young ladies to wash their feet. I have a tub of water in the back room."

"I'll show them in," Papa said quickly, as if afraid the man would go with us. The man nodded and smiled.

We followed Papa through a narrow doorway and down a long passage between two rows of stacked boxes. The large room was spooky, warm, and stuffy, lit only by the daylight coming through two narrow windows up near the ceiling. A metal tub half full of water sat in a corner.

Papa told us to wash our feet, and dry them with some of the brown paper there on an old chair next to the tub. Then we were to follow the passageway back to the shoe store, where he'd be waiting.

We did as Papa had said and hurried out to find him sitting on a bench, talking with the shoe man who had several open boxes of shoes near his feet.

We sat across from Papa, and the man began to twist and

push the shoes onto Emilia's feet. I waited anxiously for my turn. Emilia's feet refused to go into a pair of shoes, and I saw her face change from red to pink and back.

When none of the shoes fit her, the man tried them on me. The shoes were all too big for my feet. He went to the shelves and brought back some more, and one pair of black shiny shoes with shoelaces fit me perfectly. I stared at my shoe-covered feet, and could hardly wait to hear the tapping of the wooden heels on the floor. I stood up much too fast. The shoe soles slid on the slippery floor, and I went down on my backside with a loud bang.

I felt fire spreading over my face and ears as the man reached to help me up. Besides feeling like I wanted to die, I feared that Papa would yell at the man for helping me. We usually had to get up by ourselves whenever we fell.

"It takes time to break in a new pair of shoes," Papa said. Then he turned to Emilia. "You like those shoes over there?" She had been staring at a pair of parakeet-green shoes in a glass case.

"Yes, I do," she said.

"Those are velvet shoes," the man said through his thick moustache, "to be worn on special occasions, like weddings."

Papa said, "I see. She'll try them on."

"I don't think . . ." The man stopped when he saw the expression on Papa's face.

"Don't think," Papa said. "Just get the shoes."

The whole time, I had thought that all that conversation was to help me get over my embarrassment. But the man got the green shoes, put them on Emilia's feet, and buckled the little belts. The shoes fit, and Emilia's face lit up.

"We'll take them," Papa said. "What's the total?"

"Six dollars and fifty cents, señor." The man didn't seem happy to have sold the green shoes.

Papa handed over the money and thanked him for his help. The man nodded without a word and took the money.

"Let's go," Papa said. "But be careful. Don't land on the floor again."

I made it across the floor and out the door, loving the tapping sound of the wooden heels, but feeling my squeezed toes rubbing on the leather. I wished for my feet to get used to their confinement.

When we reached the fabric store, I gasped at the brilliant colors. Never had I seen so many shades of blues, pinks, reds, purples, lavenders, yellows, and a whole lot more. They all hung from brackets on the walls and danced in the breeze coming through the open doors.

A tall, skinny lady with red lips and thick glasses, wearing a black and white striped dress, greeted us at the door. "Come in, come in, *señor y señoritas*," she said in a fine, delicate voice. "May I show you some fabrics?"

"Well . . . I think we can find some among all of these," Papa said with a smile.

The lady smiled back and told him to take his time and let her know if we needed help.

Papa told us we could only buy enough fabric for one dress each, but he would let us choose the colors. By then, I had forgotten the discomfort in my feet. My gaze had traveled from one wall to the next, and I had seen a dozen of my favorite colors. I knew better than to tell Papa that, so I settled for a yellow fabric with a small print of red roses and green leaves. Emilia chose pink with white dots.

"You both made good choices," Papa said as we walked out with our fabrics. "We'll go have coffee, then head for home."

As we followed Papa, I wondered what was going through Emilia's mind. She appeared comfortable with her green shoes, but at times I thought she would explode. I had seen the face she made when we first left the shoe store, as if she realized that green was an unusual color for shoes. All the girls and women we saw were wearing brown or black shoes. She probably wished she had made a different choice, but felt afraid to say it. But then again, maybe she was thinking about Papa's changes from cruel to nice and back. That's what was going through my mind, anyway.

The streets and sidewalks were more crowded now. Men,

women, and children hurried up and down the sidewalks, dodging elbows and packages, crossing the streets in front of cars, and entering stores while others walked out.

I was still hoping to see a girl with blonde hair. There were some with red hair and some with light brown, but none as light as mine. Everyone who walked past us looked at my hair, then at Emilia's shoes. Some people smiled and others murmured under their breath. I felt bad. I knew everyone could tell that we were from the jungle.

We came to a street corner where a man stood frying pork skin in some kind of portable kitchen on wheels. The aroma filled the air, and people stood in line to buy his crispy *chicharrónes*.

We walked past all that good-smelling stuff on our way to the cafeteria. Papa and Emilia never remarked about the aroma, and I wasn't going to be the first to break the silence.

The cafeteria smelled of onions, garlic, and bread. The floor had been scrubbed, and it shone like black marble with white and beige streaks. The tables had white metal tops with black iron legs to match the chairs. Everything appeared polished clean, yet we walked in like mutes.

Papa chose a table in a corner, which was good because I didn't have to turn my head to watch the people at the other tables eating rice, red beans with chunks of bell peppers, potatoes, and meat. Even the rice and beans looked delicious, so much different from the food Mama cooked at home.

When a young man dressed in white came to our table, Papa ordered three coffees with milk and sugar, and a small loaf of sweet bread. Emilia and I would taste sweet bread for the first time ever.

There were two couples a few tables away, and each had a boy and a girl who were around my age. Yet those kids weren't shy. They talked, giggled, and ate like the grownups, and they were clean, without scratches and cuts on their arms and legs. I imagined that they lived in town and didn't work on a farm.

Papa said we would use the washroom before heading home. He motioned to a door with the word *Damas* written on it. At first I thought he meant a room for washing clothes, and we had nothing to wash. But Emilia seemed to understand, and Papa told me to follow her.

She pushed open the door, and we entered a dark room with a concrete floor and a narrow, trench-like depression in the middle with water running through it. Somehow, Emilia knew this was where people squatted down to relieve themselves. I guessed that Mama had told her, but she denied it, saying she had figured it out for herself.

The trench wasn't easy to use for someone with short legs like mine. I had to put one foot on each edge, then squat down, and I almost fell backward into the water. When we came out of the washroom, Papa asked us if we had any trouble understanding how the washroom worked. Emilia answered quickly, "Oh, no."

"Good. Now we'll go home."

I felt sad when we rode out of town in the station wagon, leaving all the exciting things behind. Worse yet was the thought that maybe Papa would turn mean once we reached home, and never bring us to town again.

But he had still another surprise.

"Now, girls," he said as we started on foot for the walk home. "You should take off your shoes to keep them clean. I might bring you back to church in December, on the day of the Immaculate Conception. You'll want clean shoes for that."

Emilia and I were overwhelmed. We looked at each other, and I was sure she was thinking the same thing I thought: *What in the world has gotten into Papa?*

Chapter Twenty-Seven

Felipito

The coffee harvest ran from August through mid-November. This time, Emilia and I had something good to look forward to, so leaving the sewing to spend the days under the trees with ants and other bugs crawling all over us didn't hurt so much. If Papa stayed nice, we would be going back to town on December eighth.

Life was still good when we finished picking the coffee berries. Without further delay, we returned to our sewing, finishing the last gloves on December first. The next day, Papa told us that we could go to Don Estrada's by ourselves. In fact, he seemed eager for us to leave early that morning.

We left the house when the boys and Alicia left for school. During the walk between the house and the school gate, Emilia and I didn't talk much because we knew we couldn't trust the boys. But as soon as we parted at the gate, she started.

"I bet Mama's going to have the brat today. That's why Papa was anxious for us to leave. He wanted us out of the way.

"Ah, but isn't it good that he didn't come with us?"

"Sure, but it's too close to December eighth, and we might end up spending that day at the creek washing shit-covered rags."

My feet suddenly felt too heavy for me to take another step. My sister was right. Mama had seemed awfully nervous just before we left. Her belly had grown huge. We sure didn't need to add more rags to our wash load. And I would die if we ended up at the creek on the day we were supposed to go back to town.

We found Mama in bed with a tiny baby when we returned home, but Doña Ana wasn't there. Papa came out from behind the house and ordered Emilia to cook lunch, me to carry water, and the boys to tend the animals. None of us mentioned the baby; we didn't even ask where it had come from.

Gloria told us later that Papa had hung a hammock in our sewing hut and sent her there to swing Alejandro. From there, she'd heard Mama moaning until the baby cried. Gloria wasn't very good at giving details, so we didn't ask many questions. The fact was that now we had a fourth brother, and his name was Felipito.

From then on, Emilia and I did our daily work, afraid to mention the trip to town and worrying that we might not get to go. I was even afraid to pray that Papa would follow through with his plan in spite of the new baby. The little talk we did about it at the springs, the creek, and the sewing hut was in soft whispers. If Papa found out that we were anxious about the trip, he would for sure make us stay home.

My stomach rose to my throat when I saw Papa walking toward the sewing hut on the afternoon of December seventh. There wasn't enough time to guess what he had up his sleeve. One quick glance at Emilia told me that she, too, expected to hear something terrible from Papa.

Papa took his time walking, as if to increase our anxiety. He looked down at the ground, out toward the woods, and up to the sky. Finally he reached the hut and stopped, looking right at us. Our needles suddenly began to slip out of our sweaty and shaky fingers.

Finally he said, "You girls should fill up all the water barrels today so we can leave early in the morning."

My heart leaped for joy.

"You might even want to wash a few rags for your mother so she has clean ones for tomorrow." With that, Papa went back to the house.

Emilia and I stared at each other, speechless. I felt my heartbeat slowly return to normal. Once Papa was inside the house, we put away our sewing and ran around the house and into the kitchen for the *calabazos* and cans. Then we ran even faster toward the springs.

About midway down, Emilia set down her can and covered her mouth with both hands. Then she started an Indian dance around a tree trunk, and I copied her with delight.

Life was still good the next morning. Emilia made the morning coffee, and I milked the goat. At last we could get ready to leave. Our lifestyle had changed, and it had to do with the money we were earning for Papa. Even though he didn't let us keep any of it, he had bought us shoes and fabric for new dresses, and we were going to town for the second time. Most importantly, he hadn't gotten drunk lately or beaten any of us.

Two days earlier, Emilia had decided that she no longer wanted green shoes. She painted them black, using some of the tar Papa used on the roof. She had put the shoes out to dry in the sun for a couple of hours, but the shoes were still sticky when she brought them in for the night. She hung them from a nail under the *fogón* so Papa wouldn't see them.

That morning before leaving for town, she reached for the shoes and found that they were stuck together. When she pulled them apart, we saw the green spot left on one shoe. From then on, every time the shoes touched, another green spot showed. She kept trying to push some of the black over the green spots, but the tar stayed on her fingers instead.

Papa didn't see the mess Emilia had made until we reached the paved road. We had wrapped the shoes in the rag we would use to dry our feet after washing them near the road.

Papa's eyebrows went up. "What the hell happened to those shoes?" He shook his head. "So that's why that damn man wasn't eager to sell the green shoes. They were black to begin with, and he'd painted them green."

I saw Emilia's face blush. Then she said with a shaky voice,

"No, Papa. I painted the shoes with some of your tar, but they never dried."

Papa stood back, stared at her shoes, rubbed his chin, and, seeing that a lot of people were coming toward the road, said, "It will serve you right if they all laugh at you."

I couldn't believe what I'd heard. This was not the father we had known. In the past, Papa would have rubbed those painted shoes on Emilia's head.

As the people merged onto the road, Papa joined them, and we hurried to put on our shoes. From then on, Emilia walked carefully, but everything her shoes touched received a sticky speck of black. We thought that people didn't notice the black-and-green shoes, because no one pointed or laughed. But Papa shook his head every time he looked down at the shoes.

Lares didn't look like the town we had seen months earlier. Music blared from a round roof of different colors, with people riding wooden horses around and around. A huge wheel with seats filled with screaming people went up in the air and down, then round and round. The crowds laughed, clapped, and cheered.

Papa told us it was a festival that came to town every year in December. Then he said we'd better hurry into the church before all the seats were taken.

I had seen the church from the outside the day we came for our shoes, but I didn't know what it looked like inside. As we walked in, I noticed that it was packed with people, and I smelled more face powder and perfume. An aisle began at the door and ran all the way to what Papa called the altar.

At the center of the altar stood a crucifix much larger than the one we had at home. I froze, facing the stiff, tortured man I had been taught to fear all my life. Mama always told us that Jesus had the power to pop out from anywhere and punish us for doing bad things. I shivered at the thought of Him lifting His head and coming loose from the nails that held Him with His arms extended against the huge black cross. Would His blood run again, after it had dripped from His hands and feet and dried around the nails?

The people murmured, sitting on long *bancos* (pews) that extended on each side of the walkway, shoulders touching, fanning themselves with papers and pieces of cardboard.

Papa motioned us to follow as he squeezed through those who were standing. At a little water well, he dabbed his finger, made the sign of the cross, and told us to do the same, for this holy water would wash away our sins. All the saints were there, bigger than ours, standing rigidly on shelves alongside the walls: the Virgin Mary and Joseph, San Antonio de Pauda, San Pedro, and many others.

Candles flickered around the crucifix, and poinsettias in tall containers stood around the altar like ladies dressed in brilliant red. When the priest entered through a side door, those who were seated stood up, placed their right hands over their hearts, and waited for the command to cross themselves.

After a moment of silence, a multitude of hands bounced from foreheads to shoulders, and the word "Amen" drowned the happy sounds of music coming from the carnival.

"Be seated," the priest said, and apologized to those who would have to stand through his long sermon.

I could see more standing up, so I felt glad that the pews were full. My gaze traveled from one girl or lady to another, noting the pretty colors of their dresses. I saw cotton and silk dresses, solid colors and prints, reds, pinks, purples, greens, and many others. I looked for ruffles, lace, buttons, and sequins, which were things we never had. And of course, I was also still looking around for a girl or boy with hair the color of mine.

Suddenly, I felt Papa pinching my arm. "Pay attention to the priest!" The pinch set my arm on fire. I felt that everyone, including Jesus, was watching me be scolded, and my face felt hot.

I had been under the impression that Papa brought us to the church so we could see it, not to pray. Praying was something we did at home. He and Mama had practically beaten religion and prayer into our brains. We learned to recite the rosary on our knees, while Papa whacked us with his leather belt or his rosary every time the tiring repetition put us to sleep. Now he was telling me to listen to the priest's message—in Latin?

When the procession began, Papa volunteered to carry the statue of the Virgin Mary and baby around the church. Before starting out, he told us to walk in the procession, staying as close to him as possible.

We disappeared from his view right away, walking to the beat of drums, horns, and trumpets. I caught a glimpse of him now and again through the crowd. He looked thoughtful and dedicated with the end of the heavy pole on his shoulder. Three other men, supporting the rest of the weight, walked with Papa. They also looked righteous, but I wondered if they were drunkards who beat their wives and children and were doing this to earn points from God.

After the procession, the priest gave another sermon and said a few prayers, and everyone walked down the aisle to receive communion. That was followed by a blessing, and Mass was over.

While other people hurried out to enjoy the festival, the three of us walked up and down the sidewalks for a while, then rode a public car out of town.

"Papa, I thought you'd let us watch the wooden horses, maybe give us a ride," I said, knowing that I might get hit.

Papa gave me a heavy look, his eyebrows meeting at the bridge of his nose. "I brought you girls to church to honor the Virgin Mary, not to watch or ride the merry-go-round like those crazy people."

Anything else I would say could jeopardize a future trip to town, so I kept my thoughts to myself. *I don't need to go to town to honor the Virgin Mary. I can do that while working in the fields or sewing in the hut. But riding the wooden horses would be an experience worth remembering.*

Chapter Twenty-Eight

The Saint Painter

On the last day of December, we children had another extraordinary surprise. An old man dressed in a black suit and a red necktie appeared at our door as we were finishing our lunch.

"That's the saint painter," Mama said as she hurried to greet the man and calm our barking dogs. Evidently Papa had hired the painter, and Mama knew that he was coming, but she had not mentioned anything to us.

Intrigued by the man's attire, Emilia, Gloria, and I ran to the wall and pressed our faces over the spaces between the boards. José and Lorenzo were already outside watching the stranger. Never before had we seen anyone around these hills dressed in a suit and tie. Besides the black suit, the man wore a black hat and black shoes, had a bushy black-and-white moustache, and carried a shiny black box.

He put the box on the step, pulled a white handkerchief out of his pocket, and wiped his face, carefully dabbing around his eyes, which turned the color of chocolate as he faced the sun.

"I'll bring you some water," Mama said, hurrying to the kitchen. The man lifted his hat, ran the moist hanky over his bald head, and smiled. A silver tooth sparkled in his mouth.

Mama returned with a shell of water, and the man gulped it

down. "I wish to begin right away," he said, handing her the empty shell. "I must be out of these woods before dark."

"I'll get the saints right away," Mama said, and went to the niche. The three of us girls moved to the next wall so we could look into the sitting area. Alicia squeezed herself in next to us. We watched Mama as she reached for the Three Kings, the crucifix, and the Virgin Mary, and carefully placed them on the table.

Now the saint painter stepped into the house, took off his jacket, and hung it from a nail near the door. He rolled up his sleeves and propped open his black box, pulled out a soft blue cloth, and spread it on the table. He reached into the box and brought out one small tin can after another, placing them on the cloth and prying off their lids with a small screwdriver.

I moved up to a higher crack so I could look down. He reached back into the box and brought out a fine stick, which he used to stir the oily contents of his cans. The thick, light-colored contents suddenly turned into brilliant colors. I saw lavender, blue, black, red, pink, purple, and a lot of other colors. The cans were probably four inches high, so what I saw from above was a display of colored dots on a blue cloth. I knew then that this image of brilliant colors would never fade from my mind.

The man painted the Three Kings first. With a fine brush, he made Gaspar's and Baltazar's faces and hands light pink. Changing brushes, he colored their lips red, and their hair black. Then he painted Mechor's face and hands black, and his horse white. Gaspar's horse he painted brown, and Baltazar's black.

Emilia and I couldn't stay and watch, as we had to return to our sewing, and to the place where we could talk and try to understand what was going on. Our saints had looked dingy for years. Why was Papa having them painted now? Was he spending the money we had earned? Yet he wouldn't give us a ride on the merry-go-round!

We talked until the painter left. Still unable to solve the mystery, we ran inside to see the painted saints. Our Three Kings' vests were now lavender and purple. Their trousers were blue and brown, their crowns gold, and their eyebrows and moccasins were black. The Virgin Mary's gown had turned creamy white, and her cape soft blue. Her hair was shiny black, her eyes blue, and her cheeks pink.

Even the crucifix looked bright and new. The cross had been painted brown; Jesus was beige, His hair black, the cloth blue, and red for the dripping blood.

Surrounded by our rough, grayish walls, our saints stood out as brilliant as a huge bouquet of flowers—a miraculous multitude of colors that took my breath away.

But our surprise didn't stop with the painted saints. Papa came home with another idea. He stared at the colorful statues, and said, "Since the saints are freshly painted, we'll have a celebration—a religious celebration like my parents used to have when I was a boy."

Mama had told us about religious celebrations, so the news made us children turn toward each other with wide eyes and open mouths. It was the most exciting thing we had ever heard.

From that moment on, our parents murmured in the sitting area about the preparations for the celebration, and we girls whispered to each other in the sleeping area. We would wear our shoes and new dresses, and comb our hair this way or that.

Later, Emilia whispered to me from her gunnysack, "I'll believe all that talk about a celebration when I see it. Papa doesn't believe in celebrating. He won't start now just because the saints are painted."

"You didn't believe he'd take us to town and buy us shoes, either," I reminded her. "I think Papa has changed since we've been sewing gloves and bringing him the money."

"He'll change again one of these days, so I'm not building up my hopes to be let down. If he celebrates, fine. If he doesn't, I won't be disappointed."

The celebration would take place on January fifth, the eve of Three Kings' Day. On the day before the celebration, Papa rode his horse to his brother's store and brought home four cans of soda crackers, sweet chocolate, wine, and anise, which he would serve to the ladies. The men would drink rum.

The day of the celebration, everyone woke up in a good mood. Papa whistled while repairing the front steps. José and Lorenzo hummed to Papa's tunes as they swept around the house, chopped wood for the *fogón*, and fed the cows and horses.

Gloria and Alicia swept the floor and watched Alejandro. Mama fed and cleaned the baby, then cooked for us and for the pigs. Then she folded her bed and piled all the blankets, hammocks, and gunnysacks in a corner of the sleeping area. Since the celebration would last all night, Alejandro and the baby would be the only ones to get sleep.

Emilia and I headed for the springs at daybreak, filled up the barrels, and then sewed gloves most of the day. At dusk we went back to the springs to replace the water Mama had used throughout the day. We felt too excited to mind the hard work this time.

The dark of night spread through the woods at the bottom of the hill as Emilia and I climbed it with our last cans of water. We put our cans next to the full barrels and went to the front room. There we found our brothers and sisters all cleaned up, gathered around Papa and Mama, who stood next to each other facing the canopy of poinsettias and bougainvillea they had put over our table.

The freshly painted saints were in the center of the table, which had been covered with a piece of green fabric. Papa had shaved and changed into his black trousers and white shirt. Mama had put on her white-dotted black dress, pinned her hair into a bun on the back of her head, and had done something special to her face that made it glow. She placed two tall candles in front of the saints, and Papa lit them with a match. The flickering light reflected in everybody's eyes, and for the first time in my life, I saw us as a healthy and happy family.

Emilia and I had washed at the springs, so now we hurried to put on our dresses and shoes. I thought my chest would explode as I combed my hair and tied a bow to match my dress. Then I tied a scrap of fabric on Alicia's hair, and Emilia tied one on Gloria's. They both looked pretty that night, and seemed as excited as Emilia and I were.

We finished getting ready only seconds before the first couple arrived at our door. I jumped up and whirled around at the sound of their voices. After days of waiting and wondering, the wonderful night had finally come.

More friends, relatives, and *compadres* arrived, one couple after another, until our house was packed with people dressed in their best outfits and shoes. The women had powdered faces, and the men were shaved and had *brillantina* (a fragrant hair cream) in their hair. Our cousins Pola and Maria Elena looked beautiful, with red lipstick and red crepe roses in their hair.

There were enough boys and girls from different couples to pair off with our brothers and sisters. Everyone seemed happy right from the start. Our parents would be too busy to keep tabs on us, so we knew we would get to have some fun.

Papa's cousin Bartolo would play his guitar, and his son would play the *guiro*, an instrument made out of a long gourd. It had grooves across it which made scratchy sounds when rubbed with five pieces of wire.

After shaking hands and wishing each other a happy and prosperous new year, we listened to Bartolo and his son stroke the strings of the guitar and scratch the *guiro*, and our house vibrated with the sounds of music and singing. They sang *aguinaldos de navidad* (Puerto Rican Christmas songs), and everyone clapped and cheered.

The three rosaries to be sung would follow the *aguinaldos*. Papa and one of his cousins positioned a long bench in front of the table where the religious statues waited. A man and a woman sat at each end of that bench, facing the altar. Behind them sat the musicians. My parents recited a prayer to the saints and made the sign of the cross, and everyone said, "Amen!"

The guitar player stroked the strings, and one of the two couples began the rosary. They alternated back and forth with the "Our Fathers," "Hail Marys," and "Glorys." A sung rosary was something Mama had told us about, but this was the first time I'd heard it. The beautiful sound of music and singing lifted me out of myself, and I floated in a dream all night.

While the couples sang that rosary, the other men and the bigger boys sat quietly on benches around the singers. The women congregated in the kitchen, while the young girls and smaller children stayed in the sleeping area.

We had people all over the place, and I wanted the night to never end. For the first time in my life, I felt like a regular person instead of a child being told what to do, how to walk, how to smile, and to keep my mouth shut. Now I could talk with my cousins. I could wear my shoes all night and look at everyone as long as I wanted, and still not get hit.

I didn't want to miss a sound, so I kept my ears tuned to the music, the singing, the murmur, and chuckles coming from the kitchen. I saw Mama at the *fogón*, chattering with the other women, her eyes sparkling. I turned to look at Papa. His eyes were shining like black marbles as he admired the painted statues and listened to the singing.

Everyone appeared to be bursting with joy. There was no anger on Emilia's face that night. Her eyes picked up the light from the lantern as she talked and giggled with Maria Elena.

Even Gloria seemed happy that night. And for the first time ever, I noticed how pretty and dainty she was. Her curly black hair framed her oval face and brown eyes. She had deep dimples when she smiled, and soft, delicate hands. She and I had existed apart from each other; she had always been either sick or sleeping, while I worked in the fields or sewed gloves in the hut.

I had paired off with Tatí, the daughter of one of Papa's cousins. We had met at my godfather's wake and liked each other right away. She was my height, with light skin, soft brown hair, and hazel eyes. More importantly, she didn't seem to mind that I was so white.

"I'm going on eleven," she said.

"So am I. Is your birthday in August, too?"

"No. Mine is in June," she answered.

I wondered if she really knew her age, but I didn't want to admit that I wasn't sure of mine. Then I lied about going to school. She lived on the high mountain across the river and was in fifth grade.

"I'm glad to be back in school," she said happily.

"Me, too," I said.

"Fifth grade is fun, don't you think?"

"Fifth grade? Oh yes, I love it. It's great." Knowing that my school days were over hurt so much, and admitting it would hurt even more. Besides that, I didn't want her to feel superior, especially on this fun night.

When the first rosary ended, Papa served rum to the men and anisette to the ladies. None of us children would get to taste any of that, but other people's children, including Tatí, were allowed a few drops of anisette. That didn't bother me, because we had always been warned to never even taste the rum Papa made.

For a while after the drinks, those who had a good ear for music sang verses they had put together about Jesus, the Virgin Mary, and the Three Kings. Then two new couples sat on the bench and started the second rosary. Another break came after the second rosary, and then the third was sung.

The first rooster crowed as the singing ended. Now the aroma of hot chocolate spread from the kitchen through the rest of the house. The women passed cups or gourds of steaming chocolate and plates of soda crackers to the men and boys and girls here and there.

After the refreshments, the music continued, but with rumbas, tangos, and boleros instead of religious tunes. Those who knew how to dance did so. The married men called their wives out to the front room, and with arms around each other, they moved around the room in step with the music. Even Pola and Maria Elena were out there dancing with sons of their parents' *compadres*. Now our house really trembled with the thumping and clapping. Dancing looked like so much fun, I wished for daylight to take its time coming.

Since Gloria and the younger children had fallen asleep on the pile of gunnysacks, the doorway to the front room was clear. Finally, Emilia and I could stand there, leaning on the doorjambs, and watch the people dance. The sound of the music vibrated in my chest, and I could feel myself dancing inside my head. I wondered if Papa would ever let his daughters dance.

I could tell that Emilia felt thrilled, too. She had a soft smile and sparkling ayes. Below her skirt, I saw her polka-dotted shoes tapping the floor—slowly, so no one else would notice. She, too, felt like dancing; I was sure of it.

Suddenly, one of Papa's *compadres*, named Carlos, came up and invited her to dance.

Emilia shrugged. "I don't know how to dance." She smiled shyly, casting her eyes to the floor.

"I'll teach you," Carlos said.

"You'll have to ask my father," she answered, keeping an eye on Papa, who sat nearby.

Carlos went straight to him.

Papa looked up with fierce eyes. "Absolutely not!" Carlos opened his mouth, but Papa cut in, "And, *compadre*, please don't ask again."

The man lowered his head and didn't return to Emilia. Papa didn't even look our way.

Emilia stamped away from the doorway. "That's another thing we'll never get to do!" Her voice was loud, but Papa didn't hear her. He stood up and served more drinks. The crowd danced until the bright sun came shining over the roof and the treetops.

Gradually our guests, with smiling faces and sleepy eyes, said their goodbyes and dispersed up the hill and through the woods. It left our house nearly empty, the sound of the guitar and voices ringing in our ears.

For weeks afterward, I felt gloomy and lonely. Then, as Emilia and I reminisced about that night, she admitted her feelings.

"I felt numb after everyone left," she said. "I still feel numb and hopeless. I don't care if Papa never has another celebration. It wouldn't be for us, anyway."

From the look on her face, I could tell she meant what she said. But although I knew that any celebration Papa had would not be for us, I would love having the house filled with people and music again. I loved groups of people, music and singing, pretty clothes, and the smell of face powder and perfume.

Chapter Twenty-Nine

Emilia's Rage

The religious celebration sent us back to our old ways. Emilia kept a long face, snapped at me and our brothers and sisters, and cursed our parents behind their backs.

Papa became aware of Emilia's attitude, and to show her who was boss, he accompanied us on our next trip to Don Estrada's. Without saying that he'd go, he shaved, dressed, and went along. As before, he grabbed the money before it reached our hands.

Emilia was as stubborn as Papa. She answered whatever he said with "Uh-huh," "No, sir," or "I don't know, sir."

I felt as if a storm was coming, and I had no place to hide. If I walked close to Emilia, Papa would say that I was taking her side. Walking next to Papa would mean to Emilia that I was trying to befriend him. I tried walking between the two, but one of them always caught up with me. This trip became torturous, but the torture didn't end with the trip.

We reached home to find Mama staggering around the *fogón*.

"Nothing but a slave," she muttered. "A goddamn slave." She looked up and saw us. "Here comes the king and his prettied-up princesses, while I slave in the heat." Her eyes were red, and one eyebrow was curved up as it always did when she'd had too much rum.

Here we go, I thought miserably. I saw Papa's face turn bright red and heard him sucking air through his teeth. I turned to look at Emilia, but she had disappeared.

"Things couldn't stay nice," I said when I found her in the sleeping area, changing out of her good dress.

"I never thought they would," she said bitterly, her face twisted with anger.

I found Gloria and Alicia in a corner of the living room with Alejandro and the baby. I knew by the look on their faces that Mama had ordered them out of her way.

"Mama's really mad," Alicia whispered.

"She's been drinking," Gloria said softly, her eyes fixed toward the kitchen. "She sent José and Lorenzo to tend the cows and the horses, and told them not to come back until supper time."

Papa came out of the kitchen, his lips pressed together into a hard line, and walked into the rum room. Seconds later, we heard him banging something and stamping the floor. Then he came out and flew through the sleeping area and into the kitchen, roaring with rage. *"How did you get into that room?"*

We hurried to the sleeping area and peeked into the kitchen just as Mama turned from the *fogón*.

"Oh, are you talking to me?" She put her hands on her hips. "Well, of course you are. How did I enter your precious room? I'll be happy to tell you. I reached through that crack with a long stick, pulled off the key from the nail, unlocked the door, and walked in. That's how I did it." She laughed.

The two stared at one another like two mad lizards ready to reach for each other's head. Then Mama turned back to the steaming pot, and Papa scratched his head, sucked air through his teeth, and started toward the front room.

"Why are you two standing around?" he asked us on the way. "Better get to work before I start banging heads."

The minute he reached the front room, Emilia and I grabbed our cans and headed for the springs.

"She deserves a beating for getting drunk," Emilia said.

I shook my head. "Maybe she wasn't that drunk."

"She's drunk, all right. Didn't you see the eyebrow?"

"Well, maybe she's drunk—but . . . well, things have been so nice." It was hard to know the right thing to say.

"What things have been so nice? If you mean the stupid shoes and the dumb trip to church . . . well, I talked to Pola and Maria Elena, and I realized that we should have had all that and more a long time ago. They get shoes and go places whether they work or not. Better yet, they get to spend the money they earn on themselves. They don't have to give it to their father." By now, Emilia was shouting, swatting the air and snapping branches.

I stood back, nodding, gasping, shocked. She'd been keeping all that information about our cousins to herself. No wonder she'd been mad ever since the celebration. Now I realized why Maria Elena and Pola seemed so much better off than we were.

"You are so right, Emilia. Other girls our age have it better than we do. But Mama getting beat is not going to help any of us."

"Nothing's going to help us!" Emilia yelled. "Mama is right— she is a damn slave. What makes me mad is that she wants us to be slaves, too."

"You're right, Emilia. You're a hundred percent correct."

As if my words were magic, Emilia calmed, and we lifted the cans to our heads and started up the hill. We didn't speak on our way up, but all kinds of thoughts about Emilia's rage went through my mind. I wondered then what she was thinking, but I didn't dare ask.

All seemed peaceful when we returned with the water. Mama was dishing out rice and beans. Papa lay in his hammock, drinking rum from a gallon jug and sucking air through his teeth.

"It's only a matter of time," Emilia whispered as we entered the kitchen.

I didn't answer, but I hoped silently that she was wrong.

Seconds later, we watched Mama stagger from the kitchen to the front room with a heaping plate of food for Papa. For years, she had sent his food with one of us girls. But this time she carried the plate herself, as if to prove something to him. She didn't hand the plate to Papa. She put it on the floor within his reach, then returned to the kitchen and began to fill gourd shells for the younger kids. We older girls were the last to be served.

Suddenly, we heard the rope of Papa's hammock squeak. Quick as a flash, he barged through the sleeping area into the kitchen, the plate of food in his hand.

"What in hell is this salty shit, eh?" The plate flew across the kitchen, hit the wall, and spilled the steaming rice and beans all over the floor.

Mama ducked, covering her head with her hands. Papa grabbed her hair and pulled her up, but she managed to get away and headed for the door. He grabbed her skirt and held her between the doorway and the ground.

The devil must have entered Emilia's mind, because without any warning, she shouted, "Stop! Let her go!"

Papa froze, his startled eyes on Emilia. Most of the kids ran into the next room, some with their gourds of food and others without.

I stayed in my corner, paralyzed. Had Emilia changed her mind about Mama deserving a beating? I didn't know what to think, or what to do. Emilia's rage might bring about the end for all of us. Somehow I felt obligated to help her out of whatever she was getting into. But did I really want to find myself among those three?

Papa kept the grip on Mama's skirt. "Don't you tell me what to do!" he yelled at Emilia.

Emilia held her place at the doorway. "Let her go!"

Now I knew she was in trouble. Papa would kill her.

While I trembled in my corner, José walked slowly across the sleeping area and put his gourd shell up on the *fogón*. Then, with an ear-piercing shriek, he jumped on Papa's back.

Papa lost his balance and landed on top of Mama. The pigs came out from under the house and ran squealing toward the woods. Papa got to his feet and grabbed Mama with one hand and José with the other.

"Good! Now I'll bang mother's and son's heads together!" The two heads sounded like two coconuts being banged one against the other.

Lorenzo wasn't going to stay out of it. He put his shell next to his brother's and flew out the door onto Papa's shoulders. Papa let go of Mama and José long enough to shake Lorenzo off. Then he grabbed Mama by the hair again.

The boys ran up a slope. "Let her go!" one of them yelled. I looked at them in awe. The two together were still smaller than Papa. What would become of them? Of all of us? Never before had any of us dared to get in Papa's way.

"We're not going to watch you beat our mother anymore!" José yelled, his voice cracking.

Papa ignored him and slapped Mama's face. "You drunken pig!"

Still wondering what to do, I saw Emilia reaching for the can of fresh water. Without hesitation, she dumped it over our struggling parents. "There! That will cool you both!"

Papa released Mama, wiped the water from his face, blinked hard, and jumped up into the kitchen. He looked around for something to hit Emilia with, and all he found was the flat, dried catfish he had brought home a day earlier. He grabbed it by the tail, took Emilia's arm, and whipped her across the back with the long, flat fish.

"What's going to cool who? This will teach you not to ever try anything like that again!"

Emilia kept going around in a circle, reaching to grab the catfish as she screamed, "I hate you! I hate Mama! I hate your stupid rum! I even hate God and the whole world, too!"

"Well, you little shit!" Papa's face turned purplish red as he growled like a mad dog. He swung the fish at Emilia's back until it shredded into pieces. Then he shoved her against the wall and hurried to his rum room.

I had gotten to my feet, but my legs trembled as he walked past without taking a swing at me.

He spent that night in his rum room. The rest of us stayed close to the kitchen door, ready to run if he came out. Meanwhile, I became my brothers' and Emilia's target.

"You're a coward!" Emilia snarled. "Stood watching like an idiot and didn't jump in to help us."

"Yeah, and you're supposed to be so smart," José added with a grin.

"You should have done what I did," said Lorenzo, waving a finger at me.

"Emilia, you said Mama deserved a beating!" I cried. "When did you change your mind? If you had told me, I would have been prepared."

Mama came in and plopped herself between us. "Keep that up, and he'll be back here in no time."

We stopped arguing, but we gave each other dirty looks until the light went out.

*   *   *

Papa left the house early the next morning, and I wondered all day what would happen when he returned. Emilia cursed and snapped branches on our way to the springs, then murmured and cursed some more in the sewing hut.

We ate lunch in a hurry that day, some of us nervously watching for Papa. As Emilia and I started back to the sewing hut, Mama decided to exercise her authority.

"Not so fast, Emilia. You have to roast the coffee beans you were supposed to roast last night."

Emilia rolled her eyes and drew her lips into a tight line. "You want me to do that now?"

"Right now!"

Emilia looked at Papa's hammock. "I'll tell you what, Mama. I'm going to rest for a few minutes, since I didn't get much sleep last night. Then I'll roast the coffee beans." She pulled down the hammock, shook off the dust, and stretched out in it.

Mama hit the rope of the hammock. "Who do you think you're talking to, young lady?"

Emilia crossed her arms under her head. "I'm talking to you! Who else?" The look on her face reminded me of a mad dog, all sharp white teeth and a wrinkled nose.

"You're asking for a good whipping!" Mama leaped to the corner and grabbed the leather belt. "You've gone far enough!"

Emilia looked at her and said, "Use that belt on me, and I'll use a machete on you!"

Mama stopped. "What did you say?"

"You heard me."

Suddenly, Alejandro trotted out of the sleeping area. As he passed near the hammock, Emilia snatched him and sprang to her feet, holding him over her hip like a chopped piece of log. Alejandro squirmed, but Emilia held him tightly. "Drop the damn belt, or I'll break his neck."

Mama's face turned white. "Put the baby down!" She raised the belt, her lips quivering.

"Not until you drop the damn belt." Emilia wrapped her hand around Alejandro's neck. Alejandro was still trying futilely to wriggle out of her grasp. "Throw it down!"

"Let him go!" Mama demanded.

"Drop the damn belt!" Emilia yelled. "Drop it!"

The belt fell to the floor.

Emilia shoved Alejandro at Mama and grabbed the belt. Stepping back, she said, "You'll never see this stupid belt again." She reached up and grabbed a sharp knife from the wall, and short pieces of leather began falling to the floor.

I had been standing against a wall, unable to utter a word, afraid that Papa would show up and finish the fight. I couldn't figure out what had gotten into Emilia, especially after she had defended Mama the day before. More puzzling was the fact that my strict and domineering mother walked away defeated by her own daughter.

I had been afraid of Emilia all my life, but after that scene, I wanted to be far away from her. Yet I had to return to the sewing hut with her and act as if nothing had happened. If she challenged Mama like that, I could not imagine what she would do to me if I ever stood up to her.

When Mama made supper that night, she didn't call us to eat, and we didn't go back inside until the sun went down. I had been hungry, but afraid of what Emilia would say or do if I said it.

As I walked through the sleeping area, I noticed that the other kids seemed nervous, as if they expected Mama or Emilia to take out their anger on them.

I ate my cold supper in a corner of the kitchen, waiting for Mama and Emilia to attack each other. But Emilia roasted the coffee beans while Mama bathed the smaller kids, and neither looked at the other.

Papa came home late that night and said he had eaten dinner with his brother. All he wanted now was peace and quiet, and a good night's sleep.

Everyone heard Papa's words, and stillness fell through the house. Ready or not, we all hurried into our sleeping sacks.

But I lay awake for a long time, feeling a thick cloud of fear around me, and wondering how soon another madness would erupt and destroy us all.

Chapter Thirty

Fifty-Two Eggs

We had developed a pattern of going to sleep mad and afraid, then waking up to start our chores as though nothing bad had happened.

The morning after Emilia's rage was no different. We all had our morning coffee and hurried to begin our work. Emilia and I hauled water up the hill, washed everyone's clothes, sewed gloves, and helped with the harvests. The other kids had their own designated jobs to do throughout the day, too. And that schedule remained much the same through the rest of that spring and summer.

Picking coffee berries was harder that year than ever before. Not only did it rain a lot, but we were allowed to stop only during the downpour. The minute the rain stopped, we were sent out, barefoot, into the saturated forest again.

"God!" Emilia cried each time we stepped on the cushions of rotting leaves. "Please send a flash of lightning and set this damn jungle on fire!" She threw the coffee berries into her basket with such force that they bounced back out and scattered on the ground. Then she challenged the Devil. "Why don't you pop out of the ground and drag my parents into your pit of fire!" She'd reach up, and then down, calling, "Do you hear me up there? Down there? Anywhere? Damn you!"

I shivered with fear of both God and the Devil, so I prayed silently that neither would listen to her. Then I prayed to find a way out of the hills before I became as old and bitter as my sister.

"Do you ever think about running away?" I asked her.

"Where do you think any of us could run to?" She turned to me, both hands on her hips. "A place where Papa wouldn't find us and drag us back by the hair?"

"I have no idea," I said. "I'm only asking."

But I did have an idea. It was something I had been thinking about for over a year. The next time we were sent to return the finished gloves, I would trick Emilia somehow and run toward the paved road with the money I had earned. I'd get into a public car and ride to town, then transfer into one going to the sewing factory in Mayaguez. I knew about the factory by reading the old newspapers Papa brought home wrapped around the codfish. All I would have to do to get a job was claim to be fourteen.

I wanted to ask Emilia to go with me, but I knew that she could not be trusted. If she told our parents that I was planning to run away, they would cripple me and I'd be their slave forever.

By the first day of November, the rains had stopped and the ground was quickly drying. The sun shining through the branches didn't seem as hot as it had been, and the breeze blew gently and cool. Emilia hummed instead of cursing as we picked the last of the coffee berries for that season.

"That's the breeze of Christmas," she said suddenly. "Can you feel it?"

She delighted me with her enthusiasm. "I feel it, all right. Think Papa will take us to church again? Maybe even buy us new shoes and fabrics for new dresses, and have another celebration?"

"Yeah," Emilia said, "he might." She reached for a twisted branch and found a hidden red coffee berry. She ran her thumb over the marble-sized berry, punctured its red skin with her thumbnail, and sucked the sweet syrup. "Yeah," she repeated, her gaze on the dry leaves near her feet, "he might take us to church again. But on the other hand, he might get drunk before Christmas and throw all of us out. Remember, he has two barrels fermenting as we speak—he doesn't make rum for bathing. You can mark my words."

That statement became Emilia's worst curse.

Papa made the rum on Sunday, four days after we had finished picking the last coffee berries. All of us had worked hard all day, and had just finished eating supper when he came home, his face red and his veins bulging.

"You," he said to me as he walked in. "Get in there and count those eggs. I'm taking them to the market tomorrow."

It would have been better if he had clobbered me on the head. Counting the eggs had been Alicia's job since she had started school, so I knew that he was fuming about something else. He always went to town on Saturdays. Why was he going on a Monday this time?

"Get going!" he yelled, his eyes red and glossy.

Feeling confused and scared, I ran into the rum room and started counting, placing each egg carefully on the floor grooves so that none would roll away and break. I knew Papa had left the door ajar to watch me from his hammock, and that made me more nervous.

"Fifty-two eggs, Papa," I said, hearing fear in my voice.

"How do you know?"

"I counted, like you told me to."

"Count again! And don't break even one."

I counted the eggs again and again, as carefully as I could, with shaky hands and sweating. Each time, I called out, "Fifty-two eggs, Papa."

"Count again, this time loudly so I can hear you."

"I counted six times, Papa! If I count one more time, some will break." From the corner of my eye, I saw him bolt out of his hammock. I had no way out of that room, and my legs were numb from sitting on them all that time.

He grabbed his machete on his way into the room. "What makes you think you can talk back to me, eh?" His voice roared like a bull tangled up on its own rope. Grabbing my hair, he pulled me off the floor and brought the machete to my throat. "You'll count those eggs again and again, until I'm satisfied! Do you understand?"

I had often seen my father bring down a thick banana plant with one swing of his machete, so I imagined my head falling to the floor like a melon. Trembling in his powerful grip, I cried, "Yes, Papa, I understand!" And a dark cloud lifted me away.

I don't know how long I lay on that floor, face down in the slime of crushed eggs. But the sound of my father's horrifying words awakened me to realize that I was still alive. I lifted my head slowly and, through the jellylike substance dripping from my face, I saw that only three eggs had survived on the shallow grooves between the floorboards. I had crushed all the others when I fell.

I carefully traced Papa's mad voice. It was coming from the kitchen.

"You worthless pigs!" I heard him shout. "I should kill every one of you. I should have done away with all of you years ago! Worthless pigs!"

Shuddering, still lying in the slimy mess, I heard plates and pots crashing to the floor, faces being slapped, and heads banging against the walls. My drunken father had left me to go beat on the rest of his family. I knew he would come back to finish with me for breaking the eggs he had planned to sell.

Crawling over the slippery mess, I jumped out the window, and ran. As I reached the woods, I heard the squeaky hinges of the kitchen door as it swung open, then Papa's boot steps behind me. I didn't think it was possible to run so fast, especially around the trees, over rocks and holes covered with leaves. I never looked back, but I think Papa stopped running long before I did.

The sun had already gone down, and nighttime was coming.

My father would wait, thinking that the fear of darkness would flush me out of the woods.

But he would have a long wait, for nothing could ever scare me more than his sharp machete at my throat.

Chapter Thirty-One

On a Dark Night

I stayed in the woods for a long time, quietly listening for my father's footsteps. When time passed and I hadn't heard a sound, I started through the darkness back toward the house.

At the *limoncillo* (lemon grass) bush, I stopped and looked down toward the house. I waited, listening, until I saw light coming through the two living room windows that faced up the hill. Immediately after that, light shone in the kitchen. That meant that someone had lit the kerosene lamps.

Now I could see three patches of light on the ground: two square ones from the windows, and a longer one from the kitchen door. I saw shadows moving back and forth over the longer patch. That meant that Mama and the kids were pacing the kitchen floor, ready to run if they heard Papa's footsteps. I didn't see any movement over the two square patches, so I concluded that Papa had settled in his hammock.

That thought, however, did not stop my knees from shaking. Maybe this time Papa had not consumed enough rum to pass out. For all I knew, he could be watching me.

Luckily, I reached the side of the house without getting caught. When I peeked through a crack, I saw Papa curled in his hammock, his boots still on and one muscular arm dangling to the floor. His eyes were closed.

I waited to make sure he wasn't faking to catch me off guard, then I headed toward the kitchen door.

I saw Mama and the kids on the long patch of light outside the door, and heard the boys nagging at each other.

"Move over!" one of them said.

"No, *you* move!" said another.

"Keep it up and you'll wake your father," I heard Mama say in a low voice. Then she saw me. "You!" She blocked my way to the door with outstretched arms, her voice filled with anger. "It's all your fault. You should have counted the damn eggs a hundred times. You're supposed to honor your parents, not argue with them. Because of you, he won't take me to town tomorrow. Now only God knows when I'll get to go."

I backed into the darkness where she couldn't see me, but I could still see her. I had not heard anything about Mama going to town. But even if I had, I would still have refused to count the eggs for the seventh time. I felt hateful right then, not in the mood to honor anyone—especially a father who held a machete to my throat, or my mother who didn't try to defend me.

If I could get into the house without anyone seeing me, I'd grab a change of clothing and be far away by the time Papa woke up. I would take my three dozen gloves, too, and turn them in for the nine dollars that rightfully belonged to me. I was the one who had sewed the gloves and poked my fingers with the needle hundreds of times.

I waited in the darkness until Mama and the kids went in. Then I eased my way into the kitchen, where Mama gave me a mean look, but didn't say a word. I stayed near the door anyway, so I could run if necessary.

Emilia came forward. "Hey, that was really close. I was sure he would cut your throat." She showed no trace of sympathy, so I didn't answer her. I walked across the kitchen and into the sleeping area, grabbed my gunnysack, and brought it to the corner closest to the kitchen door. The other kids did the same, then

Emilia followed them, and the whole kitchen floor became covered by gunnysacks and scared, tired kids.

I sat on the sack instead of crawling inside it; I didn't want anything to hold me back if Papa walked in.

Alicia brought her sack and sat next to me. I put my arm over her shoulder because she seemed frightened. She smiled at me, but I saw sadness in her eyes.

The shade from the *fogón* kept the light off my face, so I could see everyone better than they could see me. I watched Mama as she fidgeted at the *fogón* and up at the hanging net. Then she rolled a cigarette and sat on the floor. Leaning against the leg of the *fogón*, she aimed her chin toward the ceiling and blew smoke.

The last look I received from my mother, as she reached to put out the light, was with clenched teeth and glaring eyes more chilling than the dark of the night.

Chapter Thirty-Two

Down the River

When the second rooster crowed, I heard a thump on the floor, which meant that my father had jumped down from his hammock. "Everybody up!" He yelled. "I want everyone at work by sunrise."

I stepped out from under the house to start running, but streaks of light shone out through the cracks on the walls, so I peeked into the living room. Papa was holding a match to the lantern, his face still hard and unfriendly.

"I want both horses fed and groomed right away," he said. "I want the corral cleaned and repaired, and a pile of firewood knee-high. You two boys should get that work done by the time I get home. Sabina will fetch the water, feed the pigs and chickens, and mind the goats and cows. Emilia will take care of the house and the little kids, and she'd better make sure the rest of you get everything done. I don't want any bad surprises when I get back. And you better get busy and do whatever you have to do to get ready, because I'm not going to wait for you all morning."

I knew he was talking to Mama, and that was good, she'd be going to town, after all.

Peeking into the kitchen, I saw Emilia making coffee, and Mama washing her face in a gourd-shell of water. When she left the kitchen, I moved to another crack and looked into the front room, saw the door swing open and Papa walking out.

Quietly, I went back into the kitchen and asked Emilia for the first cup of coffee so I could start working right away. Luckily she glanced at me and handed the coffee without a word. I blew the steaming heat out to drink it fast, and when I heard the hinges of the front door again, I took the milk can and went under the house to milk the goat. From there, I heard Papa's steps on the squeaky floor. Then I saw the backs and heels of his black boots rest on the front step. He usually sat in the doorway with his feet hanging out to drink his morning coffee. I kept one eye on the stream of milk going into the can, and the other on his boots, hoping that he would not call me with instructions about particular jobs. I didn't want to look at him one more time.

I brought the milk to Emilia and headed down to the springs with the water can. It was still dark and spooky under the trees, but the fear of my father was greater than my fear of darkness.

On my second trip, I rolled myself into the pool of water to have a good reason to change my clothes. Mama was getting ready to leave when I walked in, soaked. I told her I had tripped and landed in the pool.

"Didn't break anything, did you?" she asked, holding a brown dress like an umbrella over her head.

As her head appeared through the neck opening, I turned away, wondering what she would do if she knew that I was changing my clothes to disappear.

I put on my other two pairs of underpants, my two slips, and my green dress over the yellow one. This would give me a change of clothing. I wanted to sneak my shoes out of the house, but how? I'd been lucky so far; Mama had not seen the extra clothing I had put on. I would not comb my hair either, because we never did just to fetch water from the springs, and she might suspect something. Besides that, she was using the only comb.

Before someone would see how fat I had become, I grabbed the water can and headed down the hill. Walking into the woods, I heard Mama holler, "Don't fall down again. If you break a leg, I won't be here to fix it."

I turned and saw her at the window. "I'll be careful," I yelled back, then ran, with a painful lump in my throat and tears burning my eyes. Maybe I hated to cause Mama heartache by leaving, or maybe I felt sorry for myself because I didn't believe that she loved me.

I hid the can under a bush, took off the extra clothes, rolled them into a bundle, and tied it with a flexible vine. With the little bundle under my arm, I cut across the hillside and the pigeon-pea field. When I reached the mango tree, which stood on the hill overlooking the house, I climbed up its limbs. Since I was dressed in green, no one would see me through the green leaves.

I leaned back on the main trunk to watch the house. I saw José grooming the horses outside the front room window, and Lorenzo milking the cow on the other side. I saw Papa come out in his dark trousers, white shirt, and white hat. He inspected the horses and went back into the house.

He came back out a few minutes later, followed by Mama in her long brown dress, pulling it up to step down, revealing her old black cotton stockings. She had tied her hair back into a bun, the same way she wore it to work around the house.

When they reached the horses, they began the same argument they always had.

"Spread your damn legs over that horse!" Papa's voice echoed back from the canyon.

"I'm a lady." Mama sat sideways and spread her skirt to cover her legs all the way down to her old black shoes.

"I don't know why I bother taking you to town. You embarrass the hell out of me, still bundling yourself up like women of the eighteen hundreds." Papa slapped her horse, and the horse almost threw Mama off as it ran up the hill.

Papa took off his hat and scratched his head, looking all around then up the hill. My heart stopped when I saw that he was looking at the mango tree. Then he said something to José, swung his leg over his horse, and off he went.

He caught up with Mama where the path made a sharp turn before the mango tree. She had been looking down toward the springs, probably expecting to see me climbing up with the can of water on my head. She said something to Papa, and he looked down, then quickly swatted his horse. I watched the tops of my parents' heads as they bobbed on their horses and disappeared into the woods.

Holding my breath, I climbed down from the tree and ran all the way to the river. Even if I heard Emilia calling me, I would not look back. I felt sure that by walking next to the river, I would reach the city on the west side of the island long before my parents came home.

The river looked wider and swifter than it did from afar, and I wished that I didn't have to run away. But I had no other choice. It was run and try to have a life, or stay and die, or be a slave to my parents for the rest of my life.

If I waited until we took the gloves to Don Estrada, and ran away from there with money for transportation, Papa might threaten me with his machete again. I couldn't take the risk. Next time, he might not stop with just a threat.

I couldn't help wondering what effects my disappearance would have on Mama. For as far back as I could remember, she had complained about her miserable life.

"My parents married me to a madman," she had often said. "At age twenty-three, only nine days after we met. They interviewed him and decided that he was 'somebody' because he owned five acres of land and planned to buy all the land north of the river. He's only two years older than I, but he'd been around, had his share of women before me. I didn't know I would become nothing but a slave. If that wasn't bad enough, God punished me with a lot of kids so I couldn't run away.

"Damn the night I met your father," she would say, leaning on the *fogón*, smoking, while we listened sadly. "I should kick myself a thousand times for liking him. Your father with his charm . . . he flashed his sparkling brown eyes, and I let the devil blind me. God, how I wish I had my life to live over again. You wouldn't find me anywhere near these woods."

I shook the thoughts about Mama out of my head and ran beside the water. It didn't take me long to leave the familiar grounds where we watered the horses and cows. Here, the low grass was replaced by thorny bushes and vines that wrapped around my legs like ropes. Some of the bushes were tall, with intertwined branches that housed many birds and spiders. Struggling to get through that web was suffocating.

I feared getting trapped there and being found by my father. He would whack the bushes with his sharp machete and drag me out by my hair.

Frantically, I broke branch after branch with my hands until I cut a tunnel through to the other side. I found a clearing of gravel where the river made a sharp turn. A wooded hillside began at the edge of the gravel, so steep that even when I threw my head back I still could not see its top.

The river became a threatening, gigantic monster, moving rapidly away from the mountain, leaving only a narrow space between the foot of the hill and the water.

If the fear of the river and whatever awaited me beyond the mountain wasn't bad enough, a swarm of bluebelly flies suddenly rose from a tangled mess of vines, banging into my face and buzzing in my ears. I thought my heart would fly out of my chest as I swatted the sticky pests away from me. The whole time I knew that if I ran into more of these kinds of obstacles, my dream of reaching the city before dark would never become reality. That was an agonizing thought.

Staying on the river's edge, I stumbled over potholes, fighting more flies, running into bushes, swatting honeybees, tripping on thorny vines, and brushing spider webs from my face. I walked into a patch of tall, thick grass with sharp leaves that cut my arms as I pushed them away from my face. From there, I stumbled over trailing vines under a canopy of bushes. These vines were deep green and cushiony, and to my disappointment, I discovered that they were over water.

My feet went through the web of vines and into the water so suddenly that I felt sure I would drown. I didn't know how to swim, and my feet were not touching bottom. Somehow, as my feet went in, I had grabbed a branch that extended from a tree at the river's edge. If miracles did exist, this had to be one, because there I sat on a hammock of vines, holding onto the branch, and the water didn't even reach my waist.

As I wondered how to get out of that death-trap, I saw that the river which had been running west had met with the mountain, and turned sharply like the letter L, and was now running south.

Praying that the branch would not break, I pulled on it a little at a time. When I felt sure it could hold my weight, I pulled myself out of the water, slowly, afraid to breathe. When I reached the trunk, I wrapped my arms and legs around it and looked back to see the water through the two holes my legs had made. The deep water whizzed like a snake under the net of vines.

Walking along the water's edge, I clung to whatever grew at the foot of the mountain. The loose dirt and stones slid from under my feet, splashing into the water while I grabbed another branch to save myself. A black bird shrieked and sprang off, brushing his wings over my head. I watched the branch swing back and forth. It had a nest with three speckled eggs.

It took a long time to get to where the river moved away from the mountains. It spread out wide, which made the water shallow enough for me to cross to the other side.

"How can I learn to swim?" I had often asked my mother.

"Swimming is not for girls."

"It might keep me from drowning."

"Stay out of the water, and you won't drown."

The water quickly came up to my waist as I started across. I knew that one more step could send me under. Still, I had to reach the other side. Desperate, I kept reaching with my arms, fighting the water, looking only toward the green valley on the other side. It was a horrifying struggle, but I made it before the water cascaded over rocks.

Walking on this stretch of flat land wasn't any easier than on the sloping ground. The thick grass and shrubs were tall, and cutting through was almost impossible, especially in the heat of the sun, which was now directly overhead. I had only half a day left to reach the city, hardly enough time to walk out of this rough terrain. I thought about my godparents and hoped they were watching over me.

The river twisted again around another mountain, and I had to cling to more vines and bushes. I knew that stepping on a loose rock would send me into the waiting river. The sun reflecting in the water blinded me, while grasshoppers and butterflies swarmed around my legs and under my skirt.

"Children who run away from their parents will be cursed," my mother had often said. I refused to believe that God would be that cruel.

I hung onto a shrub with one hand, swung my foot slowly over the weed-covered rocks, grasped another branch, and prayed with all my soul. I waited for branches to break as I watched the loose stones slide all the way down and hit the water with a splash. Small birds and bees brushed their wings over my head, reminding me that this was their territory.

A valley unfolded, and the river spread out to run wide and serene again. Yellow flowers that looked like bells dangled from vines over the bushes along the riverbed. Ducks quacked and shrieked as they scattered away from me. I rejoiced silently and ran to cross the river again where the water reached only up to my waist.

I walked away from the river when I reached the other side, following the sun rather than the water. The ground inclined here, but not too high, leading me through more bushes and trees.

Rats shrieked and ran from their hiding places as I stumbled over potholes.

When I reached the highest point of this hill, I had to climb down the other side in order to follow the sun westward. I didn't get very far before a root caught my foot and sent me flying, face down, over the shrub-covered hill.

I found myself hanging by my feet with the skirt of my dress flipped over my head so that I could see only the river below with the sun shining on it. I realized that the river had bent around this hill as it had the mountains. And if it continued curving around more hills, I would never reach the city.

At that moment, I surrendered to the fact that I might die.

Then my worst fear became reality. The weeds or vines I had grabbed as I fell snapped, and my body made a quick turn and slid all the way down to the river. I tried desperately to plant my feet on the river's floor, but the current swept me away. My arms went one way, and my legs another.

I was carried downward fast. My eyes were burning, and my ears and nose filled with water. I felt my body moving in a circular motion, then it spun faster and faster in a whirlpool that sucked me down, down into a dark, cool tunnel. I saw bubbles floating upward and away from me.

I tried to follow them, but something pulled me further down; hands reached from everywhere. I saw the transparent faces of my godparents floating around me, smiling, inviting me to go with them. I fought them for a while, but they grabbed my hair and spun me into a warm, bright light.

Chapter Thirty-Three

Out of Darkness

Coughing out gushes of warm water, I forced my eyes open against the glaring sun, and realized that I was clinging to an old tree limb at the river's edge.

Confused and disoriented, I asked myself why I was there. And soon my brain awakened and the bad memories unfolded. I had been lucky to escape the whirlpool, and I didn't know how many more were ahead. But I had to keep running and trust in more good luck.

Grabbing vines and bushes, I pulled myself farther up from the river, which at that particular spot was narrowed by two steep hills and appeared deep and serene. I told myself repeatedly that a miracle had saved me from drowning because God wanted me alive.

When I felt far enough from the water, I turned to look back and saw the old tree limb drifting slowly downstream. I felt sad watching it disappear. I thought of the transparent faces of my godparents I had seen in the whirlpool, and decided that they had sent that tree limb to pull me out of danger. I didn't feel so alone anymore.

My dress was torn, I had lost my change of clothing, my legs and arms were covered with cuts and scratches, and I still had no idea how much farther I had to go to reach the city. I pulled sticks and leaves out of my hair, and struggled through the thick bushes and vines, climbing up and away from the river.

Soon I walked into a swarm of buzzing wasps. But I had been stung by wasps many times before, and I knew that staying still was the safest thing to do. I squatted down with my hands over the back of my neck and my face between my knees.

My head throbbed, and I felt sick to my stomach by the time the angry wasps stopped stinging me. But I pushed forward, still hoping to reach the city before dark.

I spent the rest of the day crawling up that steep hill, reaching for one small tree after another. I heard more rocks rolling down behind me and splashing into the water. I fell into one vine-covered hole after another, and heard more rats and squirrels shriek and run. I noticed that the sun was falling fast behind the tall trees at the top of the hill.

I finally reached the top, but then I realized that the river was curved like a horseshoe around this steep hill. That meant that I would have to cross it one more time.

I was too worn out to climb down again. I felt trapped then, and darkness was on its way. My choices were few. I could spend the night up in a tree, or down on the thick cushion of dry leaves, with the scorpions, spiders, and centipedes.

I chose a tree with white bark and a wide trunk so I could lean back. I should have been terrified, but I had done enough shaking in the past two days to last me a lifetime. My heart had pounded so hard so many times that I knew it had to be cracked and bruised.

The fear of the dark I had felt all my life had somehow vanished. The darkness came in as I sat on the branch, rubbing my sore legs. Then I listened to hundreds of birds chirp and screech as they flew into the woods to settle for the night.

According to my mother's teachings, the Virgin Mary watched over little girls. I counted on the Virgin to keep me safe, even if running away from home was wrong. God knew I had been a good girl.

When I could no longer see my own hands, I wrapped my arms and legs around a tree limb, closed my eyes, and thought back to the many reasons that had made me run. I thought of my parents coming home and finding out that I was gone. I wondered if Mama cried.

Soon the bird waste began to come down on my head like raindrops and spattered on my shoulders. I couldn't take my hands off the branch to cover the back of my neck for fear of falling off the branch and rolling down to the river. All I could do now was pray for the night to pass.

The bird droppings coming down on me brought back the horrible memories of Emilia and our older brothers smearing cow manure on my clean hair because someone had commented that it shone in the sun. "Let's see who's going to rave about your hair now!"

I felt anger toward Mama as I remembered that she didn't do anything to stop the cruelty my sister and brothers inflicted on me. One ugly memory followed another. I thought of the time I collected silk cotton to make myself a small pillow. The silky, pinkish flakes floated from the trees only for a short time in the spring, and many were needed to make an eight-inch by twelve-inch pillow. Then I had to wait until my mother gave me a piece of fabric to make the bag.

I was thrilled when I finally sewed the bag closed, and ran to show the pillow to Mama. She held it in one hand, ran her other hand over it, and said, "Now make one for me." I had never been so proud of myself. Mama's request for a pillow meant that I had done a good job. I walked away with my chest bursting with joy.

My thrill died when Lorenzo barged through the door asking to see the pillow. In a flash, he snatched it from my hands. Just as quick, José joined in, and the little pillow traveled through the air with great speed. I jumped up, trying to retrieve it, but could not. I yelled, "Don't! You'll break it. Give it back!"

The two demons ran around the *fogón*, throwing the pillow

and laughing. When Mama reached for her belt, Lorenzo lifted the pillow and slammed it on the woodpile. A sharp edge pricked a hole in the old fabric, and my precious silk flakes rose up and gradually floated down onto the wood.

Both boys ran outside. I jumped out after them and chased them until I grabbed Lorenzo by the arm. I shook him, then punched his upper arm a few times. He threw himself to the ground and screamed that I had broken his shoulder.

Papa heard the commotion and came running. Mama told him that we were fighting "over a stupid pillow." I stood frozen. I couldn't believe what was happening. I had broken my brother's arm, for which I would be whipped, and my mother called my little pillow "stupid" after asking that I make one for her.

"She broke my shoulder!" Lorenzo kept saying as he writhed on the ground.

"Well, we'll fix her," Papa said, grabbing Lorenzo by the shirt and pulling him to his feet. "Beat her up. Here, I'll hold her." He grabbed my hair and held my face over his belly while my brother pounded my back with his fists. I felt as though my lungs would detach from whatever held them in place, for Lorenzo had inherited his big hands from his father.

After a dozen blows, Papa ordered his son to stop. He then let go of my hair, and I fell to the ground, breathless.

Then Papa grabbed Lorenzo, turned him around, and pounded his behind for lying. "So she broke your shoulder, did she?"

Feeling a little vindication that he had spanked the brat, I stayed on the ground catching my breath. I saw Mama coming toward me and thought she was going to comfort me.

"That's what you get for fighting," she snarled. "Now go milk the goats."

As Mama walked away, I swore that I would get even with all of them. And I did. When I milked the goats, I let my tears mix with the stream of milk coming into the can. The next day, my whole family drank my tears in their morning coffee.

I thought of the times Papa made me hold a pan to catch the blood of the poor pigs he butchered. "Hold it under the stream," he had always yelled, not caring how I felt. The smelly blood gushed from the cut in the pig's throat. Red drops spotted my arms, but I wasn't allowed to pull my hands away and wipe them off.

The pig, lying on a wooden bench, tried to kick off the rope around his legs, but he weakened as the blood came to a trickle. His eyes stared, glossy black surrounded by white, as if begging for mercy.

After the blood stopped dripping, Papa had me pour boiling water on the dead pig while he shaved off the hair. I had to hand him the knife he used to cut open the pig, and watch him separate the stinky, coil-like tubing. The foul steam rising from bluish-purple and pinkish flab made me gag, but Papa thought it was funny and ignored my feelings.

I wondered if Mama was missing me. *Would you help me, Mama, if you knew where I was?*

Then I remembered when Julio disappeared. He was a little boy from a hill beyond ours. His mother had died when he was born, and a year later his father was killed in a fight with another drunk. Julio's grandmother raised him "for her old age," she said, and the boy became her slave.

One gloomy September day, the old woman sent Julio to Don Castillo's store. Upon reaching our house, he smelled Mama's soup and would not go further without having some.

"That poor boy is starving," my mother said. She filled a shell with soup and handed it to him. Julio, standing barefoot outside the kitchen door in the chilling drizzle, brought the shell to his lips. His big brown eyes moved as though he expected someone to reach out and snatch the shell of soup away. I saw that his trousers had one patch over another and hung by one dirty strap. He was naked from the waist up, and I could see his ribs as he licked the shell clean. He ran his tongue over his lips, gave the dish back to Mama, and ran.

Days later, someone said that Julio had not returned to his grandmother that day. He had disappeared. Perhaps he had fallen into the river and had washed away, people said.

Did his grandmother care? I decided that she probably did; after all, she had lost her slave.

And so had Papa. I thought Papa might be up and down the river looking for me. Mama might be crying. Maybe Emilia and the other kids were crying, too. The thought was heartwarming, and I cried for myself, until another glob came from above, splattering on my head, slowly dripping down the back of my neck.

I finally let go of the branch, brought my knees to my chest, wrapped my arms around them, and lowered my head to hope and pray for the night to end.

Chapter Thirty-Four

Out of the Jungle

I awakened on the ground, my head resting on my arm, my knees close to my chest. I could not remember coming down from the tree.

Opening my eyes slowly, I noticed sunlight coming through the branches. I stayed still a little longer to get my bearings. I felt like shouting that I had survived the night, but I had to find the way down to the river and hurry toward the city.

My legs hurt when I stood up, and they were swollen from all the cuts and scratches. But I had to hurry to the river and wash the bird waste out of my hair.

Hanging onto small trees and bushes, I started down the steep hill. Through the branches, I saw the river running through a green valley. Since it was shaded by the mountain, I knew it was still flowing west.

The river was wide and shallow there because of the flat land, so I plunged into it as I reached its edge. The water felt cold on my skin but soothing to the cuts and scratches. I looked around as far as my eyes could see, making sure that no one was anywhere near the river and its valley. The bushes and trees on each side of the water were deep green and dense. And except for the soft gurgling of the moving water, all was quiet on that early morning. For a moment, I felt that I was the only person left in the world.

I shook that chilling thought out of my mind and crossed to the other side of the river. I reached a wide expanse of sand, gravel, and rock, where white birds with long, skinny legs and long necks hid their beaks in their wings. Beyond the gravel, the bushes had been crushed by heavy hooves. Cow and horse droppings lay crusted alongside the hoofprints—a clear sign that people lived nearby.

I knew I was far away from home, but I still feared running into someone who might know my parents. I surely would be returned home in exchange for a bottle of rum.

I followed the animal droppings and hoofprints to a path leading into a coffee farm. The branches of the plants were twisted, and green leaves lay on the ground. I knew from this that the coffee beans had been picked recently. That was good; once the last coffee beans had been picked, there would be no need for anyone to come around. I would be able to find oranges and bananas to ease the cramps of hunger in my stomach. I had been too scared to think about food, but now I felt so hungry I would eat anything.

Sniffing for bananas and looking around for orange trees, I heard roosters crowing somewhere up ahead. Then I saw yellow feathers clinging to the green grass alongside the path. The hoof marks were still prominent, with little curved ridges, unbroken for horses and split for cows. *I must be approaching a farmhouse. Someone can be watching, waiting until I get closer so they can grab me.*

I listened for the sound of people and peered around the tree trunks. More feathers appeared, moving slightly in the breeze—black, white, brown, and orange feathers, as if somebody had plucked chickens and scattered the feathers.

In the distance, I saw a mound of something in the middle of the path—something that looked like a black cow lying in the shade. I approached slowly, taking a few steps and stopping to look around, expecting the thing to jump up suddenly. My chest hurt from the hard pounding of my heart.

The object turned out to be a huge black boulder, and the path divided around it. I imagined someone hiding behind it, ready to jump in front of me. The closer I got to the rock, the bigger and scarier it seemed.

Then suddenly, a flock of chickens burst out from behind it, and almost startled the life out of me. I stumbled backwards and fell against the bank of earth at the edge of the path. I slid down to the ground with my legs folded under me and watched the flock flutter away, shrieking and clucking as their feathers whirled to the ground.

I stayed there with stars floating in my eyes and wondering how much more thumping my poor heart could take before it would shatter completely. It dawned on me then that my heart had been startled into a hard pounding too many times in the past years. I knew it would wear out soon, and I would never reach old age.

I finally rose to my feet, brushed the dirt off my dress, combed my hair with my fingers, and ran past the boulder. I kept climbing until I saw blue sky through a funnel-like hole in the green ceiling of branches. I was approaching the opening to a clearing at the top of the hill.

I found a *pana* tree at the edge of the path, and climbed it to look down at the clearing. I spotted a weathered cottage on stilts next to a huge red bougainvillea bush. The little house had two windows facing my tree, but only one stood open, with swinging shutters and creaking hinges. The closed window had a wooden box attached to the outside of it—*el fregadero* (the kitchen sink) filled with dishes.

Since I could not see daylight through the open window, I concluded that the door was on the other side, and closed. So I sat on a branch and watched. I took my eyes off the little house only to look down and around, making sure no one caught me by surprise. I felt much too hungry to worry about who might live there, but I still wanted to see the people before going to their door.

I saw an old woman dragging a dry branch from behind the bougainvillea bush, her long skirt sweeping the ground behind her. When she reached the house, she dropped the branch and pulled open a door. I suddenly could see through the window and out to the front yard through that open door. The old woman picked up her skirt with one hand, reached for the doorjamb, and pulled herself up into the house. She flashed past the open window, then went back outside with a short machete and chopped up the dry branch. I watched her gather the wood in her arms and carry it inside.

Minutes later, I saw blue smoke filtering through the rusty tin roof, and the closed window swinging open over the dish-washing box. Now the old woman peeled green bananas and sweet potatoes over the dishes. Since the sun was still high in the sky, I guessed that she was fixing the noon meal. I noticed that she peeled too many vegetables for one person. Maybe she had a husband, hopefully an old man. I would not be afraid of an old couple.

The lady left the window with the peeled vegetables. Seconds later, she returned, poured water into a pot, and began to wash the dishes. She scrubbed a plate with a dark rag, then poured clear water over it. The water ran through a hole in the wooden sink and streamed down to the ground, where it formed a little mound of suds.

Staring at the pile of foam, I thought how we washed dishes at home: in a corner or on the *fogón*, with ashes instead of soap. Papa would only buy a pound of soap every few months, to be used only for washing clothes and bathing. That soap was usually blue and came in a long bar like a two-by-four piece of wood, sold by the pound, and by the ounce to those less fortunate.

The lady took the dishes inside and, shortly afterward, the aroma of onions and codfish reached my tree. Suddenly my mouth became a pool of water. I forgot everything else and jumped down to the ground and headed for the clearing. Upon reaching the small yard, I took a quick look around, then followed the smell to the kitchen door. The palm-board floor was as high as my chest. Quietly, I looked in, searching from one corner to the other.

The woman had returned to the window, and stood with her back to me. I saw her bare heels, dry and cracked, under the hem of her long skirt. She had her black-and-white hair rolled into a bun on the back of her head. The sleeves of her blue-and-white print dress stopped at her bony elbows, and a black, twisted rope hugged her tiny waist. I felt lucky, because I would not fear such a small lady.

I turned my head to make sure there wasn't someone sneaking up behind me. When I looked back inside, the lady had moved to the *fogón*, and stood stirring the sizzling codfish with a long wooden spoon. Next to the frying pan, I saw another pot on three rocks splattering onto the fire. The woman took two burning pieces of wood and walked to the door.

She saw me looking up at her, and froze. While blue smoke rose from the burning wood in her hands, my knees trembled below the hem of my dress. I tried to speak, but the words didn't come.

"*Santo Dios!*" she said at last. "Do you make a habit of looking into people's kitchens? Do you? Close your mouth. Answer me—do you?" She stepped closer to me and threw the burning wood over my head and out the door. I watched the sparks fly up as the burning wood hit the ground. "You must be my new neighbor's girl. Are you?"

The old woman smiled, but I stood mute, wondering what she was talking about.

"Tell your mother to come see me as soon as she's settled in her new house—well, new to her, anyway. The place has been locked up since the owner died. Well, he didn't die the normal way—hung himself, that's what he did. No one wanted to live in the place after that. Well, come in. Don't just stand there. How old are you? You don't talk much, do you?"

I nodded, and then shook my head.

"I know what you're thinking," she said. "I talk too much, right?"

I nodded again, then quickly shook my head.

She laughed and turned toward the *fogón*. "You might as well come in and help me eat this food."

If I go in, will she lock the door and keep me trapped inside? Terrible thoughts came to mind as I peered beyond the kitchen, fearing I might see someone crazy or drunk coming out, swinging a machete. I saw a wooden rocking chair in a corner of the next room—the living room—and a white metal table with three rusty legs. A faded black-and-white picture of a couple with a small boy hung on the wall above the table. A brown hammock, rolled tightly, hung nearby on a rusty nail. A narrow doorway led to another room, which I imagined was the bedroom.

"Well, are you coming in or not?" The old woman turned from the *fogón* with a wooden platter full of cooked bananas, sweet potatoes, onions, and fried codfish. "Come, sit next to me and eat." She sat on the floor beside the food, folded her legs, and covered them with her skirt. "Is it true that your mama has nine little ones?" She took a piece of hot banana, blew on it, and put it in her mouth.

I nodded and pulled myself up to the floor. I sat on one leg, letting the other one hang out in case I had to run.

"I didn't tell you the food is hot, did I?" she asked as I struggled to blow out the heat from the hot chunk of sweet potato I had stuffed into my mouth. "Remember that nothing holds the heat in like sweet potatoes," she said with a laugh.

As the piece of potato burned slowly down my throat, I wondered how she could talk while eating such hot food, and without a tooth in her mouth that I could see.

"It's too bad about your father getting killed by lightning like he did. Tell your mama to come see me once she's all settled. Poor thing, a widow, with nine children. That place was locked up for such a long time. It must have been full of roaches and mice, wasn't it?"

I nodded again, with my mouth full. The food was delicious, and it was a lot of codfish and onions for just the two of us. At home, we children were given a tiny sliver of codfish to eat with a lot of cooked green bananas. And we never had onions with lunch. Papa had insisted that onions were to be used only with chicken soup and rice and beans.

"What's your name?" the woman asked.

I filled my mouth to avoid answering.

"It's okay, you don't have to tell me. My name is Marta, if you want to know. Poor little thing, you really were hungry, weren't you?"

I smiled so she would know that I liked her and appreciated the food.

"It must be hard to feed nine children with no father around to help. Such a pretty girl, you are. But how did you get all those cuts and scratches? Running through the bushes? You sure could use a comb through that hair. Such blonde hair. Are the other children as blonde as you? And look at your poor dress. It needs washing and mending."

Marta had dark, wrinkled skin and a long, fine nose. Her eyes were dark and deep in their sockets, with a filmy rim framing the iris. She reminded me of my godfather's mother, and for a moment I wondered if the two might be related.

"You probably think I talk too much. That's what happens when you live alone after having a companion for over fifty years. I almost went crazy when my man died. He was just resting on that hammock." She pointed to the tied-up bundle on the nail. "I was in my rocker mending his trousers when he called for help. I jumped up right away, but he was gone before I reached him. It's bad when something like that happens to you."

I wanted to say I felt sorry for her, but I knew if I started talking, I would have to answer all her questions.

"My son wants me to move closer to town with him and his family, but I tell him I'll be carried out of here in a box. Poor Ramon, he gets mad and says I'm stubborn. You should have heard him yesterday. He nagged all the way to the river on his horse, and pulling a poor cow behind him. He'll be back tomorrow to give me a hard time again.

"Oh, I guess I'll have to leave this place one of these days. I'm getting old and going blind. But I'm staying here as long as I can." She smacked her lips and smiled.

I licked my lips and looked into her eyes, smiling so she would see that I liked her very much. She patted my shoulder.

"God bless you. You're a good girl."

I put my hand over hers and squeezed it gently.

When she picked up the platter and took it to the window, I quietly slid to the ground and walked away. On the other side of the bougainvillea, the path divided into two. I stopped to decide which way to go, and heard Marta talking as if I were still there.

I felt a lump in my throat, and guilt for not thanking the nice lady for the food. I would visit her someday. Then I would tell her my name and explain the scratches on my legs and my reasons for running away.

Chapter Thirty-Five

Who's Blanca?

The path branching to the right looked wider and more traveled, and it went in the same direction as the river. I could hear the water way down there when the breeze blew toward me. Sometimes, when the water picked up the sun just right, I could see the sparkles through the branches. I soon noticed the color of the earth changing from brown to red. Shortly afterward, I walked out from under the trees into a fern-covered plateau divided in the middle by the red path.

I had reached the top of the mountain. Now, like standing on a bald head, I could look around over the treetops. The wooded hills way out there looked like green clusters. I saw some small clearings and rooftops, and the river zigzagging and sparkling through the indentations around the clusters. I felt safe this far from home, where Papa wouldn't find me.

I ran until I heard dogs barking and the voices of men and women coming from the woods ahead. I quickly hid behind a tall fern to trace the voices, and to think about what to tell people who might ask where I was going.

At that moment, I realized that I needed to know what to say to anyone who might try to help me once I reached the city. I would ask for directions to the sewing factory, and then what? Who would even look at a ragged girl? If I looked as bad as

Marta said . . . Well, I might have to run back to her; she would be kind to me. I could keep her company, but that wasn't what I wanted.

I even wondered if I could still go back home. *Maybe Papa will only give me a whipping. No, he'll do more than that.*

I had no choice but to keep running. I heard the sound of hooves and ducked back behind the fern just before a skinny young man in blue trousers and a big straw hat rode by on a brown horse. As soon as he passed, I took off again. I found a barbed wire fence around a herd of cattle, and then noticed a white house up on a slope. More than one dog barked, but they seemed fenced in and never reached me.

I soon saw some houses with smoke rising from their rooftops dotting a hillside on my right. From there on, I couldn't walk fifty feet without passing another house. Dogs came out, some barking, others wagging their tails. I saw chickens in flower gardens scratching the ground, and two little girls under a tree, playing with rag dolls. They smiled and asked where I was going.

"To town," I answered, and kept running.

A patch of thick vegetation separated two nice concrete homes from three wooden ones on stilts bunched together at the foot of another hill. Cars had turned around here, probably earlier that morning, matting down the grass at the edge of the path. Farther ahead, I saw a *cantina* between two homes with their doors wide open. The road became wider in front of the three dwellings, then continued straight into the wooded hill. Hoping no one would see me, I flew past the three buildings and stopped only when I reached the woods.

I heard someone moaning down in the ditch, so I tiptoed to the edge of the path and looked down. I saw the black, curly hair and shoulders of a woman squatting near a tree. A large brown bundle rested against the tree trunk. There was no one else around, so I watched her.

She stood up, pulled her underpants over a huge belly, and adjusted her skirt. Still groaning, she reached for the bundle and placed it over her hip and under her arm. Then she looked up and saw me.

"Oh, aren't you pretty!" she exclaimed, her big brown eyes checking me from head to foot. "You must be Doña Concha's girl Blanca. She said your hair is blonde, almost white. But it's a rat's nest! What happened? You poor girl! And look at your dress, all torn and stained." The woman reached the edge of the path, breathing hard, her belly extended and her navel pushing into the fabric of her brown cotton dress.

"I'll take the bundle," I said, without answering her questions.

"Ah, your mother said you're a hard worker," the woman panted. "Ay, I climbed down that hill to pee, and now I need to go again."

"How do you know my mother?" I finally asked.

"We met at the clinic last week. Didn't she tell you?"

"Maybe she did and I forgot. I even forgot your name."

"Ah, don't worry. My girls forget everything, too. Ana . . . my name is Ana."

I thought of Marta talking about the widow with nine children. This woman might be talking about the same person. "Did my Mama tell you what happened to us?"

"About how your father was killed by lightning? Yes, she told me. I felt sorry for her. Nine children! And you the oldest? I feel sorry for all of you. On top of that bad luck, the poor woman breaks her leg! *Misericordia* (mercy)! At least she can spend her time sewing gloves. Six dozen, she wants you to bring her. Is that right?"

"Yes, six dozen," I said, going along with her, hoping that the real Blanca would not show up. "Can we walk now?"

"Yes, but not too fast," she said. "This baby is getting too heavy." She hugged her belly and laughed.

We walked past little houses on stilts with rusty roofs, coffee and mango trees, orange, *pana*, and other fruit trees on both sides of the dirt road. Ana gasped and talked while I looked left and right for the real Blanca.

Even though I was still afraid, I felt blessed by meeting this lady. She was headed for the sewing factory, the place I had hoped to find. My prayers had been answered.

"Your mother said you've never been to Mayaguez before, is that right?"

"Yes."

"You must be careful not to get lost. It's a big city."

"I'll stay close to you," I said, wondering how to lose her once we got to the factory.

At last we heard a horn from around the bend. "Thank God! Here comes the *publico*," Ana gasped.

A brown and yellow station wagon appeared and stopped. Two ladies and a boy got out. Then Ana got in and I followed her, sitting at her side as though I were her child. Two old men were in the back seat, and a woman with a small boy sat next to the driver. The station wagon turned around and continued on.

After a few stops, the station wagon filled up. Each time a new passenger got on, I worried that it might be Papa or someone who would know that I was his daughter. When the woman in the front seat talked to the driver, I turned to listen, suspecting that they could tell that I was on the run. I imagined being on the lookout for the rest of my life, always in fear of getting caught.

Ana seemed nervous, looking around as if she, too, suspected that I was doing something wrong. I kept hoping that no one would ask her if I was her daughter. I imagined her saying that I was Doña Concha's girl, and the person saying, "I know Concha very well, and that's not her daughter."

"Are you scared?" Ana whispered in my ear.

"No, why do you ask?"

"It's on your face, and on your hands."

I looked down and saw my hands crossed in my lap, the fingers purple from squeezing. "Well, maybe I am a little scared," I admitted.

"Ah, don't worry. You'll be just fine." She placed her sweaty hand over mine. "You'll be just fine."

I wondered if she thought I would come back with her, and I felt guilty that I couldn't tell her the truth. At that moment, a tear splattered on my knuckles, but I didn't know if it came because of Ana or because I didn't know what would become of me if I couldn't find a kind person to help me. This was a desperate moment, yet I couldn't tell anyone, nor could I turn around and go back home.

I saw a blue line way ahead meeting with the sky, and whispered to Ana, "Look at that blue valley up there."

"Shh." She leaned over and whispered, "That's the ocean."

"Oh! But why do you whisper?"

"So they won't think you are a *jíbara* (hillbilly)."

"But that's what I am, a *jíbara*."

"Yes, but you don't need to sound like one."

"Does that mean that we are almost there?"

"Yes, we're almost there," said Ana.

I nodded and looked straight ahead. We were moving down-hill, the station wagon rolling fast. The brakes squeaked to stop for a red light. I could see huge buildings, high and low, one next to another, and a lot of people on street corners and sidewalks.

Soon the light changed to green, and the car rolled on, only to stop for another light, and another, until the city swallowed us.

Chapter Thirty-Six

A Dark Room

There were stores connected to other stores, and people of all ages crossed the streets in front of cars, hurrying to get somewhere. I knew Papa had never been here, but I looked for him in every crowd. I sure didn't want him to drag me home now, not after all I had gone through to reach this town.

My stomach turned at the thought of the coming night. *Where can a girl hide and not be found by some mean and cruel person?*

I knew I could make a living sewing gloves. If only I could find another nice lady like Marta or Ana who might let me live in her home until I was older.

The driver drove around the *plaza* before coming to a stop where the public cars lined up to load and unload.

We stepped out onto a blistering hot sidewalk where I stood holding the bundle, squinting because the sun was too bright on the white buildings.

Ana handed a quarter to the driver, and then shrieked, "*Un nikel!*" She held the nickel between her thumb and index finger. "I gave you a quarter, and you give back a nickel?"

"Ten for you and ten for your daughter," the driver said, and turned quickly to collect fares from the other passengers.

Ana stood holding the nickel, mumbling something that made me feel guilty.

"My mother forgot to give me money," I said, too ashamed to look her in the eye.

"She probably didn't have any to give you." Ana dropped her hand. "*Vamonos* (let's go)," she said, and took the bundle from me. "You earned it anyway by carrying this for me."

I followed her across the plaza, where white pigeons flew off the statue of Cristóbal Colón on a black iron horse. We walked down a narrow street with sidewalks and red geraniums growing in pots. There were stores that had beautiful dresses and blouses hanging from the walls and racks, and doctors' offices with balconies and doors that opened toward the sidewalk.

We walked past ragged people who leaned against the corners of buildings begging for pennies. I noticed their weathered skin, their hungry eyes, and the sores on their legs and feet. I saw a small girl who had no arms and a young man without legs on a square box with wheels, waiting for pennies to fall into his tin cup. I wondered how they had lost their limbs, and then felt a jolt in my stomach.

How would I run without legs, or eat without hands? I hoped to have a lot of money someday. If I did, I would give some to those poor people.

"If I give you my last nickel, I'll be begging, too," Ana repeated again and again. Most of the beggars didn't respond, but one old woman, wrinkled and ragged, sneered and spat at Ana's legs. The brown saliva missed her shoes and splattered on the concrete.

"That's why I would hate living in town," Ana said. "Putting up with beggars. Dogs, too. A lot of them with mange are roaming around town. If they bite, you get rabies."

"I hope to have a lot of money someday," I said. "I'd give some to the girl who had no hands, and to the man who had no legs."

"I'll pray for your good fortune, then," Ana said with a laugh. "Usually people who have money don't give it away."

A few feet beyond the beggars, the smell of hot grease, onions, and codfish filled the air. Sweaty men stood near wooden carts on wheels, selling food. "*Bacalaitos!*" some yelled, referring to codfish wrapped in flour. Others sold fried plantains. "*Tostones fritos!* Only five cents. Buy them here. They are delicious!"

"Now that's what I wish I could buy!" Ana cried. "I'm so hungry I could eat a whole pig."

"I'm hungry, too," I said as my stomach twisted and growled.

A man swung a plate of golden fried bananas. "*Tostones?*"

"Tempt me again, and I'll grab that plate," Ana told him.

"Hurry back after you get paid," he urged, moving on to the other passersby.

"Oh good! We are almost there," Ana gasped. "That's the sewing factory over there." She pointed to a huge concrete building with many large windows and two wide doors facing the street. Next to the building, I saw a few benches under a circle of trees.

"That's where the workers take their *siestas*," Ana said.

"What's a *siesta?*"

"A *siesta* is a short rest, or sleep, that city people take after they stuff themselves at noon."

Our shadows were long beside us as we reached the door, and inside a clock on the wall read a few minutes after three.

"We'll be here until dark," Ana whined. "Look at the lines of women waiting to have their sewing checked."

I counted five lines of girls and women, each holding a bundle, shifting their weight from one foot to the other. Some of them smiled as we entered, but others stared and blinked their eyes like frogs waiting to catch flies. I looked at the lines of faces, and saw some brown with dark eyes, and others white with hazel or green eyes.

There were even some with eyes as blue as the sky, and I didn't feel so strange anymore. I noticed their red lips, and the flowers in some of the younger girls' hair. I saw skirts that flared like umbrellas, which had bunnies or cats sewn on them. Everyone in the lines was wearing shoes—some black, others brown, and a lot of them white.

I felt overwhelmed by so many strange faces, and by actually being in the place I had dreamed of reaching someday, but had not expected to reach so quickly. A steady hum from low voices seemed to be lingering somewhere between the high tin roof and the concrete floor. I saw the women's lips move, but could not make out their words. I pictured myself as a tiny bug at the bottom of a barrel, and all the women as big scorpions and spiders around the rim, ready to swallow me. I thought of running out and going back to Marta, where I would not feel so afraid.

"Hold this spot and my gloves while I run to the toilet," Ana said.

I took the bundle and watched her. She couldn't run with her knees tight together, hands to her side, grasping the hem of her skirt.

When she disappeared down a long hallway, I looked around again at the many women waiting to have their work checked. I wondered where they lived and what they were thinking as they looked at my scratched legs, my tangled hair, and my torn dress.

"Too late," Ana whispered when she returned. "My panties were already wet. If you have to go, the place is empty now."

I did as she suggested, and found four white toilets filled with water lined up against a high wall. There were short walls separating the toilets, and canvas hanging as doors. A wooden box with a long chain hung above each toilet.

Having no idea what purpose the boxes served, I looked for the toilet that seemed the cleanest, stuck one foot in it and washed my leg from the knee down. Then I washed my other leg and dried them both with paper towels. I moved to a sink, which had a rusty mirror above, washed my arms and face, ran my wet fingers through my hair, then returned to Ana.

The lines of women on the concrete floor faced a square area in the middle of the huge room. The square was enclosed with short walls and countertops. Every couple of feet, the counter had openings called *ventanillas* (little windows). Through those windows, the glove-makers had their work inspected and received their pay.

The women inside the enclosure were nicely dressed, wearing shoes and fine stockings, makeup, and lipstick. They were called *inspectoras*. The knowledge these inspectors had about gloves, and the way they dressed, put them in a powerful position. They were "city people," and city people were better than the hill people who did the sewing.

"I've never seen this place so crowded," complained Ana.

I had counted the women; there were fifteen to twenty per line. With so many waiting, nobody would stop their work to listen to me. And if I waited for Ana's turn to come up, the truth about me would be out. When she asked for work for the woman she thought was my mother, the *inspectora* might ask me questions I couldn't answer.

By now I felt like a little puppy surrounded by dog catchers. I was suffocating.

"Stay in line and hold my place, sweetie. I have to go again," Ana said and hurried away.

After she had gone, I asked the lady behind me if she knew which of the women inside owned the factory.

"I don't know, but those two up there are the managers," she said, pointing at two ladies at a desk a few feet above the *inspectoras*. Neither of them looked friendly, so I decided not to talk to them about a job. I would leave with Ana when she left, find my way back to Marta's, and take the chance that she would let me stay with her for a while. I felt too scared to spend the night on the street, and too scared to hide inside and be alone when everyone left.

The woman ahead of me had reached the *ventanilla*, and her work was being inspected by the time Ana returned.

"We're next," I said.

Ana smiled, but her face was shiny with sweat.

"Are you okay?" I asked.

She rubbed her hands together. "I'm fine . . . just fine."

We watched the *inspectora* shove the wooden scissors into each finger of the black gloves. She squeezed the handles, and the tips spread open, showing perfect stitching. Without a blink, she reached for the next glove, until three dozen gloves had passed through her hands. She wrote something in a booklet, reached into a drawer, counted money, and handed it to the worker ahead of us. Placing four more bundles in front of the woman, she yelled, "Next!"

Ana stepped forward, smiling, and still sweating. She lifted the bundle up to the counter, and I waited to hear her ask for gloves for my mother Concha. Was Ana going to produce Concha's card? Or ask me for it? I noticed my wet hands and my shaking knees, but still I waited, keeping one eye on the door. One question about Concha, and out I'd run.

I felt sweat running down my spine when the *inspectora* reached for the last dozen of Ana's gloves.

Suddenly, Ana let out a shriek and grabbed her belly with both hands. Just as I stepped back to look at her, a gush of warm, yellowish water hit the floor and splashed the people around her. All the lines broke, and people scrambled around in panic, screaming, shouting, running, pushing and shoving. A big woman in the next line pushed me until I could no longer see Ana. I heard Ana calling "Blanca!" but the crowd was too thick for me to get to her.

Someone yelled, "Call the hospital! This woman is having a baby! Stay back, she's having a baby!"

Another woman from inside the enclosure shouted, "Get back in line! Back to work! Everyone calm down!"

I watched the waves of women trying to form new lines, but the area near Ana was blocked by a circle of ladies assigned to keep others out of the way. I felt too confused to think, or to run out, so I kept backing into any space I could fit into.

A few minutes later, a loud siren blared near the factory, and two men and a woman, all dressed in white, ran in through the door with a folding bed. They ordered people out of the way and busied themselves with Ana.

In all the pushing and shoving, I ended up at the bottom of three steps leading to a partially opened door. Thinking that if I were higher up, I would be able to look down and see what was happening to Ana, I walked up the steps. I still could not see her, but I discovered that this was a storage room filled with sacks of gloves and other fabrics. A dim light hanging from the ceiling made the room cool and cozy.

It was the perfect place for me to sit and watch the commotion, then figure out what to do before dusk. If they took Ana to the hospital, I didn't want to go with her.

The two men in white came through the crowd carrying Ana away on the narrow cot. I heard her mumbling something about "Blanca," so I ran past the agitated women and caught up with her outside.

"Doña Ana," I called, "don't worry about me! I can go back by myself." She started to say something, but grabbed her belly and let out another scream.

The men were pushing her into the ambulance when she yelled, "Tell your mother I am sorry to let her down. And be careful on your way home."

I ran back inside. The place was wild now, everyone still talking and laughing about the emergency. I don't think anyone saw me go back in. Those who saw me running out must have thought I had gone with Ana, because I didn't hear anyone mention the girl named Blanca.

I found my way to a semi-dark room, higher than the workers, looking out into the lighted enclosures. I sat back on a sack of gloves and watched the people work, talk, and laugh.

Chapter Thirty-Seven

The Uncertainty

"Wake up! Wake up, whoever you are!"

The voices seemed far away. They were unfamiliar to me. I wasn't at home in my gunnysack. Was I still on a tree branch in the woods?

"Come on, golden curls, we need to go home."

I opened my eyes and saw one tall and one short figure hovering over me. I finally realized where I was and jumped off the sack, shaking and mute. The light was behind the women, and I could not see their faces. They grabbed my shoulders and pushed me back down on the sack.

"Not so fast, little one," one of them said. "First you must tell us who you are and what you are doing here."

Still mute, I looked from one set of dark eyes to another.

The taller woman brought her face close to mine. "Well, are you going to speak or not? Do you have a name? Should we call the police? Your parents must be looking for you."

"Tell us your name, dear," the shorter lady said, and I immediately thought that she was more compassionate than her companion. "You need to go home. Your parents must be worried about you. And we have family waiting for us." She looked at the taller lady. "Maybe we should call somebody."

My brain woke up enough to know what had been said. "No,

please. Don't call anyone. Can you let me sleep here tonight? I have no place to go."

The tall one shook her head firmly. "Sleep here? Of course not. This is a warehouse, not a bedroom. You must leave at once, before I notify the authorities." She stepped back, and I realized that no help would come to me from her.

The short lady came closer. "We're still waiting for you to tell us why you are here."

"I got lost and fell asleep. But I can leave first thing in the morning."

The tall lady reached for my arm. "No, you'll leave now! Come, I'll show you the door."

"I can find it by myself," I said, stepping down from the sack. As I walked away, I decided to try my luck one more time, counting on the shorter woman who hadn't been as harsh as the tall one. "You wanted to know my name? It's Sabina." My voice echoed in the huge room, which had earlier been filled with many women and voices; now it stood quiet and dark. "I came here looking for a job and fell asleep waiting for the owner. Please let me explain. I have no place else to go." By now my voice was cracking and my knees shaking.

"Okay, Miss Sabina, you have thirty seconds," the tall lady said. "So start talking."

Glancing around the half-lit room, I wondered how to begin my explanation without saying that I was running away from home.

"Miss Sabina, are you stalling for time? If you don't hurry, I'll have to call the police." The tall one stepped back, hands on her hips. "Do you understand?"

"Please don't call anyone. I'll explain. Then I'll go, if you still want me to. I'm running away from home, from my parents." Suddenly my throat was blocked, and breathing became difficult, so my words came out in sobs. "My parents drink and beat us—that's why I ran. See these cuts and scratches? I got them running through the jungle—running so fast I nearly drowned in the river. We live at the bottom of two mountains. It took me two days to get here. All I want is to find a job in this factory, because I know how to sew gloves. I can make four to six gloves a day, depending on the fabric and style. So can I please talk with the owner? It will be awful if I end up sleeping out in the street." I was hyperventilating, but I could see hope in the short lady.

"You are a foolish girl!" the tall lady said, squinting at me. "There's no owner here. I am the manager, and this is my assistant. You talk as wild as you look. I want you out of here at once!"

The short woman whispered in the other lady's ear. Then they walked away and stood under the dim light, moving their arms, scratching their heads, and walking in little circles.

Please, God! I don't want to end up on a street corner begging for pennies and being attacked by mangy dogs. I suddenly wanted to disappear.

The tall lady came forward. "You might as well save your tears. I'm not going to fall for your tricks. You should be home crying in your mother's arms."

I headed toward the door, my feet heavy, my head down. *Oh please, ladies, change your mind before I walk out that door. My dream about a better life is turning into a nightmare. This is not how it's supposed to go. The people in my dreams are as nice as my godparents.*

"Wait a minute." That was the short lady's voice.

I stopped but didn't turn.

"Come back here. I have an idea."

I turned around. "You do?"

"Wait there," she said, and the two went to a corner.

"Monica," I heard the tall woman say, "you have your family to care for. Why bother with a ragged girl?"

"She can sleep on my back porch for one night. I'll send her away in the morning."

"Listen to me, Monica. Before you do something crazy, take a look at her. Her dress is all torn and dirty, her legs and arms scratched and bruised. Where in the world has she been? You'll borrow trouble for yourself by bringing such a girl into your home."

"It'll be all right for one night," Monica insisted, patting the tall lady on the shoulder. "She can sleep on the back porch."

The tall woman came toward me. "What were you planning to do if we hadn't found you? Come back in here every night? Do you know what would've happened if we hadn't found you? Tomorrow is Wednesday. At dawn, that door will swing open and several men will come to haul those sacks out to a boat. If they had found you here, you'd be in Florida in a few days. Only God knows what would've become of you."

I looked at her and wiped my tears. They were either going to help me or throw me out. Nothing I would say would make a difference.

"It's all right, Luisa," said the one named Monica. "I'll take her with me."

Luisa rubbed the back of her neck. "I can't even think straight anymore. I'm too damn tired. It's been a long day. Do whatever you wish, Monica. Call the police, if you want to. I'll see you tomorrow." She walked back into the storage room and disappeared.

Doña Monica pulled a switch, and the room turned as dark as the jungle. "I'll put you up for the night. Come this way, girl."

I followed her up and through the storage room, where she flipped another switch and darkened that room as well. Doña Luisa had left a door open. It led to a carport with two dark-colored cars in it. Luisa was sitting in one of them. When we walked out, she called Doña Monica to her car window, and the two talked in soft voices.

Fear crept up again. *Doña Luisa might still convince Doña Monica not to help me. If she does, I'll stay in this dark carport and try my luck again tomorrow. One way or another, I'll manage to survive. If I don't, at least I'll know that I tried.* One minute I wanted to run and never stop; in the next minute I felt afraid of the street beyond the alley. There were some dim lights a little ways down the street, and a lot of darkness in between.

A dog, tired and limping, came out from the shadows, nose

to the ground, and crossed the alley without even looking our way. I wondered if it had a home. Maybe no one wanted it when it was young, and that was how it ended up in the streets. If I had a home of my own, I'd take the poor little dog in. I wondered why God made children powerless, and why it took so long to grow up.

Doña Monica got into the other car, told me to sit in the back seat, and then started the engine. A panel near the steering wheel lit up, and I saw a display of red and green numbers. Two bright lights outside the car shone on the concrete wall as the car rolled back into the alley. As I stared at the two lighted spots on the wall, amazed that a car would have built-in lights, Doña Luisa backed her car into the alley, where she turned left. Doña Monica turned right.

I had always wondered what a city looked like at night, so I looked out one window and then the other. I could see lights shining down from high poles loaded with wires, and trees and buildings partly shaded the streets and walkways. The interior of the car was dark, and more so as we drove through shaded spots.

I found this to be very spooky, since I had never been in the back seat of a car by myself at night, and Doña Monica wasn't talking. It seemed as if a dark cloud was carrying me through shadows and lighted spots. The few people walking at the road-side flashed by quickly. The homes and buildings didn't look like those I had seen during the day.

I felt strange. Not sick . . . just lightheaded and empty, as if I knew the world was about to end and I had no one with whom to share the fear. It was an exhausting feeling, a gloomy heaviness consuming me. When I blinked, my eyelids wanted to stay closed. It seemed to me that I had arrived there with the lady named Ana not a few hours ago, but days earlier.

I could feel the floor of the car, rough and warm under my aching feet. I pulled a foot up and ran my hand over the dried skin and the cuts and scratches.

Doña Monica wasn't speaking to me, but she knew where

she was going. I, on the other hand, had no idea where she was taking me. Maybe I would have been better off sleeping behind a building or up a tree. *What if this lady is a drunk?* I would have to run again, this time from a stranger.

Another of my mother's rules came to mind: "Children speak only when spoken to." Sometimes she was nasty about it. "Children speak only when the chickens pee." It took me years to learn that chickens never peed. A kid could wait forever to ask a question.

"I'm sure glad you are not as mean as your boss," I heard myself say. Once I found my voice, I couldn't stop talking. "Would she really send me out to the street? I think you saved my life, Doña Monica. I'll never forget you for helping me when I had nowhere else to go."

She made a right turn at a light, and then said, "I am doing this to help my boss. You'll have to leave in the morning. Go back to your parents. They can't possibly be so bad."

"I'll leave in the morning. But I'll still be grateful to you, Doña Monica. You could have listened to your boss and sent me away, but you didn't. I'll never forget it."

"At least you have good manners," she said, making another turn. She made so many turns that at times it appeared that we were going back to where we had been. In the dark of night, I couldn't guess in which direction we were headed. I could only pray silently that this woman would not turn out to be a drunk, and that she would not have a drunk husband waiting for her. I couldn't imagine where I would run to if I met with an impossible situation once we reached her home.

"You sound mature," the woman said. "How old are you?"

"Fourteen." I lied. "And I'm a real hard worker. I can sew four to six gloves a day, depending on the style and fabric. I can read and write, and I know arithmetic. I know how to make my own clothes, and how to wash, mend, and iron. I can pull weeds, pick coffee berries from the trees, shell them, and roast them. I even milk cows and goats."

"Kind of small for fourteen, aren't you?" she asked.

"Yes. And my brothers and sisters are also small for their ages. You want to hear what else I know how to do?"

"I think I'm going to hear it whether I want to or not, so go ahead and tell me. I'm sure it's something I have never learned to do myself, and I'm much older than you."

I reached for the backrest of her seat and pulled myself forward. "I can make rum. Have you ever known a girl my age who knows how to make rum? I learned from my father. From the time I was about three, he took me with him to the creek, and I watched the whole process."

"I suppose you learned to drink the stuff, too." She was turning onto a narrow street, a darker and bumpier one.

"Oh no. My father warned me to never even think of tasting rum. That was something for grown-ups only. 'If I ever smell rum on your breath,' he'd say, 'I'll strip the skin off your back with my leather belt.' Think you would take a sip of rum after a warning like that?"

Doña Monica replied with another question. "Did your father ever strip the skin off your back?"

"No. But that's because I'd do anything to avoid a beating. That's how I became a good worker. He snapped his fingers, and I ran to do whatever he wanted. When he warned me not to do something, I never tried to find out what he would do if I disobeyed him."

"So why did you run away?"

"Two days ago, my father got drunk and held a sharp machete to my throat. He wanted me to count fifty-two eggs for the seventh time. I told him that one might break if I counted again. I wasn't supposed to talk back, so he threatened to cut my throat. For some reason, he didn't follow through with the threat, but I wasn't going to give him the chance to try again. I did what anyone would do. I ran." I struggled with the last words, wanting to crawl into something and cry myself to sleep. I wouldn't wake up until my twenty-first birthday, whenever that might be, three or four years before or after the actual date.

Doña Monica drove her car down a gravel driveway and under a yellowish house on concrete stilts. "Don't you think they'll come looking for you? They must be thinking that something bad has happened to you. I'd go crazy if one of my children suddenly disappeared."

"By now my parents must know I ran, because the worst thing already happened to me. What could be worse than having your father hold a machete to your throat? Why would they worry about something else happening to me?" I couldn't hold back my sobs.

Doña Monica got out of the car and opened my door. Her hands shook as she reached for my hand, asking me to step out. "What a horrible story. It's all right. Don't cry. You can stay here tonight."

I followed her up a stairway to a balcony, which ultimately led to a porch that had only three walls. She flipped a switch on the wall, and a bulb on the ceiling put out a dim, yellowish light. I saw a closed door on one of the three walls, which turned out to lead into the kitchen.

"You can sleep there for the night," she said, pointing to a long wooden bench against a wall.

"That's a lot better than the tree branch in the jungle," I said. "Thank you very much."

Without another word, Doña Monica unlocked the door to her kitchen and walked in, closing it again so quickly that all I saw inside was the corner of a white stove. A window faced the porch, but the louvers were tightly closed so I couldn't peek inside.

Feeling alone and hungry, I looked around carefully, in case I had to run. Facing the balcony, I had one wall to my right, one behind me, and the kitchen wall to my left. There wasn't anything separating the porch floor from the balcony, so I could look straight out and see the dark horizon and some small lights to my right and a few others to my left. I calculated that the dark open space straight ahead was the ocean, and wondered what kind of world existed beyond it.

The door swung open and Doña Monica came through it. "I have a blanket and some crackers and milk for you. I'm sure you must be hungry." She put the dark-colored blanket on the bench and handed me the glass and four soda crackers. "There's a latrine down there you might want to use, and a faucet where you can wash up." She flipped another switch, and a light shone on a wooden shack below the balcony. "Be sure you turn off the light afterward."

"Thank you, Doña Monica. You're a kind lady."

She nodded and went back inside.

I spread the blanket on the bench, then sat down to eat the crackers and drink the milk. This was the first time I'd had milk without coffee. It tasted delicious. When I finished, I went down to use the latrine, then washed my face, sore arms, and swollen legs under the faucet. I hurried back up to the top of the stairway and flipped off the switch.

I leaned on the railing to let the cool breeze dry the water off my skin. From there, I could see streaks of light through the closed louvers to my left. I imagined that would be Doña Monica's bedroom. *Maybe she's thinking about me, wondering why a little girl is running away from her parents. Maybe she'll still call the police. I'd better stay awake and be ready to run at the first sound of steps on the staircase. No, she wouldn't have brought me here to do that, and she wouldn't have given me a blanket, crackers, and milk.*

When the water on my skin had dried, I lay back on the hard wooden bench, pulled the blanket up to my chin, and stared at the darkness, thinking.

I must convince Doña Monica that I'm a good girl who deserves her help. When did I leave home? It seems like a long time ago. If a branch hadn't come along in the river when it did, I'd still be at the bottom of the whirlpool.

Is Papa looking for me? Please, God, don't let him show up here. And don't let Doña Monica send me away.

Chapter Thirty-Eight

Monica's Mercy

I woke up to the clinking of dishes, children's voices, and the smell of coffee and chocolate coming through the louvers. I folded the blanket and placed it on the bench, then went to look out the balcony.

The air felt cool, and the view was breathtaking. The sun was emerging from a faraway mountain, and it highlighted the treetops and the red tile roofs of homes on the hillside.

Way out there, meeting with the blue sky, was the wide spread of ocean. I had never seen anything like it before; it was an incredible scene that made me feel like flying from the balcony like a bird all the way to the water, where I would disappear so no one would ever find me. Even if I never accomplished anything else by running away, I would be satisfied that at least I had seen the ocean.

The kitchen door swung open, and Doña Monica came through with a cup of hot chocolate and a chunk of bread smeared with margarine.

"Eat this right away, and I'll give you a ride to town." As she turned to walk back inside, two small boys came running and screaming from the kitchen. Behind the boys came a girl about my age holding a hairbrush up in the air.

"Stop, you two," Doña Monica said, taking the boys in her arms. "Drop the brush, Mariana," she said to the girl.

"Tell them to stop teasing me, Mami. They took my ribbons."

"Give your sister the ribbons, boys."

"I don't have them, Mami, I swear it," said the oldest.

"Me neither," the other added.

"They don't have your ribbons," Doña Monica told the girl who stared at me with her mouth open.

"Ay, Mami, who's that?"

"That's a girl looking for work. Her name is Sabina. And we have to get going, or you'll be late for school." The four walked into the kitchen, and I sat back to eat my breakfast and to wonder what I would do in town. How would I walk into the factory looking for work when the manager had already decided that she didn't want me there?

I noticed a flower garden beyond the latrine, and another of fruits and vegetables, striving to survive among the weeds.

"I can pull all those weeds for you," I said as Doña Monica came down the stairway. "You don't have to pay me. Just let me stay here for a few days." I felt the blood drain from my face as I stood there at her mercy.

She looked at me over her shoulder as she turned to put some things in the trunk of her car. Then, with a raspy voice, she yelled, "How dare you try to manipulate me!" Her face tightened as she looked at me through squinted eyes.

"I'm sorry, Doña Monica, but I can't go home."

"Look, young lady, I'm already running late. I can't listen to you now, and I can't help you. Get in the car, if you want a ride to town."

"No, thank you, I can walk up there. And thank you for bringing me here last night." It was hard to keep from crying, as I had no idea where to go from there. I had been stupid to think that I would find someone to be kind to me.

"It's a long walk to town."

"Not for me. I have walked much farther than that."

"Well, I don't have time to argue with you." She got into her car and started the engine, her face still twisted and hard.

I followed her car up the driveway, watching the two smiling faces with dark eyes staring at me through the rear window. I couldn't see the girl. She sat up front with her mother, but I imagined her being thrilled that her mother had not helped me. I wondered if Doña Monica would ever make her children pull the weeds out of her garden. No . . . I knew her kids were too spoiled to do such work.

When they turned onto the main road, and I could no longer hear the car, I headed down toward the flower garden. Somehow, I would show this lady that I was worth helping. By the end of the day, she would be glad I had stayed around.

I found a small trowel on a shelf in the carport, and borrowed it to do a better job. I pulled crabgrass and pig vines, telling myself that this had to work. *Doña Monica will see how helpful I can be and keep me here. She can't possibly have the heart to chase me away.*

My chances of finding work at the factory didn't look so good anymore, not after meeting the cranky manager last night. It hurt to think of what would become of me. Yet, even though I had no idea of what was to come, I felt good being far away from my parents and my sister. I felt free in spite of the uncertainty.

A thick hedge of hibiscus separated this garden from the large yard of another house. I figured that no one would see me through all the bushes, and since I was down a hill and behind Doña Monica's house, no one would see me from above.

I was shortly proven wrong by a woman from the house on the other side of the hedge.

"Hey! What are you doing over there?" The high-pitched voice startled me. I remained quiet, hoping she was calling someone else.

"Hey! You with the yellow hair, what are you doing?"

"Pulling weeds." I looked, but didn't see her.

"It's about time she hired someone to clean up that mess."

I didn't answer. Maybe she would go away.

"That's not an easy job, especially with the sun cooking your back, poor girl."

When she didn't say anything else, I started thinking about how I hated working in the heat of the sun at home. This time the sun didn't seem to matter. I was working for my own reasons, could quit anytime, and could sit in the shade if I wanted to . . . and Papa wouldn't be there to hit me on the head.

I heard footsteps in gravel, and then saw a short woman with a cup in one hand and something wrapped in a white cloth in the other.

"Are you hungry? Want some coffee and sweet bread?"

It was the voice I had heard from behind the hedge. Still, I felt suspicious. Was she being kind? Or was she keeping me busy until the police showed up? I pulled weeds, watching her from the corner of my eye.

"I figured you might want to take a break and eat something. Got to be hungry working so hard."

I looked at her again and felt at ease. She seemed too friendly to be mean. She was short and stout, with kind brown eyes that closed up when she smiled. I noticed a lot of fine silver bracelets jangling from one wrist. She wasn't a poor woman. Nor was she someone who worked outdoors; her hands were small and soft, and her black shoes were clean and shiny.

"My goodness, what a great job you're doing!" Her face broke into a bright smile, and I saw two rows of small, narrow teeth, perfectly straight and white.

"Thank you," I said, taking the coffee and bread. "Why do you give me food while I'm working for someone else?"

"I just guessed you might be hungry."

"I am hungry." I sat under a poinsettia tree while the lady watched me take the first bite.

"Like it?"

"Yes I do. Do you have a lot of weeds in your garden?"

"No, I don't. I have a good gardener. I've been telling Monica that she needs someone to help her around here. The poor woman thought she could work in town and still keep up with the jobs her husband had done for years."

"Her husband got tired and stopped doing the work?"

"No. He was killed in the war a few years ago. It was the saddest thing, a good husband and father of three to die so young. And what about you? Are you from the hills? I've never seen you around here before."

"I live at the bottom of the mountain."

"That's far for someone to come to pull weeds, isn't it?"

"It is." I handed her the empty cup. "Thank you very much for the delicious bread and coffee. Now I must get back to work, since I have a lot more weeds to pull."

She took the cup and smiled, peering into my eyes. "Tell your parents that too much sun is harmful, especially to such light skin. Is your whole family blonde?"

I nodded, reaching for the trowel, then watched her walk away. She looked harmless and kind. I decided that I would go to her door if Doña Monica chased me away tonight.

As I was finishing the flower garden, Doña Monica drove into the carport.

"I knew you'd pull a trick like this!" she yelled. "I did you a favor last night, and now you're pushing yourself on me. I'm going to have the police take you away!"

"Oh please!" I begged, running to her. "Don't call anyone. I only did the weeding to repay you for putting me up last night. Please, Doña Monica, give me another chance. I can't go back to my parents. Please let me stay a few days until my cuts and scratches heal. Then I'll leave."

Doña Monica stood staring as I went on begging, reminding myself not to cry, to act mature, to be polite, to keep talking while she was still listening.

"Believe me, Doña Monica, I would not be standing here today if I had not fainted the day my father held his machete to my throat. Should I go back and let him try again?"

Doña Monica blinked, looked this way and that, scratched her head, peered at me, took a deep breath, and said nothing.

I couldn't stand the suspense, so I walked slowly to the shelf in the carport to return the trowel. Then I started walking up the driveway, tears streaming down my cheeks and gravel digging into the bottoms of my sore feet.

I sat under a tree, up on a slope near the main road, to think things out. *Maybe I should go to the woman who gave me coffee. If she doesn't help me, I'll jump into the ocean.*

Chapter Thirty-Nine

A Second Chance

I heard dogs barking behind fancy homes with flower gardens, and songs about love and broken hearts blaring from radios. I wondered if the women in those homes were cooking delicious lunches; the aroma of spices traveled with the breeze. I imagined a fine lady calling me in for lunch.

Then I heard Doña Monica's car crushing the gravel up the driveway. It slowed down as it reached the paved street, and I saw the window on the driver's side go down and her looking out of it. I pretended not to see her.

"I know you haven't gone very far, Sabina!"

She didn't sound too angry, so I waited.

"I know you heard me, Sabina. Don't pretend you didn't! So come out before I drive away."

I didn't really want her to leave, so I stepped from the shade and walked to her car window with my head down.

"Get in," she ordered. "I don't have much time."

"Did you change your mind? You're going to let me stay?" My voice shook, as I believed she had decided to keep me around. I climbed into the back seat, crossed my arms over my chest, and waited. She pointed her chin to the road and backed the car down the driveway and into the carport.

"Look," she said, taking a deep breath. "I don't want to help a girl who's running away from home. Pull the weeds, and I'll give you money for the *publico* fare. You must have uncles or grandparents who can help you. I have my own children to raise. I can't take on another responsibility."

"You can give me money if you want to, but I'm not going to my uncles. They are as bad as my parents. And my grandparents died years ago. I'll still pull your weeds. And I'll do a great job, too."

"Go," she said, and drove away. When she turned onto the paved road, I grabbed the trowel and headed down to the vegetable and fruit garden. I pulled weeds and vines from around the orange trees, the banana plants, and the sweet potato vines. There were red ants on this red earth, and they crawled and bit my feet and legs. I bore the agony, just to show this lady that I was no stranger to hard work.

I didn't want to think about Papa, but I felt his presence and heard his voice in my mind: *"Red ants in the middle of a hot day will set your skin on fire."*

I hated him for getting drunk, for being mean, for making me work so hard, for making me run away. I wanted to wish that something bad would happen to him, but I couldn't. I didn't feel love for him, either. I dreamed of going back to the farm someday to urge my brothers and sisters to run away, just to make my father regret what he had done to me. The thought was so vivid it gave me strength.

The woman from next door must have thought that I had left, because she didn't come back, though I hoped she would come with more coffee and sweet bread. When she didn't, I ate oranges and bananas from Doña Monica's trees. I took several breaks to cool off the ant bites under the faucet, and still finished before Doña Monica got home. I even swept the carport and walkway around the house while waiting for her.

When she finally drove into the clean carport with her children, the girl said, "Mami, why is that girl still here?"

"Because she needs a place to spend the night. Now go change your school clothes. All three of you, get going."

She walked up the stairway without so much as a word about the cleaning or the work I had done. Since I had never been praised for the work I did at home, it didn't bother me that Doña Monica didn't acknowledge my efforts. But her snotty daughter really bothered me. She was as repulsive as my sister Emilia, calling me "that girl" and looking at me as if I were the ugliest thing she'd ever seen. Still, I let her get away with that for fear that her mother would send me away for good.

I washed the dirt off my legs and arms under the faucet, and sat on a little slope overlooking the flower garden. The plants swayed in the breeze free of the weeds. Thoughts about the many times I had pulled weeds in the fields back home kept burdening my mind, even though I wanted to forget. I wondered which one of the kids got stuck doing my share of the work. And I wondered if anyone was still looking for me, or if they thought I'd drowned.

I pictured Papa in his hammock drinking and threatening to poison his whole family. I hoped that my disappearance would be a lesson to him and make him stop drinking and beating everyone.

The sun became a bright orange ball touching the horizon, and I was still there feeling sad. What would I do if Doña Monica didn't invite me to come up to the porch? I knew she had started dinner, because the smell of onions and garlic reached my nose, making my stomach hurt with hunger.

When the sun disappeared and the horizon turned orange, Doña Monica came out with one of her daughter's old dresses, panties, a towel, and a pair of brown shoes. She held out a piece of blue soap.

"You can bathe under that faucet and put on these clothes. It's dark now, so no one will see you. Here's a comb you can use after you wash your hair. Then come up to the kitchen. You must be hungry."

She put the brown comb on top of the folded dress and left. The comb was missing two teeth in the middle, but I was thrilled to get it. I thanked her as she walked away. She looked back with a trace of a smile.

I placed the things she gave me on the carport's railing and stuck my head under the faucet, with my dress still on. The cold water over my sun-warmed skin made me shiver as I quickly scrubbed my head, making a lot of suds that ran down my neck and inside my dress. After rinsing off the suds, I went to a corner of the carport, removed my wet dress and panties, dried myself, and put on my new clothes, which fit as if they had always been mine. The shoes were tight, but I figured it was because my feet were still swollen, and by morning they would fit better.

I rinsed my old clothes under the faucet and hung them on a line behind the latrine. Then I toweled my hair and combed it outside the carport so the breeze would dry it fast. Afterwards, I headed up the stairs, hoping that Doña Monica would let me keep my new clothes and shoes. Those new things, although they were given to me, made me feel that I was a person, too.

Doña Monica saw me walking up and held open the kitchen door. "Well, look how pretty you are!" She seemed really friendly for the first time. "Come inside and eat with us."

I walked into a beautiful kitchen filled with a spicy aroma, and watched her stir rice in a white pot. My mother had always said that white rice had to be cooked in iron pots. Anything other than iron made the rice mushy.

"Is everyone in your family blonde?" Doña Monica asked.

"No, I'm the only one."

She pulled out a chair across from her daughter and told me to sit. The girl looked me over and said, "That's my dress you're wearing, and my shoes."

"Be nice, Mariana," her mother said.

I thanked the girl anyway. "Do you want them back?"

The girl smirked. "Not after you've worn them. Have you ever eaten at a table like this? With tablecloth and all?"

"Never mind, Mariana," her mother said. "That's not important."

The girl stuck her tongue out at me.

I felt like ripping it out of her mouth, but I didn't want to risk not getting some of the food her mother had prepared. Peering into her eyes, I said, "Do you always stick out your tongue at people you've just met?"

Doña Monica turned from the stove. "Behave, Mariana, or leave this kitchen." She came forward and placed forks, spoons, and knives on the table.

As she turned away, the girl said to me, "I bet you can't eat with a fork."

"You're looking for trouble, Mariana," her mother said. "Behave yourself and go tell your brothers that dinner is ready."

Mariana turned her head toward a doorway and shouted, "Ruben and Adriano! Supper's ready!"

Doña Monica turned quickly. "Mariana! I will not have you behave this way, especially when we have a guest."

"But, Mami, she's not a guest. She's just a *jibara*."

"Go to your room, Mariana! Right now!"

Mariana pushed her chair back and stamped out into the next room.

Her mother shook her head. "Sometimes I . . ."

The two boys walked into the kitchen like little gentlemen and took their seats at the table.

Doña Monica bowed her head, and the four of us thanked God for the food, made the sign of the cross, and said, "Amen."

"It's nice to know you're Catholic, too," she said, dishing out white rice onto the boys' plates. She passed the platter to me. "Help yourself."

I took the platter hesitantly, wondering if I was supposed to eat it all. At home, we didn't eat at a table passing the food around. Whatever Mama handed to us we ate.

After the rice came a deep dish of beans in red sauce with cubes of potatoes and bell peppers. That was followed by a smaller plate of crispy *tostones* (fried plantains).

That was my first good meal since the vegetables at Marta's, and it was so delicious I wanted to inhale everything on my plate. Still, I forced myself to eat slowly, because it wouldn't be nice to appear starving.

Suddenly Doña Monica asked me a question that took my appetite away. "Sabina, yesterday at the factory, wasn't the pregnant woman who went into labor calling you Blanca? Some of the *operatoras* said that she's your mother."

"Oh no, *Señora*. I was standing next to her because we arrived together. We had met at the *publico* stop, and I thought she was calling me Blanca because I'm so white. By the time I realized that she had me confused with a girl named Blanca, she was on her way to the hospital."

Doña Monica looked straight into my eyes and said, "Your story sounds believable. You must have been practicing that speech for hours. But I don't believe it any more than I believe the story about your parents."

I felt as though something very heavy had come down on my head. I put down my fork, pushed myself back from the table, slid from the chair and, with my head down, walked out of the kitchen and onto the balcony.

I waited a few minutes, hoping that she'd change her mind and call me back in. I thought about how hard I had worked, and about how nice it had been to get the new clothes and shoes. But the fact was that she really didn't want me there.

I ran down the steps and sat at the edge of the carport, collecting my tears in my hands, wanting to drown in them. If the ocean had been closer, I would have thrown myself into it, to disappear in the waves forever.

I finally heard Doña Monica's voice. "Come back inside." She touched my shoulder. "You'll get cold out here."

I wanted to turn around and hug her, beg her to be nice to me, to like me, to believe me. Still, I sat there, waiting to hear her tell me that I didn't have to run anymore.

"Come back and finish your dinner. It's not only that I find your story hard to believe. It's that I have my own problems, and

I can't get involved with a runaway girl. You must admit that you are a runaway."

I dried my tears with my skirt, stood up slowly, and followed her up the stairs. "I am running away. And I don't blame you for not believing me. My mother never believed me, either. That's one of the many reasons why I ran away."

"Well, you'll be glad to know that I talked with Doña Luisa this afternoon, and she told me to bring you to the factory tomorrow. If anyone can help you, she's the one. That is, if you are sure that your parents aren't going to come around looking for you."

We were in the kitchen by then, and I wanted to ask her why she hadn't told me that earlier, instead of making me want to jump into the ocean and drown. But I said, "No. My parents think the river washed me away. That's what they believed when other people's kids disappeared from our hills."

"When children disappear, the parents assume that the river carried them away, and they leave it at that? The authorities don't come around to investigate?"

"Where I come from, nobody ever comes around."

"That's the craziest thing I have ever heard. Someday I'm going to have you tell me more about those hills of yours. But for now, just sit down and eat." She dumped my cold food into a waste-basket and replaced it with warmer food.

"I don't feel hungry anymore."

"Eat what you want and leave the rest." She went to a counter that had a white sink, turned a faucet, and began to wash the dishes. I thought about how we washed dishes back home, in a gourd-shell of water with ashes in place of soap.

I took a forkful of food, and my appetite came back.

Still, I felt bad that Doña Monica hadn't believed me earlier, so I didn't let her know that I found her cooking delicious.

I checked out the kitchen, from the white metal cabinets to the red linoleum on the floor, and the circular tube of light up on the ceiling.

I wondered if Doña Monica was rich, and what she was

thinking. She scrubbed plates, cups, and forks, rinsing everything under running water without saying a word. My eyes traveled down her back, from the top of her curly head of black hair, past her small waistline, her hips, the hem of her lavender dress, her slim legs, and finally her white sandals. I considered her a rich lady, pretty, smart, and powerful because she was a grown-up.

I listened for her children, but did not hear them. I wanted to ask her if they had already gone to bed, but I was a child, a *jibara* from the hills, ragged, bruised, unloved, and unwanted. I suddenly felt sick.

"Doña Monica, may I go to the porch? I'm awfully tired."

She turned from the sink and looked at me as if she had forgotten that I was there. "Oh yes, Sabina, you have every right to be tired after all the work you did." She turned back to the sink. "You did a very good job. Thank you. It's something I enjoy doing myself, but with my job and three children, I don't have time to pull weeds."

I nodded as I stood up, glad that she had finally mentioned the work, but still feeling hopeless. Then I saw the girl standing in a doorway.

"Mami, does that mean you're going to let her stay?"

"No, it doesn't, Mariana," Doña Monica said, turning from her dishes. "Did you finish your homework?"

Mariana made a face at her mother and walked away.

"I apologize for my daughter. She can be very rude."

"No need for apology, *señora*. Thank you." I closed the door behind me and went to my bench and blanket.

Chapter Forty

At the Factory

I lay on the hard bench with my new clothes and shoes still on, and listened to the sound of running water and the rattling of dishes and spoons on the other side of the wall.

Doña Monica apologized for her spoiled daughter. My mother would have slapped me for a lot less than rudeness. But Doña Monica knows where her daughter is. My mother is probably wondering how one of hers disappeared.

Warm tears ran down my face, for I really did not like to cause my mother any pain. I felt a hollow space in my chest, a desperate need to look through a magical window that would allow me to see what was happening back home. Were my parents looking for me? Crying for me? And were they where I pictured them: Papa in his hammock, and Mama at the *fogón*?

Tomorrow. I must think about tomorrow. Doña Monica is taking me to the factory. Doña Luisa might be able to help me. I must think about tomorrow . . .

*   *   *

My first thought the next morning was of Doña Luisa. *She might help me, but she might not. If she decides not to help me, will Doña Monica bring me back here again?*

I went to the balcony and watched the sun come up, its rays spreading over the hillside like a golden blanket, turning the dewdrops into a glistening display all the way to the ocean.

I wanted to feel excited about being near the ocean—the place I had often dreamed of—but the fear of not knowing what lay ahead was too great.

Finally, I heard voices inside the house. Doña Monica called me to come inside for a cup of chocolate. "We're running late this morning," she said, holding the door open for me. "Did I tell you that Doña Luisa wants me to bring you to the sewing factory? Come, Mariana! We're running late!"

Doña Monica didn't wait for answers. She moved as fast as she talked, her dress moving the kitchen air, her shoes tip tapping on the floor. She placed five cups of steaming chocolate and a plate of sweet bread on the table.

"Come, you three! It's getting late!"

The two boys walked in wearing ironed outfits, their hair neatly combed, and they were smiling. They pulled out their chairs slowly and sat like little gentlemen.

Then Mariana barged in, stamping her feet, with two bushy pigtails bouncing at the back of her head and an ugly grin across her face. She pulled out her chair so hatefully that the floor screeched.

"Mami, why does Luisa want you to bring her that girl?"

"I don't know, Mariana. Eat your breakfast. It's late."

For Doña Monica and her children, breakfast was a regular routine. They probably thought it was for me, too, but in fact this was my first breakfast ever. I remembered my mother saying that only rich people ate *desayuno* (breakfast). The poor had to settle for a cup of coffee with a few drops of milk, if they were lucky enough to own a cow or a goat.

I didn't share that thought with Doña Monica and her children. Instead, I ate quietly, and glanced from one pair of brown eyes to another.

When everyone finished, Doña Monica gathered the cups

and plates and carried everything to the sink. "Now you three run in and brush your teeth, fast, and hurry to the car," she said, then followed her running children out of the kitchen.

I went to the porch, got my old dress and panties, then waited at the bottom of the steps. Soon I heard the kitchen door open and saw the children run down the steps, the boys leading with Mariana behind them, swinging the hem of her skirt as if to let me know that she was better than I.

Doña Monica was the last to come out. "You can sit with the boys." She motioned to the back seat and hurried to the front. Mariana had already claimed the passenger seat, which was okay because it kept her away from me.

While Mariana chattered in the front seat with her mother, the two boys played with each other. One stood his fingers like soldiers on a notebook, and the other boy shot the soldiers with a thumb and index finger. "Pow, pow," they whispered, then giggled. They were nice boys.

I looked out the window and saw lines of homes that had been painted, some blue, some pink, and other colors, each with balconies and flower gardens. I saw a girl sweeping a walkway in front of a house, and Emilia flashed through my mind. A man standing outside a closed building, wearing dark trousers, white shirt, and a white hat, reminded me of Papa. I shivered, then wondered where I would go if Doña Luisa didn't give me a job.

The narrow road widened as we came closer to the city. I thought of Ana, and felt guilty that I had forgotten about her. Meeting her that day had made it possible for me to reach the city. I wondered if she was still in the hospital, and what I should do if she happened to be at the factory.

We passed by the plaza, where a man seated on a concrete bench read a newspaper. Then we came up to the zone where the public cars dropped off and picked up passengers. The image of my father flashed through my mind again. I felt a sudden urge to run again.

"You can get out here, Sabina," Doña Monica said as we

reached the factory. "Go inside. Doña Luisa should be there waiting. Tell her I'm taking my children to school and will return shortly."

I nodded, but I couldn't find a word to say to her. My mouth felt dry, and chills ran up and down my skin. This was probably my last chance. *Where will I go from here?*

I watched her drive away, and then I looked at the building. It stood partially in the shade and quiet. I walked slowly through the wide door. The large room with the enclosures was ghostly, dark, and cool. I pictured the lines of women I had seen two days earlier.

I saw the door to the back room and shivered, remembering Doña Luisa saying that I'd end up in a place called Florida if the men who came for the sacks of gloves found me there.

A woman's voice startled me. "Come up here."

I looked up and saw Doña Luisa in the area above the enclosures. Her tone wasn't friendly, so I waited.

"I'm up here, girl. Come right up!"

Please, Lord, help this lady like me. I don't know where I can go from here. I trembled as I walked up the steps.

"Good morning," I said at the door, trying to sound like a grownup.

Doña Luisa didn't look like the lady I had met earlier. Her hair seemed more red than brown, tied back in a bushy tail, and her face looked plain and pale.

She sat behind a desk and pointed to a chair across from her. "Have a seat. I need to ask you some questions." Without looking at me, she shuffled some papers, filled a jar with pencils, and piled up some notebooks.

"I'll answer your questions the best I can," I said, politely and hopeful.

Doña Luisa straightened her back. "My assistant tells me that I should give you a job. She says you are a good worker, and very bright."

"I'm glad she said something nice about me."

She pushed back her chair, and her small, dark eyes scanned my face. "You look human today. And what beautiful hair you have. Is everyone in your family blonde?"

"No. I'm the only blonde."

She leaned forward over her desk. "So, you're running away from home and looking for work in the city?"

"Yes."

"You're too young to live alone. What are you, ten? Twelve?"

"I am fourteen. Small for my age, but I know how to sew gloves and dresses. And I know how to embroider roses like the one on your blouse, although I would have made it yellow, which shows prettier than red on a pink blouse, and I can even make better leaves than those."

Doña Luisa looked down at the three green leaves and red rose over her left breast. "I made the rose," she said, her chin still down and a roll of skin bulging over the collar. "*Mi sirvienta* (my maid) embroidered the leaves. Embroidery is one of the few things Manuela can't do well."

"I'm also good at arithmetic. I can add, subtract, divide, and multiply. I can even work on a farm. I know how to prepare the soil, plant beans and other vegetables. Except for going to school half days for three years, I have worked like a grownup all my life."

Doña Luisa raised her eyebrows, then squinted. "Where did you go to school?"

"In Perchas, for only three years. Then the school closed. Teachers didn't like to go that far into the countryside."

"What will you do if your parents come looking for you?"

"They will not look for me this far away from home. They think I drowned in the river. But if by chance they do come this far, I'll run into the ocean rather than go back to them."

"So you hate your parents?"

"No, I don't hate them. What I hate is their drunkenness and the beatings."

"What makes your parents so mean?"

"The rum Papa brews near the creek."

"*Ah, ron cañita.* Making rum is illegal, isn't it?"

"The police don't go that far back into the mountains."

Doña Luisa placed both hands on her desk, fingertips touching, and stared at them.

I waited, my own hands sweating in my lap. Then the click of high-heels coming across the big room broke the silence. I saw Doña Monica arrive at the office door.

"Monica," Doña Luisa said, "take her to the workroom and give her a sewing and math test." She went back to her papers without another word to me.

Doña Monica took me through a long, dark hallway to a large room that had two windows facing a narrow street. She gave me one glove to sew and wrote six math problems on a sheet of white paper for me to solve. She said she would be back soon, and then she left.

I looked around the room before starting the work, and saw three tables, four chairs at each table, and a lot of scraps of fabric and pieces of thread on the wood floor. I saw a black porcelain cat in a corner, staring at me. Mama always said that black cats meant bad luck.

I shook the thought out of my head and started on the math problems. When I finished them, I went to work on the glove. It was different than any I had done before, but I figured it out and was almost finished when Doña Monica came in. She checked the math problems, and then the glove with the long wooden finger.

"Perfect stitches," she said. "Someone taught you well. Was it your mother?"

"No, a friend of my parents."

"Good work," she said, smiling, "on both the math and the sewing. Wait here for Doña Luisa."

I didn't mind waiting then. With a huge bubble inside my chest, I looked up to the white ceiling and whispered, "Thank you, thank you, thank you."

Doña Luisa walked in looking a lot prettier, freshly made up with rouge and lipstick. Her hair was in a roll at the back of her head, and a wreath of tiny pink flowers circled the roll.

Taking the paper and glove from the table, she switched her gaze from one to the other. "This is good work." She studied the work for another moment. "I'm going to help you, but if your parents come around, you'll have to leave. You may work better than any fourteen-year-old I've ever seen, but you are still a child." She pulled out a bundle of twelve ready-cut glove samples from a shelf and said, "See if you can figure these out."

Doña Luisa left the room before I had finished unwrapping the package.

Chapter Forty-One

The Linereses

The twelve gloves were of different styles. They would be handed out to the sewers as samples. I figured out two right away and finished both before noon. Doña Luisa and Doña Monica came in and inspected the gloves.

"Perfect stitching," said Doña Luisa.

"Work of an expert," Doña Monica added.

I let out a sigh of relief and couldn't hold back a smile.

The two ladies didn't say that I had a job, but they shared their lunch with me. They cut open a loaf of bread and stuffed it with cheese and ham, then cut it in three equal pieces. It was the first time I had ever eaten cheese and ham on bread, and it was delicious.

As we ate, the ladies asked me more questions about my family and about why I had come to this particular city.

I told them the truth about why I ran away, and that I had come to their town because of the sewing factory. I also told them that I hoped to go back to school part time, and someday return to the hills to rescue my brothers and sisters.

"If things were so bad in your family, how come no one else has run away?" Doña Monica asked.

I felt ashamed and stupid, but said nothing.

"Some children are easier to brainwash than others," Doña

Luisa said. "This little girl is brighter and stronger than her brothers and sisters. That isn't uncommon. Every family has one child who is different from the others."

"I know you're right, Luisa, but what about the mother? Why hasn't she run from that horrible man and his rum shack?"

The conversation went on between the two ladies as I sat there, eating and looking at one and then the other. Doña Luisa had suddenly taken my side. It sounded wonderful, but I couldn't understand the sudden change.

"A woman can find herself trapped in a marriage," she said, "and since she feels she has nowhere to run, she takes her frustration out on her children. It's unfair to the poor children, but it's true." I heard compassion in Doña Luisa's voice, even though her words were directed to Doña Monica.

The two stayed quiet for a moment, as if searching their minds for answers.

Finally Doña Luisa turned to me. "I may be making a big mistake, but I'm going to take you home with me. I'm going to trust that you're telling the truth, just to give you a chance. I know what it's like to live with drunken parents. But if your father shows up looking for you, you'll have to leave. I don't need any more problems in my life."

I sat staring at her, speechless. The manager of the sewing factory was taking me to her home? Now I felt positive that God loved me. I didn't even wonder where Doña Luisa lived or how she would treat me once I got there. I just looked at her and at Doña Monica, who sat smiling and nodding.

"Time to get back to work," Doña Luisa said. She got to her feet and left the room.

Doña Monica started out, and then stopped at the door. "I talked her into giving you a chance. You'd better be telling the truth about your parents. I want no regrets."

"I'm not lying," was all I could say.

"We'll see," she said and walked out.

I sat there, staring at the closed door. *What if Papa knows*

*more about the mountains and this city than I think he does—
and somehow figures out that I didn't drown, but ran away
instead?*

The thought was so painful, I could hardly breathe. Then I
saw the unmade gloves and decided not to let the fear of Papa
stop me from trying to do the best I could with what I had accomplished so far. I would still be careful, and I would look around
and over my shoulders. But I would not allow myself to live in
fear that he would catch up with me.

I decided to go to the washroom before getting back to work
on the gloves. There were two women using the toilets, so I got to
see them reach up and pull the chain. I heard a lot of water
rushing down the pipe, dashing around inside the toilet and gurgling away. At last I figured out the use of the wooden tank without
embarrassing myself by asking someone how to flush a toilet. I
saw this as something new I had just learned, and I hoped to
someday tell my sister about it.

Feeling good and sure of myself, I returned to the room upstairs, pulled a chair close to the window, and began to work on
the third glove. I made four of them that afternoon, which Doña
Luisa thought was remarkable. Making six gloves in a day, all of
a different style, was a record even for an adult woman, she said.

I didn't feel intimidated by Doña Luisa by the time we left
the factory at sunset, even though she had me sit in the back
seat. She and Doña Monica stood at the carport talking before
getting into their cars. I knew the talk was about me.

She followed Doña Monica out of the alley and onto the street.
Then, beyond the plaza, she went one way and Doña Monica
another. I felt something—maybe fear or sadness, or both. I wasn't
sure. Or maybe it was that the road Doña Luisa turned into was
dark, and it curved like a snake under a canopy of trees. Her
car's engine roared as she maneuvered the curves, and the headlights shone onto the street and quickly moved to the banks, as if
they were searching for something.

I had one scary thought after another. *What if Doña Luisa is taking me to the bottom of a hill, to a houseful of mean children? Maybe she has a drunken husband. She might be a drunk herself. She's not talking. Is she thinking? Is she wondering what to do with me?*

I had to break the painful silence. "Doña Luisa, do you live far from Doña Monica?"

"Not too far. Monica lives over there." She pointed to her right, but I saw only darkness. Then we emerged from the trees into a clearing. The headlights shone on an incline downward, and I saw a huge open space in front of us.

"The ocean! You live near the ocean?" I couldn't contain myself.

"Yes, I live near the ocean," Doña Luisa said. "You've seen it before, haven't you?"

"Only twice," I said, leaning forward. "From the *publico* the day I arrived in town, and from Doña Monica's balcony."

"You'll see it better from my house," she said, turning right onto a narrower road that cut across the hillside. The houses there were farther apart, and I saw them only because of their lights. Looking out the window to my left, I saw the line where the water met the horizon. I could hear the exciting sound of waves pounding against the earth at the foot of the hill.

With the bending in and out of the curving road, a big white house with brighter lights kept coming in and out of view. As we came closer, Doña Luisa slowed down and followed a driveway lined with bougainvilleas. A husky man with a dark mustache and a brilliant smile opened a black iron gate.

"*Gracias*, Carlos," she said, and drove down, steering the car around the house and pulling in under it. "I have some bags in the trunk," she said to Carlos, who had followed the car. "Please bring them up." She handed him the keys and motioned for me to follow her up a winding stairway with a black iron railing.

A stocky woman dressed in blue with a white apron and dark-framed glasses opened a door, and we stepped into a kitchen filled with a spicy aroma.

"Manuela, this is the girl I told you about. She'll be staying with us for a while. Her name is Sabina. Please take her downstairs. Have her shower and change into these clothes." She handed the bag to Manuela and walked across a red, shiny floor.

"This way, Sabina," Manuela said, as if a girl coming to stay a few days was routine. "What beautiful hair she has," she told Carlos as she walked past him. He nodded.

I followed her downstairs, my hands sweating and with a knot in my stomach. Too much was happening at once, and I had to fight against panic. We walked through a dark hallway, passed two closed doors, and came to a small room that had only one small window with louvers and dead bugs stuck on the screen. A plastic yellow curtain hung in a corner of the room, and a rusty pipe with a faucet coming through a wall was the shower. Behind another yellow curtain, I saw a white toilet under a wooden box.

"This faucet makes a loud noise when you turn it," Manuela said. "And this chain gets stuck sometimes. But keep pulling until it works." She smiled at me, which made me feel much better. "Gee, I love your hair. Is your whole family blonde?"

"No, I'm the only one," I said, and laughed for the first time since I had been on the run.

"What's so funny?"

"That's the same question everyone keeps asking me."

She giggled. "Well, you have beautiful hair. Can you find your way back upstairs when you're finished? I've got to go serve dinner."

I told her that I could, and thanked her for being nice.

She giggled as she went down the hallway while I stood at the door watching her. I wondered how much Doña Luisa had told her and Carlos. I felt sure that Manuela and Carlos liked me. Better yet, I felt sure that Doña Luisa was rich. Not only was she the manager of a factory, but she had a car, a big home, and Manuela and Carlos working for her.

I felt overwhelmed with joy and fear mixed together. Then I felt an urge to see Emilia and tell her about all the things that had happened to me. Of course, she would never believe me. I couldn't blame her, since nobody else would, either. Even I could not believe that I had any right to be so lucky. Everything that had happened to me in only a few days seemed incredible and frightening.

I pulled the old chain and then jumped, startled when the water rushed into the toilet like the waterfall back home. I was still shaking when I got into the shower, then I shivered because the water was cold. After the shower, I pulled a beautiful dress and panties out of the bag. I remembered seeing Doña Monica giving this bag to Doña Luisa in the carport at the factory. I wondered if Mariana knew she had just lost another dress and panties.

The dress was pink and soft, with a small print and buttons down the back, and the white panties were almost new, with lace around the legs. I had never had panties with lace before. I combed my hair with the comb Doña Monica had given me, and whirled in front of the mirror. I looked beautiful! Then I opened the door, looked into the hallway left and right, and walked as fast as I could past the two closed doors and up the stairway.

Manuela must have heard me coming, because she opened the door, still giggling, and told me I would have supper with her and her husband. "Sit here," she said, pulling a black chair to a white metal table.

Carlos walked in from another room and sat at the head of the table. "Doña Luisa said your name is Sabina? Mine is Carlos." He extended his hand. "You are new in the city?"

I took his rough hand and said yes, wondering how many more questions I would have to answer. Manuela put three plates of rice with red beans and chunks of beef on the table.

"We say grace," she said. "Do you?"

I nodded, and we bowed our heads, thanking God for our food. Silently, I thanked God for everything else, too.

During the meal, Carlos and Manuela only asked a few questions. Did I have a middle name? How old was I? Had I ever before been to Mayaguez?

I answered their questions, ate, and looked around. The kitchen was even prettier than Doña Monica's. The floor was red and shiny, and the ceiling, the cabinets, and the two sinks were white. A long countertop matched the floor. And above the sink was a large window facing west.

"Can you see the ocean from that window?" I asked.

"Miles and miles of it," Manuela said. "You can see it in the morning. It's too dark now. Have you ever been to the ocean?"

"No."

"We'll take you there someday," Carlos said.

"You will? Thanks!" They smiled at each other, and I felt convinced that they did like me.

Doña Luisa walked into the kitchen. "We enjoyed our dinner very much, Manuela. Only you can prepare such delicious beans." She opened the refrigerator and took something out. "Manuela, when Sabina's finished eating, please show her to the balcony." With that, she left the kitchen.

Following Manuela to the balcony a few minutes later, I felt as though I was walking through a dream. We walked through a room where there was a huge table wearing a white lace cloth that draped around it like a full skirt on a lady. I counted eight black, glossy chairs with red velvety seats around the table. Two plates smeared with red sauce and food pieces had been left on the table. Next to the plates, I saw two drinking glasses with some water still in them. Hanging from the ceiling, a lamp shaped like a crown with glass leaves shone down and made the water glasses, smeared plates, spoons, and forks sparkle like dewdrops in the morning sun.

I concluded that Doña Luisa had a husband, and that they were truly rich. I didn't belong in a place like this.

As we reached the balcony, I smelled the ocean and heard its waves pounding. Then I saw Doña Luisa rocking back and forth on a chair that had long, pointy wooden runners. The light bulb from the balcony's ceiling made her hair seem more red and her dark eyes twinkly.

"Pull out that chair and sit down." She pointed to a bamboo chair in the corner. "It's heavy, so you'd better drag it."

It made the black and white tile floor squeak, so I stopped.

"It's all right, go ahead and drag it," she said. Although her eyes appeared cheerful, she seemed rather unfriendly.

I sat in the squeaky chair and waited for her to speak. Then I heard a strange sound in the dining room, and turned. I saw Carlos pushing an old man in a chair with wheels, a blue blanket draped over the man's legs.

"*Querido*," said Doña Luisa as they reached the balcony. "This is the young lady I spoke to you about. Her name is Sabina."

The man smiled, reaching for my hand. "Felipe Linares."

I took his hand, and nearly fainted. His smile was warm and friendly, and his eyes were duplicates of my godfather's eyes. I felt sure that this man was going to like me.

"You are right, *Querida*," he said. "She does resemble Teresita. Please sit down, child. Tell us about yourself."

I took back my hand and sat down, still speechless, unable to look away from his kind eyes. He reached into his shirt pocket, pulled out a pair of black-framed glasses, and put them on, looking me over again.

"Yes, *Querida*, she does look a lot like Teresita."

"Teresita was our daughter," said Doña Luisa, her voice trailing off.

"*Was* your daughter?" My voice shook.

"She died three years ago," Don Felipe answered.

That really spooked me. "I am so sorry," I managed to say, in spite of the chilling feeling spreading through me.

"So you ran away from your parents?" Don Felipe asked.

"Yes, sir, and I almost drowned in the river. I even got lost in a jungle and had to sleep up on a tree branch."

The couple looked at each other, and Doña Luisa said, "I think she's tired, *Querido*. She's a hard worker. Why don't you talk with her tomorrow?"

He nodded. "Yes, of course. She should get some rest."

Doña Luisa called Manuela and told her to show me to a room where I could sleep. I said goodnight to the couple and thanked them for taking me in.

They were right: I felt tired. But the uneasiness I had about Doña Luisa had disappeared. I felt that she liked me more than she had shown. It felt good to be liked and helped, but I wondered why strangers were kinder to me than family.

Maybe I would wake up and find out that this was all a dream. But if it were real, someday I'd want to tell Emilia and our parents all about everything I had experienced.

Manuela took me downstairs again, to a small room next to the shower. The door squeaked when she pushed it open, and the air inside smelled musty. She flipped a switch on the wall, but the dim light bulb hanging from the ceiling made little difference. She cranked open a small louvered window, and the outside air came in lazily.

"Leave the door open so the musty smell will clear," she said, pulling a narrow bed away from the wall. She took a white sheet out of a box and spread it over the thin mattress.

"I can do that," I offered. "You're probably tired."

"No, I'll do it. But you're right, I am tired." She dropped the sheet and backed away.

"I can help you anytime you have a lot of work to do, if Doña Luisa lets me stay here."

Manuela smiled. "Thanks. She'll let you stay. Don't worry. She's a good-hearted woman."

I kept the light on after Manuela had gone. I sat on the bed, leaning against the bamboo headboard and staring at the walls. The yellow paint was peeling off, hanging like dry skin after a bad sunburn. The concrete floor was stained, and the round straw mat in front of the bed was badly worn.

Still, this was the nicest bedroom I had ever slept in. Thoughts of Emilia and Mama came to mind. It would be nice if they were worrying about me. I prayed that by now Papa thought of me as dead, and would never, never show up here.

*　　*　　*

I awoke to the sounds of footsteps and voices somewhere outside the room, becoming clearer as they came closer. Daylight streamed through the louvers, and branches brushed back and forth on the window.

My heart thumped. I noticed that the light bulb had gone out. Something wasn't right, and it took me a few moments to realize where I was. I heard the voices again.

"She looks like Teresita, but she isn't her. You must remember that." I recognized that as Manuela's voice.

"I know she isn't Teresita. No one can take her place. I am not foolish enough to think otherwise." That was Doña Luisa's voice.

"I just don't want to see you hurt again." Manuela's voice faded away, and a door opened and closed. Then I heard a car start and roar away.

"She looks like Teresita," Manuela had said. I look like Teresita? Is that why Doña Luisa decided to help me?

I jumped out of bed, smoothed down my dress, opened the door slowly to look into the half-dark hallway, and hurried to the shower room. I went upstairs after freshening up, and found Manuela in the kitchen. As she opened the door, I saw magic everywhere. Everything looked nicer and brighter than it had the night before.

I looked out the kitchen window. "Is that the ocean? My Lord! I had no idea! All that water!"

Manuela grinned, her eyes like shiny black marbles. "Your first real look at the ocean, bless your heart. How about some hot cocoa and a doughnut? Doña Luisa left you some gloves to sew. She'll come for you at noon."

From the breakfast table, I saw brilliant red hibiscus, yellow chrysanthemums, pink carnations, and other flowers I had never seen before. "This must be the most beautiful place in the whole world!"

Manuela chuckled. "You went to sleep right away."

"How do you know?"

"I stopped in on the way to my room. You had fallen asleep sitting up with the light on."

"Wasn't the door locked?"

"It was, but I have a key."

That scared me. I slept so soundly that I hadn't heard her come in? "I'll sleep with one eye open from now on."

Manuela laughed. "You don't have to. I'll stay out of your room from now on."

My room?

"You can sew on the balcony," Manuela said. "I have to wash the kitchen floor."

"Want me to help you?"

"You're very sweet, thank you, but you'd better start on your sewing. Luisa will be back before you know it."

I thanked her for the breakfast, took the gloves, and walked through the dining room. My eyes went everywhere. Not even in my wildest dreams had I hoped to one day be walking through a place of shining floors, with the morning sun coming through the louvers, highlighting the paintings on the creamy white walls. This was much too good, so soon after years of existing in the mud and thorns.

When I reached the door to the balcony, I drew in my breath. The view of the ocean was the same as I had seen from the kitchen, but more spectacular. The houses left and right of the balcony were far apart, with trees between them. But I could still see the red roofs, which reminded me of my old school. The blue sky was dotted with fluffy white clouds over the ocean, some shaped like poodles and others like angels with wings. Below the balcony, I saw a field of fruit trees and banana plants that stretched all the way to a narrow plain of sea bushes and vines. I looked as far as my eyes could see, and could not believe the beauty. I wanted to live the rest of my life in a place like this.

I sat in the bamboo chair and began sewing the gloves, taking in quick glimpses of the ocean, afraid it would disappear if I didn't look at it.

I heard the sound of Don Felipe's chair coming down the hallway, with Carlos pushing it. They both smiled and said good morning as they passed the balcony on their way to the dining room. I heard the clinking of forks and knives, and knew Don Felipe was having his breakfast.

A while later, he wheeled himself onto the balcony. "Now I get to visit with you before Luisita comes back," he said.

I had made up my mind to answer any questions he asked, but his questions weren't about me.

"Do you ever stare at the clouds to find different images?"

"All the time," I said. "Watching the clouds is one of my favorite things to do."

"I didn't appreciate clouds as a young boy," he said, a little wistfully. "But since I've been in this chair, I have discovered the beauty in them."

I wanted to know why he was in a wheelchair, but I didn't want to embarrass him by asking.

"Maybe I should learn to sew gloves," he said with a laugh, as if to keep the conversation going. "It would be another way of passing the time."

"Yes, and you'd poke your fingers a lot. But I'll teach you, if you really want to learn."

He laughed again. "Thank you. I'll let you know when I'm ready."

This was the first time I had ever talked with an older person for more than just a few seconds. It was the beginning of a close relationship with a man who became a true father figure to me.

Don Felipe and I talked until Doña Luisa returned. Manuela had walked back and forth past the balcony, peeking in with a smile, and Carlos had wheeled Don Felipe to the bathroom twice, always bringing him back to the balcony. I finished two gloves and started on the third throughout our exchange of the things we enjoyed doing.

"Sounds like you're having a good time, *Querido*," said Doña Luisa, joining us at the balcony.

"Yes, *Querida*. This young lady is a pleasure."

"I'm glad," she said, and winked at me.

I felt good knowing that I had brought someone happiness. And I loved hearing the way the couple talked to each other, calling each other *Querido* and *Querida*, which meant Dear, an expression of love. My parents called to each other with words like, "Hey you!" They referred to each other when speaking to us children as "your father" and "your mother."

I went back to the factory with Doña Luisa after lunch, and we didn't return until after 8:00. I found out that Fridays would be the longest days because of all the cleaning and organizing after the other workers left. Doña Luisa, Doña Monica, and I were the only ones there for the last two hours. During that time, the two women agreed to let me do the little jobs they felt too old and too tired to do.

I knew they were trying me out, but I did everything they asked of me, and stood ready for their next request.

Chapter Forty-Two

Who's Teresita?

On Saturday morning, I helped Manuela with the wash while Doña Luisa and Carlos took Don Felipe to the hospital for some treatment. We washed the clothes with a bar of blue soap in a metal tub that had been placed on a sturdy bench under a mango tree.

"I never washed clothes in a tub before, especially with a board to scrub the clothes on," I said as Manuela gazed at my busy hands.

"You washed over a rock in the river?"

"Over a rock in the creek, with a little piece of soap."

Manuela smiled. "I thought you lived near the river."

"Yeah, but we weren't allowed to wash in the river. That was where men bathed, and we might see them naked." That made Manuela laugh, and I felt close to her.

We washed, wrung out the soapy water, rinsed twice, wrung out that water, and hung everything out to dry on lines—not the bushes as we had done at home. By the time we finished with the dark clothes, the sheets and towels were dried. Manuela showed me how everything had to be folded to fit in the shelves. I watched and copied her carefully, but never told her that we didn't have sheets, towels, or shelves back home.

We carried the linen to the shelves upstairs, where family

pictures adorned the hallway. I saw a picture of Don Felipe and Doña Luisa standing with a little girl between them. They were smiling, and the girl looked like me, if I were dressed up and had ribbons in my hair.

"She was killed in a car crash when she was only ten," Manuela said. "But don't mention it to Doña Luisa. She'll tell you about it someday. She loves to talk about her only child. It saddens her, but she enjoys remembering."

"She was in a car crash?"

"On their way home from a wedding. That's why Don Felipe is paralyzed. He has treatments every Saturday, and is hoping to walk again. It'll be a miracle if he does, just as it is a miracle that he's alive." Manuela's lips curved downward, and she headed back downstairs without another word. Her sadness wrapped itself around me as I followed her, wanting to say something that would make her feel better. But I didn't know the right words.

"Be a dear and help me pick the pigeon-peas for supper while the rest of the clothes dry," she said at the bottom of the stairs, as if to erase the sad story from my mind.

"I'll help you with any work you need to do," I said, and brought the spark back into her eyes.

"Do you have any children?" I asked as we pulled down the branches and carefully chose the ripe pods.

"No. I was a *jamona* when I married." She giggled.

"What's a *jamona*?"

"A girl who reaches thirty before getting married."

"Have you always lived with the Linareses?"

"No. We came thirteen years ago. Teresita was two months old, God love her."

I saw the sadness in Manuela's eyes again, and tried to change the subject quickly. "I saw a church across the plaza. Do you ever go?"

"Every Sunday. You'll get to go with us tomorrow, unless you don't believe in religion."

"Me? Oh yes, I do. I really do. Thank you for including me."

I couldn't believe my luck. I had found nice people who were treating me as a person, not just a runaway, and I'd get to go to church with them, too.

While bubbling about going to church, I thought about Papa. Even if I knew for sure that he would never come this far to go to church, I'd still look over my shoulder for him.

*　　*　　*

The church was bigger than the one in Lares, but it wasn't as crowded, which made it easier for me to look around. My heart skipped a beat every time I saw a man dressed in black pants and a white shirt like Papa wore.

Getting into the car after Mass, Manuela asked, "Were you looking for your father in church? You seemed nervous."

"I felt nervous, but I knew he wouldn't come this far, especially to look for me." The last part of that sentence hurt, for I felt deprived of my father's love.

Doña Luisa looked into the rearview mirror. "So you think he won't come here looking for you, is that right?"

"I *know* he'll never come here looking for me . . . but I will always be on the lookout for him."

"That's the saddest thing I have ever heard, *Querida*," Don Felipe said. "A little girl afraid of her own father."

"I was afraid of my old man, too," added Manuela.

Her husband reached for her hand. "And I of mine, until the day he died."

The conversation took off from there, everyone telling a little something about their childhood and their drinking parents. I felt blessed knowing that these people understood my reasons for running away.

We didn't go to the house right away. Doña Luisa drove Carlos and Manuela to their relatives' home, where they would spend the rest of their day off. I went home with the Linareses and helped Doña Luisa take her husband out of the car and lift him into his chair.

We had corn bread, ham, and coffee for lunch at the kitchen table. The Linareses talked about their daughter: how much I reminded them of her, how old she would be now, and how they'd never stopped missing her. They mentioned her with such love, I could feel their pain. I wondered why my parents couldn't have loved me like that.

"I want to show you something," Doña Luisa said, after helping her husband down for his afternoon nap. She unlocked a door, pushing it open slowly, as if afraid to bump into someone inside. "I keep this room locked. I'm always waiting for her to come back."

I saw a single bed made up in soft pinks and lace. A pink blanket was folded neatly at the foot of the bed. The doll leaning on the pillow looked like a two-year-old girl dressed in pink organza with ruffles and lace.

"This was the last doll we bought for her," Doña Luisa said, picking up the doll and smoothing its hair. "I packed away most of her dolls, but this one I had to keep on her bed. I know she's not coming back, but I like to believe she will." She placed the doll on the bed carefully, as if it were a real baby, spreading the skirt so that it opened like an umbrella, forming a circle around the body. "I'll show you the rest of the dolls another time," she said in a choked voice.

I looked around and kept silent, in awe of all that I saw, and at the same time saddened by Doña Luisa's loss.

"I have another room I want you to see," she said, and then locked the door. We passed two other closed rooms, and then she opened a third one. "This is where my little nephew slept when he came to visit us. I'm thinking of putting you in here."

"Me? What about your nephew?"

"He and his parents have moved to New York. It'll be a long time before he comes back. So you can sleep here until he does. No sense in leaving the room empty for years."

"It'll be fine with me, Doña Luisa. Staying in any room here is—well, I don't know what to say. 'Thank you' is not enough."

"You can stay here as long as you like. Here are towels you can use." She pulled open a drawer. "Here are the sheets for the bed. You can make it by yourself?"

I assured her that I could.

"When you finish, go down and get your things. You can put them in these drawers."

"All I have is what you and Doña Monica have given me."

"You'll be surprised at how fast four drawers will fill up." She opened a tall cabinet in the corner. "Your dresses go here."

A bell rang in another room.

"I need to go help my husband. Come back to the kitchen when you're finished."

It didn't take long to get my things and put the sheets on the bed. Then I hurried to the kitchen and helped Doña Luisa prepare the evening meal while Don Felipe read the newspaper. We ate together again at the kitchen table.

Afterwards, the couple went to the balcony, and I cleaned up the kitchen. This was a thrill. For the first time in my life, I washed dishes in a sink, with soap instead of ashes, and dried them with a soft white towel.

I went to the balcony when I finished. "Doña Luisa, if you don't need my help for anything else, I'll go to the blue room and read for a while. That is, if you'll let me borrow one of the books in your nephew's room."

"*Your* room, Sabina," Doña Luisa said. "It's your room now." Her smile was warm, and Don Felipe looked as though he knew what she was talking about. I thanked them and said goodnight.

In the room, I looked around and felt unworthy of their kindness. I closed the door behind me and sat at the little desk with a novel in my hands, but I couldn't move beyond the first page.

I thought of Mama's warnings. "Don't trust anyone. No one will give you anything for free. People earn your trust, then stab you in the back. No one will care about you. Their only interest is what they can get out of you."

I thought about the hours I had worked at the factory. *Doña Luisa has not mentioned payment. What if she expects me to work all day just to pay for my food and a place to sleep? How would I have money to go rescue my sisters and brothers?*

Chapter Forty-Three

A Brighter Day

At the factory on Monday morning, Doña Luisa had me separate three hundred pennies into piles of ten cents each. She left the room, closing the door behind her. I didn't like being alone in a closed room with all that money. Then I wondered if maybe she was testing me.

I was almost finished when she came and said, "Oh, Sabina, be a doll and do me a favor. Go into my office and bring me my purse. I'm too tired to go myself." She'd been walking back and forth, giving the *inspectoras* orders, but it was still before lunch, too early to be tired yet.

I went right away and found her purse on her desk, open, with loose bills of fives, tens, and twenties exposed. I closed the purse and carried it to her.

"Doña Luisa, your purse was open with your money right on top. I hope you know how much you had. This kind of thing makes me nervous."

She took the purse and said, "You don't want to be accused of stealing?"

"I don't want to be accused, and I won't steal."

"Wait here," she said with a smile, and walked out. Moments later, she returned with a few folders and asked me to carry them and her closed purse to her office. I did as she said and left her office right away, convinced that she had done that to see if I would be tempted to take some of the money. I felt proud that I wasn't.

After lunch, she had me take unmade gloves out of boxes and put them into pairs, then tie twelve pairs into a bundle. I emptied three boxes and made twelve bundles. I knew she had me do that to make sure I could count. My next job was to match the right thread to the right unmade dozens of gloves.

"I love doing this kind of work much better than pulling weeds in the fields back home," I told her. "Thank you very much for giving me a chance."

"I'm glad I did," Doña Luisa said. "Now let's go home."

At home, she told Manuela to set an extra plate in the dining room. From that night on, I ate my evening meals with her and her husband.

"I thought we should discuss your wages," Doña Luisa said after we had said grace. "I'm sure you must have plans, and I doubt that you'd want to work for free. So go ahead and tell me how much you think you should be paid."

I didn't need to think about it for too long. I would not ask for wages from people who had been so good to me. "You two have taken me into your home and are feeding me, so I should not be paid as a regular employee. You even gave me your nephew's room. I can't ever pay you for your kindness."

I knew that one day I would want money to go back for my brothers and sisters, but that was a long time away. Right then, all I wanted was for the Linareses to feel good about me.

"Isn't she appreciative?" Don Felipe asked his wife, his smile making him look ready to hug the whole world.

"Yes, but she needs more than shelter and food."

"Perhaps an allowance would be appropriate," he said.

"Yes, an allowance for clothes would be fine," I said. "I can even make my own dresses if you let me use your sewing machine."

Doña Luisa's face lit up. "I am becoming very fond of this

young lady, *Querido*. Not only is she a good worker, but bright and thoughtful, too. And I admire her courage."

"Admire?" I said. "Why?"

"I'll tell you another time," she said. "I only wish that I had been able to do what you have done." Her voice faded away.

"I don't understand," I said.

"She had drinking parents, too," Don Felipe answered while Doña Luisa wiped her eyes.

"Drinking, cruel parents!" she exclaimed bitterly.

I couldn't believe what I was hearing. She hadn't been very sympathetic toward me the night she found me in the storage room, yet she had been a victim of drinking parents herself.

"I like your decision, Sabina," she said. "We'll treat you like a relative rather than an employee."

"You have a good head on your shoulders, Sabina," said Don Felipe with a wink. "You'll be more like a daughter." He leaned forward, tiny creases forming around his kind eyes, emphasizing his words as if he thought I needed persuasion.

"We'll tell people around here that you are my niece's daughter," said Doña Luisa. "Otherwise, they'll drive us crazy asking questions. Almost everyone around here knows that I have a niece in New York whose husband died in the war, leaving her with five children. All my neighbors know that we had considered having some of her children here for a while. The older girl changed her mind after all the plans were made, and since none of these people have seen my grandniece, they'll assume you are her. I don't like to lie, but this is an exception. People won't ask too many questions, and you'll be accepted in the community and in school when you sign up."

I thought my heart would fly out of my chest. "Doña Luisa, are you saying that I might be able to attend school?"

"I can't promise, but I think so. I'll check after Christmas vacation. While you wait to begin school, you can use my sewing machine. It has been collecting dust for years. I even have some fabrics you can have—a red and white checkered print, which will look beautiful on you. One day we'll get a pair of white shoes to go with the dress."

I sprang from the chair, breathless. "I can even make dresses for you, if you would like me to." I hugged and kissed her on the cheek, then did the same to Don Felipe. "You two are the most wonderful people I have met since my godparents died. I'll be grateful to you for the rest of my life." My throat felt blocked and my eyes filled with tears, so I returned to my chair, shaking.

Don Felipe's eyes were twinkling. "We are happy to have you here, too," he said. "Since we lost our precious Teresita, our lives have been empty. Having you come to us as you have is a blessing." He reached for my hand and kissed it, his thin moustache pressing into the back of my hand. "There are some bad people in the world, young and old. But there are many more good ones. We believe you're one of the good ones. You'll make a difference in the world someday, if you're given the chance."

"We can't understand people like your parents," Doña Luisa said. "They take their children for granted, abusing them instead of feeling lucky to have them. We wanted many children, but could have only one. Now she's gone." She stared at the family picture on the wall, and once again, her voice faded away.

Later in my room, I thought of Mama's warnings. "People earn your trust, then stab you in the back." Mama had better be wrong.

*   *   *

The next Saturday, while the Linareses were at the hospital, I helped Manuela with the wash and other chores.

"Manuela, I have been wondering why Doña Luisa would have me eat with them. Why not you and Carlos, too?"

"They want to get to know you better," Manuela said. "As for Carlos and me . . . Well, we have always eaten in the kitchen, so now we don't feel comfortable anyplace else."

Manuela's answer made sense. I had read about the rich

people's servants eating in the kitchen, usually after they had waited on their masters. However, I felt a little sad for them, because to me they didn't seem to be any less than the people they worked for. I decided that I would never be a servant or have any if I became rich someday.

"I'm worried about Doña Luisa," Manuela said, hanging a sheet on the line. "I'm really worried."

"Why? Is she sick?"

"No. But I think she's borrowing trouble for herself. As if she didn't have enough problems already."

"What kind of problems?"

Manuela turned toward me. "I think she's reaching out to you to fill the empty spot Teresita's death left in her heart. One day you'll leave, and she'll be crushed."

"Don't worry. I'll stay as long as they want me, though I know I can never replace their daughter."

"It was a devastating accident," she said. "They were coming home late one night from a wedding in San Juan, and a drunken man driving a truck ran the light. He rammed their car into a utility pole. Teresita was asleep in the back seat behind Don Felipe, who was driving, and the two were crushed together. Doña Luisa was unconscious for two weeks. She woke up calling for Teresita, and they told her that the girl was dead and buried. Her screams were heard across town. Relatives and nurses held her down to keep her from jumping out the window. She didn't want to live without her baby."

Manuela's tears fell like raindrops on the grass, and I felt sick for making her cry, and sad for the Linareses.

"The only way I would leave them is if they abused me."

"Doña Luisa and her husband aren't abusers. They have hearts of gold." Manuela put the emphasis on *hearts of gold*. "Don Felipe was in the hospital for over six months. He still has problems, takes a lot of medication for pain, and returns to the hospital every Saturday morning for some treatments. Poor man. He was a businessman who kept himself busy all the time. Now he has to spend the rest of his life in that wheelchair. All because of that damned drunk who shouldn't have been driving."

Now that I knew how the accident happened, I understood why Doña Luisa had taken me in. I couldn't help wondering what would have happened to me if Teresita hadn't died. I felt lucky to have found a couple who were longing for someone to love. And I would never do anything to hurt them. I felt love for them.

No, I will not leave these people, I told myself in my room later. Then I thought about my mother's sayings: *"No one owes you anything. If people give you something, it's because they want twice as much in return. Don't think you are special, because all you are is a female for men to clean their asses with when they can't find anything better. God made men in his image, but He made women in the image of something men could use."*

My mother was wrong. I wasn't just a female. I was a human being. I refused to believe that God sent me into the world only to be used and abused. Someday, I would tell my mother that.

*   *   *

For the next four years, I would go to the factory with Doña Luisa every day. I sewed new samples, worked in her office writing notes and recording messages, ran errands, and counted money for the payroll.

In two months time, I had learned enough new things to make a smart decision. I would become a woman of power like Doña Luisa, not like the poor women outside the enclosure, standing in line with their bundles of gloves, hungry and sweating while they waited to reach the little windows where their work would be inspected. If they did their work correctly, they would be paid. Then those poor, starving souls headed for the cafeteria, where for twenty-five cents they could treat themselves to a plate of rice and beans with little chunks of beef.

Some of these women could not even afford to eat lunch in

the cafeteria. They owed their money to their local grocery store. You could always tell where the women came from by their appearance. The country poor wore cotton dresses, some with patches, and old muddy shoes without stockings. Their legs with bulging veins were badly bruised and covered with open sores. Sweat, black with dirt, dripped from these women's heads down their necks while fat brown lice crept in and out of moist nets of hair.

The better-dressed women wore high-heeled shoes with fine stockings and silky dresses. Their hair was styled, and their fingernails were painted red or pink. They kept their distance from the sweaty *jíbaras*. These ladies kept one eye on the *inspectoras*, who always wore makeup and were nicely dressed. They smiled brightly at the women on the other side of the windows. Somehow, that smile gave permission to the clean-looking, well-dressed ladies to jump the line. That meant the sweaty, poor women had to wait even longer.

"Let me inside that enclosure and I'll stick that damn thing up your ass," one ragged, sweaty woman shouted furiously. She had been watching the *inspectora* stretch one glove after another, throwing them down into the *made wrong* pile. The poor woman would have to take the gloves back, undo them stitch-by-stitch, and then sew them over again if she ever wanted to be paid. "Ugly bitch! You're squeezing that damn wooden thing extra hard to find my work wrong! You're made up like a damn clown, making eyes and granting favors to the better-dressed bitches in line. Well, I may not be dolled up, powdered, and perfumed, but I'm as good as any of you."

"Lady, please," said the woman checking the gloves. "I'm doing my job the same as always. Your work is too loose. I have no choice but to find it wrong."

"Too loose, my ass! Come out here and I'll show you what loose really is!" The woman swung her arms wildly, making the others in line duck her elbows.

She was still crying and yelling when the police walked in.

Two big men in blue uniforms dragged her out for creating a disturbance. She didn't come back for her gloves.

That picture of desperation driven by poverty and necessity was glued to my mind forever.

Chapter Forty-Four

My Second Carnival

Coming home from the factory one day, we noticed some big trucks parked near the plaza and several ragged men dragging out pipes and wires.

"Ah, the carnival," said Doña Luisa. "That time of year again." She slowed down, and I noticed that the sweaty men worked frantically, as if someone was snapping a whip behind them, keeping them always moving. Their eyelids were red, their hair greasy and stringy. They looked as if they never slept.

"I didn't know this town would have a festival, too," I said, remembering the one in Lares.

"Carnivals move from one town to the other to celebrate that town's saint. They usually last eight days."

"My father took my sister and me to one once—but he didn't let us have a ride, even on the wooden horses."

"Carlos and Manuela usually go to the festival. You might want to go with them."

"Will you be going, too?"

"No, I don't go to things like that with Felipe in the wheelchair."

"I would love to go, Doña Luisa, if it's okay with Manuela and Carlos, and if you don't need me to do some work."

"They'll go Saturday night, after all the work is done."

That night and the following nights, I thought about my upcoming trip to the festival. I would wear my new checkered dress and my white shoes. Maybe Doña Luisa would give me some money for a ride on the wooden horses. I kept thinking back to how excited Emilia and I were about going to the carnival that time. Then I remembered how disappointed we had felt when Papa didn't even let us watch the merry-go-round.

Things will be different with Manuela and Carlos, I told myself. *And I'll have fun without fear.*

On Saturday evening, Doña Luisa drove us up to the edge of town. She even gave me a dollar bill as we stepped out of the car.

"For rides," she said lovingly.

This was my very first dollar bill. I nodded and folded it carefully, then closed my hand tightly around it.

My skin tingled with excitement as I walked through the crowded plaza with Manuela and Carlos, hearing the music, the voices, the screams, and the cheers.

Then a dark shadow came over me as I saw the long line of *publico* cars across the street. Among the cars pulling in, I saw two from Lares. My heart thumped. I imagined Papa bolting from one of those cars. Even though I didn't think he would come this far, my fear of him made me think he would pop right out from any car or building.

"What's the matter, Sabina?" Manuela asked. "Are you afraid?"

I nodded.

"Ah, don't worry!" Carlos said, making his face hard and angry. "If your old man shows up here, I'll punch his nose out of shape." He held out his huge fists, ready to swing the first blow.

This made Manuela laugh, and I couldn't help but join her. Carlos wasn't much taller than my father, but I felt good because he seemed strong enough to back up his statement.

"We'll start with the horses," Carlos said. "Follow me."

Manuela took my hand, and we followed Carlos to a line of people buying tickets.

"I have my own money," I said, bubbly. "Doña Luisa gave me a whole dollar."

"You hang onto that dollar, little one. This is my treat." Carlos reached into his pocket and pulled out a five-dollar bill.

I couldn't help thinking about my father again. He had refused me a ride on the wooden horses, a dime for Mother's Day, and a toothbrush to keep my teeth clean. Yet Carlos, who wasn't even related to me, would pay for my ride.

"Come on, you two," Carlos said, shuffling the tickets. "The horses are waiting."

"Stop remembering things and have fun," Manuela suggested as we joined Carlos at a small gate.

I nodded that I would, but deep inside I was wishing that Emilia were there with us. It seemed odd that I would miss her, considering how mean she'd been to me. "Manuela, how do you know I'm remembering things?"

"It's written all over your face."

A smiling young man motioned us to step up to the revolving floor. "Watch your step," he said, reaching to help us in.

Carlos helped me onto a horse close to the center. He helped Manuela to the one in the middle, and he took the outside one. Once all the horses were taken, the floor picked up speed and increased with the loud music. Suddenly I was traveling through the air, my hair flying, my heart pounding, and my stomach sinking and rising. I saw Manuela and Carlos looking at me with bright smiles and glistening eyes, as if I were their daughter whom they loved dearly.

I saw boys and girls, parents and lovers, laughing and cheering as we flew round and round. The ride wasn't very long, but the memory of it would last forever.

"Well, how did you like it?" Carlos asked as we stepped down from the platform.

"It's the most thrilling thing I've ever experienced,"

I said, wondering what it would be like if I had Carlos and Manuela as my parents.

Carlos rubbed his hands together and smiled. "Good, I'm glad you liked it. We'll try the Ferris wheel next. Follow me, ladies." He started off with a little dance in tune with the music from the merry-go-round. Manuela chuckled behind him, and I followed the two through the crowds. I saw anxious men and women with sun-baked skin urging people to play their games.

"Here, right here! Win this doll for your little girl! This ball for your son!" Their voices were hoarse. "Right here, folks! Take this sparkling gold chain home to your sweetheart!"

I saw small stands with different items for sale: little dolls dressed in colored feathers, ribbons swinging in the night breeze, and barrettes displayed in glass cases. I noticed an open box of girls' socks of many colors, and another box with necklaces and rings. Small toys like tops and spinners also hung from hooks within the stands, waiting to be sold for pennies and nickels.

I saw nicely dressed women and girls, men and boys. And I even noticed some blonde hair and green and blue eyes. I heard a lot of cheering, laughter, and music. This was a world filled with life.

We reached the Ferris wheel and sat on the swinging seat, Manuela next to Carlos, and I next to her. When the big wheel began to roll backward, loading and unloading other people, I thought that our swinging seat would come off its brackets and we'd plunge to our death. But this was a thrilling experience, so I wasn't going to let Manuela and Carlos see that I was scared. Of course, they could see my knuckles turning white from squeezing the bar in front of us.

The wheel took us up backward, then forward, and back again. It began moving faster and faster as my stomach went up and down like a yo-yo. I heard people yelling and screaming, and I noticed other machines turning and spinning nearby. I heard music blaring from everywhere, and I saw the outskirts of the city, pitch black because we had all the lights.

As our ride came to an end, I realized that I had been missing my sister. The bad memories about her disappeared momentarily, and I thought of the fun we would have had together if things had been different.

Perhaps I would never feel like going to another carnival again. The joy of such fun had gotten lost somewhere between the mountains and the city.

I didn't tell that to Manuela and Carlos. Instead, when we arrived at the house, I thanked them with a hug and a kiss.

Chapter Forty-Five

Fifth Grade at Last

"I registered you in school today," Doña Luisa said one day on our way home from work. She turned the steering wheel one way and then another, as if she had just made a common statement. "The second semester begins on the third week of January. You'll attend classes from eight to twelve, then go to the factory to work the rest of the day."

I smiled at her, but the right words wouldn't come.

Doña Luisa continued to drive without taking her eyes off the road. "I registered you in fifth grade as my niece. No one will ask questions that way, and you'll be respected, since most of the town knows me. I told them you had been in New York for a couple of years and had not attended school there, but that prior to New York, you had attended four years in Perchas."

"Fifth grade? Don't I need fourth grade first?"

"You won't have any trouble doing fifth grade work."

"You registered me with your niece's name?"

"I gave them your name and my niece's New York address."

"Doña Luisa!" I folded one leg under me so I could turn on the car seat and face her, my chest bursting with excitement. "I am the luckiest girl in the whole world, and you are the most wonderful person I have ever met. If you weren't driving, I would give you a great big hug. Thank you, thank you!"

Doña Luisa laughed loudly. "You are welcome, welcome!"

The joy of going to school was accompanied by worry. I wasn't going to a little country school to begin first grade. This school was in the city. The students would be more sophisticated than the ones near the mountains. They might not treat me as one of them, but as a *jíbara*. Worse yet was the thought that Doña Luisa had lied to get me in, and I would be attending school as her niece from New York.

"I'm really excited about attending school," I said, "but I wish I could sign up in my own name. If the truth comes out later, I would not want people to find out that you told a lie to help me, as much as I appreciate it. Do you understand?"

"I understand, and I appreciate your concern, Sabina. But sometimes it's necessary to twist the truth just a little. The fact is that if I said you were running away from your parents, the school would not accept you."

"What you say is true," I told her. "But I'll feel awfully bad if you get in trouble because of me."

"I don't expect any trouble, so don't worry. Go to school as my niece, and we'll take things one step at a time."

Since I wanted to attend school more than anything else in the world, I had no trouble complying with Doña Luisa's idea. In fact, thinking of myself as her niece made me feel important, not just my parents' runaway daughter.

As for Doña Luisa, I knew she would rather tell people that she was helping her niece instead of a ragged girl from the hills. I concluded then that we both came out with a pretty good deal.

*   *   *

On the first day of school, when I was getting dressed, Doña Luisa came into my room.

"Let's make a pretty girl look even prettier," she said, holding out a green ribbon. "It'll match your uniform." She had me stand in front of the mirror while she combed my hair. "Such beautiful hair, fine and curly. You are as pretty as a flower in the spring."

I thanked her for saying nice things, but thought of my mother with her wooden comb years earlier. Then I remembered Papa saying that my hair was soft and my scalp so white. I felt sad that I wasn't missing them. I wanted to feel love for them instead of fear. I wanted to feel a desire to be with them, rather than feeling glad to be far away.

"What are you thinking about, Sabina?" Doña Luisa asked.

"My first day of school so long ago."

"It wasn't that long ago," she said, turning me toward the mirror. "There. How do you like it?"

"I like it! Thank you. Do I remind you of someone else?"

"You do, but I know you are not Teresita."

"I know it, too, but . . ." I hesitated. ". . . may I think of you as my mother?"

Doña Luisa smiled. "Yes, you may. And may I think of you as my daughter?"

"Of course," I said. Then I saw her teary eyes, and opened my arms to her. She took me into hers, and we both struggled to hold back our sobs, but our tears could not be restrained.

We held onto each other until we heard the sound of rolling wheels.

"*Querida*, is there something wrong?" Don Felipe looked startled, his hands reaching for the doorframe as if he were trying to pull himself out of the chair.

"Ah, *Querido*, no. We're just a little emotional today. Sabina reminds me of Teresita. But we are going to be just fine, aren't we?" She looked at me with a wink.

I winked back and felt warmth wrap around me like a comforting blanket. I took one more look in the mirror, and then followed the Linareses down the hallway to the kitchen.

Doña Luisa and I left after breakfast.

The school was a three-story building in which the fifth and sixth grades were held on the first floor, seventh and eighth on the second floor, and ninth and tenth grades on the third floor. A short distance away stood a long white building, only one story high, with a red roof and many windows. First, second, third, and fourth grades were taught there.

The students in the upper building were called *los de la hi* because they were smart and outspoken. I noted with mixed feelings that the girls wore lipstick, colored their nails, held hands with boys, and chewed *chicle* (gum).

Doña Luisa walked with me to the classroom, where she introduced me to my new teacher, Dolores Moreno de León, a tall woman wearing glasses with frames that matched her straight black hair. She reached to shake my hand as if I were someone special.

"It's very nice to meet you, Sabina." She bent down to look into my eyes, and I worried that she would guess my true age. "Such lovely green eyes. What beautiful hair! I can see the resemblance. You must be thrilled to have her with you, Luisa."

"I am, I am," Doña Luisa said with a bright smile.

I felt thrilled. Being back in school was a dream come true. Having Doña Luisa in my life was a miracle.

"You're going to like this school," Doña Luisa said to me. Then she turned to the teacher. "Sabina's a good worker. You'll be glad to have her in your class."

When Doña Luisa left, Mrs. Moreno said, "Your aunt is a wonderful woman. You're lucky to be related to her. The whole town loves her and Don Felipe. There are no other two people in the whole world like those two. I'm glad she brought you in early. It gives us a chance to get acquainted before the mob arrives."

As I listened to Mrs. Moreno, I thought about the classroom of the little country school back home. Then, for a very short second, I wished Emilia were here with me. However, the thought of how mean she had been made me glad she was miles away.

Putting her out of my mind, I studied the outline of the room, wondering how many thousands of students had been educated here. The desktops were carved with black numbers and letters.

I couldn't imagine placing a sheet of paper on these tops and being able to write smoothly.

Boys and girls began to arrive, and before long the schoolyard was a huge, noisy arena. The girls were as active and noisy as the boys, screaming, shouting, pulling, punching, and climbing the trees around the yard. I couldn't tell which students were fifth graders and which were sixth until the bell rang and they came in, fifth graders through one door, and sixth through another.

"We have a new student today," the teacher said. "Her name is Sabina. She's the grandniece of Doña Luisa, the sewing factory manager. Sabina comes to us from New York."

While the teacher talked, thirty pairs of eyes gazed at me. Among those eyes, I saw two sets of green and three sets of blue. Better yet, these students had light skin. One of the blue-eyed boys had curly red hair, and the other two had black hair. One of the green-eyed girls had light brown hair, and the other had hair almost as light as mine. This was the most gratifying discovery for me. I finally felt good about being blonde.

I hadn't been in class for an hour when Mrs. Moreno started talking about the war and the shortage of food it caused, especially for people who lived in cities.

"We are fortunate to have Sabina here," she said. "She can tell us how the shortage of food affected the people of New York City."

Every head in the class turned toward me, and I felt as if someone had hit me on the head. I felt my heart thump and skip a few beats. Luckily, I remembered that Doña Luisa had registered me as her niece from New York.

"We didn't have much food in our house," I said. "But I really don't know much about the war because my parents kept a lot of that information from us. We didn't have a radio, and we weren't allowed to read the newspaper." My throat felt dry by the time the last word came out, and I prayed that I would never have to tell another lie.

"That's right, students," the teacher said. "There are some

parents who think they are protecting their children by keeping information from them. But I disagree. I think children should be aware of what's going on in their world. Don't you think it's better to know what happens around you?"

The class agreed, and I felt that I had not lied, since my parents did keep us from learning. Still, I wished I could tell the truth without hurting Doña Luisa. I had been lucky to be able to give that answer in class, but the teacher's next question might not be as easy to answer. The whole school would know the real Sabina, and that would prove that Doña Luisa had lied.

During recess, some of the girls asked me questions about life in New York, and I always said that talking about home made me feel like crying. That was not a lie, but it didn't help me make friends. From then on, while the other girls played, I read under a tree to avoid having to answer questions. Consequently, I didn't make many friends.

Springtime came quickly. It hardly seemed possible that so much time had passed and no one had come around looking for me. All the effort my parents had put into keeping their children from being seen by outsiders actually had helped me disappear into the hustle and bustle of a big city. If anyone from the hills had come to the factory, I knew they wouldn't have recognized me.

The cotton tree at the edge of the road near the entrance to Doña Luisa's home triggered the painful memory of my brother bursting my little pillow. The pinkish silk cotton was flying through the air when we returned from church on Palm Sunday. Doña Luisa stopped the car just to watch the feather-like flakes float and dance in the mid-morning sun.

"Look how light and soft they are," she said, putting her hand out. The flakes would barely touch her hand, and up they went.

I, an expert on gathering the silky flakes, caught one and held it between my thumb and index finger, remembering my pillow, and hurting inside. I ran my finger over it gently while the memories flashed through my mind.

"That brings her bad memories, *Querida*." Don Felipe's soothing voice broke my thoughts.

I let the flake go, watching it lift into the wind, fluttering, until it got lost among many more.

The Linareses were my family now. I felt lucky to have met them, and I felt loved for the first time in my life.

When the car began to roll again, many flakes floated behind us, threatening to stick onto the rear window as if to ease any grief that might still be hanging over me. I kept my eyes on the beautiful flying signs of spring.

We went back to church on Thursday night, Good Friday, Saturday morning, and Easter Sunday. Each time, I thought about the time Papa took Emilia and me to the little church in Lares. I didn't miss anything about my family anymore. Instead, I looked at the two couples at my side and felt strong and very lucky.

*　　*　　*

School ended the last Friday in May. Come the middle of August, I would begin sixth grade. I'd have a birthday, which might be my thirteenth, but my new family would think I was turning fifteen. Someday, when I was much older, I would admit to them that I had lied about my age just to get a job.

Summer was hot in the city, especially under the tin roof. Even though the ceiling was higher than a two-story house, it crackled and popped in the heat of the noon sun. A few fans moved the warm air but did not cool it. Women stood in the lines, red-faced, fanning themselves with pieces of cardboard. Their tempers flared at any crossed eye or at any elbow that accidently poked their ribs.

"Poke me one more time, and I'll break your damn arm," one woman yelled to the one behind her.

"Back up a few steps," Doña Monica announced, holding a speaker over her mouth. "You have to give each other room to breathe."

"That's easy for you to say," another woman shouted from the back of the line. "You're up there with that damn fan blowing under your skirt. Why don't you go out there and stand under the blistering sun for a while?"

Doña Monica tried to say more, but the crowd drowned her voice with their jeers and claps. Doña Luisa came out of her office and pulled a string that set off an alarm. The crowd quieted, but only for a few seconds, while she warned them through the same speaker that the temperature in the city was over a hundred degrees. If people didn't cooperate, she would close the factory.

The lines broke and women scattered, shouting and screaming like chickens when dogs chase them. Doña Luisa pulled the string again, and two policemen ran in, clubs in hand and sweat pouring down their faces.

The women weren't intimidated by the police. They ran around screaming, waving their arms up in the air.

"Close the damn place and we'll set it on fire!" someone's loud voice pierced through the commotion.

Some of the women cheered and yelled. "Burn the damn place down with everything in it!"

When the crowd finally quieted, there were only enough women left to form three short lines. All the locals had gone home to escape the heat and stay away from the sweaty *jíbaras* from the remote countryside. The locals would return early the next day to be first in line and leave before the mob rolled in.

"We're very sorry for the disturbance," Doña Luisa told the police, who apologized for not being able to be of more help. "Those poor souls are in such need for their little amount of money that waiting seems like an eternity to them."

"We know, *señora*. That's why we didn't arrest them."

Another afternoon, when everything was running smoothly, the horrifying scream of a man outside made everyone in line turn. He ran down a narrow driveway behind the factory, screaming and waving his blood-covered arms, some of his fingers dangling and blood streaming out of his head. As his screams came closer to the factory, the lines broke apart, and women headed for the rear doors to see the commotion. The bloody man ran into our building, across the huge room, and out the front door, leaving a trail of blood on the factory's floor.

Later, we learned that the poor man had been outside a couple's home asking a woman for directions to someone else's house. The woman's jealous husband appeared from behind the house and began swinging his machete at the unsuspecting visitor. The man tried to protect his face with his hands, but most of his fingers fell to the ground. When he turned to run, the machete hit his head, almost splitting it in two.

In his fright, he took a shortcut through the factory, hoping to reach the plaza where the police on the corner would help him. He had barely made it to the sidewalk when he fell to the hot concrete. His body jerked and trembled until no sign of life was left in him.

While the police questioned some witnesses, loud shrieks came from the jealous man's house. Finally, someone told the cops that the crazy husband was now beating his wife because her flirtations had driven him to murder.

The police kicked in the couple's door and found the man with his pants down and the woman tied to her bed. The neighbors told police that the man's biggest thrill was to beat his wife, tie her down, and have sex while she fought to get away.

During the excitement, some of the women in the lines screamed. Others fainted and fell to the floor.

I trembled as I watched, holding onto the railing above the enclosures. I thought of the night Papa beat Mama with his machete, and of the time he held it at my throat. For many nights after the incident at the factory, I lay awake praying that Papa would not do something crazy before I could get back there to save everyone.

Chapter Forty-Six

Over and Around Me

My education about human sexuality started at the sewing factory when I heard the women tell each other secrets in soft voices. They substituted words with some I wasn't supposed to understand. *Estoy así* meant they were menstruating. The period was *la cosa*, the thing. *Tengo la cosa*—I have the thing. *Me lo hiso*—He did it to me. *Di aluz*—I gave birth.

They often asked me if I knew what they were talking about, and I always said I didn't. Then they asked if I was a *señorita* yet, and I said I wasn't. But I didn't know that a girl became a *señorita* when she had her first period, and a *señora* when she gave away her virginity, married or not.

When I finally figured out the whispering and secrets, I prayed that no such thing would ever happen to me. Whatever "the thing" was, it didn't sound very pleasant.

My prayers did not work. One day I woke up with a strong headache and felt like crying. I couldn't concentrate in class, and my hands felt cold and wet all day. The headache grew worse, and I had to tell the teacher. She told me to go home. I struggled all the way to the factory and collapsed in Doña Luisa's office.

"I think your visitor is coming soon," she said, splashing cold water on my face.

"Who?" I mumbled.

"Your monthly friend."

"What friend?" Then I remembered the women's whispers, but I felt too embarrassed to say anything else. I lay around the office with an ice pack on my painful head.

"We'll stop at the drugstore on our way home and get you some Kotex," Doña Luisa said, and I thought she meant something for my headache.

"Is that better than aspirin?"

"I'll tell you what it is later."

I stayed in the car while she went into the drugstore. She returned with something in a paper bag, which seemed too big to be aspirin. Inside the car, she reached into the bag and pulled out a blue box with the picture of a white rose on it. The word *Kotex* was written on one side of the box in big black letters.

"These are sanitary pads," she said. "Every female uses them sooner or later. I think your time has come to use them. You'll find the instructions inside the box."

I thanked Doña Luisa, but I still felt too embarrassed to tell her that I didn't know much about the menstrual period. That night, I felt too sick to eat supper, so I went to bed early.

I dreamt that Uncle Luís was butchering my pet goat, Cielo Azul, all over again. I saw the blood dripping from the goat's throat. Desperately, I held a rag against the wound to keep my little pet from bleeding to death, but the rag got soaked and the blood dripped to the floor.

I woke up in a sweat, gasping for breath, my throat dry, and my body shaking. I turned on the light and looked for Cielo Azul under the bed and around the room. Glad to realize that it had been a dream, I tiptoed to the bathroom, and nearly died when I saw a huge spot of blood in my underpants.

This was the worst moment of my life. I would bleed to death, just like Cielo Azul.

It seemed that once I discovered the stain, the blood flow increased. I knew my heart was pounding hard, and that would make me bleed more. I would be dead by morning. Even if I didn't die, my life was forever ruined. I'd never be able to step out of my room again.

I shook while cleaning up, and then ran to my room to read the instructions in the blue box. Afterward, I lay in bed, furious with my mother. She should have told me that someday this would happen.

Every girl should have a mother or a friend like Doña Luisa. She came to my room in the morning.

"Feeling any better?" She saw the open blue box on the table. "Ah, so I was right?"

"I feel awful," I said, "and embarrassed."

"Still have the headache?"

"Yes, and cramps."

She sat at the foot of my bed, and in a soft voice said, "Well, the headache and cramps will go away soon, but don't make yourself sick with embarrassment. Your menstrual period is a normal process. It happens to every healthy woman. It feels strange the first time, but you'll get used to it fast. It's a development. Your body will blossom, and shortly you'll be a beautiful woman instead of a girl."

As I listened to Doña Luisa, I saw compassion in her small, dark eyes, and a delicate smile that made me trust and adore her.

"I'm sure you're nervous, but let me tell you what happened to me." She covered her mouth with her hand and laughed. "It's funny now, but at that time I felt embarrassed and scared. My late sister and I had been planting beans with our father and his brother all day. It had been very hot, so I blamed my stomach cramps and headache on the sun. All of a sudden I felt something trickling down my leg. Luckily, my dress was long, so no one saw anything. I went behind a tree and looked under my skirt. I felt as if fire spread through my face. I didn't tell my father or my sister. I just ran home, crying and praying that the bleeding would stop before my father found out."

"Did your father run after you?"

"My sister told me later that he and his brother stopped digging holes and watched me run, then looked at each other and went back to digging."

"Did you tell your mother?"

"I didn't need to. She guessed it when she saw me."

"What did she do?"

"She gave me a bunch of rags—no Kotex in those days—and told me to clean up and go to bed. I stayed in bed, hiding from my father for a week."

"A whole week?"

"Yes, but you don't do that nowadays. Stay home today, to get used to being a woman. Then return to school and work as usual. You'll be fine."

"I don't want anyone to know. Please don't tell Don Felipe. Don't even tell Manuela. She might tell Carlos."

"It'll be our secret." She smiled. "Now I need to go to work."

As she walked away, I thought about everything she had said. Then I realized that if I had not run away from home, I probably would have had my first menstrual experience out in a field with my father, and maybe even with my horrible uncle Luís. I also realized that my headache had vanished, and the cramps were bearable.

Chapter Forty-Seven

Luana

In sixth grade, I became friends with a girl named Luana who sat in the seat next to mine. She was quiet and shy, and didn't seem very popular with the other students. I felt safe talking with her, since she didn't seem to be someone who would betray a friend. She was small and skinny, and she had beautiful hazel eyes that looked heavy with sadness, and brown hair that had lost its shine.

We would sit together under a tree during recess, read and discuss what we read, then we would talk and watch the other students hang around with their own kind. Luana told me about her life, and I told her a few things about myself. She said that her mother had died of tuberculosis when she was five. Her father sent her to live with his mother, then ran off to New York with a new love. He had promised to come back for her once he made enough money. Eight years later, Luana still waited to hear from him.

I told her that my father had been mean every time he got drunk, and that my mother had felt burdened with too many children. That was why she had sent me to live with Doña Luisa.

Luana didn't ask me details about the things I told her, so I shared stories without mentioning names. I told her that my godparents had died, and they had been the only people who had shown me love.

She told me about losing her other grandmother, who had been nicer to her than her paternal grandmother. Then I talked, with tearful eyes, about how my mean uncle had snatched away and butchered my little white goat.

Luana listened with sadness, and then said that she had an uglier story about one of her uncles. Someday when we had more time, she would tell it to me. I couldn't imagine what could be worse than the things my uncle had done, so I waited curiously.

One day when school let out at noon, we sat under a tree to talk for a while before heading home to our work, and she told me the earth-shaking story.

"My nasty uncle got my cousin pregnant," she explained.

This was a shock to me. I had believed that a girl had to be married before she got pregnant. "Luana! What are you saying? Uncles don't do things like that, do they?" Thoughts of my ugly uncle Luís came to mind, so I immediately said, "Never mind, Luana. Don't answer that."

"I believed the same thing for years, until I saw it happen to Lili," Luana said with pain written on her face. "I hate my uncle! He ruined Lili's life, and she's only my age."

"You saw him do that to her?" Memories of Emilia and me watching the horses mate flashed through my mind. "He did that while you watched?"

"I didn't see when he did it the first time. I didn't even suspect anything when Lili's breasts swelled and her belly grew."

"You mean . . . he did it more than once?" By now I felt afraid and curious at the same time. If men did things like that anytime and anyplace they pleased, then a girl should never be with men anywhere.

"Oh, yeah. He grabbed her every time he found her in the shack milking the goat."

"Didn't she run? Didn't she tell her parents? I'd hit him on the head with something heavy."

"My uncle warned her not to tell. If she did, he would kill her and her mother. At that time, Lili and her mother lived with us because her father had abandoned them. I remember waking up to hear my grandmother and my aunt asking Lili all kinds of questions. 'Just tell me who did it,' my aunt kept saying. 'Tell me, and I'll kill the bastard.' Poor Lili just cried and cried without answering. 'Leave the girl alone,' I heard my grandmother say. But my aunt said a few more things before she finally gave up. 'You'll tell me sooner or later. When you do, I'll kill the son-of-a bitch.' After those harsh words, my aunt shut up.

"A few days later, after my aunt left for work, my grandmother sent Lili to milk the goat, and me to bring water from the public fountain. When I reached the fountain, I saw Uncle Pedro coming from the woods behind our neighbor's house. He ducked around and ran into the shack. When he didn't come out right away, I put down my can and hurried to the shack. I peeked inside through a crack in the wall, and to my shocked surprise, I saw that my uncle had Lili pinned to the wall. It was the ugliest thing I had ever seen, yet I froze. I couldn't run to get my grandmother. He had one hand over Lili's mouth, his pants down to the floor. I watched him wiggle his naked bottom really fast against her front.

"He finally stopped moving and quickly pulled up his pants. Then he waved a finger at Lili and said, 'Don't forget. If you tell, I'll kill you, your mother, and mine.' Lili's eyes were as big as saucers. I finally found the nerve to run, yelling for my grandmother to come quickly.

"But then I felt myself being dragged by my hair into the shack. 'You want to be next?' He slapped my face. Then my grandmother came through the door, swinging a broom at him. He snatched the broom, shoved her to the floor, and ran."

I had been holding my breath, speechless, watching the pain in Luana's face. "Did he ever come back? Was he ever punished?"

"He didn't come back for a long time. Lili and her mother went away that night. When I got up the next morning, they were gone. My grandmother said that they had gone to Las Marias, to Lili's other grandmother."

"What about your uncle? Was he ever caught and punished?" I had pictured my mean uncle Luís while Luana talked, and I felt ready to strangle all living uncles.

"One night after Lili had been gone a few weeks, my grandmother and I woke up to the sound of gunshots. We didn't suspect that it had anything to do with my uncle, but later on, two policemen knocked on our door. They said my uncle had been shot by the woman who lived two houses down. She had been awakened by the loud cry of her goat under her house.

"The policemen told my grandmother that the woman grabbed her gun and ran out to save her goat. There she found my uncle hooked up to the goat's rear. The woman fired the gun and missed. My uncle lunged at her, so she fired again and shot him in the leg. He hopped into the woods, and the lady sent for the police. They didn't have to look too far to find my uncle. He was leaning against a tree trunk wrapping his belt around his wounded leg.

"The police walked him to the lady's house so she could identify him. She also told police that my uncle had forced himself on her a week earlier. Now he's in jail with a wounded leg. Have you ever heard an uglier story than that?"

I had to admit that I had not, and I felt sick and confused. Suddenly I didn't have much to say, but I hugged Luana and told her that I felt sorry that she'd had to experience such ugliness. We would talk some more tomorrow. For now, I had to hurry to the factory, and she to her home.

The story Luana had told me wasn't one I could repeat, especially to Doña Luisa, so it stayed in my mind the rest of the day and night, along with the feeling of disgust. I had felt that all the ugliness about life had stayed back in the hills. Now I had learned that ugliness existed among humans everywhere, and I might not always be able to run from it.

My friend Luana didn't come to school the next day, which was Friday, so I didn't see her until Monday. She said that she'd been sick over the weekend. She looked pale and tired for the rest of the week, which was the last week of school for that year. After school that Friday, we said our goodbyes, telling each other that we would be back in class in a couple of months. In August, both of us would be in seventh grade.

I had always liked school, but having a close friend in the same class would be so much better. She would be like a nice sister to me, and I would help her to be stronger and feel better about herself.

August came, and Luana didn't show up for class. Finally, the seventh grade teacher announced that Luana had advanced tuberculosis and had been confined to a sanitarium on the other side of the island.

The news was like a hard punch to my stomach, but I still had hope that she would be okay and would return to class. But a couple of weeks later, we were told that she had died.

For days, I walked around in a daze, wondering why everyone I loved ended up dying.

Chapter Forty-Eight

Skipping Grades

Seventh grade seemed like a torture to me. I couldn't concentrate on the schoolwork. I felt terribly alone, and constantly thought about Luana.

"Make new friends," my teacher suggested.

"What I would like is to skip seventh grade."

Those words came up by themselves; I had not even wondered if it was possible. As I heard myself making that statement, I concluded that the challenge of keeping up with a higher grade would help me forget Luana. I would not become close friends with anyone else.

"Skipping seventh grade would mean you'd have to do a lot of extra work," my teacher said. Still, she provided me with a series of tests and, two weeks later, I became an eighth grader.

I also faced another set of problems. There wasn't any room in that class for a girl genius. So to a lot of the students, I became "The Talented," "The Expert," or "The Know-It-All."

"Don't let them bother you," said Don Felipe. "They're only jealous. In time they'll come around."

"I'll talk to the principal," said Doña Luisa.

I was sure that would make things worse for me, so I told her I would talk with the teacher first. And I did.

The teacher, Miss Sanchez, gave a short speech to the class

about how some people wasted their energy being jealous of those who work hard to accomplish their dreams. "It's easier for some people to ridicule an achiever rather than to admit their own lack of ability to learn."

I got a few looks as she talked, some with smiles, others cold and unfriendly. I ignored them and started working as soon as the teacher finished her speech. She had never mentioned my name, nor had she stared at me while talking, but the students guessed why she was lecturing.

At recess, I stayed in the classroom reading. A boy named Rojelio came back in and said, "I know you feel bad, and it's our fault. We were being so stupid and jealous."

"Jealous! I worked day and night to make those grades."

"Well, I felt bad because I knew Miss Sanchez was talking about you, about all of us. It's one of the things I like about our teacher. She never scolds us for anything, but gives a talk which makes the guilty confess."

Other boys and some girls talked to me after Rojelio, admitting that they had acted silly. I told them that I understood and would forgive them. The name-calling stopped, but I still kept myself too busy to make another close friend in school.

Back at the house, however, my relationship with Don Felipe became stronger. He helped me with my homework every night, and never tired or sounded irritated in any way. If I didn't understand something at first, he would explain with a kind and soft voice. Sometimes, before falling asleep, I would go over the times Don Felipe had spent helping me. Then I would compare him to my father, who could not teach us kids a thing without clobbering us on our heads and calling us stupid pigs.

I couldn't understand why a nice person like Don Felipe had to end up in a wheelchair while someone as mean as Papa could live in perfect health day after day. I wondered then if he would have been nicer to his family from a wheelchair.

I finished the first semester with high grades, and Miss Sanchez congratulated me. "I had my doubts at first," she said, "because of all the extra work involved. But you applied yourself and made it. You should feel proud of yourself for your strength and determination."

Those words gave me more energy to keep on working; they were the kind of words I never heard from my family back at the farm.

When I showed my report card to Doña Luisa at the factory, she hugged and congratulated me. As soon as we got home, she told Don Felipe, Manuela, and Carlos. They all applauded and said they were happy for me.

"I wouldn't have done that well without help from all of you," I said, and gave each a hug.

Don Felipe smiled with his whole face and said, "I believe that you are capable of accomplishing anything you make up your mind to do, with or without help from any of us."

I gave him an extra hug, then went to my room feeling ten feet high. I thanked God for bringing me to this family. Then I prayed that one day I might be able to help my sisters and brothers escape the jungle so they, too, could have a better life.

*   *   *

When the Christmas holidays came around, I decided to try again to have some fun. I agreed to go with Manuela and Carlos to a party at Manuela's brother's home in a village outside the city. Carlos's brother picked us up about 7:00 that night and brought us back when the party was over.

I had agreed to go because I thought it would be like the Christmas celebration my parents had, where the rosary was sung all night. I expected to hear a guitar and a *guiro and aguinaldos de navidad* (Christmas songs).

The party at Manuela's brother's house was much different. The music came from a small radio on a shelf with poor reception. Couples went around the room with arms wrapped around each other. Women's skirts flared and whirled like umbrellas of brilliant colors.

The people were nice and friendly. They told me they were glad I had come to their party, for they had heard nothing but good things about me. Some of the men asked me to dance, but somehow having a man's arm around my waist and his sweaty cheek against my hair didn't seem very exciting. Besides that, dancing didn't look like something I would learn on the spot. If I tried it, I would be remembering all the bad feelings I had accumulated about most men. So I smiled and told them no, but thank you for asking.

I went back to looking at the girls and boys standing or sitting around. I searched for girls who might look like Emilia, Gloria, or Alicia. I saw brown eyes, dark hair, and pretty smiles, but no one who looked like my sisters. None of the boys resembled my brothers, either.

I felt out of place, and I didn't know how to have fun without the fear of my parents and my sister. I had wanted freedom, but now I didn't know how to enjoy it.

I asked myself: *Will I ever enjoy anything but work?*

Chapter Forty-Nine

Nose to the Books

Classes on the second semester lasted until 3:00, but I was allowed to leave an hour earlier so I could work at the factory for a couple of hours.

When I got there, Doña Luisa gave me a Coke, and I worked until closing time. The work I didn't finish there, I took home and did after supper. Afterwards, I did my regular chores, then my homework. Sometimes I was still studying at 2:00 in the morning.

I wondered then if any of the other students had work schedules like mine. They all seemed worry-free, and too energetic for their own good, always starting fights over silly little things.

Boys' fights were always about girls. One boy claimed a girl for himself, and warned other boys not to even look at her. They sang verses back and forth, each implying that the girl in question had given her heart to the singer when she was still in her mother's womb. Soon the punches flew, and the boys ended up with black eyes. Sometimes one boy sat on another and squeezed his throat until the victim turned purple. One time, a fight got so hot that the superintendent was pulled to the ground when he tried to break it up. By the time the fighting stopped, the police had been called, and the boys' fathers came to drag their sons home by their ears.

The girls' fights usually started with an argument in the washroom over which boy threw the first punch. Before long, fingers were pointed, hair was pulled, feet went up in the air, and the floor got cleaned with their dresses.

I saw the fights among the girls as a disgrace to women, and I vowed never to fight a girl for any boy. It looked downright ugly!

Still, I understood why the boys had the impulse to fight each other. They had seen adult men fighting on the streets. It was common in the bars and *cantinas*. Men drank until the late hours of the night, and then stepped outside to punch and slap each other. And often one guy pulled out a knife and cut the other.

Fighting between men became more intense during election years. They argued about who was the best political figure and who would do more for the working man.

One time a guy pulled out a gun, but his bullet went in the wrong direction and hit the back of a classmate's father. He was crippled for life. After hearing that story, I walked around scared that a bullet meant for someone else would cripple me.

I also learned during that semester that I had to worry about my virginity. A *señorita* could lose her virginity even if she had never been touched by a man. All she needed was an accusation by a man's jealous wife.

Men of all ages noticed when a girl's body developed. They would flirt with her even when they were working in a ditch, knowing that they had a half dozen children and a pregnant wife at home.

If the *señorita* made a mistake and looked toward the men, and by chance a jealous wife saw her, the rumors started. One word from a jealous wife would start the accusations. The girl had flirted, too, the women claimed. Before long, each woman told the story her way, and the accusation became a long line of gossip that spread like a contagious disease. A girl's reputation would then be ruined forever.

The words men said to the *señoritas* were called flowers. The dialogue was always the same: "I want you. I love you. I'll give my soul for you." From boys aged ten to little old men in their eighties, the flowers flew. "Your tiny waistline makes me dizzy. I'm hungry for you." It was accepted male behavior to flirt with girls until they grew too old to speak.

That wasn't fair, I concluded. It meant that girls were what people thought they were, and they could grow old waiting for time to prove the gossipers wrong.

I stopped to tell a classmate, Juan, that I didn't appreciate his "flowers," especially when I knew he had a girlfriend, and that I didn't need him or anyone to carry my books.

Before I knew it, someone ran to Juan's girlfriend, Dolores, and told her I had been talking with him.

Dolores confronted Juan, and he convinced her that I had been the one who went to him and confessed my special feelings for him. He had rejected me, he told her. To sound convincing, he told her that he wasn't attracted to blondes.

The next day, Dolores came after me. "I heard about your stupid attempt to seduce my boyfriend." Her black eyes peered at me. "Let me warn you, freckles, try one more time and I'll pull your pale hair out by the roots." Her own black hair hung like a bushy horse tail, and the dark skin of her face blushed with red spots.

"I have never heard a more stupid accusation," I told her. "Me seducing that boyfriend of yours? I wouldn't waste my time on him."

"You'd say anything to get out of it." She came closer to me. She was tall and big all around. I thought about Emilia, and about the time Lorenzo tore my pillow. He had lied about me breaking his shoulder. I received a terrible beating while he ran free.

But my parents weren't here now, so I could handle this problem without their interference.

"Just a minute!" I yelled. "Be smart. Bring that idiot and have him repeat his story to you in front of me. You'll see how fast he'll change his tune."

Juan decided to be clever. He told Dolores he wasn't about to participate in a female scuffle. He didn't know I could make decisions too, and my father wasn't there to punish me. I picked up a big rock and met him as he came out of the boys' bathroom.

"Tell Dolores the truth, or I'll smash your face!"

Juan squirmed and cried out to Dolores that he had been the one who flirted with me. "Only once—to make her mad—you know I don't like blondes."

I walked away, still holding the rock. Days later, I heard that Juan had told Dolores that he would admit to anything when someone held a rock to his face. I didn't hear whether she believed him, but she never bothered me again.

*   *   *

We didn't have class during holy week, and the sewing factory closed from Thursday until Monday. I used all those days to catch up on my studies. And the hard work paid off. I passed to ninth grade. In August, class would be on the third floor. I would wear a pink and gray uniform.

During summer break, after working hours, I made an umbrella skirt for Doña Luisa and embroidered a gray poodle on it, which stood out on the pink fabric. I made two dresses for myself, larger sizes now that my body was changing fast. I even made a sheath dress for Manuela. She insisted that her waistline was too big for other styles.

I finally went to the beach with Manuela and Carlos. As we walked downhill along a narrow path of rocks and holes, I realized why we hadn't gone before. The ocean didn't look so far from the balcony, but walking down to it took forever. Still, I felt thrilled that for once I'd be able to wet my feet in ocean water.

We took off our shoes and stepped down onto the heaps of sand. We laughed while walking like drunks. Carlos rolled up his trousers and walked into the water until it reached his knees. Manuela gathered her skirt and stepped in where the water went a few inches up her legs. I walked on the wet sand where the waves came in, covered my feet, and then quickly backed out again.

I saw some young boys in cut trousers running around, jumping into deep water and disappearing. Seconds later, they would come back on a foamy wave. It looked like a lot of fun, but I knew that swimming was another thing I might never learn to do.

"Manuela, do you know how to swim?" I asked.

"Oh no. That wasn't allowed when I was a girl."

"Well, can't you learn now?"

She shook her head firmly. "I'm too old."

"This isn't a good beach for swimming," Carlos said, water up to his knees. "Too many barracudas."

"What's a barracuda?" I asked, feeling like a little girl asking questions to loving parents.

"It's a big fish that eats people who get in its way."

"In that case, I'll never go in that water," I said jokingly, not knowing that this would be my only visit to the ocean in the four years I lived there.

I looked like a cooked lobster by the time we returned home, and the painful sunburn blistered and peeled.

That same summer, while working at the factory, I heard more stories of things I had never known could happen.

"My neighbor's daughter ran off with her boyfriend," one of the *inspectoras* said. "She threw her bundle of rags out the window when her parents were sleeping, and jumped into her lover's arms."

Another *inspectora* said, "My niece was really mad and aimed right for her husband's balls. If the trigger had not gotten stuck, he would have lost his precious jewels."

Everyone laughed, while I tried to figure out what the woman referred to as "his precious jewels." I didn't dare say it, but it bothered me that they laughed because someone had pointed a gun at another person. Anything about guns reminded me of my parents' first baby, the one I never met. He had died because there was a gun in the house, which the owner used as a toy.

By the end of that summer, I had heard so many weird and scary stories that I couldn't remember who told which. Still, when I returned to school in August, I heard more gossip, like this unforgettable and cruel story from a girl named Menta.

"My sister Rita's life is ruined," she began. "Papi found her behind the house yesterday, kissing her boyfriend Paco. What made Papi really mad was that Paco had his hand inside Rita's dress, squeezing her breast. Papi sneaked behind them and grabbed Paco by the hair. Paco's hand got caught in Rita's belt, and Papi almost broke it trying to pull the hand out. 'Go into the house,' he ordered her while he slapped the you-know-what out of Paco.

"Afterwards, Papi dragged Paco to his father, then came back home and locked Rita in her room and chained her to the wall, where she spent the whole night.

"This morning he told Mami to get Rita ready while he went to town to make arrangements for Rita and Paco to be married. I know my poor sister's life is ruined. Paco is nothing but a lazy bum. I don't know how Papi can be so mean to marry her off because of a stupid kiss."

The story made me sick. To think that a parent would ruin a young girl's life over some old-fashioned belief. It seemed to me that it was time to have a law against those kinds of parents. I thought about my mother. Her parents had married her to Papa, and she ended up having a miserable life.

I concluded not to ever let a boy touch me, even though my parents weren't around to force me to marry before I felt ready to do so. If I ever married, it would be only for love.

Chapter Fifty

A Blow to the Heart

One day in May, I arrived at the factory from school and found Doña Monica in Doña Luisa's office.

"Sabina, I'm glad you're early. Luisa had to leave at eleven. Don Felipe's in the hospital. He's very sick."

I froze. "In the hospital! He was fine this morning." I heard Doña Monica talking, but my mind had gone back to the day my mother told me about my godfather's death. Then I thought about my godmother, then about Cielo Azul, and Luana.

"Sabina! Come on! Don't cry. He'll be okay. Help me finish straightening up. Then we'll go to the hospital." Doña Monica's hand rested on my shoulder. "Make yourself strong. Luisa will need your help."

I felt hot tears running down my face. I didn't tell Doña Monica about the thoughts that had flashed through my mind. Maybe I didn't want to make her feel bad for me. Or maybe I didn't want my words to come out in sobs. I couldn't feel anything but fear at that time. I moved around in a daze, doing whatever Doña Monica told me to do.

We locked up the factory and headed for the hospital as soon as the last *inspectora* left. I had learned that hospitals existed in most towns, but I had seen this one only from a distance. I had concluded that hospitals were places where people went to cure their illnesses, and eventually everyone came out looking and feeling better.

On our way there, Doña Monica said, "Don Felipe has been in poor health ever since the accident, but he seemed better and happier since you came. You lifted his spirits."

I squeezed my words through the lump in my throat. "But he will be all right if he's in the hospital, won't he?"

"I hope so, for Luisa's sake. His death would hit her pretty hard. He's her whole life."

"She will always have me!" I cried.

Doña Monica reached over and squeezed my hand, and I knew she was weeping inside.

We walked through a wide door into a huge room where mothers held whimpering children, and the air smelled like urine and rubbing alcohol. A young woman dressed in white came from behind a desk and told Doña Monica to go down the long hallway and turn right at the third door.

As we walked past some open doors, I saw lines of high beds with white sheets. In most of those beds, I saw old women, some sitting up, wearing plain blue shirts that exposed their bony backs. Some moaned, while others stared into space, their eyes dried out and their white hair in need of a good comb. I thought then of my mother's stories about purgatory before entering heaven.

We found Doña Luisa on her knees facing the statue of the Virgin Mary, her black rosary dangling from her shaky hands. This was the praying room, where relatives of the sick would line up to wait their turn and pray to the Virgin.

Doña Luisa stood up as we entered the room and, reaching out to us, cried, "The doctor said that Felipe had a stroke!"

I felt a blow to my heart. I had heard the women at the factory talking about people who had suffered stokes, and were paralyzed and mute. All I could do was hug Doña Luisa and pray inside my head.

Leaving the room so others could pray, we went to the large waiting room.

"I hate to say it, but I'm afraid I might lose him," Doña Luisa sobbed with raw-looking eyes.

I looked at her as she held onto Doña Monica's hand, but I had no words to express my own sadness and concern. It would be terrible for everyone if Don Felipe died. Even though it seemed selfish, I had to ask myself how his death would affect my future. Would Doña Luisa continue working? Would she let me stay with her? I felt helpless, and wondered why bad things happened to good people.

An older lady dressed in white, with a stiff white cap over her head, came and told Doña Luisa that we could see Don Felipe. We followed the nurse down a hallway to a long room where yellowish curtains hung from the ceiling to provide privacy to the men in the two lines of high beds.

In one of those beds lay our Don Felipe with his head turned to the side. His mouth hung open, and saliva dripped down to the white sheet. With startled eyes, he lifted his left hand to touch his wife.

"*Ay mi pobresito! Mi Querido Felipe*," she cried, rubbing his right arm, which lay stiffly against his body.

Doña Monica stood at one side, patting Doña Luisa's back and saying comforting words. I stood at the other side, choking and wishing for the power to make everything good for the hurting people I had come to love.

*   *   *

Don Felipe was sent home five days later, for there wasn't anything the doctors could do for him. For the next two months, we took turns giving him all the love and care possible. Doña Luisa slept with him and fed him breakfast every morning. Carlos bathed, shaved, and dressed him, then wheeled him to the balcony for fresh air and stayed with him most of the time. Manuela fed him lunch and kept him company while Carlos did the outdoor work.

On the days when Doña Luisa had other commitments, I fed Don Felipe, combed his thin hair, rubbed his arms and legs, and read to him. I told him that I loved him, and that I would have a good future because of all the help he had given me. Even though his eyes had lost their sparkle, I could tell by the way he moved them that he felt pleased with my words and the things I did for him.

It became painful for me to watch Doña Luisa struggling to help Don Felipe squeeze out a word or two. Sometimes, I feared that she would suffer a stroke herself and end up like her husband.

Seeing Manuela and Carlos walk around with teary eyes made me think I was losing everyone who cared about me. Perhaps this was my punishment for running away from home. Maybe my mother's stories were true, that children who ran away from their parents would be cursed forever. I prayed that it wasn't so, for I had no intention of returning to the mud pit to stay.

*   *   *

On a Sunday afternoon in mid-July, a strong wind blew from the ocean, followed by heavy rain. Thunder boomed and lightning flashed.

This was the heaviest rain I had seen in the city.

Carlos and Manuela were visiting relatives, and Doña Luisa was down for her *siesta*. I was reading in my room. Suddenly I felt frightened, and thought of the time my godfather drowned.

I ran out of the room and down the dark hallway, feeling the same fear I had felt at the bottom of the mountain years earlier. My feet couldn't move fast enough; I imagined hands reaching out from inside the walls.

My heart pounded as loudly as the storm as I ran through the kitchen and downstairs to *la sala* outside Manuela's room. As I reached the lower step, a loud clap of thunder shook the house. I flew across the dark room to a corner directly under the kitchen—the side of the house that was underground without windows. I sat on the little wicker sofa with my knees against my chest, facing the only window on the opposite wall, and relived the storm near the creek years earlier.

Manuela had closed the blinds before she left, but the lightning still flashed through the tiny cracks where the louvers met. I couldn't hear the rain behind or above me, but I heard it splashing against the window.

The door to Manuela's room and the ones to the bathroom and laundry room were closed, and nothing was spookier to me than closed doors facing a long, dark hallway. I wanted to run back upstairs, but my legs felt numb. I stayed there, shifting my eyes back and forth from the closed doors to the louvers, waiting for ghosts or monsters.

A long time passed before I heard the kitchen floor squeak above my head. My heart made another attempt to leap from my chest. I tilted my head and heard the squeak again. Finally the door at the top of the stairs opened, and I heard the chilling squeak of each step. I knew that my mother's monsters had finally caught up with me. I waited with my eyes tightly closed, holding my breath.

"Where are you?"

Thank God! The voice sounded familiar. I opened my eyes and saw Doña Luisa, in her long white robe, standing like a statue at the bottom of the stairway.

"I figured you would be hiding from the storm," she said.

I stared at her as my trembling subsided. Finally, I asked, "Did the thunder keep you awake?"

"The thunder, the rain, the lightning, and Felipe."

"He can't sleep either?"

"Oh, he's asleep. It's the noise he makes in his sleep that keeps me awake. I'm going to have to move him to another room. I hate to do that, but I need my rest, too. I'm going back. Are you staying here?"

"No, I'll go up, too."

Something hit the floor on the other side of the house as we walked into the kitchen. We gave each other questioning looks and listened for more.

"Was that thunder?" I asked.

"No, it wasn't," she said. "Felipe!" She ran across the front room and down the hall. I was behind her when she ran into her bedroom. "Felipe!"

He was not in the bed.

"Felipe! Oh God, no! Sabina, help me get him back on the bed."

I leaped to her side, looking down at the floor between the bed and the wall. Don Felipe had fallen from the bed. His eyes were wide open, and white foam spilled from his mouth.

We lifted him up to the bed and called out his name. We rubbed him and shook him, but he was gone.

Chapter Fifty-One

Moving to New York

Doña Luisa cried during the wake, fainted at the cemetery, and continued crying through the novenas. She dressed in black, stopped wearing makeup and lipstick, and forgot how to smile. She put Doña Monica in complete charge of the factory and didn't return to the job for two months.

My heart ached for her. I wished I could take away her pain, yet all I could do was watch and cry with her. I was hurting, too. Losing Don Felipe was as bad as losing my godparents and my Cielo Azul. I couldn't understand why wonderful loved ones had to die.

Manuela did the housework with pain in her eyes. She loved the Linareses, and hated to see Doña Luisa suffer such grief. Carlos didn't seem to know what to do with the free time he had after finishing the outdoor work. The time he had spent taking care of Don Felipe was now spent with his hands in his pockets, as if waiting for someone to tell him what to do.

Sadness hung heavily around all of us, even after school started in the middle of August. I began tenth grade knowing that I would have a difficult time without Don Felipe's help. I left for the factory thirty minutes before class was over, only to find out that Doña Luisa had gone home. I then had to ride a public car part of the way home and walk for a long ways.

Doña Monica complained constantly about all the extra work that was dumped on her. "I can't carry on by myself. If she doesn't get over her grief soon, I'll quit. I can't go on doing her job and mine."

The bitter sound in Doña Monica's voice made me think she had stopped being a friend to her boss. Still, I didn't know which one to feel more sorry for. The ambitions I wanted to achieve no longer seemed important. The people who had cheered me on were no longer there. One had died, and the other spent her time in her room or on the balcony, rocking and staring at the sky.

I spent a lot of time and energy walking from one place to another. By the time I reached home, I felt too tired to think about homework. Soon I began to fall behind in my studies, feeling the constant pressure to catch up, but unable to do so.

One day I walked into the factory and heard the women talking about the possibility that Doña Luisa would sell her house and move to New York. Fear traveled through me like fire. *Where will I go?*

"You can come live with me," said Joséfina, an *inspectora*.

"Oh no, she'll live with me," Doña Monica said. Even Maria, another *inspectora*, suggested that she would gladly take me in.

Arriving home one evening, I found Manuela at the kitchen sink with tears running down her face. "What's wrong?" I asked, thinking that someone else had died.

Manuela wiped her tears with the back of her hand. "Go see Doña Luisa. She's in the dining room."

I walked slowly, afraid of what I might find, and saw Doña Luisa at the table, sorting through a pile of papers. This didn't seem to be the reason Manuela was crying.

"Excuse me, Doña Luisa. Something's wrong with Manuela."

"I know she's crying, but nothing's wrong." She hesitated. "Well, I mean, she's not sick, and no one has died." Doña Luisa didn't look at me. Her hands kept reaching for papers, putting some in folders and to the side, and dropping others into a brown bag on the floor.

"What about you, Doña Luisa? Are you all right?" I stood confused, books in hand. "Is there something I can do to help?"

She lifted her head and stared at me for a few seconds. Finally, she drew a breath and released it in a long sigh. "My sisters want me to move to New York, and I'm considering it." Her face looked drained, and her eyes were red.

I felt as if a bolt of lightning had stricken a corner of the house. "Move to New York? What would I do?"

She tilted her head. "Go with me."

"Go with you? Doña Luisa, this is so sudden!"

"No, it isn't. I've been thinking about it for months. Please, tell me you'll go." Her voice faded as she turned back to her papers.

"New York, you said? Isn't that far away?"

"Not anymore," she said, moving one handful of papers to one side, another to the bag. She seemed in a hurry, as if she were planning to leave soon. "Airplanes fly fast. You can have breakfast here and supper in New York the same day."

"New York! Airplanes! I have never thought of going that far." I waited for more from her, but she kept sorting papers. I walked quietly to my room and stretched out on my bed with my hands behind my head.

What does an airplane look like inside? And how does it feel to actually fly in one? Traveling through the air in something that looks like a big fish from the ground must be invigorating. I would be the first person from the hills fortunate enough to fly in an airplane.

I imagined the look on my parents' and Emilia's faces when they heard that I had not drowned, but had flown to New York in an airplane, had learned English, and had become a real American.

I'm already a United States citizen, as all Puerto Ricans are, and with green eyes and blonde hair, I'll look American.

I jumped off the bed and hurried to find Doña Luisa. Between my room and the living room, a thought flashed through my mind: *What about the promise I made in the jungle? If I don't go back to help my brothers and sisters, will I be punished? Is breaking a promise a sin?*

I knew it would soon be four years since I had left home. That meant that everyone was that much older. I might not be able to help my older sisters and the two older boys. But I would feel really good about myself if I could give the three younger ones a chance to get away from their enslavement.

I found Doña Luisa still sorting papers.

"How soon will you move to New York?" I asked.

"As soon as I sell the house and most of my things." Doña Luisa wasn't one to waste time.

"Well . . . I would love very much to move with you, but I feel that I need more time here. At least until I graduate from high school."

"Graduate!" She closed the box, her eyes on me. "Why can't you graduate in New York?"

"I don't know English. Isn't that what they speak there?"

"It is what they speak, but you can learn."

"Learning a new language would take a long time, don't you think? I'd like to graduate before I'm too old."

"An older person would take a long time to learn a new language, but a young girl like you could learn in a few months."

"To be honest, Doña Luisa, I do have another reason for wanting to wait. You might think I'm crazy, but I would like to go back to the hills—just to see if I can help my brothers and sisters escape."

"That's the stupidest thing I've ever heard you say." She stepped away from the table, looking as she did the night she found me in her storage room. "You want to go back there, knowing that your father might kill you? That's insane!" She picked up the box and carried it to her room.

I felt torn between what I believed and what I thought Doña Luisa wanted for me. It was an uncomfortable feeling. I didn't want to hurt the woman who had done so much for me. Yet there was the nagging desire to go back to the hills. Would I really be able to help my brothers and sisters? Or did I want to go just to show my parents and Emilia that I had survived and had done well in spite of their cruelty?

We had supper in the kitchen with Carlos and Manuela. Only the soft clicking of forks could be heard after saying grace. There were frequent glances and the lazy reach for the glasses of water, followed by the dull tap as we placed the glasses back on the table.

The silence was killing me, and finally I had to break it.

"I thought about what you said, Doña Luisa, and you're right. I would be risking my life by going back to the hills, and my graduating would be fine in New York. Thank you for wanting me to go with you. However, I still want to think a little longer before giving you an answer."

She put down her fork. "I'm glad you think I'm right, but don't wait too long. I need to know who's going with me and who's staying."

"All I need is a few days. Then I'll let you know my decision. There's one other thing, though. What about you and Carlos, Manuela? Where will you go?"

"We're following Doña Luisa to New York. She'll go ahead to find a place big enough for all of us."

"That's great!" I said, clapping my hands. "We'll stay a family!" This made the three of them chuckle and clap, which sounded very nice.

For a short time afterward, I pretended that all my problems had been resolved.

Chapter Fifty-Two

On Second Thought

Doña Luisa resigned from her job, which made the factory workers cry.

"Things will not be the same without you! We know you should be with family, but it hurts to lose you. You'll probably never come back. We'll never see you again." They cried, and the whole place was in mourning for weeks.

Trying to decide what to do became a torture for me. I wanted to move to New York and forget about my family. But even though I loved Doña Luisa, deep inside I longed to see my mother. Perhaps the grief of losing me had made her a kinder mother. For all I knew, even Papa could have changed. The only way I would know was to go there.

I couldn't give Doña Luisa an answer, even when she expressed concern about what my father would do to me if I showed up after such a long time.

I couldn't turn down her invitation, either. It was as though I expected time to change everything before I had to make the decision.

The women from the factory who had offered their homes were also waiting for an answer. Even the pharmacist who bought Doña Luisa's house had asked me to stay and work for his family. When I told him that I didn't want to quit school, he said that I could do both, attend school half a day and work after class.

I couldn't concentrate on my school work in class or at home with all the decisions pending. The uncertainties kept me worrying day and night. Some nights I couldn't fall asleep. When I finally did, I had terrible dreams about flying over water—dreams in which I struggled to make it to the other side, then would lose momentum and fall through the air, waking up in a sweat just before touching the water.

Finally, one night Doña Luisa called me to the balcony and insisted that I give her my decision. She needed to make the flight reservations.

"I really want you to move to New York with me, Sabina. I care about you as if you were my natural daughter. Have you forgotten that on your first day of school, we both agreed to treat each other as mother and daughter?"

I felt a sudden jolt of guilt. I had not shown consideration to the woman who had taken me in and treated me with the motherly love I had never known.

"Oh, Doña Luisa, I am so sorry. I'll never forget our agreement, and I don't want to disappoint you. Please don't be upset. I'll move with you. I really will."

Doña Luisa sighed, opening her arms to me. "Felipe would be pleased if you move with me. He had never wanted me to end up alone."

I rested my head on her chest and told her that I didn't want her to be alone, either, and that she was the most loving mother in the whole world, and that I worried about her living in New York without me.

She pulled her head back and looked into my eyes. "You do? You really worry about me?"

"Of course I do. You're all I have." We sobbed together.

Later, in my room, I felt torn and confused. To avoid hurting Doña Luisa, I had turned my back on my promise. New York seemed so far away. How could I help my brothers and sisters from there? What if I couldn't come back for five years? How much older would the poor kids be?

I broke into a sweat. New York would have to wait.

Early the next morning, I knocked on Doña Luisa's door and told her that I wanted to go to the farm and see my mother before I left for New York.

"Then I'll go with you," she said without hesitation.

With great effort, I convinced her that without her I could hide in the bushes for days if I had to. "I can run fast if Papa sees me. But how fast would you be able to run through vines and over rocks?"

At first I thought she felt rejected, but then she smiled and said, "I get the point."

"Oh, it's not that you aren't fit," I said quickly, seating myself at the foot of her bed. "Those hills are treacherous, and you aren't familiar with them. I'd die if something happened to you because of me."

She thought for a moment, then asked, "So are you going just to see your mother? What if she doesn't let you leave again?"

"I ran away before. I'll run away again."

"What if your brothers and sisters do follow you?"

"If they do . . . I would want to help them."

Her face turned sad again. "What about me, and New York?"

"Maybe I can rent a house, get them settled, and then join you in New York. I can get a job there and send them money. What do you think?"

Leaning back against the headboard, she stared at me with wide eyes. Then she said, "I have an idea." She stroked her chin, thinking. "You can bring them to Aguadilla."

"Aguadilla?"

"That's where the new Air Force base is, and they're hiring civilians. It's only twenty-five miles from here. My friend Inez lives right outside the main gate. You met her at Felipe's funeral, remember? She owns a restaurant there, and she has several homes, too, which she rents out. I know she can help you get them settled. I think you should check the possibilities. I can take you there while I still have the car. I want to see Inez before I leave, anyway."

"Doña Luisa! Going to visit your friend is a wonderful idea, but my family might not be that easy to help."

"Take it one step at a time," she said. "Go with me to see Inez. While we're there, we'll tour the base. If you see possibilities, you can persuade your family to come away with you. If they refuse your help, you'll be free to move to New York. At least you'll know you tried."

"Great idea! Aguadilla, here we come!"

Chapter Fifty-Three

Borinquen

On Sunday morning, we headed for Aguadilla and the base on the northwest tip of the island. We had dressed in dark colors, since we were still in mourning, yet I fantasized that we were on a pleasure trip rather than checking something so I could begin a new struggle.

Keeping busy with work and school for the past four years, I hadn't been outside the city limits. Everything I would see on this trip would be new and exciting to me.

Doña Luisa seemed happier this morning, too. Even though she didn't wear makeup, her skin glowed and her eyes looked bright and cheery.

Soon after leaving the city, Doña Luisa said, "We're coming up to the river you followed here."

Suddenly, we were on a bridge—the first one I had ever seen. As the car started across, I looked far to my left and saw where the river met with the ocean. Far to my right, I saw the narrow valley on both sides of the river, and the line of distant mountains. The memories of my father telling me where the river began and where it ended came back. Little did he realize that one day I would follow that same river to run from him.

Leaving the bridge, we entered a street that was lined with

flamboyant trees rich in green foliage. The branches touched each other over the street, creating a green canopy.

"Oh, how beautiful!" I said.

Doña Luisa nodded. "Yes, it is. You should see it when the trees are in bloom. It's like driving under a red roof."

"Gee . . . we'll miss that if we move to New York."

"Ah, I've seen it. And you can always come back."

"Come back to Mayaguez? Without you?"

"Well, just come to see the trees, and then turn around."

We both laughed at that, and the sound was good.

There was silence after the laughter. Then Doña Luisa asked, "You aren't thinking of going home through the mountains and up the river, are you?"

"No. This time I'll travel by public car. I've saved some money from my allowance, which I'll use for transportation. I'm sure no one will recognize me, since I look more like a woman than the skinny little girl who disappeared four years ago."

"Aren't you afraid your father will hurt you? Maybe even kill you for running away?"

"He has to catch me first, but I won't let him."

"How will you visit without him seeing you?"

"To be honest, I haven't made any plans. But I think I can figure out a way. Please don't worry about me, Doña Luisa. I'll be okay."

"Good. You know, Sabina, in New York you'll learn to speak English."

I laughed. "I don't think you'll stop worrying about me until you see me come back from the hills."

"All I said was that you'll learn English."

"I know, but you were thinking about my trip. Besides, English sounds like a hard language to learn."

"Bah! You'll be talking like an American in three months."

"I hope you're right," I said. "But it's hard for me to imagine speaking anything but Spanish."

"You'll end up marrying an American and living the rest of your life in the United States."

I laughed at that, too. "No American would want to marry someone like me. Anyway, I might not ever get married."

"You don't have to get married. But what makes you think that an American man would not want to marry you? You're a good girl, bright and beautiful. What else would a man want?"

"I think you give me more credit than I deserve."

"I don't know anyone who deserves more credit than you do. Look at what you've done! You ran away from your parents, did well in school, and now you're going back to help your brothers and sisters. Wait and see. A few years from now, you'll look back at your life and wonder how you accomplished so much."

"I'll have you to thank for whatever I accomplish," I told her.

"Fine, but don't forget that I didn't go to the mountains to rescue you. You came to me. I wasn't very sympathetic when I found you in my storage room, either. What a mess you were! I didn't want to take the time to help anyone. I had enough problems taking care of Felipe. The only thing that kept me from calling the police was that you reminded me of my Teresita."

"Even with my messy hair, I resembled her?"

She nodded. "I saw beyond the hair and the torn dress."

"What would the police have done to me?"

"They would probably have taken you back to your parents."

I shivered at the thought. "Thank you for not calling them. I'd be dead by now."

A road sign read *Aguadilla 9 kilometros* and an arrow pointed to a narrower road curving to the right. Doña Luisa took that road.

"We'll go through town so you can see it," she said.

The street was lined with wooden houses on stilts and *cantinas* with jukeboxes blaring. Children dressed in torn, dirty clothing played outside and on broken-down balconies. Dogs with patches of hair missing lay in the sun while others, skinny and shaggy, roamed along the edge of the road.

"This is an area you must stay away from," Doña Luisa said. "It's called *el mondongo*, a place for prostitutes." She turned right, and on that street the houses were halfway over water, with short stilts on the street side and long ones on the ocean side.

"How can they sleep with waves crashing on the houses?"

Doña Luisa chuckled. "I don't think they sleep much, anyway."

She pointed out the places of interest: the main street, the huge old church facing the plaza, the courthouse, the municipal building, the theater, and a fabric store.

Finally, she turned into a street called Borinquen, and we were on our way to the Air Force base.

"Start looking for *Americanos*," she said. "They usually come down this road by the truckloads on Sundays on their way to the beach. They'll be wearing short pants or swimming briefs, so you'll see a lot of bare legs and chests."

The minute she finished speaking, a blue truck with gates around its flat bed and *U.S. Air Force* printed in orange on the side came barreling down the hill filled with laughing *gringos*. They waved and whistled, and I saw their blonde, shiny hair and beaming blue eyes. They were traveling fast, going one way and we the other, so we passed in a flash. But I saw enough to want to see more.

We came up to a small square building in the middle of the road, where Doña Luisa obtained a visitor's pass from a tall man in a blue uniform.

Entering the base was like going into another world. I had never seen such a beautiful place. Huge expanses of grass spread like green velvet on both sides of the street. There were palm trees and blooming hedges of hibiscus everywhere.

We passed the military airport, where I saw airplanes for the first time and American men walking around, some in khaki uniforms and others in blue, looking tall and confident.

We passed a fenced area where women wearing short pants and summer tops swung rackets at bouncing balls. Doña Luisa said they were playing tennis. I couldn't believe the wealth of the Americans. The women actually had time to play games. That wasn't how it was for the women I knew.

Approaching a large field of green grass, I practically bounced off my seat. "Men wearing women's colors! Look at that! Red, bright yellow, and green!"

Doña Luisa laughed again. "Golfers usually wear bright colors. But American men don't have the hang-ups Puerto Rican men have, so you'll see them wearing bright-colored shirts, and even some with prints. They don't believe that they might lose their *machismo* by wearing colors."

The farther we went, the more impressed I was by the appearance of the base. I had heard about people coming here from all over the island to find jobs, but I had no idea that it would look like this. Everything looked so clean, bright, and beautiful. There were no shacks on stilts with rusty roofs or little huts made from palm leaves.

"Thank you, Doña Luisa, for bringing me here."

We reached an area where there were concrete buildings, four and five stories high, with many louvered windows with screens. Doña Luisa said these were barracks where the soldiers lived. I found this extraordinary—a luxurious place in my island of so many poor people.

"We're coming up to the base exchange," Doña Luisa said. "We'll see a lot of American women. This is where they shop. We'll have lunch in their cafeteria, so you can look them over."

She couldn't have brought me to a better place than this. It was incredible. The women pulled up in cars and parked between white lines in a huge parking lot. They stepped out, some dressed in short pants with sleeveless blouses, others in slacks or summer dresses. They wore pretty sandals, and I could see their clean white feet with red toenails.

I felt embarrassed to be staring, but I couldn't help it. I had thought of Mayaguez as a rich city, but it couldn't compare to this base.

"Let's have a hamburger for lunch," Doña Luisa said. "Have you ever eaten one?"

"What's a hamburger?"

"It's meat with tomatoes and lettuce between two slices of

round bread. You'll like it. They know how to make good ones here."

We walked into a huge, clean, and airy restaurant where many tables were occupied by Americans. Some of the women had small children with them—beautiful children with blonde hair and blue or green eyes. This made me feel even better. I knew no one would make fun of my hair and eyes here.

We went to a counter, where Doña Luisa ordered two hamburgers with french fries and coffee. A young Puerto Rican man wearing a white jacket and cap took the order and said he would call our number.

Doña Luisa seemed relaxed and sure of herself, as if places like this weren't a big deal. But to me, this seemed like a foreign country.

We chose a table and waited for our meal. I glanced from one face to another, listening to the strange language. It didn't sound like the few English words I had learned in school, or like something I would be able to learn in three months, as Doña Luisa had suggested.

Eating my first hamburger turned into an embarrassing experience. I bit into the bun, and a green disc mixed with catsup and mustard ejected onto the plate with a splash. My face felt hot, as I wondered what this green disc was. Of course, I later found out it was a slice of pickle.

When I looked from under my brow and saw that no one was laughing, I retrieved the green disc and quickly stuffed it into my mouth. As I bit the pickle, my whole face went into some kind of spasm. I knew I would die of embarrassment, and if I didn't die, Doña Luisa would probably disown me. But she ate as if nothing had happened, so I covered my nervousness by eating my messy hamburger as delicately as I could.

After lunch, Doña Luisa drove around the base, past the officers' club and its beautiful beach. She drove on residential streets where I saw many concrete houses on each side of the street. These houses had manicured lawns and trimmed shrubs around them. I even saw fenced backyards with children hanging on a couple of chains and swinging back and forth, laughing and singing as their light hair blew in the wind. I envied them, and wondered what it would be like to grow up like that.

"We'd better head on toward Inez's place," Doña Luisa said, "if we want to get back home before dark."

"Thank you, Doña Luisa, for bringing me here. I had no idea that such a place existed."

"You're welcome. And I hope you'll like New York, too."

We reached the main gate, and Doña Luisa returned the visitor's pass to the M.P. on duty. She thanked him in English, and it sounded strange to me. A short distance from the gate, she pulled into a parking space in front of a business that read *Inez's Restaurant and Billiards*. Above the entrance, I saw a picture of a young woman wearing a white apron over a short black dress, carrying a tray with a mug of golden beer with white foam spilling over the rim.

Doña Luisa told me this was a popular place for civilian men working on the base. They came here for their meals and entertainment. Soldiers who liked activities outside the base also came here.

The popular love song *Entre Copa y Copa* was blaring from a jukebox, while men played billiards in the middle of a large room.

Doña Inez saw us from the kitchen and came out with a brilliant smile and open arms. "Luisita! What a wonderful surprise! And you brought the young lady with you. How nice! Please follow me into the kitchen. We are preparing the early Sunday dinner for my regular customers."

We walked into the warm smell of onions, garlic, and other spices. A younger woman stood at the cooking counter, stirring red rice with ham in a huge iron pot. She smiled brightly when Doña Inez introduced her as her "right-hand helper."

I offered to help so Doña Inez could visit with her friend.

"What a doll you are to offer a hand. Thank you," she said,

and Doña Luisa winked at me. I felt so good; I almost forgot why I had come here.

I washed some pots and other dishes that the girl, who was named Ida, kept bringing to a deep concrete sink in a corner. I could hear the two friends chatting at a table in the opposite corner, but with the noise from the pots and the running water, I couldn't make out their words.

By the time we left, Doña Luisa had given her friend a ten dollar deposit on the only rental available in the area. It was the old grocery store she had used before starting this restaurant and billiards.

"This will give you a place to bring your family until a house is available," said Doña Luisa. "I told Inez about your plans, and she understands completely. Like me, she wishes you could forget all about your family and move to New York. But if you go on with your plan, she will help you with information about finding work on the base. Inez is a good woman. You can trust her."

I couldn't find the right words to say how grateful I was. I felt excited about the possibility of bringing some of my brothers and sisters here. But I could only picture Alicia being happy and friendly about the move. I knew she would be fun to have around. I didn't know much about my two younger brothers, for they were quite young when I left. As for the older siblings, what I remembered most were the nasty things they did to me.

But I knew that if I told Doña Luisa about my mixed feelings, she would insist that I leave well enough alone. Ironically, I felt determined to do something I really feared doing.

Doña Luisa unlocked the door to the old grocery store, a wooden building with a tin roof and a concrete floor. It was dusty and occupied by cobwebs. Two tall shelves divided this room into three spaces: one for sleeping, one for cooking, and the other for washing clothes and bathing. The latrine behind the building would be shared with two other families.

Living here would not be easy, but as Doña Luisa said, it was a start.

"Now, Sabina," she said, "I want you to listen to me. I can't talk you out of going through with your plans, although I wish you could forget your family and go to New York with me. It might sound cruel to you, but I don't think you should sacrifice your life for them. They were mean to you, and they might not have changed. You're probably making trouble for yourself by bringing them here."

"Don't worry. I don't think they will come."

"Then why bother going?"

"So that I can be satisfied that I tried."

"You are a stubborn young lady," she said, shaking her head.

"You wouldn't like me any other way, I'm sure."

Doña Luisa stretched open her arms, and we embraced.

Chapter Fifty-Four

Going Home

On the third week of November, a Friday morning, I left Mayaguez in a pickup truck full of furniture and household goods. Pancho, the owner of the truck, was an acquaintance of Doña Luisa. She had hired him to drive me to Aguadilla, where I would catch the first *público* and start out on the journey to the farm.

He would continue on to Doña Inez's in Borinquen, and she would show him where to unload the furniture. With the furniture were two boxes with all my clothes and the things I had accumulated in four years.

One smaller sealed box was to be delivered to Doña Inez by Pancho. I didn't know what was in that box, but this was the advice from Doña Luisa: If my family refused to go with me, I was to return to Mayaguez and leave with her two weeks later. If my family left with me, I was to report to Doña Inez for instructions from Doña Luisa.

Before leaving Mayaguez, while Pancho and Carlos loaded the truck, I said goodbye to Manuela and Doña Luisa in the event I didn't come back. This was painful. I had written a note of thanks for each of them to read after I left, but I knew that they read them before they went to bed. All three of us had red eyes that morning as we hugged one another goodbye, each trying to be brave for the sake of the others.

I wore an outfit that I had made especially for that trip: a brown skirt over short pants with elastic around the legs and hidden pockets to carry my transportation money. The blouse was green and yellow, with sleeves down to my elbows. The colors I had chosen would blend with the bushes if I had to hide. I wrapped a brown turban around my head to hide my blonde hair, and I wore brown shoes with thick soles and heavy shoelaces.

In a bag I had made out of brown gabardine, I carried a canteen of water, a small box of saltine crackers and a bag of raisins, a spare blouse and underpants, a pair of socks, a toothbrush, and a comb.

The crackers and raisins were Doña Luisa's suggestions. She said they would give me energy. She also gave me her old binoculars.

I would be traveling all day on narrow, winding roads, changing *publico* cars in two different towns, and then walking some distance down hills to reach the farm.

I had never been on the road between Aguadilla and San Sebastian, but I knew that Papa didn't come this far, so I didn't worry about running into him.

However, my feelings changed when I reached San Sebastian. I knew this was his town. He would be here tomorrow, selling his beans and eggs. I half-expected him to be around the next corner. I became nervous and suspicious. I imagined that everyone who looked at me knew me, and they would run to tell my father.

In spite of my shaky knees, I reached the *publico* stand and, avoiding eye contact with others, sat in the middle seat next to the door for a quick exit. I knew my outfit drew attention; the *señoritas* around here didn't dress like this and didn't carry bags like mine. Still, I believed that my disguise would keep hill people who might come aboard the *publico* from recognizing me.

A woman passenger sat next to me and immediately asked if I knew the time, if I was hot "with that thing" around my head, and where I was from. I shook my head to one question, shrugged at the other, and murmured, "Aguadilla" to the third. She kept trying to see my eyes, tilting her head to the side like a pigeon. I looked out the window, hoping she would get tired and leave me alone.

We reached the end of the paved road at about 1:00 in the afternoon. From then on, I had to be very careful. I didn't think anyone would recognize me, but I didn't want to take any chances. So I walked, stopped and listened, and hid behind bushes at the sound of voices, horses, or footsteps.

Everything looked the same as it had years earlier: tall trees, coffee fields, little wooden houses with dogs barking, and ragged little children playing in the dirt. I felt like a thief, hiding and waiting for the right moment to step out and run.

I reached my old school, and felt shocked and sad to see that weeds and bushes had grown tall around it, blocking the windows and doors. The only parts I could see were the red roof and the flagpole. I couldn't believe that the school had closed again after it had reopened. That meant that my sisters and brothers, as well as the other kids from the hills, were not attending school.

I walked past the old house where the crazy old man had lived, realizing that in three years of running past here, I had never seen him. The only things left of the house now were the stilts and the bougainvillea vines climbing up a tree. Next I came up to the fern field, where the view was still spectacular, the ground was level, and the yellow butterflies still flew.

Leaving the fern field, I headed downhill into the forest. A thousand memories flashed through my mind. I remembered the first day of school, when I followed Emilia and Papa, afraid of both. I thought of the many times we were caught in storms. We would slide, fall, and roll until a tree trunk stopped us. The woods seemed so scary then.

Today the sun filtered through the branches, and I could see around the tree trunks without worrying about monsters. Of course, I still had to worry about running into Papa. He could appear from behind any tree. But somehow I felt confident that I would see him before he saw me. I didn't stare at one spot; my eyes were everywhere, my head constantly turning.

Coming up to our property line, I heard voices way down by the creek. I hid behind a tree, listening to the sound of machetes or axes chopping wood, and roosters crowing.

I should have listened to Doña Luisa.

I tried to walk quietly, but that wasn't easy with all the dry leaves crackling under my shoes. I kept telling myself not to panic, but when I saw a moving branch from the corner of my eye—stirred by the wind or a small forest creature—my heart sounded like a galloping horse. I saw the woods as beings, coming slowly toward me to capture me and imprison me.

I walked away from the trail and found a little slope where I sat to think. I had two choices: I would either become stronger and continue down toward the house, or I would turn and run back to Doña Luisa.

She was right: Coming here was a stupid idea. After four years of living in the city, I had forgotten what these woods were like. I had even forgotten about going in the bush instead of using the toilet. God, I couldn't believe how different and difficult everything seemed to me. The best thing for me to do would be to head back up the hill and forget all about this part of the world.

That was an appealing thought, but I couldn't act on it right away. I ate a few crackers and raisins, then took out the binoculars and scanned around the trees. Everything was clear ahead, so I continued forward on my mission.

Still, I struggled with two voices inside my head. One told me to run out of the woods and go back to where people were civilized. The other voice reasoned that as long as I had come this far, I might as well satisfy my curiosity and see what I had run from four years earlier. I had longed to see how everything and everyone in my family looked after four years. I had wondered how much bigger my sisters and brothers had grown. I wanted to see if the house looked as bad as I remembered, and if Mama had another baby, or maybe even two.

Most importantly, I wanted to find out what everyone thought and did the day I disappeared.

I didn't want to go too far down the hill until four o'clock. That was the time Papa would stop working and head for his hammock. Hopefully, I wouldn't run into barbed wire, holes in the ground, or pig pens around the house. I knew that a lot of changes could have taken place in four years.

I started across the hillside, staying close to the property line, aiming for the gorge above the springs. From there, I would be able to watch the house, then go down to the springs where I hoped to find my sisters fetching water.

I had to be very careful, for one loose rock would quickly send me to the bottom of the hill. I had once walked across this gorge like a cat, but after four years on level ground and paved streets, I found it very difficult.

I don't know how long it took, but I eventually made it to the spot I had wanted to reach. I was sweating, my knees were shaking, and I had sore fingertips from grabbing branches and rocks.

Leaning against a tree, I looked through the binoculars. When I spotted the house, my heart thumped. I felt happy and scared at the same time. Maneuvering around the branches, I saw the kitchen side. The door was open, but I didn't see anyone around. Then I saw chickens and heard pigs squealing.

The house appeared smaller than I remembered. It was hard to believe that so many traumatic incidents had taken place in such a small house.

I checked around frequently, afraid that Papa would pop out from behind a bush. Had it not been for the binoculars, I would have felt terrified and might not have come this far.

The next time I looked toward the house, I saw one of my brothers hurrying around the yard. It was either José or Lorenzo— I couldn't be sure which. Then one of the two younger boys, Alejandro or Felipito, came out from under the trees with a bundle of wood on his shoulder. I thought I would fly out of my shoes, I was so eager to get closer.

Then I almost dropped the binoculars when I saw my father appear in the yard on a black horse from behind a line of trees. I quickly lowered the binoculars, gasping loudly, as if he were right in front of me. I felt my heart fall into my stomach. Heat rushed through my body, and my heartbeat echoed in my ears.

I had to look again before he disappeared. With shaky hands, I brought the binoculars to my eyes, only for a fraction of a second before removing them to look around me, and then taking another glimpse. Papa still looked mean and strong, with a straight back and broad shoulders, his head turning left and right, his face stern. He wore brown clothes and a beige hat. The old machete lay across his lap.

Feeling powerless, and very small, I shoved the binoculars into my bag and hid behind the tree, where I could take deep, deep breaths and think. Momentarily, my brain refused to move beyond two questions: Why had I not listened to Doña Luisa? Why had I come back to this jungle of fear, thorny weeds, and crawling insects?

Unless Papa had changed his routine, he would be inside now, settling in his hammock for the night, hopefully with his bottle. If my predictions were right, I would be able to reach the house without him knowing it. The trick was to keep track of him. Guessing that he might not even wonder what had become of me, I felt that I had an advantage over him: I knew where he was.

I had been lucky so far. Not even a drop of rain had interfered with my plans, and I felt sure that God would not abandon me now.

I hurried down the rest of the hill, sliding and tripping all the way to the springs. Everything looked as it had when I had left: dry leaves covering the ground, clear water filtering from the huge rocks, and the runoff hissing over its pebble-covered path.

I knew that I had changed in the past four years, but I hadn't expected to feel so strange being here. Even the water filtering through the rocks tasted strange, as if it contained rust or metal.

I remembered that it had taken me a long time to get used to city water.

The sunlight had disappeared, and I knew that the woods would soon be dark, yet no one had come for water. Maybe the routine had changed. Maybe no one would come around anymore.

Feeling sad and disappointed, I washed my arms and hands, then sat on the rock above the stream to wait a little longer.

Time passed, and fear crept in. The birds flew in for the night, noisily taking their places in the trees, and the *coquí* (a little frog) serenaded from the banana plants.

I decided to head up toward the house and hide just before reaching the yard. Then, to my delight, I heard the dry leaves shuffling, and through the branches I saw my little sister Alicia coming with the water can. Our old dog, Canela, followed her, lifting her paws in slow motion as if feeling her age.

I wanted to jump out and hug my sister, but I didn't want to startle her. If she screamed, someone might hear her and come to investigate.

I sat back and watched her as she put the can under the stream only a few feet from me. She sat on a rock to wait, looking smaller than I had imagined. I guessed that she was the age I had been when I left, but she didn't look twelve.

Canela pointed her nose up, let out a lazy bark, and plopped herself down beside Alicia.

Finally, when I felt sure that nobody else was coming, I called Alicia's name and slowly stepped down. "Alicia, don't make a sound. I'm your sister, Sabina."

She sprang to her feet, eyes wide as if she'd seen a ghost.

"It's really me, don't be scared. You were only eight when I left. That's why you don't remember me."

"I remember you," she said, stepping back. "But you're supposed to be dead. Stay away from me! You're a ghost." She kept backing away.

"I'm not a ghost. Please listen." I stepped closer so I could grab her if she ran or screamed. If she did, I would have to fly out of there or be killed. "Please let me explain. I'm really alive, see? Feel me. Pinch me." I took her hand. "Pinch me—I'm alive. I need to talk with you before someone comes looking for you."

Alicia stood still, staring. "But you look so different. Bigger and—prettier! Didn't you drown in the river? Where have you been?"

"No, I didn't drown, and I'll tell you where I've been later. For now, I need to know some things." I felt the moisture on my palms, and the fear that she still might run.

"Nobody will come looking for me," she said.

"Why not?"

"Because they never do."

I stared at her. She was dressed in a skimpy little dress made of flour sacks and dyed with *jengibrillo* (wild ginger roots). Her skinny legs were covered with scratches and open sores. She hadn't grown much.

"Why would nobody come looking for you?"

"Why would they? Nobody cares what happens to me."

This simple statement, sounding so much like something I might have said four years ago, brought a lump to my throat. But I swallowed it down. I didn't have time for sentiment.

"Listen, Alicia, we have to talk quickly. I need to know where Papa and Mama are right now, and what they're doing."

She looked puzzled. "Why?"

"Because I came to take you and the others away."

"Take us away? Where could we go that Papa wouldn't find us?" Alicia waved her skinny arms. She looked in pain. "Where could we go?"

"Don't worry about that. I have a place, and I'll deal with Papa on my side of the fence."

"You have a fence? Are you rich?" Her eyebrows went up, and her big brown eyes grew bigger. "Are you rich? Where have you been?"

"No, I'm not rich. Not yet, anyway. Now tell me quickly, before it gets much darker."

"Papa is in his hammock, drinking and blubbering about how he's going to do away with all of us one of these days."

That sounded like Papa, all right. "And Mama?"

"Mama is cooking supper and asking God to take her away."

I shook my head. "So nothing has changed."

"Oh, it has," she corrected. "It has gotten worse."

"What about Gloria? Does she still faint?"

"No, she hasn't fainted for a long time. Mama said that she outgrew her fainting spells."

That was one bit of good news, at least. "Okay, listen, Alicia. Can you help me find a place to hide for the night? Are there any other dogs? Holes I might fall into? New shacks, or barbed wire?"

"No dogs, no shacks or barbed wire. Just a few holes for banana plants, but they're on the hillside facing the front room. There aren't any goats under the house, and the pigs go into pens for the night. You can hide under the house."

"What about tomorrow? Will Papa be home?"

She thought for a moment. "What day is tomorrow?"

"Saturday."

"Papa goes to town every Saturday. Are you staying until then?" Alicia's sad face broke into a brilliant smile.

"Alicia, you mustn't tell anyone I'm here. If Papa finds out, he'll chase me away, and you'll have to spend the rest of your life in this mud hole. Do you understand?"

"I'll never, never tell," she promised, "'cause I want you to take me away. You can hide under the house, under the sleeping area."

"Why the sleeping area?"

"There's a loose board under my cot. I can hand some food down to you. That's what I do for Mama when Papa throws her out."

I couldn't help giggling when Alicia said that, but inside, my heart ached. Apparently, my disappearance had made matters worse for everyone. I had thought the loss of one child would make my parents appreciate the others more. I had been wrong. My anxiety grew; I could hardly wait until tomorrow.

We had to leave quickly. Soon it would be pitch black in these woods, and only the owls would be able to see anything.

Staying at a distance, I followed my little sister and Canela. I wanted so badly to carry the heavy can of water Alicia held on her head. She looked so fragile, her bare feet with rough, leathery toes grasping the soil to climb the hill. Her arms were thin and barely reached the rim of the can on her head. She took a few steps, turned to make sure I was still behind her, then took a few more steps, repeating the pattern all the way up. Each time she turned, she flashed a smile, giving me courage to follow through with the promise I had made to myself in the jungle four years earlier.

When we reached the yard, I stayed under the trees as she looked back one more time, and then went inside the kitchen. A few minutes later, someone lit the kerosene lamp, and I saw my mother walking to the *fogón*. She reached up for something, maybe a plate or a gourd cup. She handed out a dish, and I wondered which of my brothers or sisters would have to wait for a dish or spoon to be available. Since Papa had refused to buy more dishes or utensils, there were never enough to go around.

I remembered the many times I had sat hungrily waiting for someone to finish eating so I could have my food. Sometimes the one who was eating deliberately took his or her time to make the one waiting suffer a little longer. Sometimes I fell asleep when the wait was too long after I had worked all day in the fields.

From under the tree, I saw Emilia plant herself down in the doorway, as she had done for years, to eat her dinner with one leg hanging down, swinging back and forth. I recognized her immediately, but I couldn't tell if she had grown any taller. I wondered what she would do if she knew I was watching her.

I was now surrounded by darkness, which made it possible for me to see into the lighted kitchen through its open door. Still, there wasn't much I could see in the narrow space. This made me anxious; I wished I could widen the doorway so I could see where everyone sat eating their evening meal.

In the meantime, my mouth watered and my stomach growled. I could smell the food, and I imagined tasting it. Alicia would push a shellful through the space under her bed. I wondered how she would keep a straight face as she sat in a corner, eating her meal and holding a secret. I hoped she would be strong. If she told, I would be dead.

The waiting dragged on for a long time. Finally, Emilia stood up and left the doorway. A while later, she came out with the iron pot in her hands, went straight to the pig pen, and dumped the contents for the squealing pigs.

As she hurried back into the kitchen, she closed the kitchen door, and now I could only see little spots of light through the wall cracks. Here and there were some longer streaks of light spilling onto the ground from longer cracks. However, that wasn't enough light to help me. I had been left alone in the dark.

When my eyes adjusted, I looked left, right, and straight ahead, and then swiftly headed under the house. Canela wagged her tail as I passed her; she had curled up for the night. I located the sleeping area and chose my spot, listening for voices and steps above my head.

I heard Mama scolding one of the boys. Then her footsteps moved across the room, making the boards squeak, and dust fell on my shoulders. My eyes followed the row of stilts under the center of the house where the sleeping area ended and the front room began.

I heard the sound of the rope rubbing the wooden hook as Papa's hammock swung back and forth. I estimated that he was about four or five feet to my right, with only the floor between us. I trembled as I imagined what he would do if he knew I was this close to him. I warned myself not to sneeze.

Mama's steps traveled across the floor to the front room, and some of the boys ran to the kitchen, squabbling. Emilia ordered them out of her way. The boys carried on in low voices somewhere between the kitchen and the sleeping area.

I heard a soft scrape above my left shoulder, then a faint

streak of light lit the ground near my hip. A brown hand holding a bowl of rice and beans poked through.

I grabbed it quickly, giving the wrist a little squeeze of appreciation. When the hand pulled away, the board moved slowly, covering the hole, leaving only a few streaks of light on the dry, loose earth around me.

The aroma of the food reached Canela. She sniffed and made an attempt to stand up, but then she lowered her head and yawned. I would have shared my food with her, but I felt relieved when she didn't come forward. I scooped the delicious rice and beans into my mouth with my fingers, being careful not to lose a single grain or bean. I wondered if Alicia had forgotten to include a spoon, or if perhaps our family had no spoons left.

I practically licked the bowl clean, and then set it beside me. Gathering my skirt tightly around my thighs, I pulled my knees to my chest, wrapped my arms around them, and waited. Why hadn't I asked Alicia for a gunnysack?

During my four years in the city, I had forgotten about roaches and mice. Now the aroma from the rice and beans brought roaches from their hiding places, dragging their wings across the streaks of light. As they found no food, they headed in a single file toward the kitchen, where they would lick the dishes once everyone had gone to sleep. I shivered, knowing the mice would be the next to come out.

I decided to recite the rosary to keep from going crazy under this old house, with mice and roaches and pitch darkness everywhere. The night would be long, but praying would help. At the first sign of daylight, I would run back into the woods and wait for Papa to leave.

I heard a slow scratching sound again, so I turned my head and saw a streak of light. It grew wider as two fingers wiggled through the opening of the floor. They slipped away when I touched them. Then a corner of a gunnysack poked through. It came down slowly as my little sister pushed it an inch at a time.

"Oh, what a nice girl you are!" I whispered, but Alicia

squeezed my finger, and I knew to be quiet. I caught the sack as it came a little at a time, gathering it into my hand to keep it from falling on the loose dirt. When the last corner came through, I held the hand and kissed it. When the hand wiggled, I knew it meant "Goodnight." I put the rice bowl in the hand and watched it disappear. A painful lump blocked my throat, and hot tears rolled down my face.

I got into the sack feet first, smoothing it up to my armpits, then pulled the string to fit snugly around my upper back and chest. I left the string loose in case I had to jump out and run into the woods. Later on, I would lean back against my gabardine bag, and maybe rest my eyes for a short while, but not before reciting the rosary.

I heard a lot of complaints, arguments, and cries in the kitchen—and footsteps in the sleeping area. Urine trickled down the stilts around me. What I had known as common practice for years shocked me now. I had not expected to find my family still urinating through the cracks on the floor and walls. Males aimed at the walls, and females squatted over the cracks in the kitchen floor.

The smell lingered in the air under the house for a long time, then lessened as time passed . . . or maybe I became used to the odor after a while. Canela moved from her spot and settled herself down next to me, smelling worse than the pee. But I let her stay so she could scare the mice away.

Looking out into the black of night, hearing the owls hooting and the wild cats fighting, I wished I could fit through the cracks like the gunnysack. I would snuggle up to Alicia and run out at dawn.

For the moment, I leaned on my side, my back close to Canela, and listened to the chirping, hooting, and shrill meows coming from the woods. Even the pigs squealed in their smelly pens, bringing unpleasant memories of the times Papa made me catch the blood from the pigs he butchered. I shivered in the darkness, and wondered if Alicia had to hold the pan now that I had left.

The light went off. No more streaks came through the cracks. The voices quieted, and the rasping sound of the hammocks' ropes increased. I pictured Papa's hammock on one side of the front room and my brothers' four hammocks occupying the remaining space.

I heard another slow scratch above my head, then a soft whisper. "Are you there?"

I stretched out my arm, feeling around in the dark, and took my little sister's hand, letting her know that I was still there. She squeezed mine back as if saying, "*I'm glad.*" We shared a dialogue of squeezes until her hand relaxed. I didn't want her to be caught sleeping with one hand through a hole in the floor, so I squeezed one more time and pulled my hand away. She did the same, and the board scratched for the last time.

The snoring stopped and started again. Even Canela snored, lifted her head, and went back to sleep. Someone stirred in a hammock. A rope squeaked. Footsteps moved across the floor. Urine trickled down the stilts. The steps returned to the hammock, the rope squeaked, and the snoring continued. I closed my eyes and listened to the sounds of the night.

Chapter Fifty-Five

The Second Run

When the roosters crowed, I realized I had been asleep. It was the stupidest thing I had ever done. Had it not been for the roosters' crowing before daybreak, I might have slept until Papa came out of the house and caught me.

I sat up straight and waited for daylight, noticing the quiet upstairs. They all seemed to be still asleep. This was great, but I felt the churning of anxiety in my stomach. I had made it this far, but I had no idea what the rest of the day might bring. I might have to run up the hill with my family chasing me with brooms and machetes.

I saw Canela rise, point her nose toward the woods, and stretch. Yawning, she walked out from under the house and was gone. I rolled the gunnysack into a small bundle and put it up onto a floor joist. Then I held my gabardine bag and moved closer to the outer stilts.

When I heard the floorboards squeak, I walked softly across the yard and up the hill. I hid under the mango tree which overlooked the house, and waited. The grass around the tree was tall, cold, and damp. I was shivering by the time blue smoke rose from the kitchen's roof. The front window swung open, then the front door, and Papa stepped out. My heart stopped.

He went behind the house, and seconds later came back

buttoning the front of his trousers. He picked up something from the ground, then walked around the corner toward the kitchen door. He returned with a gourd of coffee, sipping it and walking, inspecting the ground as though he could sense that something was different.

I felt the hands of fear choking me. It was almost unbearable—my years away had not lessened my fear of my father. I surely didn't want him to find me now.

The sun finally rose over the mountain like a bright orange ball. Papa finished his coffee and disappeared behind the house. One of the boys came out. It was José, but he was not as big as I had pictured him in my mind. He walked across the yard and down to the corral.

Papa must have gone into the house through the kitchen door, because he walked out through the front with his shaving kit and a pan of water. He hung his little mirror from a nail near the front door and began to shave, his razor blade flashing in the sun. I remembered his machete and shivered.

José returned, riding his brown mare and leading a white horse. He gave them water sweetened with molasses, and brushed them with a brush made from a short grass called *matojo*. Then he went behind the house and came back with the harness gear. While José got the horses ready, Papa finished shaving and went back inside.

I had no idea how things would go beyond this point. If Papa left without spotting me, and the rest of the family didn't gang up on me, my four-year-old dream could become reality.

But getting everyone away from the farm was only the beginning of another series of problems. I couldn't imagine any of the kids or our mother working anywhere outside the farm. I wished I had listened to Doña Luisa, but it was too late now to run.

When José finished with the horses, he went back inside, and Papa came out in his black pants, white shirt, and Italian hat. He inspected José's work and mounted his horse, walking it slowly around the yard. Finally, José returned wearing a different shirt and pants, but no shoes. He rode his mare up the hill, following Papa on his white horse. They trotted up the path only feet from where I waited, and disappeared into the forest.

I stayed hidden and watched for the rest of the family. My mother went out with a bucket to milk the cow, and Alicia headed down to the springs with her water can. She looked around as she walked, probably wondering where I was hiding.

When Mama went back into the house with the milk, Lorenzo came out and took the cow to pasture.

Now I headed toward the springs. I found Alicia up on a rock watching for me.

"Here I am," I whispered.

Alicia jumped from the rock, and we hugged each other.

"We don't have much time," I said. "Can you help me approach Emilia and Mama? If I can convince them to leave with me, the boys and Gloria won't be a problem."

At first I didn't think Alicia was strong enough to help me. Her face turned pale, and I could feel her uneasiness.

"Be brave, Alicia. Take a chance, like you did last night. You gave me the rice and the gunnysack, and that took a lot of courage. I have never been as proud of anyone as I was of you last night."

She looked up and smiled. "I'll do it. This morning when I get back to the house, Emilia's going to the creek to wash clothes, and I'm supposed to go with her. You can hide there and come out when I give you this signal." She pushed her hair behind her ears. "I don't think you'll have much trouble convincing her, because we have all been wishing we could disappear where Papa would never find us."

"What about Mama?" I asked. "Do you think she'll leave?"

"Mama is always talking about leaving, especially after Papa slaps her around."

"What about Lorenzo? Will he give me any trouble?"

"Maybe," she said. "Sometimes he talks about running away, so he might help you. You'll have to watch him. Whatever happens, I'm going away with you."

About an hour later, I met Emilia and Alicia at the creek. I waited for them behind the bush Alicia had recommended. Emilia looked more like a mature woman than a señorita, but she giggled a few times while talking with Alicia. I couldn't hear their words, but I felt that Emilia wouldn't be a problem.

When Alicia faced the bush and pushed back her hair, I recognized the signal and stepped out.

"Ah, you weren't lying!" Emilia said to Alicia, and they both walked toward me. "You're supposed to be dead," Emilia said, with a smile and a hug. "What did you do? You look so different!"

"I'll tell you later," I said. "We don't have much time. I came to take you away."

"Take me away?" She stepped back and stared at me.

"Not just you," I said quickly, worrying about time passing. "I want to take the others. Mama, too. Do you think she'll go?"

She looked shocked. "Take Mama? Are you crazy?"

"No, Emilia, I'm not crazy. The question is, do you want to spend the rest of your life here?"

Emilia thought while Alicia and I waited. "I don't want to stay here. But where can we go?"

"I have a place in a city for all of us."

"What city?"

"I can't tell you the name of the city until we get there. You'll have to trust me. It's a good place for all of us. We can find work there, and one day everyone can live free of Papa."

"What would become of him if we left?"

Emilia's concern for our father shocked me. I didn't think she cared. "I can't worry about Papa. He's a grown man. He can take care of himself."

"He's our father," she said, raising her voice. "We are supposed to honor our parents, no matter what."

"I'm going to honor my parents," I said, "but from a distance."

Alicia clapped and laughed. "I'm going with her," she blurted through the laugh. "I'm tired of being a slave."

Emilia stared at the moving water, then at the load of dirty clothes, and back at the water. Alicia watched both of us, encouraging me with her smile.

"Let's go," Emilia said, picking up the bundle.

"Leave the clothes," I said, "so you can run faster."

"I'm just going to hide it." She laughed as she carried the clothes to a vine-covered rock, lifting the vines and shoving in the rags. "I'm not saying that I'm going with you, but I want to see Mama's reaction."

As we ran up the hill, my sisters asked me questions. I answered without saying where I had a house waiting for them.

We reached our yard and saw Mama picking oregano near the kitchen door.

"We'll stay behind the trees," Emilia whispered.

"You think Mama will hit me?"

"I don't think so. She always cries when your name is mentioned."

"What about Papa? Has he ever cried for me?"

"Of course not," Emilia said softly. "Men don't cry. He'd probably kill you if he found you here. Then he'd kill us for helping you."

I patted her shoulder and stepped into the yard. "Mama?"

My mother cupped one hand over her eyes. "Ave Maria!" she cried, leaping toward me with her arms wide open. "I knew you weren't dead!"

Kisses spread all over my face. My chin rested on her collarbone. I smelled wood and tobacco smoke, oregano, cilantro, and chicken feathers. This was the mother I remembered.

"I knew you weren't dead, I knew it!" she said over and over. Then, quick as a flash, she held me at arm's length. "And how are you going to explain yourself to your father?" Her face had turned pale, and there were tears in her eyes.

I wiped away my own tears. "I'm not here to explain anything to Papa. I only came to take you away."

"You what?" Her eyes grew wide.

"I came to take you and everyone else, except Papa, to live

with me in the city. I have a place for all of us, Mama, but I can tell you about it on the way. You'll have to trust me, and we have to hurry before Papa comes home."

"Listen to her, Mama," Alicia said as she and Emilia approached. "We can't go on as slaves forever."

Lorenzo appeared with a sack of vegetables on his shoulder. He stopped for a moment, then lowered the sack and ran toward us. "You're alive! Oh my God! You're alive!" He wrapped his arms around me, telling me that he cared about me.

Hugging him back, I couldn't help but recall my little pillow and the punches he had given me after he burst it open.

Lorenzo's words brought Gloria and our two younger brothers out. "Is that you, Sabina?" Gloria looked strong and energetic. Alejandro and Felipito stayed back shyly until Alicia reminded them who I was.

A few minutes later, we were all in the kitchen and sleeping area, asking each other questions, laughing and crying. Even Alejandro and Felipito, who were only four and two when I left, talked and asked questions as if they remembered me well. They kept us laughing by saying, "Let's run away right now! Even with empty bellies!"

Alicia and I didn't tell anyone that she had seen me the night before, and had fed me and helped me pass the night under the house. We let everyone think that I had just met her at the springs.

I wasn't too sure Emilia would leave. She kept changing her mind. One minute she said she would leave, and the next she wanted to stay. "Somebody has to be here for Papa," she said.

"Papa is too mean to need anyone," Lorenzo told her, but her look of warning stifled him. There were a lot of things I wanted to tell her about loyalty, but I was afraid she would get mad and try to beat me. I also worried about time passing and having to spend another night hiding.

"This is something I have to think about," Mama said, her face now marked with lines of anger. "You ran away like a bad girl. We thought you had drowned. We even had a vigil for you, for God's sake!"

"So what, Mama?" Lorenzo blurted out. "You can hold another damn vigil when she dies for sure. For now, let's get the hell out before the old man gets back."

Mama gave him a dirty look. "What about José? Don't you care what happens to him?" She reached into her pocket and began to roll a cigarette, her fingers moving quickly.

My mother's reaction left me speechless. I saw a woman who looked much older than she should, with broken teeth that had never seen a toothbrush, and feet like those of a gorilla, fighting to hang onto a brutal lifestyle. I remembered the time I had read her an article from an old newspaper about a woman who tortured her husband for abusing her and their children. Mama's hard hand had sent me to the floor with bleeding lips.

Now I had to become stronger than ever before, or else be dominated by my mother and Emilia. "I did not run away like a bad girl," I said firmly. "I ran because I appreciated life and I wanted to live, so that someday I could help you, Mama. So that someday I could help my brothers and sisters."

The words worked like magic. No one blinked. Eyes gazed at me from all sides as I moved around while talking, afraid that I would lose my nerve if I stopped.

"I don't want them to be slaves forever, unless they choose to be. I want a better life for you, Mama, with real cigarettes instead of tobacco rolled in old brown paper. I want to see shoes on your feet. And I want to bury you in a shiny casket when you die of old age. Papa would wrap you in an old gunnysack and put you in a hole he'd dig near the creek. Is that what you want, Mama?"

Sweet Alicia stepped in. "Listen to her, Mama. She's your only chance."

Mama lifted her hand to slap her, but Lorenzo caught it. "You can stay here and rot with Papa and Emilia, but I'm leaving," he said.

"Me, too," added Alicia, jumping over next to Lorenzo.

"And so am I," said Gloria.

The two younger boys stepped into the action and claimed that they had no intention of staying behind.

"Just a minute!" Emilia came forward. "I haven't said that I'm not going!"

Mama was staring down at the floor, her left hand around her chin, and her right hand cupped around the burning roll of tobacco. "What about José?"

"We'll wait for him, Mama." I walked over to her and placed a hand on her shoulder. "We'll wait for José."

She lifted her chin, tears rolling down her cheeks, and nodded.

All the kids except Emilia clapped and yelled, "We're leaving, we're leaving." A frown from Emilia cut off the voices. Alicia burst out laughing, and the rest of us joined in. Then Emilia couldn't hold a straight face.

"Pay attention, everybody," I said. "Let's get organized and be ready to run once José gets home. You should all get cleaned up and wear your best outfits. Take only a few changes of clothing, especially underwear."

Everyone laughed.

"We won't be carrying much," said Alicia.

"I'm taking the sewing machine," Mama said.

"No, Mama, it's too heavy," I told her. "I have a better one for you, the kind you work with your feet. Now get your things and let's decide where to meet if we're separated. We have to avoid getting caught by Papa. He'll drag you back here, and you'll never be able to leave again. When he gets back today, he should find all of you doing what you usually do. Otherwise, he'll suspect something."

"We won't be able to run very fast through the woods," Emilia said, "especially at night, with so many holes and rocks under vines!"

"If Papa is still afraid of the dark," I said, "he won't follow us as he would in the daytime."

"He'll leave for the cock fight early tomorrow," Mama said.

"We'd be better off leaving then. He won't get home until dark, and he'll be drunk. By then, we can be far away."

It was settled. We would leave the next day.

We all sat here and there on the floor, each with a heap of cooked bananas and codfish, and I was the center of attention.

I looked at the scratched-up legs extended outward on the floor. Lorenzo had the most cuts, and one foot was turned. He had cut himself and developed an infection, which took a long time to heal since it was beneath the outer joint of his ankle, and was never treated. Everyone's feet looked painfully dry. Emilia and Gloria had nicely shaped legs, but with curly black hair and a lot of scratches. They both had large breasts, loose for the lack of brassieres. I felt almost guilty for wearing a bra, for looking cleaner and feeling prettier.

As bad as everyone looked to me, I wanted, if only for a short time, to feel a sense of family—something I had missed all these years. I wanted to belong here, with a mother and brothers and sisters. Yet I knew to be careful about what I said. I couldn't talk about where I had been or where I had rented a house. If everything suddenly went wrong—say Papa came home earlier than expected and caught me there—I would have to run fast. I knew he could drag the information out of his scared slaves and find me.

As the only one who didn't sit on the floor, Mama ate leaning against the *fogón*. She had been thinking, her eyes traveling from one of us to the other, as if comparing my appearance to that of the other kids.

"Tell me, Sabina," she said, "what did you do to survive—a young girl out there by yourself?"

I looked up and saw that ready-to-judge look in her eyes. She was God, and I the sinner. A draining feeling crept up on me, and my appetite disappeared. I cleared my dry throat.

"It's an interesting story, Mama—a very long one which I want to tell you. But this is not the best time. You all should hurry to do your work so Papa won't suspect a thing."

"A story is right," Mama said firmly.

"Never mind, Mama," Lorenzo cut in. "Let's just leave and be far away before Papa gets back."

"Hey, maybe I'll get to attend school," Alicia said, so bubbly it made everyone laugh. "Well, what do you think?"

"I think it's possible," I said, "but only if we get going."

With this, everyone sprang up and went about their chores. I went back to the creek with Emilia and Alicia, where we squeezed the water out of the garments and spread them on the rocks and bushes to dry. Then we took off our clothes and jumped into the clear, cool water.

I captured a moment of tranquility, a fearless moment. "This is how our lives should have been. We should have been free to do this more often. Instead, we were forbidden to bathe in this creek. Actually, we were forbidden to bathe anywhere when we wanted to. Incredible! We had to get permission to bathe."

"Yeah," Alicia said, her face glowing with a smile that didn't want to quit. "And we still have to ask permission, as if we were slaves, right?"

"That's right," I said. Then I looked at Emilia, who scrubbed herself and stared at the water as if unaware of us. "You're not thinking of changing your mind, are you, Emilia?"

"No, but I think we should hurry out of the water. We don't really know that Papa's in town. What if he changed his mind and is up under those trees watching us? Imagine having to run through those bushes naked."

The thought was chilling. We put on our clothes, gathered the laundry, and headed up to the house.

"Does Papa still make rum?" I asked.

"Of course he does, and drinks it, too," Emilia said, the muscles on the back of her legs bulging with her steps.

"Does he still castrate pigs?"

"Oh sure, but now the boys get to hold the poor creatures."

"Who holds the blood pan when he butchers one?"

"The boys and I do," Alicia said.

"So things have not changed much since I left."

"Not for the better," said Emilia as we reached the yard.

We found Mama at the *fogón* starting supper. She didn't hear us come in. Her face looked as if she had just bit into a sour lemon. I knew she was afraid to leave.

"Mama," I said, "nothing could be worse than living here in the dirt with rats, roaches, and insects that suck your blood. Have you seen the termites under this shack? One of these days, the stilts will crumble and you'll end up in the river."

She nodded. "Fine, fine, I'll leave, I'll leave."

Then it seemed that everyone heard the sound of hooves at the same time. We looked out toward the hill and saw Papa and José. Everyone looked at me with wide eyes and open mouths. My throat went dry.

"Something's wrong," Mama said hoarsely.

Then we saw José's red face and his look of despair. We found out later that a *compadre* had made sugar cane rum and had traded a gallon for a gallon of Papa's molasses rum. Papa had made José carry the gallon, and José had dropped it. By the time they arrived home, Papa had slapped the boy dozens of times. That was only the beginning of what was to come.

When they reached the front door, Papa dismounted and ordered José to feed and water both horses. Then he headed for the rum room.

Once he closed the door, I grabbed my bag and ran out the back door and up the hill to the mango tree. From there, I watched the house, paying close attention to the front door and Papa's hammock, which still hung empty.

As the breeze changed, I smelled the aroma of my mother's cooking. It made my mouth water, but I knew that I would not get to eat any of her cooking tonight. I didn't plan to sleep under the house again. If one of my brothers or sisters broke down and told Papa about me being there, he would have to find me somewhere else. I felt that I could trust Alicia, but I couldn't be sure of the others.

I leaned against the tree and waited. Finally, Papa came out of the rum room with a gallon jug in one hand and a coconut shell in the other. He stretched out in his hammock with his feet to the door as he had always done, for he would never sit or stand with his back to a door or window.

I could see him well with the binoculars, but a close-up of his red face made me shudder. It had that harsh look that was so familiar to me, with one corner of his mouth pulling toward his ear. The two veins over his eyebrow bulged as they did every time he had cruelty in mind.

I watched my brothers and sisters come out one or two at a time and look up and down the hill and around the house for me, but I didn't wave or make a sound. They looked and went in again.

José came back from the corral, dragging his feet, his head down to hide his face. He went around the house to reach the kitchen door. I imagined him inside whispering to the others about Papa's rage.

I waited for the explosion. Knowing my father as I did, I knew it could begin at any moment.

Mama stepped outside, spreading corn and calling the chickens in the usual way: "Pee, pee, peeee!" When the flock rushed in to devour the corn, she went back inside. Shortly after that, I heard the sound of plates and spoons.

I imagined my brothers and sisters sitting on the floor eating their dinner, some with spoons, others with pineapple leaves. Emilia would probably sit in the doorway swinging one leg. Gloria would be at the window in the sleeping area, facing the woods, wondering if I was still hiding there.

The sun would soon disappear behind the mountain. I had seen it come up in the morning. Where had the day gone? I didn't want to be inside the house with my family, but I felt lonely, hungry, and terrified. I knew that at any moment, evil would burst through the house, and the sparks would reach the sky.

Suddenly, my father's voice rang out once, twice. Then I saw his plate fly from the hammock, hitting the wall, then the floor. He jumped to his feet, shouting and calling names.

I shoved the binoculars into my bag and stood ready to run. But the familiar banging on the walls began, and I knew my father was banging heads. Nothing had changed since I had gone. Papa was still a monster, an evil man. Why had I thought that things might be different?

I heard more thumping, more banging, slaps, shouting, sobbing, and shrieking. Then I saw José fly out the front door, landing face down on the ground with Papa on top. Papa had José by the shirt and was about to punch him again when Lorenzo jumped out the window and hopped on Papa's shoulders, yelling, "Run, José! Run!"

But José, seeming disoriented, had a hard time standing. Every time he stood up, his legs wobbled and he fell to the ground. Finally, as Papa tried to shake off Lorenzo, José got to his feet and staggered up the hill.

Watching my brother had to be the most intense moment in my life. If I tried to help him, Papa would see me, and I would soon be dead. I had to stay still, my heart aching for José, and with one eye on Papa, who was walking around in circles with Lorenzo on his back, swearing that he would kill everyone before midnight.

I saw Alicia bolt out of the house and run up the hill toward the mango tree. Then she changed her mind and headed for the water springs. Papa threw Lorenzo on the ground and went after Alicia, grabbing her skirt. José saw him and turned back. Papa let go of Alicia and started on José again, but Lorenzo surprised him from behind once more.

Finally, Emilia came out shouting, "Papa, stop! Stop at once, unless you want me on your back, too!"

My father's hand froze in mid-air. He stared at Emilia, then ran into the house yelling, "Heads will fall to the ground tonight!"

Evidently, when Mama saw Papa come in, she shot out of the kitchen door. The other kids jumped behind her, and they all scattered through the woods like chicks after their mother hen. Papa came a few steps behind them with his machete in one hand and a sword in the other.

"I'm going to chop off your heads, you lousy pigs! I should have killed every one of you years ago!"

I stayed by the tree, frozen, my heart racing like a wild thing inside my chest. I remembered the time Papa held the machete at my throat. At that time, he hadn't gone through with his threat.

Perhaps my father was merely a bully, one who enjoyed pushing his family around as long as they allowed it. This made sense to me now. He would not kill his family. He needed them. Who else would he have to kick around during his drunken spells?

Finally, Papa returned from the woods, still shouting, "I'll fix all of you when you come crawling back! You'll come running when the darkness scares the shit out of you! You'll see! You are all sleeping outside tonight!" He stepped up into the house, closing the front door behind him. A few seconds later, the back door banged shut.

I gave him enough time to stretch out in his hammock with his bottle, then I ran down past the house and toward the springs.

Darkness had fallen quickly in the thick woods, but I found Mama, José, Lorenzo, and Gloria bunched up around the trunk of a tree above the springs, overlooking the path where Papa would walk if he came that far.

"Come!" I said. "Let's find the others before it gets darker."

"Your father!" Mama cried. "He might be hiding anywhere."

"No, he's back in the house with both doors closed."

We all knew that Papa was afraid of the dark. He wouldn't come out this far and take a chance of getting stuck here all night without his jug. We also knew that it would soon be too dark for any of us to see a thing. We started our search for the others, worrying about the younger children falling into a vine-covered hole or stumbling down to the bottom of the ravine.

When we could no longer see our own hands in front of us,

we clung to each other around a tree trunk to wait out the night, vowing to go back for the others in the morning.

"My thumb is throbbing," José whispered.

"Did you cut yourself?" I asked.

"Yeah, a long time ago."

"And it still hurts?"

"He's got an infection," Mama said.

"Is it serious?"

"He might lose his thumb. We need to go back home and put some ointment on it."

"Mama, I'm not going back home," said José.

"Me neither," said Lorenzo.

"And neither am I," added Gloria.

We whispered questions and answers to each other, until Lorenzo told me about some of the crazy things Papa had done during the past four years.

"Don't talk bad about your father," Mama said sharply. "Children are supposed to honor their parents, no matter what."

"Children need to be honored too, Mama," I said. "When parents mistreat their young ones, they are not even honoring God, because children are gifts from God. That's something I learned in church, not from my parents."

"Hush up!" she warned. "He could be around here."

"No, he's probably snoring by now," Lorenzo said.

"I feel sick," José whispered, and then vomited.

"I knew that would happen," said Lorenzo. "Every time Papa beats him, he pukes."

"I'm so cold," José whispered through chattering teeth. His skin felt hot with fever when I touched him.

"We have to get him out of here while he can still walk," I said. "Do you know where we are? Can we go to someone's house?"

"I can find Uncle Luís's house in the dark," said Lorenzo.

As we started across the gorge, I suggested that only Mama, José, and Gloria go to the door. Lorenzo and I would hide under the house.

"Don't leave there until one of us comes for you in the morning," I said. "And don't tell anyone I'm here or that you're going away. If Uncle Luís tells Papa, we won't get away."

Chapter Fifty-Six

Dragging José

Lorenzo said that he knew Uncle Luís's house well, so with help from the streaks of light coming through the cracks, he chose a corner under the living room, away from the pee corner. It would also be easy for us to run out if someone came looking for something under the house. We felt fortunate that Uncle Luís didn't have dogs, and his pigs were in pens away from the house.

We sat back to back and whispered. Lorenzo asked questions about where we were going.

"I'm sure glad you came back," he said. "You have always been so smart."

This wasn't the time to remind him of my pillow. Right now I needed him more than he needed me. He knew this area well. I wouldn't know which way to run.

"We'd better be quiet," I said. "Whispers can be heard through the cracks."

We heard Mama tell our uncle all about the beating over a gallon of rum. "And look at the poor boy, sick with an infected thumb."

Then we heard the boards squeak as people walked from one room to another. We heard the ropes of the hammocks rubbing on the hooks from which they hung. It sounded as if José had stayed in the front room with Uncle Luís while Mama and Gloria went to the kitchen with Aunt Natalia.

We heard the pigs squealing in their pens, cats fighting in the woods, and the owls hooting. We shifted our weight from one side to the other.

Finally, Lorenzo stretched himself in the dirt. "Don't let me fall asleep," he whispered.

"I hope I do," I said, and leaned back on my bag.

*　　*　　*

At daybreak, Lorenzo and I went back to the springs, hoping to find the rest of our brothers and sisters. Before starting out, we agreed to run in separate directions if we encountered Papa. He couldn't chase us both at the same time. We would meet at Uncle Luís's later, where Mama and Gloria waited with José.

Daylight filtered through the tree branches when we reached the springs, and birds were flying out of the woods. We expected Papa to jump from behind every bush and tree; each sound of leaves moving might be his footsteps.

"Let's wait here," Lorenzo whispered. "The kids will come looking for us if they're still out there." We went up the slope where he and the others had waited for me last night.

Time moved slowly as we held our breath, hoping to spot Papa before he spotted us. Finally, the dry leaves shuffled, and Emilia appeared from under the coffee trees, dragging the water can. Lorenzo stepped down and asked her if Papa was up.

"You scared the hell out of me!" she whispered crossly. "He wasn't up when I left, but where did you and the others hide last night?" She stamped around Lorenzo as though she wanted to take her anger out on him. "We couldn't find you, and it got so dark we had to go back. When Papa fell asleep, we climbed into the house through the hole under Alicia's bed."

"Emilia, calm down," I said, climbing down the slope. "We couldn't find you either, and we've been scared for you all night. But José is really sick. We had to get him some help."

This stopped Emilia. "Is it his thumb?"

"It's his thumb plus a high fever and an awful headache," Lorenzo told her.

"The poor thing cut himself a long time ago, and the thumb won't heal," Emilia said. "It's because he's always working with the horses, and he's probably gotten horse pee and manure in the cut. You two had better get going and find help for him before he loses his whole hand. You'd better hurry. If Papa catches up with you, he'll do something crazy, and José will lose more than his hand." Emilia put her hands over her face and wept.

"I'm not leaving without you and the others," I said.

"Then no one's leaving!" Emilia gasped. "Papa will catch up with you. Don't you see? Once José is well, you can come back and get the rest of us."

"Maybe she's right," Lorenzo cut in. "It's probably better that we don't all leave at the same time."

"Besides that," Emilia said, turning to me, "have you ever wondered what Papa would do if he found out you were here? I think you should run before he shows up. Come back for us once José is better."

"I will," I whispered. "But please explain to Alicia that I will be back for her."

Emilia promised to deliver the message, and we had nothing else to say. Lorenzo and I hugged our big sister goodbye and ran.

When we reached our uncle's yard, I sent Lorenzo to get the others. "Be sure Uncle Luís hears that you're taking José to the hospital in Lares. He'll run to Papa to tell him, and we'll be far away by the time Papa begins looking for you."

Uncle Luís stood outside his house, watching José struggle up the hill, hanging onto Mama and Lorenzo. Gloria followed quietly, looking around for me.

I imagined Papa waiting for the rest of his family to return from the woods, his brother running to him with news about José, and the two on the front steps with a bottle of rum. Papa would expect Mama and the rest of the children to return from the hospital with ointment on José's bandaged thumb.

He had a big surprise coming.

I caught up with Mama and the others, and found that José was burning with fever and complaining about a headache.

"I'm not going to make it," he cried. "Save your energy."

Still we pushed on, past the old school without anyone seeing us. This was the advantage of leaving early on a Sunday morning, the only day of the week when people didn't have to be up early. I don't know what we would have done if we had run into some friend or relative. Mama would probably have collapsed. She looked pale, sick, and worn out.

We couldn't walk very fast with José feeling so sick, but we were sure that Papa was still in his hammock waiting for the rest of his family.

When we finally reached the paved road, I offered to pay the *publico* driver the full fare, a dollar, if he would drive us, without stopping for anyone else, to the San Sebastian hospital.

"Got someone sick?" the driver asked.

"Very sick," I said, "and contagious."

"I sure don't want to catch whatever he's got," the driver said, staying way back while we helped José into the back seat. As soon as we shut the door, the driver got in and drove off.

We reached the hospital quickly, since we were ahead of the churchgoers. I gave the driver his dollar, and he wished us good luck. He hurried off to avoid contamination.

I asked José if he could still walk. "I guess so, but how far?" He looked worse now, his voice fading and his legs trembling.

"I'm taking you to Aguadilla," I said. "Their hospital is bigger and better than this one. Papa won't go that far looking for you."

José smiled faintly. Even Mama smiled, seeming pleased.

Lorenzo and I put José's arms around our shoulders and practically dragged him to the Aguadilla *publico* stop. I paid this driver the full fare, too, so he would take us to Aguadilla without stopping for other passengers. The driver asked if the illness was serious, so I gave him the same story I had told the other driver. He smirked at me and sped up.

Several times during the ride, I caught Mama looking at me, her eyes soft, as if she felt good about the way I had handled things. I had told her earlier about the rest of the children, and that I would go back for them once we took care of José.

She agreed that the whole family should not have left at the same time. That would force Papa to hunt us down. "The younger ones will be okay. Emilia's like a mother to them."

I felt reassured that the younger children would be all right, but my heart ached for Alicia. She wanted so much to leave with me. I wondered how many times Papa would beat them before I could return. Maybe he would ease up on them; then again, maybe he would be twice as mean because Mama was gone.

José's head hung low, bobbing up and down every time the car hit a bump. Mama pulled him over to lean on her shoulder, and I remembered when he was younger and almost died with an illness that lasted for months. Fever blistered his lips and mouth and made his hair fall out. No one took him to a doctor, hospital, or the drug store, where a pharmacist could have given him something to bring down the fever.

The only time Papa came near his sick little boy was when he was drunk. He brought home two rotten bird's eggs which someone told him would cure his son, and he forced the stinky things down José's throat, shells and all. José vomited throughout the afternoon and night while Papa slept without hearing his son's agony.

"What's wrong?" Mama saw my tears.

Pushing away the memory, I said, "Nothing."

"So where have you been for four years?" she asked, as if she thought that was why I was crying.

"I'll explain later. This isn't the time or the place."

"That's what you said before."

"Don't worry, Mama," I said. "As soon as we take care of José, I'll tell you the whole story."

She looked at me the same way she used to when she didn't believe me.

The sign *Hospital* came into view, and the driver pulled into the driveway, stopping near the entrance. He took the dollar, but didn't offer to help us with José.

We got José inside, where I wrote his name on a writing tablet and we waited in a crowded room that smelled of alcohol. Embarrassed at our appearance, we found our way to a washroom, where Mama and I washed José before a doctor would see him. Then the rest of us took turns making ourselves presentable before returning to the waiting room. There were only two chairs available, one for José and the other for Mama. The rest of us stood around, hungry, knowing it would be a long time before we would have any food.

Mama motioned me to come closer so she could ask what I intended to do for her and all my brothers and sisters. "I sure don't want to end up living under a tree," she said.

"You won't," I promised her. "But if you do, at least you'll be free."

Gloria spoke up. "She said she's got a place for us, Mama, remember?"

"I'll live under a tree any time, as long as I'm free," said Lorenzo. "Anywhere away from crazy Papa."

"I will not let you children talk that way about your father," Mama whispered loudly, and many eyes from across the room turned to stare at us.

"After what he did to me, you defend him?"

We could barely hear José's whisper, and I worried that he might be dying. I thought about Doña Luisa and what she would do. Then I walked to the little window and told the woman working there that my brother would die if he didn't get help soon.

"Bring him through," she said, with a stern, cold face that made me feel guilty. When Lorenzo and I brought José through, she looked us up and down, pointed to a chair, and said, "He can sit there. You two wait outside."

A short while later, she called me back.

"Your brother has a bad infection, making him very sick.

Take him into that room. A doctor will be there shortly." She pointed to a closed door across the hallway.

I waited with José for a long time before a doctor came in. He looked at José's hand and said he had gangrene traveling up his arm and needed immediate attention. He sent me back to the main desk to sign some papers, in which I wrote my brother's first name with a different last name, and my new address on Borinquen Road. I gave the false last name in case Papa came this far looking for his family.

"You're lucky we have a bed for your brother," the doctor told me when I returned. "Sometimes a patient has to wait weeks for a bed. This boy would be dead in a few days without treatment."

I looked for José's reaction, but he was hunched in the chair, hands on his lap, his eyes closed.

"Go back outside and wait until a volunteer shows you to the infirmary," the doctor said. A man dressed in white came with a wheelchair and took my brother away.

I walked out of the room, blinded by tears. A tight feeling in my chest took my breath away. I had barely reached the waiting room before I burst into sobs.

"He's going to be okay," said a woman who had also been waiting for help.

Another lady reached for my hand. "They will take care of him. He'll be all right."

I couldn't tell anyone that I wasn't crying because my brother might die, but because of the beating Papa had given him the day before. Nor could I admit the anger and hate I felt in my heart.

None of us had realized how serious gangrene was, or that José would be in the hospital for several weeks. After they took him upstairs to a large room where three long lines of beds were separated by thin yellow curtains, we were told to go home and come back during visiting hours. The hours were from 2:00 to 3:00 in the afternoon, or 7:00 to 8:00 at night. We were given the 2:00 to 3:00 schedule.

"If we were still at home, I could take care of him," my mother complained as we waited for a ride to our new home on Borinquen Road.

"You had plenty of time to take care of him," Lorenzo said, "but you didn't!"

"Watch your tone," Mama warned him. "Just because your father isn't here, don't think you can talk to me like that."

"So, Mama," I said, "what were you waiting for, the thumb to rot and fall off?"

"I didn't even know it was infected!" she cried.

"Stop making her feel guilty, you two," Gloria said.

"How could she not know the thumb was infected?" Lorenzo insisted. "Couldn't she see it?"

"All right!" I said. "Stop arguing. Here comes the *publico*."

By the looks my family gave me, I knew the days ahead would be difficult. They were wild and reluctant to adapt.

"One important thing we all have to learn is to respect each other," I said. "Without respect, we won't get along. We won't get anywhere."

"Oh, now you're going to educate me!" my mother said, showing me once again that her age had power over us.

"No, Mama," I said. "I am not going to educate anybody. I do hope that everyone can learn, as I have, that respect goes hand in hand with love and caring.

"This *publico* will take us to our new home. I'll pay him the regular fare, so he'll make frequent stops and we'll get to see our new neighborhood. You'll want to look around, and not be arguing. This environment is a lot different from the one you've known. It has more people and more of everything else. Keep your eyes open, because you'll want to see as much as you can."

The regular fare from Aguadilla to Borinquen was five cents per person. I gave the driver twenty cents for the four of us. I got one of those *you must be rich* smiles from Gloria, which made me feel tall and smart. I winked at her, and off we went, the breeze coming through the open windows, blowing our hair.

We were flying to a new beginning, free of Papa. I knew times would be rough for a long time. But I had interrupted Papa's lifestyle, and that was gratifying to me. Still, I knew I would have to go back for the others, especially the little ones. My heart ached for Alicia. She wanted desperately to leave. I prayed she would be all right until my return.

Mama sat between Gloria and Lorenzo. She seemed stiff, as if refusing to look around, yet her eyes rolled from side to side. I knew she meant to show me that she would not take advice from her daughter. After all, she was still the mother.

To my satisfaction, I saw that Gloria's eyes were beaming, her smile fixed as she looked out one window and then out the other. She glanced at me often, as if to let me know that my efforts had paid off. It pleased me to see that all the dizzy spells and tumors had not left her crippled or retarded. I knew she would be beautiful once she learned how to groom herself and had nicer clothes.

The middle seat in which we sat was the shortest of the three in this station wagon. Once the back seat was filled, though, a little square stool could be placed on the small space at the end of the middle seat. That was where I sat, turning the stool to ride backward so I could watch my family's expressions as they took in the sights.

Lorenzo had always been full of character. He could be stubborn and mean enough to cause a lot of pain. Of all the boys, he would be the one to take on Papa some day. Then there was the side of Lorenzo that inspired us and made us laugh. He sat there, in spite of righteous Mama, hardly able to sit still, his bony knees sticking out of the holes of his dingy beige trousers.

Of all the kids, he had the most beautiful eyes. Highlighted by thick, dark eyelashes, the sclera (the white of the eye) had a grayish tone that made the brown iris sparkle, whether he was happy or mad. Each eye had, between the iris and his nose, a brown freckle that gave his eyes a daring look. When he looked down, one could see the back of his upper lids, a lighter skin than the rosy color of his face.

G

Keeping his elbows close to his body, Lorenzo pointed left and right. "Look at that! Amazing! Incredible!" He pointed to a grassy open space where boys his age hit balls with wooden clubs and sent them flying up in the air.

"Don't get your hopes up," Mama mumbled.

That didn't intimidate Lorenzo. "Boy, I'm glad you came back for us. I didn't know the world was so big."

I couldn't help smiling. I felt important, smart, clever, and accomplished. Still, I knew that Lorenzo would be a handful with all his energy.

More importantly, I knew that Mama would try to be the head of the family. Lorenzo would be her challenge. And I would get the blame for everything that might go wrong. I knew it. I could see it coming.

Chapter Fifty-Seven

A Place of Our Own

"So this is where you've been for four years?" Mama asked when the driver stopped in front of our place.

"No," I said, hurrying to open the door.

"Where were you, then?"

"In Mayaguez. I came here two days ago. I'll talk about it later." I pulled out the old broom and a rag from the pile of furnishings Doña Luisa had sent, showed Gloria how to dust the shelves, and proceeded to knock down the cobwebs and sweep out the dust. "We'll make this place our home until a better house becomes available."

"I never thought I'd end up living in an old *cantina*," my mother said, walking from one corner to another.

"This was not a *cantina*," I told her. "It was a grocery store. But we'll make it our home for a while."

"It's better than the one we left," Lorenzo volunteered. He had been checking out the shelves. "Any groceries hidden around here? A can of sardines the owner left behind? A loaf of bread? Anything?"

I finished sweeping and moved on to the next task. "Stop being a clown, Lorenzo, and help me unfold these beds. Mama, you and Gloria open those boxes and put everything up on the shelves. We'll go get something to eat when we are finished."

"We'll get to eat in a restaurant?" Lorenzo asked, glowing.

"Maybe," I answered.

Doña Luisa had given me two single folding beds. They had wooden frames, with hinges so they could fold for storage. In place of a box spring was a wire net. The mattresses for these beds were quilts about a half-inch thick.

We put the beds against the wall, across from each other. "One bed for you, Mama, and the other for me. Gloria, you and Lorenzo will sleep on the floor tonight. Tomorrow I'll buy fabrics to make you each a hammock." I felt so proud of myself, I wanted to pat my own back. Here I was providing for a family who had been mean to me. I wasn't going to point that out to them, but I wished they would soon realize it and ask me to forgive them for being so cruel.

Doña Luisa had given me three straw chairs and the small wooden table from her laundry room. She had also given me her sewing machine, which delighted my mother.

"Where did you get all these things?" she asked.

"She'll tell us later, Mama," Lorenzo reminded her.

Doña Luisa and Manuela had packed a box of their old clothes and shoes.

"Mama, in that box you'll find some clothes to wear. Gloria will wear one of my dresses. But first we need to go across the street and buy some water."

"Buy water?" Gloria blurted out. "Water can't be sold! It's a free gift from God!"

"Nothing is free in the cities," I said. Then I explained about the latrine. "We have to share it with some of the neighbors."

"Now I've heard everything!" Mama exclaimed. "Sharing a latrine!"

"Ah, but at least we have a latrine." Wide-eyed, Lorenzo got everyone laughing. The sound of laughter was uplifting.

We used our first can of water to wash ourselves. Then Mama dressed in one of Manuela's old dresses and shoes. At first she insisted that nothing would fit. Then she said, "Oh well, can't look a gift horse in the mouth."

I didn't respond to that, but I wished she would show more gratitude.

I let Gloria wear my blue dress and black shoes. She giggled and said, "These poor feet are in for a punishment. Ouch! They don't want to be in prison. But the shoes fit okay." She buckled the strap and stood up, stuck out her shoe-covered foot, held the toe to the floor, and turned her leg this way and that. "They are beautiful! Can I keep them?"

"They're yours," I said. "I don't have anything for you, Lorenzo, but I'll buy you something tomorrow."

"Oh, don't worry. I'm so happy I can even go naked."

Mama looked at Lorenzo from under her brow and pressed her lips together, but the laugh she had been hiding burst out. This started a reaction, and we all laughed, holding our bellies. We would try to stop, but one look at the other one's distorted face and teary eyes added to the unstoppable laughter.

During that short time, as we staggered in circles around each other, bending and reaching for something to hang on to, I felt the closeness to my family I had always wanted.

It took a while to get serious, but when we did, Mama shook the dust out of Lorenzo's trousers and shirt, and we started out to Doña Inez's place.

"We'll eat in a restaurant!" Lorenzo couldn't keep his mouth shut, even after Mama threatened to do it for him.

"I don't think I could eat where people might see me," Gloria said, smoothing her dress.

"You'll get used to it," I said. "The first time I ate in front of people, I was too hungry to be embarrassed."

"Well, aren't you going to tell us about it?" Lorenzo asked.

"Yes, Lorenzo. When we get back, I'm going to tell you everything I've experienced in the past four years."

He rubbed his hands together, eyes ready to fly out of their sockets. "Oh, I can't wait!"

We entered the restaurant through the kitchen door, and Doña Inez welcomed us as if we were close friends.

"My dear girl!" She opened her arms. "You made it! Are you all right? Of course you are! How silly of me. You wouldn't be here if you weren't. And this must be your mother. My dear lady, come in and sit down. You must be hungry. Oh, and here are your brother and sister. Didn't you have others? Six or seven, Luisita said?"

"Yes, seven," I said, wondering how much Doña Luisa had told her about us. "Let me tell you their names. My mother is Carmela, and this is my sister Gloria and my brother Lorenzo."

Doña Inez shook one hand after another. "You poor souls! Don't worry about a thing. You'll be just fine. I'll get you some food. Sit down, sit down, poor souls." She moved as fast as she talked, a short, plump woman with friendly, dark eyes that narrowed with her smile. She turned quickly and was behind the cooking counter before anyone could say a word.

I glanced at my mother, who sat with raised eyebrows and lips formed into an 'O'. Beside her sat Lorenzo with a brilliant smile, sniffing at the aroma coming from the stove. Meanwhile, Gloria sat quietly, her eyes traveling from Doña Inez to the stove, to the white refrigerator in a corner, to the huge counter loaded with unwashed dishes, and up to the open shelves on the walls. I remembered thinking that Doña Monica and Doña Luisa were rich when I first saw their homes. I knew that Gloria saw this kitchen as luxurious.

"Excuse me, Doña Inez, let me help you," I said. "I didn't bring my family here to give you extra work, or cause you any inconvenience whatsoever." I hurried to her side. "Please let me wash the dishes and clean the kitchen for you. It's the only way I can ever pay you for being so kind to us."

She put a hand on my shoulder. "That's nice of you to offer. Luisita told me that you're a hard worker. But please, eat something first. I'm sure you must be hungry. Here, this is for your mother, and this is for your brother." She gave me two plates of white rice with red beans and little chunks of ham. Two more plates followed, one for Gloria and the other for me.

While Doña Inez and her helper carried plates of food into the diner, we savored our delicious meal. I knew that Lorenzo would have licked the plate, had he been alone. My mother and Gloria ate with delight, but seemed shy and pitiful. I felt extremely sorry for my mother, but hopeful for Gloria. At her age, Gloria could learn anything, if she wanted to. But our mother . . . well, she would have to put aside her old-fashioned ways and open her mind to changes and new ideas.

I started washing dishes as soon as I finished my meal. Then I showed Mama and Gloria how this had to be done. "We have to earn our meal," I told them, and they smiled and agreed. Mama washed, while Gloria dried and put the dishes up on the shelves. I took Lorenzo outside, where he and I swept the leaves and papers off the patio and around the building.

"Oh, my dear," Doña Inez said from the kitchen door. "My daughters are going to love you for doing that. I usually have them sweep that every night, and they hate it. They're at the movies today, and they'll be glad to find out that someone else did their sweeping."

A long concrete stairway led from the patio to Doña Inez's residence, where she lived with her two teenage daughters. Lorenzo and I swept that stairway, too. Then we took a bucket of soapy water and two rags and scrubbed the concrete patio floor, and all the way up the steps. Doña Inez was delighted with our work.

My mother and my sister had washed the pots and pans and most of the dishes. They had put things up on the shelves, and wiped and dried the counters and the floor. Now Doña Inez could finish her work earlier than usual and have some time to sit down and rest. We had made a wonderful friend for life.

We said goodbye to our new friend and thanked her for the wonderful meal. She thanked us again for our help, which made me feel so good, especially when I saw the look of fulfillment in my mother's and my siblings' eyes.

"Wait! I almost forgot. Luisita left something for you." Doña Inez reached up into a tin box, pulled out a white envelope, and handed it to me. "Come by anytime," she said, with the sweetest smile I had ever seen. I thanked her with a hug, and we left.

Chapter Fifty-Eight

The Whole Story

Our walk from Doña Inez's restaurant would take about ten minutes. The sun was bright and warm when we had left our place, but now the streetlights had come on, and the area looked like a carnival. There were bars and *cantinas* everywhere. Loud music came from radios and jukeboxes. Men and women walked up one side of the street and down the other, out of one *cantina* and into another, talking, laughing, and whistling. Cars with bright lights rode up toward the base, and others down toward the city.

This was the first time I had seen this *barrio* at night, and it seemed more crowded and busier than the big city of Mayaguez. As Doña Luisa had said, people moved here from all over the island, and were living in houses and huts, over stores and restaurants, and some under houses that stood on high stilts.

Later, we learned the second name for this *barrio*: *Punta Revolución* (Point Revolution). It lived up to its name. People were in a festive mood all the time.

"This is the most exciting place I have ever seen!" Lorenzo exclaimed. "I feel like dancing." He whirled at the edge of the street.

"Yeah," Mama said, "but it's not a place for you. So don't even think about it."

Gloria said, "Mama, how can he not think about it when it's

right here, sparkling and full of life? It looks like heaven to me. Totally opposite of the old farm."

"The farm is home—a place where children grow without the influence of city people," Mama said firmly.

"The farm," I said, "is an inferno. We need to go back soon and get the others while they are still young."

"It's a hell of an inferno, and I never want to see it again." Lorenzo had the last word, and we were home.

I opened the door, reached in, and flipped a switch. This was our new home: an old grocery store divided by a partition of shelves. The wallboards and the beams had never been painted, and with age they had a grayish color. There was no ceiling, so when we looked up, we saw the tin sheets of the roof and many rafters. A light bulb hung from a rafter on each side of the partition. Walking in made me feel sad. I thought of the warmth of the Linareses' home.

For Gloria and Lorenzo, this was the best they had ever seen. I couldn't guess what Mama was thinking. She seemed burdened with thoughts and sadness, or maybe questions. I feared asking her how she really felt. Her answers might lead to arguments and more bad feelings. She sat on a chair and stared at the floor. Gloria sat across from her, and Lorenzo was on the floor raving about electricity.

I went behind the shelves and opened the envelope from Doña Luisa. Five ten-dollar bills were wrapped in a letter. For a moment, I stared at the money in awe. Then I stashed the money in my bra and unfolded the letter.

> Dear Sabina,
>
> I'm praying that you'll return unharmed. If your family came back with you, the money will help until you find work. As we had agreed, I'll wait for you here in Mayaguez. If you don't come, I'll know you've taken your family out of the farm. In that case, I'll stop by to say goodbye on my way to the airport on Thursday.
>
> Love,
>
> *Luisa*

By the time I finished reading, the paper was dotted with tears. I couldn't believe Doña Luisa's generosity. How could she be so kind and loving after all the tragedies she had suffered? Fifty dollars on top of everything else she'd given me was hard to believe. This was the first time I'd ever had that much money.

My mother came around the corner and saw my tears. "Crying about the others?" Her own eyes were red.

"Yes. Are you crying, too?"

Mama nodded, and her sobs brought Gloria and Lorenzo to our side.

"Okay," I said, "are you ready to hear my story?"

"It's about time!" Lorenzo's arms went up. "But can we sit someplace?"

I sat on the edge of one bed, Mama and Gloria on the other, and Lorenzo stretched out on the floor between the beds with his hands under his head. The light shone down on us, reflecting in Lorenzo's eyes.

"Talk," he urged. "I can't wait."

I started with the day Papa held the machete to my throat. "Imagine how I felt, knowing that my head would hit the floor like the banana plants I'd seen Papa cut down. Imagine what I thought when none of you even tried to stop our drunken father."

"He would have killed all of us!" Mama cried. "Besides, I knew he wouldn't cut off your head."

"Get on with the story," Lorenzo ordered. "We can argue about it later."

"No, we are not going to argue or even talk about it later. I'll tell it to you now, then we'll go on with our lives."

Mama had her hands over her face, but I ignored her. I had Lorenzo's ears, and Gloria sat waiting, elbows on her knees, chin on her hands, two brown eyes gleaming.

I told them how I cried as I milked the goat, letting the tears fall into the milk can. I described being up in the mango tree, watching my parents mount their horses and ride past my tree.

"I followed the river and almost drowned because I didn't know how to swim. I spent a night on a tree branch in the pitch black jungle." I told them about meeting Marta, the lady in the wooden hut who gave me lunch.

As I talked, I relived every detail of my experiences, feeling the pain and the fear. I looked at my mother's frozen face, her mouth partly open, her unblinking eyes on me. I glanced at my sister. Her tears were running down her cheeks. And there lay Lorenzo in a daze, waiting for more details.

I sprang from the bed and walked back and forth between the two beds, my arms moving up and down like wings, the huge lump in my throat choking me. "Imagine me doing this, Mama, at age twelve! Or was it ten, eight, thirteen . . . Which was it, Mama? Do you know? Or didn't it matter?"

I described meeting Ana, the pregnant lady who called me Blanca.

"I carried her gloves, Mama." I was sobbing now. "And that day, I became a liar. From then on, I lied. I lied to survive, because I was running from my own father. Imagine that. A little girl running from her own father!"

I knew I had spoken loudly at times. I had feared that maybe the three would get mad and attack me right there. Then I felt ten feet tall and believed that I could whip them all for being mean to me.

"Leave the rest of your story." My mother made an attempt to reach for me. "I can't listen to any more of it now. We've been through a lot today, and I am old and tired."

That struck me the wrong way. "No, Mama. You may be tired, but you are not old. And yes, we've been through a lot today—actually, we've been through a great deal all our lives. But if I don't finish the story now, you might never hear the rest."

This brought everyone to the edge of the beds. This time, Lorenzo sat beside me.

"Let me tell you about the people God sent to help me." I started with Doña Luisa and Doña Monica, and then I talked about Don Felipe, and Manuela and Carlos. I talked until my throat dried out and my voice became a raspy whisper.

"Maybe you should stop now," Lorenzo said softly. He put one hand on my shoulder. "You never have to talk about it again, if you don't feel like it."

I felt like mentioning the time he burst my pillow, but he looked so sad. So I took a deep breath and let myself fall back on the bed. "You can turn out the light now," I whispered.

I heard the switch, and the light faded away. Then I noticed that all was quiet outside. All the lights had been replaced by the break of a new day. I had talked all night. I heard sniffing and deep inhaling. The beds squeaked as tired bodies tried to find relaxation.

Then Mama murmured, "It all amounts to one thing. Children are supposed to honor their parents, not disobey them and run away. The people who helped you were wrong. They should have whipped you and sent you back to your family."

"Mama!" Lorenzo jumped off the bed. "If those people hadn't helped her, we would still be home, by the kitchen door, ready to run from Papa. José would be dead! Forget about the stupidity of honoring mean parents and be glad that one of your children had the guts to run." He walked out of the room, opened the door, and stepped outside.

I stayed in bed, too mad to move and too tired to talk. I heard Lorenzo outside, close to the wall, walking back and forth. I could hear his heavy breathing as he exhaled his frustration.

Soon I heard a car speeding up the road, and another one went by minutes later. I knew people were on their way to their jobs on the base. Then I heard people talking, and walking past our house.

The revolution of a new day had begun. We had to decide our next step. We had a few dishes Doña Luisa had given me, and a heating plate. We had no coffee or food, but I had money, and the store was just across the street.

I stood up and spoke, my voice hoarse. "Mama!" She lifted her head. "You might be right about honor and obedience, but I found out a long time ago that it didn't work for me. You can go back to the farm and die there, but I'll keep running. That's one choice. The other is that you can stay with me and work with me, and together we can help the other children. Think about it and let me know."

I walked out of the room, and then met Lorenzo outside, and the two of us walked up and down along the side of the road, quietly at first. We saw station wagons filled with people racing by, stirring up the dust at the edge of the narrow road. Men came out of houses and huts and walked toward the Air Force base. We noticed dogs roaming around, and heard music from radios. When the sun peeked from behind a distant mountain, we headed back to our home.

"Mama can do whatever she wants," said Lorenzo, "but I'm never going back to the farm. Even if I have to eat dirt, I'm staying right here."

We found Mama and Gloria ready to do whatever I wanted.

"We aren't going back," Mama said, her face drained, her eyelids red. "I'll do whatever I can, so long as we can go back soon and get the others."

To save my voice, I nodded. Then I went across the street and bought coffee grounds, bread, a piece of cheese, and milk. Using the hot plate Doña Luisa had given me, I made coffee, which we drank in real cups also from Doña Luisa. The bread and cheese was our first breakfast together. The whole time, Lorenzo raved.

"Breakfast! Bread and cheese! I love everything about being here. I'll get a job sweeping. I'll even wash dishes." His enthusiasm made Mama smile, and I knew there was hope.

I visited the office of employment that day and applied for work on the base. In the afternoon, we all went to see José. We found him asleep, but he soon opened his eyes and smiled.

"They scraped my thumb and put some ointment on it. Then they wrapped it up in all this material and gave me some pills to cure the infection." His lips quivered as he lifted his wrapped hand off the bed. "I've been thinking about Papa. What if he finds me here? I won't be able to run."

"He won't find you here," I said, wanting to set his mind at ease. "Don't worry about anything. You'll be out of here and home with us in no time."

"You'll love the place she got for us," Lorenzo said. "It's right on the street. We can feel the breeze the cars make as they speed by. There are many stores around, with bright lights at night and a lot of people going in and out. Loud music comes from each place. It's the most exciting place I've ever seen!"

"I can't wait to see it," José said. A moment later, his eyelids fell, and he was asleep.

"You did the right thing bringing him here," my mother said on our way home.

I felt good and proud of myself, but I wanted her to say more, maybe tell me that I had saved his life, or something of that sort. It had taken her too long to say something positive about what I had done.

*   *   *

Doña Luisa stopped by on her way to the airport.

"Congratulations!" she said as we hugged. "I was afraid for you, but I knew all along that you would pull it off." She turned to Mama. "I'm Luisa Linares. You must be proud of your daughter."

Mama took her hand. "Carmela Santos, at your service."

"I don't want to seem disrespectful, Doña Carmela," said Luisa, "but I hope you know how lucky you are to have such a fine daughter. She can come to live with me anytime."

For a moment, I felt sorry for Mama. Her eyes filled with tears and she nodded, but words wouldn't come.

Doña Luisa turned back to me. "Manuela and Carlos sent their love. They'll come to see you before leaving for New York. I must go now, but I'll write to you soon, so you can join me as soon as you're ready. I'll be waiting for you."

She gave me a long hug, which I returned with many thanks for everything, and for the fifty dollars. She kissed my forehead and was gone.

Through my tears, I watched her walk to the waiting car and ride away. I grieved over her for weeks after she left.

"So that's your angel lady," Mama said when I walked in. "Quite a lady, too. Strong, beautiful, and smart."

"I'm glad you noticed that," I said, but I didn't feel like saying anything else.

I went to the employment office on Monday morning and was hired to do alterations in a sewing shop next to the base laundry, beginning that day. Fifteen dollars a week was a lot of money in those days—more than I had ever earned before.

Two weeks later, I found a job for Lorenzo as a caddie at the base golf course. In the meantime, Doña Inez hired Mama to help her with cooking and washing dishes at fifty cents a day, plus meals for her and Gloria. We all went home happy at the end of each day.

A few weeks later, I found a better job for Mama as a maid at the base, earning $1.50 per day. Doña Inez kept Gloria as her helper, and Mama didn't have to worry about leaving her alone. More importantly, that gave Gloria a sense of self-worth and her own income.

Finally, after five weeks in the hospital, José came home, minus a thumb. The doctors had cured the infection, but could not save the thumb. Still, José felt well and strong, and eager to work. I found a job for him as a busboy in the base cafeteria.

We all had to get our blood tested to work on the base, our first experience with a needle in our veins. Then we had to learn about orders in a strange language.

* * *

The most difficult thing we had to learn was how to live with each other without fighting. Mama kept saying that she was too old to learn new things, and that one day she would take her rags and go back where she belonged. Gloria said that she hated working in a greasy kitchen, but she refused to work on the base with Mama.

All of them refused to contribute part of their earnings to the household expenses. Mama spent her money on cigarettes and rum, and then tried to boss us around. Time and again, I had to remind them that we were all consuming as well as working and earning money, and that this was not the farm.

One Friday afternoon, since everyone had just gotten paid, I told them that they had to help me with the expenses or stop eating and using water and electricity.

Mama cried, mumbling that she was going to end up living on the streets.

"We'll all end up in the street if I don't get some help with the expenses," I said.

"If Mama ends up on the streets," Lorenzo told me, "I'll fix you with this." He held the kitchen knife I had bought with my own money.

"Now I'm really shocked!" I said. "All this time, you led me to believe that you appreciated being here, that if it hadn't been for me, you would all still be at the farm.

"Now, only months after I rescued you, you have the nerve to threaten me? In my own house with my own knife?" I was practically shouting now, my eyes going from face to face. Mama's jaw hung open, her eyes wide and startled as if she had been stripped of her rights to rule over her children. I noticed Gloria in a corner wiping tears from her face. Then I saw Lorenzo return the knife to its place. As long as my power was holding, I decided to yell a little bit longer. "I didn't expect any rewards from any of you, but I didn't expect to regret all I've done, either." With that, I left the house and ended up at Doña Inez's place.

When I returned that evening, Lorenzo said that he was sorry, and promised never to talk to me like that again. Then Mama said that I was right, that everyone had to pitch in and help pay the utilities. I didn't feel like talking then, so I nodded and went into the kitchen for a glass of water.

Later, when we all went to bed, I admitted to myself that I could not count on any of my family, and I definitely could never trust Lorenzo. I would go back for the others soon, then I would move to New York, where my best friend Doña Luisa waited.

Chapter Fifty-Nine

Goodbye Humble Beginnings

As a blonde working on the base, I had a different set of problems. The Americans expected me to speak English. Only when they heard my Spanish did they understand that I wasn't an American. Most of the time, when I waited at the bus stop, the military bus stopped for me. That infuriated the Puerto Rican maids, and they shouted dirty words at me. They had to wait for the old civilian yellow bus, which cost them ten cents to ride into and out of the base. I rode in the clean, newer, blue bus for free. The soldier driving the bus never asked me for an I.D., and I didn't tell him I was a civilian.

During the first week in this location, I had no trouble walking from home to the main gate and back. All I knew up to that point was that Borinquen was noisy from morning until late at night—a wild place where little boys played dice on the street and grown men wore boxing gloves to fight each other.

While men patronized the *cantinas*, the lights flashed, music blared from jukeboxes, and the local *señoritas* walked up and down the street on Saturdays and Sundays. All dressed up, they hoped to meet an American soldier who would marry them and take them to the rich land across the ocean.

The local men, who flirted constantly, resented the American soldiers who attracted their girls. So any local girl who dated or married a *gringo* received her share of harassment. Then there were the jealous wives of the flirting men. These women had something bad to say about any single girl who made their husbands' heads turn.

Things got bad for me when the *barrio's* people discovered that the new blonde in the area wasn't an American, but a Puerto Rican. Now the men made a special effort to flirt, making the jealous wives and the *señoritas* hate me.

"What a gorgeous blonde!" the flirting men exclaimed as I walked to and from work. "She's beautiful—looks just like an *Americana.*"

Soon, the married women watched through the cracks in their walls, threatening to dump boiling water or pee over my head if I didn't stop walking past their homes. The dark-skinned *señoritas* didn't like to see a young blonde *señorita* get extra attention. They constantly suggested that I color my hair black. "Before we shave it off."

When Doña Inez told me that one of her homes was vacant, we packed quickly and moved. The house stood on a slope, off a dirt road a half-mile from the paved street. It was a wooden house, but it had a real kitchen, a living room, and two bedrooms—one for the boys, and the other for Mama and us girls. We even had our own latrine and a bathing hut. This would give us privacy away from the noisy street.

Besides all that luxury, our new home was fenced in with barbed wire and a hedge of wild pineapple bushes, which would keep Papa out if he ever caught up with us.

*   *   *

Now that we had more room, and three months had passed since my trip to the farm, it was time I went back for the others. This time I wasn't afraid. I had more money, and I knew where to look for Papa.

I got lucky, and found him in the outdoor market in San

Sebastian. He didn't see me, so I hurried to the *publico* stand and paid the driver a dollar to take me directly to the point closest to the farm without stopping.

I reached the old house at 11:30. Emilia saw me running down the hill, and ran up to meet me.

"What has taken you so long? I thought you'd forgotten us. How's José? Did he die? Didn't you think I would be worried?" She looked filthy and out of breath.

"Stop, Emilia. I'm here now. It hasn't been easy, and no, José isn't dead. He lost his thumb, but he's okay. Now, how soon can we leave? I saw Papa at the market, but he could be on his way home."

"You won't believe the hell we've gone through since you took the others away. Wait until I tell you Papa's reaction when Mama and the kids didn't come back!"

"Tell me later," I said. "Let's get the kids and leave."

We both laughed as we entered the kitchen. There was the pile of green bananas Emilia had been peeling, the butcher knife standing straight up, a big banana stabbed to the floor.

"That's how excited I got when I saw you," she said.

"Where are Alicia and the boys?"

"Alicia's fetching water. The boys are gathering wood."

"I'll get Alicia," I said. "You call the boys. We have to clear out of here fast."

I ran through the woods and down the slippery hill, where I had fallen so many times before. Memories flashed through my mind, but I had no time to relive them.

I saw Alicia coming up the hill, huffing and puffing with the heavy can of water on her head. I hid behind a tree and said, "What's the one thing you have always wanted to do with that can?"

She stopped to look toward my voice, and I stepped over the underbrush. She dropped the can to the ground. We laughed and hugged, and hurried to the house.

"I knew you would come for me," she said over and over.

"I couldn't forget you," I said. Alicia grinned.

When we reached the house, it was all I could do to keep Alejandro from setting the place on fire before leaving. The night before, Papa had whipped him with a rope for tripping on a tree root and breaking the basket of eggs to be sold.

"Without a home to get drunk in, he would look for you until he found you," I said. "Just get your things and let's go."

We headed up the hill before 1:00, each of us with a small bundle of clothing under our arms. We stopped at a slope about eighty feet from the house to look back to where our lives had begun. Our emotions overwhelmed us. Without a word, we stared, our teardrops falling to the grass beneath our feet. The old house, with its windows and doors closed, looked humble and lonely, without a sign of life in it or the usual stream of blue smoke that had always made it appear warm and alive.

None of us seemed eager to abandon our humble beginning— but neither were we willing to return to the turbulence within the walls that hid our misery from the rest of the world.

As we looked at each other, speechless, two of our piglets, oinking and wagging their short tails, emerged from under the coffee trees. We tried to laugh, but our laughter turned to sobs. The poor babies had followed us, expecting that we weren't going too far.

Emilia squatted down, rubbed the piglets, and then slapped their behinds, yelling at them to go back to their mother. The piglets ran, squealing, and once again we headed up the hill. None of us looked back again.

We reached the paved road just before 3:00 and looked around for Papa. If he had left town earlier than usual, we didn't want him to surprise us—it would spoil the surprise we had left for him.

In San Sebastian, I paid the driver an extra quarter to take us straight to the Aguadilla loading zone instead of dropping us off at the plaza, where Papa would see us if he was still in town. Then I paid the driver his full fare to drive nonstop to Aguadilla.

During the entire ride, we hardly spoke. We looked at one another and motioned to point out people or things we wanted the others to see. Each of us was burdened with the same question: What would Papa do when he got home?

In Aguadilla, we hurried to the Borinquen zone, where I again paid this driver the full fare to drive straight through to our new home. We got there before 5:00 that afternoon.

Mama had prepared a feast, as if she knew that I wouldn't come back alone. There were a lot of hugs, kisses, and tears.

Then fear, like a poisonous fog, came over us. We looked at each other.

"He'll never find us here," I said.

"He will, sooner or later," Mama answered.

"Then we need to decide how to handle him if he dares to show up at our front door," I said. "For now, let us follow the good smells into the kitchen." The smiles returned.

We stayed up most of the night talking, laughing, and crying. The little kids told us about Papa's reaction when Mama and the others did not return home the day he beat José. They said that Papa could not figure out where everyone was hiding.

"He looked like a mad bull," Emilia said, "walking circles around the front room, one hand in his pocket, the other in a fist, his finger drilling into his temple. 'Where in hell are they? They'll be damn sorry when they get back.' He sucked air through his teeth and asked all of us, 'Where did they go, eh?' Sometimes he looked mad enough to spit fire, but for some reason he didn't beat us. He cut down on his drinking, as if he was afraid we would leave, too."

Mama nodded. "Good! And now he has lost everyone. But he'll find us. It's only a matter of time."

"He won't find us unless someone tells him where we are," Gloria said.

"Someone will. We aren't the only people who moved here from the hills," Mama insisted. "All he has to do is tell his brothers and cousins that his family left him, and for a few shots of rum the gossip will spread like fire. Those people who moved to this barrio still have relatives in the hills. When they go back to visit, they'll tell that they have seen us. Once the news reaches your father, he'll ask questions all the way from the river to the end of the world until he finds us."

I felt the blood drain from my face. I could picture Papa at our door. Still, I didn't want us to live in fear.

"Listen to me, Mama," I said. "We live near the city now. If he finds us, we can send for the police."

"Yeah!" Lorenzo said, rubbing his hands together, his eyes like huge brown marbles. "We'll have him locked up in jail!"

"Locking him in jail would only work if they kept him there for the rest of his life," Emilia said. "He'll bribe his way out and come after us."

"Okay, then," said José. "We'll get together and beat him like he did me."

"Yeah," said Alejandro. "We'll whip him with a wet rope, like he whipped me yesterday."

"Stop! You don't beat your parents, no matter what they've done to you," Mama said, eager to take control of her family.

"Don't worry, Mama," I said, holding back my anger. "We'll only beat him if he makes us defend ourselves."

We had been sitting on the kitchen floor, eight of us children and our mother. I wanted to hold this moment a while longer.

"Let's pretend that we are a happy family, for once in our lives all together sitting so close to each other without anger or fear. Let's pretend, if only for a moment."

I let my eyes travel from face to face. José was holding a smile, showing perfectly straight, but yellow, teeth. Lorenzo sat with sparkling eyes, a bundle of energy ready to hit the streets and do whatever boys his age were already doing. Across from me were Emilia and Gloria. Emilia needed some help with her appearance, but I could imagine her looking quite attractive once I had time to show her a few points. She was probably twenty years old, although our ages didn't matter at that moment.

Gloria was probably eighteen. I had already plucked her eyebrows and cut her hair, which curled around her oval face like a permanent, highlighting her big brown eyes. I thought she looked beautiful.

Next to me was Alicia, maybe twelve, all eyes and smiles, eager to have her hair cut, and to heal the scratches on her legs and arms.

Alejandro and Felipito, probably eight and six, bright-eyed, ragged, and skinny, sat next to Mama, waiting for more stories. Mama, looking much better than she had a few months earlier, waited anxiously to boss around her family again.

This was the coziest and most loving time we had ever experienced. Some of us talked, others listened. Our knees touched, then our feet, when our legs got tired and we stretched them out. We shared stories, cried, and laughed.

Every now and then, Mama would try to remind us about honoring our parents. Each time, Emilia or Lorenzo would cut her off with something like: "That horse manure got us nowhere, Mama!"

Mama's face would crease, and she would try to stand up, but Alicia would tug at her. "Mama, please! We are done being slaves. Let's hear more stories."

"Okay," I said, "let's talk about who will stay home with Alejandro, Felipito, and Alicia while the rest of us work."

"I'll stay," Emilia said. "I'm an expert at taking care of kids and doing housework."

"Good," I said. "And the three younger kids can go to school."

My mother's hand came flying toward my face, but I caught it before it smacked my teeth. She quickly covered her mouth as she realized that I wasn't the little girl she used to slap around.

"Don't ever do that again!" I warned her. "You're not in the woods now, and I'm not so little anymore. Besides, this is the city. If you don't send them to school, the law will come around and you'll have to answer to them. You might end up in jail if you deprive them of an education."

Chapter Sixty

See Him Run

The walk home from the paved road after work was delightful this afternoon. The coconut trees alongside the dirt road were rustling in the breeze. The dust had settled between the stones after yesterday's rain, and the air smelled fresh and clean. The sun still shone brightly on the tin roofs, but the shade from trees everywhere else made everything appear cool and peaceful.

I felt happy and proud of myself. I had rescued my mother, my sisters, and my brothers from the mud pit. As soon as they were able to support themselves, I would join Doña Luisa in New York.

Reaching the narrow walkway up to our house, I heard a man shouting, but thought it was the guy two houses down. A few more steps brought me closer to the angry voice.

My heart stopped, then it began a loud pounding in my ears. I felt my stomach rolling itself into a tight ball. *Is that Papa? Oh my God! Who told him where to find us? What am I going to do? Where can I hide?*

I wanted to run for my life, but I also wanted to see if he was outside the fence or on the other side of it. I knew that Alicia and the younger boys would not have unlocked the gate for him. Yet I feared that Emilia might let him in. *If he's inside, we are as good as dead.*

I took the next few steps like a cat moving in on its prey:
quietly lifting a paw and slowly stepping forward. The trouble
was that I didn't feel as light as a cat. My shoes made grinding
sounds on the gravel, as if I weighed a lot more than my 110 pounds.

I looked up as I reached the walkway and my knees started
shaking. I squeezed my little wallet so hard that it popped open
and the few coins I had in it flew out. It was all the money I had
left, and payday was two days away, but I didn't dare bend over
to retrieve it.

Standing outside the fence, facing the house, was my father
in his dark trousers, white shirt, and white hat. He looked like a
raving black and white bull with a red face, waving his fists toward our front window and stamping the ground with his black
boots. I knew that if he turned his head and saw me, I would
have to run faster than ever before, and this time he would not
stop until I was dead.

"So you went back to get the rest of the kids. Was it because
I didn't come after you the day you abandoned us? Well, surprise, surprise, it took me three weeks of asking questions, but I
tracked you down. You can stay away until you rot, but send out
the younger kids. If you don't send them out, I'll come inside,
smash your heads together, then drag the little shits by their ears
all the way to where they belong!"

I realized that he was yelling at Mama. *Did she come home
early today? Was Papa already there when she arrived? Oh my
Lord! Are the older boys home, too?* Scary thoughts flashed through
my mind as I slowly stepped back, holding my breath and hoping
that my father would not turn his head toward me.

I backed down to the road, and then walked slowly past the
house and into the neighbor's yard. I didn't have to knock on
Doña Matilda's door. She was at her window talking with my
mother, whose face was as white as a peeled potato as she leaned
out my bedroom window.

"Oh, I'm so glad to see you!" said Doña Matilda. "Your poor
mother is scared to death."

I stood between the two houses, trying to figure out how to jump over the thorny hedge and climb up through my window. I could feel the two frightened women, one at my right and the other at my left, waiting for me to solve a huge problem.

I felt embarrassed hearing Papa shout on the other side of the house. I knew that in the short time we had lived there, Mama had told Doña Matilda a lot about our stormy background. I had come home from work other times to find the two having long conversations through the open windows.

"How long has he been there?" I asked Mama, turning my back on Doña Matilda—not to be rude, but out of shame. Now the whole world would learn about our miserable lives. I felt my face turn red, but there was no place I could hide.

"He showed up a few minutes after I got home from work," Mama replied. "He's been trying to jump over the fence ever since. I'm afraid for José. He'll be home soon. Your father will drag him back to the farm. God have mercy!"

"José and Lorenzo will not be home until dark," I said. "But go talk to him through the living room window. Keep him arguing there while I figure a way to get inside."

Mama was too afraid to talk to Papa, even though she was up in the house with the doors locked, and with Emilia, Gloria, Alicia, Alejandro, and Felipito at her side. "Talk to him? The way he yells?"

"So don't talk," I said. "Just stand at the window and let him do the talking."

Mama sent Emilia instead.

"You little bitch!" he yelled at Emilia. "I always trusted you, and you ran out on me just to follow your stupid mother!"

"You're nothing but a miserable old man—a drunk! None of us want to ever see you again." Emilia's voice rang as loud as Papa's.

"Shut your filthy mouth and send out the younger kids!" he shouted. "You can stay with your mother and rot together, for all I care! Send them out before I jump over this damn fence. If I have to come inside, you'll be sorry. I'll bang your heads together until your chicken-brains spill to the floor!"

I knew a lot of the neighbors could hear the shouting, but I also knew that no one would come around to help us. It was too early for drunks who would enjoy punching the anger out of Papa, and the men who were sober would not want to get mixed up with a strange madman.

Meanwhile, the more time that passed, the chances were greater that the boys would come home. I didn't worry about Lorenzo, because he could outrun Papa any day. But José was weaker, and Papa would surely drag him back to the farm. Someone had to stop Papa, but by the looks of my mother and sisters, I would have to be the one to do it.

I borrowed the neighbor's stepladder and climbed through our bedroom window just in time to hear Papa yell that he should have poisoned us years earlier, that we were stupid pigs like our mother.

"You're a miserable old man!" Emilia shouted. "A mean drunk. We all hate you, so go back to your rum shack."

Before Papa could yell another insult, I pulled Emilia back and took her place at the window. Now I had the pleasure of seeing Papa's mouth freeze open. His eyes blinked once, then stretched open so wide that I thought of two brown cups on white saucers.

"Gee! You look as if someone hit your head with a hammer," I shouted.

I felt my heart racing, as if it were trying to fly out of my chest. This fear, however, was mixed with joy. While I confronted my mad father, Mama and the kids could see how confident I had become. They would realize that I would no longer let anyone push me around.

"Did I hear you talking about surprises a few minutes ago?" I heard my voice shake, and felt heat spreading over my face and ears. I knew that Papa could jump over the fence somehow and try to finish what he'd started four years earlier.

Waiting for my shocked father to answer me with one of his insults, I felt a tug at my skirt. Turning halfway, I saw my mother's bloodshot eyes.

"Now that he's seen you, he'll really go crazy. You shouldn't let him see you. He'll get tired and go away if you ignore him. Please! Ignore him, for my sake, please!"

"He won't come in, Mama. There are seven of us."

"Look!" Alicia cut in, pointing out the window.

I turned and saw Papa reaching up to the fence post. With one twist of his solid body, he jumped over the mess of wire and shrubs. I heard the stamping of feet behind me. From the corner of my eye, I saw Mama and the girls stumbling into each other, desperately looking for places to hide.

Then I saw Papa reaching for the windowsill. I knew he would pull himself up into the house. Trembling, I quickly slammed the wooden shutter and locked it.

"Where in hell did you come from?" I heard him shout. Then I heard him running toward the little balcony and up the concrete steps. He kicked and pounded on the front door so hard I knew it would soon fly off its hinges.

"You're supposed to be dead!" his voice roared through the little square window on the door, sending chills through my trembling body.

Everything was happening so fast I could hardly think. Still, I noticed all the frightened eyes directed at me, as if expecting me to protect them. This confirmed my fear that I would have to fight my crazy father by myself. I believed that I could escape if I ran, but that meant I would be running for the rest of my life.

I heard the door hinges crack, and then I saw Mama running toward the kitchen with Alicia by the arm. Emilia took a leap and followed them. The back door flew open, and the three jumped out.

I stood there in disbelief, feeling very much alone. Luckily, Gloria jumped and pushed the door shut and locked it. In the meantime, the two little boys stood on either side of me.

"Don't worry," Alejandro said. "We'll help you fight. Even without those three chickens, we can beat Papa. It's still four to one. We're bound to win."

"Me, too," said Felipito. But I saw fear in his sparkling brown eyes.

"You can count on me," said Gloria. "All of us together can tie him up and teach him a few lessons."

I don't know why, but as I looked at Gloria, I had an amazing thought flash through my mine: If we could subdue him, I would convince him somehow that all we wanted to do was love him, not hate him, and he should stop being mean and let us teach him how to love.

As I questioned that thought, I realized that our problem had taken a terrible twist: Through the little square window on the door, Papa had seen Mama and the girls run out. He had taken off after them immediately. Now we all ran to look out the bedroom window. We saw Mama and the two girls trying to jump over the fence to reach the neighbor's yard, even though Doña Matilda had closed her doors and windows.

Papa grabbed Emilia by the arm, but she fought him off and started running. As he caught up to her, she snatched poor Alicia and shoved the frightened girl into Papa's hands.

I saw Alicia's skinny legs swinging and trying to kick Papa's hard shins, and my heart ached. He would probably hurt her just so I'd see what he would do me.

"Let her go!" I yelled. "I demand that you let her go!"

"Who the hell are you to demand anything?" Papa looked up, and I saw fire in his eyes. He had both of Alicia's wrists in one hand and a bunch of her hair in the other, tilting her head back.

The memory of Alicia's startled eyes looking at me would stay in my mind forever.

He let go of her wrists, bent over, picked up a huge rock, and held it against the horrified girl's head. "I'm going to split her head, then I'll come in to bang your head until your eyes pop like corks out of bottles."

As he yelled, I thought of the time he had held the machete at my throat. I don't know where my next burst of energy came from, but I shouted so loud that my throat felt raw for days afterward.

"Help! Somebody! Help! My drunken father is killing his own defenseless daughter! Help!"

Papa pushed Alicia to the hedge and, roaring like a mad dog, threw the rock at me. I ducked, and the rock hit the floor.

Papa jumped back onto the balcony. "You little shit! I'm breaking down this damn door, then I'll beat the hell out of you and the rest of the stinking, rotten bunch."

Unable to reach safety at the neighbor's house, Mama, Emilia, and Alicia returned through the back door while Papa was still trying to break through the front. I heard door boards crack, and I knew we were about to die. I reached under my bed and pulled out an old baseball bat I had found behind the latrine when we first moved in. I had brought it in for protection, if the time came.

I figured this was the time, so I held it by the slim end, then turned to the scared bunch. "He's coming in," I said urgently. "Arm yourselves with anything you can find and be ready to fight for your lives, or we'll die."

No one said a word, but Emilia quickly headed for the kitchen, and everyone else followed her. In a flash, they all returned, shouting and waving their weapons: the broom, the frying pan, the butcher knife, the iron, the washboard, and even the water bucket.

We stood a few feet from the door, stamping our feet and urging Papa to come and get what was coming to him. He couldn't see all of us through the little square window, so we yelled, telling him what we were holding in our hands.

"Once you drop to the floor, we'll keep hitting you until you beg for mercy!" I shouted.

"Yeah!" Emilia said. "We'll give back to you what you've given us for years."

The other kids added their own threats, and I knew, by the

perspiration and the smell of body heat, that we looked mean and tough. Never before had we shared the same fear and anger. Now we were finally prepared to fight together.

Another blow to the door sent a short board into our living room. Emilia quickly grabbed it. "Good! Now I have something new to hit you with."

Papa kept kicking and pounding. We held our weapons in position.

Then he stopped, and we saw his angry eyes peeking though the little square hole. "Ah! You're all a bunch of worthless pigs. I don't want any of you, so you can all go straight to hell!"

With those words, he moved away from the door. I hurried to the window, opening it slowly, expecting him to jump up. Instead, I saw him put one foot on the barbed wire and jump onto the walkway. He ran down to the dirt road and immediately turned in the direction of the paved street. The hedge of bushes alongside the road covered him from the waist down, but I could see his shoulders and head bobbing rapidly, and he didn't stop even when his hat flew off.

I didn't know that Papa could run that fast, nor could I figure out what made him run scared. Then I heard the sound of tires on gravel, and to my pleasant surprise, I saw a black and white police car speeding down the dirt road, catching up to Papa and leaving a low cloud of dust behind.

I motioned to Mama and the kids. "Come look!"

Emilia was the first one at the window, then everyone else followed. I stepped to the side to make room for the little boys, and to figure out what had happened. Were the police really going after Papa? Which of the neighbors sent for them? Then I felt another blow to my stomach. *If the police lock Papa in jail, he'll come after us again when he gets out.*

"So that's why he stopped pounding on the door," Emilia said with a wide grin. "Now I know why he ran. He heard a car and looked up the road, saw that it was a police car, and ran scared."

Alicia moved back from the window and burst out laughing. "He ran like a scared cat," she said through the laughter.

This made Gloria laugh, too. Soon enough, I was down on the floor with everyone else, consumed by nervous laughter. We grabbed our bellies and tried to speak, but the words would not come. I knew that in spite of the laughter, we all had the same question in mind: Will Papa come back?

We stayed on the floor for a while. I felt drained, and everyone else looked it, too. Mama's husband, our father, was out of our lives—if only for the moment.

A gentle knock at our kitchen door brought us quickly to silence and sent our hearts back to the darkness of fear. Then, as we looked at one another, we heard Doña Matilda's soft voice. "Carmela?"

Mama hurried to the door. "Thank God it's only you. Please come in. We were terrified!"

"I hope I did the right thing," Doña Matilda said, one hand in her dress pocket, the other holding something behind her. "When I heard that man pounding on your door right after you called for help, I sent my son to bring the police." The nice lady smiled and produced Papa's crispy-white hat, crushed by the police car.

Alicia puckered her lips. "Too bad his head wasn't inside the hat."

We all burst out laughing again, so hard this time that teardrops dotted the floor, and even Doña Matilda couldn't keep a straight face. Although it was a nervous laughter, the sound was great and pleasing to my heart.

Epilogue

We never found out whether the police took Papa to jail or sent him away with a warning, so we continued expecting him to show up at any time.

Then, two months later, Mama went to visit Doña Inez, and to her delight met with an old friend. It was Isabel, the lady who had taught Emilia and me how to sew gloves. She had come to look for work on the base, and had been told that Doña Inez owned rental property.

Isabel gave Mama a report about Papa that delighted all of us. Papa had brought into his home a woman who had lived in a small hut across the river. The woman had three fatherless children—one girl and two boys.

As Mama reported the good news to us, we three older girls realized that she seemed hurt. Little by little, Mama revealed to us that the three children were our half-brothers and sister, and that only God knew how many more were around our hills. Mama went on to confess that other women had been a major cause of our turbulent years.

Knowing that Papa had a new family to keep him busy gave us all a sense of peace and freedom.

Still, I had another pain to endure. Doña Luisa, my wonderful friend and mother for four years, died of a sudden heart attack. After all I had gone through, and just as I looked forward to moving to New York, I suddenly had no place to go, and no hope.

*   *   *

For the next three months, I worked, ate, and slept wrapped in a cloud of grief. I lost weight, and Mama remarked that I probably had a deadly disease. I didn't tell her that at that time I didn't fear even the possibility of death.

Finally, Doña Inez introduced me to Frank Wilson, a twenty-five-year-old American soldier who she had known for over two years.

"He's a good man," she said. "It's about time you meet someone who can take you away from here. You need a new beginning, away from your whole family. And don't even worry about your mother and your siblings; once you're gone, they'll do just fine. Getting to know Frank will help you shake off some of your grief."

I didn't tell Doña Inez that Doña Luisa had predicted that one day I'd end up with an American husband.

Frank spoke softly and appeared tranquil and kind. He had gorgeous sapphire blue eyes and blonde hair. He had learned some Spanish, and I had learned a little English, so we understood each other.

By the time I left Doña Inez's place, I had accepted Frank's invitation to see a movie the following night. One date led to another, and finally Frank declared that he had fallen in love with me. I had no idea what loving a man was supposed to feel like. But I felt comfortable going to the movies and holding hands with Frank. He had learned that a *señorita* was not to be kissed or touched, so I didn't experience any unpleasant advances from him. Frank appeared to be a totally different kind of man from my father. He would love and protect me.

Three months after our first date, we married at the base chapel. Our witnesses were Doña Inez and Frank's closest friend.

In October 1954, my husband and I boarded an Air Force cargo airplane (my first flight) to the United States. I would be far away from Papa, but also from Mama, who said that I was running off with a strange man from the other side of the world.

As I walked out of the house, suitcase in hand, Mama came from the kitchen with teary eyes. She wrapped her arms around me and cried, "What will become of me with you gone?"

I hugged my mother and kissed her forehead, but I didn't answer her question. I felt hurt that she still wanted more from me. I had spent an entire year making sure she and the kids would learn everything they needed to know about surviving outside the farm. What more did she want?

I had my future to worry about. Had marrying Frank been the right decision? What if he changed into a drunken monster once he reached his hometown in Minnesota? And how far away was Minnesota? I had never heard of it before.

As the airplane moved down the runway, I stared out the small window and watched the coconut trees, the hibiscus hedges, and the green grass of my island gradually disappear.

Fear gripped my stomach then. I could not define my feelings for Frank. Was it love? Or was it gratitude? After all, he was giving me a new identity, and he was taking me to a new country to live free from abuse and poverty.

I silently prayed for love.

Other books by Jacqueline Jorgensen:

Yearning To Be American
(Now available)

Back to the Mud and Vines
(Available soon)

9 780738 8642